Willis R. Whitney, General Electric, and the Origins of U.S. Industrial Research

Willis R. Whitney at about the age of 40, ca. 1908.

WILLIS R. WHITNEY,
General Electric,
and the Origins of
U.S. Industrial Research

GEORGE WISE

COLUMBIA UNIVERSITY PRESS
New York   1985

Library of Congress Cataloging in Publication Data

Wise, George, 1944–
Willis R. Whitney, General Electric, and the origins of U.S. industrial
research.

Bibliography: p.
Includes index.
1. Whitney, Willis Rodney, 1868–1958.   2. Research,
Industrial—United States—Biography.   I. Title.
T40.W45W57   1985   607'.2'24 [B]   84-27484
ISBN 0-231-06016-5 (alk. paper)

Columbia University Press
New York   Guildford, Surrey

Contents

List of Illustrations

List of Figures

A STATISTICAL PICTURE OF THE GE RESEARCH LAB:

Acknowledgments

I thank many people for helping me with this book. Mrs. Agnes Wendel, George Barker, and Vincent Manti provided invaluable source material. Many past members of the staff of the General Electric Research Laboratory, including Herman Liebhafsky, Louis Navias, Herbert Pollock, C. Guy Suits, and Willem Westendorp, provided invaluable insights based on their own experience. Librarians and archivists, including Ellen Fladger of the Schenectady Archives of Science and Technology, Deborah Cuzort and other members of the staff of the MIT Archives, B. Dolores Thompson of the Fenton Historical Society, Jamestown, New York, and Maryde King, Judy Lent, Julia Hewitt and Marian Smith of General Electric were generous with the books and papers in their care. Craig Waff, Leslie Bialler, and their co-workers at the Columbia University Press were kind, helpful and professional in carrying out all the steps that turned my manuscript into a book.

I gained much from discussions with many historians, including Reese Jenkins, Ronald Klein, Stuart Leslie, David Nye, Leonard Reich, Jeffrey Sturchio, and especially my teacher Robert V. Bruce. I took advantage of previous work done by people interested in the career of Willis R. Whitney, including John Broderick, Virginia Westervelt, Miles Martin, and especially the pioneer historian of industrial research Kendall Birr. I benefited from the support and help of many colleagues and managers at the General Electric Research and Development Center, including C. William Austin, Barbara Hutchings, R. Ned Landon, Gregory McGarry, Kim Reksc, Roland Schmitt, Ray Shanahan, Peter Van Avery, and Mary Ellen Walsh, and especially from the encouragement and editorial advice of Catherine Welsh. And I thank my parents George and Frances Wise, and, most of all, my wife, guide, and helpmeet, Bonnie Wise.

George Wise
February 1985

Willis R. Whitney, General Electric, and the Origins of U.S. Industrial Research

1/

The Corporation's Chemist

To a boy in the upstate New York town of Niskayuna in the Depression years of the 1930s, finding a turtle in the woods meant good luck. He could take it to an old man who lived down by the stream called Lisha Kill and get a shiny new quarter for it. The old man, whom everybody knew as Doc Whitney, had been studying turtles for more than twenty years. He would mark their shells, make a record of their migrations in a special log book, and occasionally keep them for a while in a concrete enclosure for observation. He had learned that turtles migrated annually over individual paths through the woods, reaching the same spots at the same times each year; that they would not lay their eggs in captivity; and that they liked to eat bananas. By 1935, dozens of turtles, marked with Whitney's initials and the date they had first been found roamed the Niskayuna woods.[1]

But why did old Doc Whitney care so much about turtles? That was only one of the questions neighbors might have asked about him. They knew he was, or had been, a figure of importance at the huge General Electric Works in nearby Schenectady. But if so, why did he live out on a country farm instead of alongside the other company leaders down in the "GE Plot" in the city? They knew he held a great reputation in the world for energy and optimism. But if so, why was he seen sometimes moping in his garden, wrapped in gloom. And why his occasional absences, rumored to be for hospitalization? They knew that the "doc" stood for an advanced degree in science. But if so, why did he seem more interested in simple things—turtles, goldenrod galls, arrowheads—than in nature's deeper mysteries?[2]

Those interested enough could learn from the newspapers

the basic facts of Doc Whitney's career. He was born in Jamestown, in the western end of New York state, in 1868. He earned a bachelor's degree in chemistry from MIT and a Ph.D. degree in that subject from the University of Leipzig in Germany. He became a chemistry teacher at MIT. Then, in 1900, he joined General Electric to create what that company called the first American industrial laboratory devoted to fundamental scientific research.

In other words, GE hired Whitney to carry out a pioneering experiment in the use of scientists by industry. GE would use scientists as scientists—not as inventors, consultants, engineers, or testers. They would be called on to do all those jobs. But at the same time, they would be given the freedom and the encouragement to remain members in good standing of the scientific community. They would do research bearing on the important questions of chemistry, physics, and metallurgy; discuss their findings at scientific meetings; and publish their results in scientific journals.

But could industrial scientists truly remain scientists? Would the ideals of science prove compatible with those of industry? And how would an attempt to answer those questions shape the life of an individual? A closer look at the life of Willis R. Whitney illuminates these issues from two sides, the public and the private.

On the public side, Whitney did as much as or more than any other single person to shape the institution we know today as industrial research. In 1900, there were a few dozen laboratories in American industry that employed professional scientists. None of them fit the description implied today by the term "industrial research": a place where scientists can contribute to the advance of science while they put science to work. Whitney consciously created such a laboratory, deliberately blending the traditions of the academic laboratories that he had been trained in with the realities he observed at the GE Works in Schenectady.

Industrial research of the type Whitney fostered has spread and flourished. In 1979, it required a 594-page oversized book and small print merely to list the names, locations, and activities of the industrial research laboratories of the United States.[3] The 9,600 entries ranged from the Aardvark Instrument Company in Columbus, Ohio, where four chemists and chemical engineers studied applied electrochemical processes, to the Bell Laboratories in Murray Hill, New Jersey, and several satellite locations, where a staff of 8,000, including nearly 2,200 Ph.D.s studied nearly every science from physics to psychology. Americans poured more than $40 billion annually into industrial research. They received from it in return inventions crucial to prosperity and national defense, and scientific work rising occasionally to Nobel Prize quality.

On the private side, Whitney had to give up his own career as a chemist to make a place for others in the corporation. "I would rather be a little Moses than a big Jeremiah," he once wrote.[4] He got his wish in a way he did not quite intend. He led chemists into the corporation and in the process helped lead American science into its modern institutional setting. But he personally remained behind, on the banks of the Lisha Kill, following his turtles. He would discharge into his many hobbies the tensions built up by not doing science. Whitney helped create the modern system of science-industry interdependence. But in the process the system he helped create passed him by.

In helping create a new role for American professional scientists, Whitney sailed on the tide of a changing American society. Four successive waves helped bring in the tide that converted a nation of farmers, small factories, and strong local institutions into a nation organized economically, industrially, and politically on a national scale.

The first wave was the growth of relatively small-scale manufacturing in hundreds of big towns and small cities. In one such town, Jamestown, in the gaslit parlor of a comfortable house, on a Wednesday evening in the spring of 1886, an elderly man and six teenage boys sat around a specially constructed round table. The man was William C. J. Hall, manager and part owner of Jamestown's biggest factory, the Alpaca

Mills. The boys were the students in Hall's YMCA class in microscopy. The table was built on a swivel so that its top could rotate. Hall, long a devoted amateur microscopist, would take out one of his carefully prepared samples mounted on a glass slide and put it into the stage of his beautiful binocular microscope. He would bring the field into focus, then turn the table, passing the microscope to each boy in his turn. Speed up the scene and the microscope becomes the pointer of a vocational wheel of fortune, picking out one of the boys for a life in science. The pointer stops at the place of seventeen-year-old Willis R. Whitney.

The second wave was the organization of giant corporations and powerful professions, carrying chemistry into the corporation. On a Friday evening in March 1901, a Pullman car of the Boston and Albany railroad, traveling west, held a handsome, well-dressed, clean-shaven man of thirty-two. His fellow passengers might have taken him for a traveling salesman of the better sort or a young business executive. But Willis R. Whitney held two other jobs. Behind him, at the Boston end of the line, was the class in theoretical chemistry he taught at the Massachusetts Institute of Technology. Ahead of him, in Schenectady, waited a weekend of doing research for General Electric. Four months ago he had taken on this second post. Last month he had shaved off the full beard he had been growing since 1896, when he had earned the degree of Ph.D. in chemistry from Leipzig. Now he was coming to realize that doing the industrial job right might require giving up the teaching job, as well as the beard that had been its symbol.

The third wave brought national affluence, largely based on technology. Electricity, automobiles, radios, and refrigerators became the property of many rather than the luxuries of a few. In the fall of 1921, as that wave began to come in, the members of the American Chemical Society met to honor one of their own. The tenth Perkin Medal, honoring contributions to the practical use of chemistry in the tradition of British chemist William Perkin, went to Willis R. Whitney. The record of invention and discovery Whitney had compiled as a scientist, summed up in forty U.S. patents and twenty-five published papers, had not by itself earned one of American chemistry's highest honors.[5] The medal, as the speeches accompanying its presentation made clear, honored Whitney's unique example as a manager of research.

To describe that example, chemist Arthur D. Little rose to depict Whitney as a "pragmatic scientist" driven by curiosity who "didn't want to go to heaven unless there were problems there."[6] He painted the picture of a born teacher who once responded to an industrial job offer with the words "I'd rather teach than be president." But Little did not mean to evoke the yellowed index cards or settling chalk dust of the lecture hall. Whitney, he explained, teaches by personal contact and inspiration. He has a "genius for friendship." He can more likely be found outdoors than in meeting rooms or offices. He's "a dirt farmer who knows hog cholera and manure, and what to do when his chickens get the pip." He hunts arrowheads and traces the migratory paths of turtles. But he can be one of the boys, too. "He enjoys the higher things in life," Little said, "and has even been known to sidestep a meeting of the American Academy of Arts and Sciences and go to a girl and music show instead."

But Little kept coming back to the ability to inspire. "Whitney can talk to a man three minutes and inject into him enough enthusiasm to last three months." Little even found an apt chemical term to describe this quality. Whitney, he stated, is "exothermic." That is, he is like a chemical reaction that gives off energy to its surroundings. He energizes the work of others, rather than drawing on others to fuel his own personal quest of papers, inventions, and honors.

The fourth wave put out the exothermic flame, at least temporarily. In 1932, as the Great Depression broke over the world, Whitney followed his turtles and fought his own personal depression, and a chemistry colleague, Wilder D. Bancroft, wrote a characterization that combined dubious psychology with acute observation. He applied to American chemists a pair of categories proposed by Germany's Wilhelm Ostwald. On one side were the "classicists": scientists with a "phlegmatic, melancholic nature" and a "low reaction velocity." On the other were romanticists: sanguine, choleric, exhibiting a high reaction velocity. "In this country," Bancroft observed, "Whitney is a romanticist."[7] Little had agreed, pointing out that he saw a striking physical resemblance between Whitney and the composer Franz Liszt.

Bancroft went on to summarize the fate of his second type of chemist. "The romanticist," he wrote, "is more likely to break down from mental exhaustion than the classicist and is consequently more likely to change his subject in later life." By 1932, Whitney had done both of these things.

The four images—the boy with the microscope, the man on a railroad car, the exothermic reaction, and the broken romanticist tending his turtles—sum up Whitney's career. In an era when his chemistry colleagues were increasingly modeling their discipline on physics, he remained a boy with a microscope, an observer, and a classifier. In an era when industrial and academic values warred for the allegiance of professionals, he invented an institution that combined and linked industry and academe, just as the railroad line linked Boston and Schenectady. In an era that increasingly belonged to the endothermic—the individuals who could draw energy from their institutional surroundings—he kept his exothermic flame burning. If the U.S. research laboratory largely followed the GE model, the U.S. research director did not follow the Whitney model. He was more likely to follow the model of one of Whitney's contemporaries, Frank Baldwin Jewett of Western Electric, an endothermic organizer, more comfortable in the committee room, on the telephone, or behind the desk than on the lecture platform or roaming the halls of the laboratory. As American industrial research matured, Whitney's exothermic enthusiasm became unnecessary, it appeared—perhaps even superfluous. Finally, an era of Depression, from 1929 to 1939, seemed to conclude the case against a romanticist in industry.

But if the Whitney style does not survive, the Whitney legacy does. American industrial research bears his imprint. The full story of American industrial research remains untold, perhaps untellable. But perhaps we can begin to understand it by following, out of a nineteenth-century factory town becoming a city, through the emerging profession of twentieth-century American science, and into one of the giant enterprises of the industrial age, the journey of one corporation's chemist.

2/

The Manufacturing Republic

A photograph of Whitney at age eight survives.[1] Features that would later emerge more distinctly had already begun to appear: the broad, high forehead; the heavy eyebrows over hooded eyes; the thin, straight nose, a bit too long; the beginnings of a smile at the corners of a pursed mouth; and the round, outthrust chin. Later, the face would become squarer. More intensity would gleam from the dark eyes. Two short furrows would begin where the eyebrows met the bridge of the nose, as though dug there by the effort of thinking over hard questions.

Whitney became an observer and a questioner. He observed and asked simple questions about turtles, arrowheads, worm galls, corn plants, chemical reactions, institutions, and people. He used the answers to form simple theories that he tested by experiment and experience.

For his first eighteen years, his experience remained confined within a small circle of relatives and friends in a small, though rapidly growing, town. The main influences on him during those early years included his father, John Jay Whitney, a kindly, conservative, parochial businessman; his mother, Agnes Reynolds Whitney, a homemaker who combined a love of good books with a simple, sincere religious faith; a grandfather, George Tew, a self-made banker and community leader; and William C. J. Hall, a businessman whose interests had turned to doing and teaching science. Behind each of these models and influences stood the atomsphere of Jamestown, New York, an expanding community experiencing in its limited compass some of the same forces of modernization that were more dramatically reshaping cities such as Boston, Pittsburgh, Cleveland, and Chicago.

Willis R. Whitney at about age 8, Jamestown, New York, about 1876.

In that photograph he appears to sit fishing on the bank of a country stream. But observation quickly reveals that he is posing in a studio. The riverbank is a carpet. The ripples on the stream are scratches in the photographer's negative. The trees and bushes are a painted backdrop. The fishing rod is a length of lath.

Whitney's later portrayals of his boyhood home would depict it as rural, placid, and simple, like that fishing scene. His version would be just as artificial as the photographer's creation. The Jamestown and Chautauqua County of the 1870s and 1880s did indeed contain some of the best fishing streams, lakefront beaches, and stands of maple in western New York state. But the region's most distinctive feature during those years was not its resemblance to the ideal of rural America. It was the speed and determination with which it was trying to leave that ideal behind.

Call the time and place where Whitney's Jamestown rests the manufacturing republic. Across America, small towns swelled into big towns, and big towns put in street lights, streetcars, and gas mains and called themselves cities. These new cities based their economies on modest-sized manufacturing enterprises, locally owned and controlled, yet beginning to produce for a wider market. Earlier, the towns had mainly served the needs of their surrounding farms. Later, they would join with the larger cities in producing goods for the nation.

In 1880, as historian Albert D. Chandler notes, the factories of this manufacturing republic produced boots and shoes, beef and pork, clocks, clothing, agricultural implements, firearms, carriages, and furniture.[2] Four-fifths of the three million Americans employed in these and other mechanical industries worked in factories in 1880. But in most factories of the manufacturing republic machinery and manufacturing methods remained simple, supervision direct, and control local. "For at least a generation," historian Herbert G. Gutman concluded about industrializing America, "the factory and its disciplines, the large impersonal corporation, and the propertyless wage-earners remained unusual and even alien elements in the industrial town."[3] In the big towns and small cities of the manufacturing republic, these alien elements did not dominate the scene. Factory owners typically were also factory managers, and like Whitney's father John, were city officials and boosters too.

You can still find the remains of the manufacturing republic, isolated but not erased by the industrial state. Drive southwest from Buffalo, aiming at the westernmost corner of New York state. Turn down route 60, leave the Lake Erie shore behind you, and enter Chautauqua County. Within fifteen minutes, you will climb one side of a long, wooded hill and cross a divide. The streams behind you drain northward into the lake and the industrial orbit of Buffalo: steelmaking, lake boats, and the grain trade. The streams ahead of you drain southward into the Allegheny River, bound for the Ohio valley and the west.

The abandoned silos, trailer parks, and auto junkyards of route 60 stand on what was once some of the most productive farm land in New York state. And before that it provided lumbermen with some of the best beech and maple east of Michigan. In the 1840s, those lumbermen would carry their logs to the rapids of the Chadokoin Creek, five miles from its source in Chautauqua Lake. There sawmills would cut the logs into boards to be loaded onto keelboats and shipped south and west to Pittsburgh. As those pioneering lumbermen cleared the land, they sold it to the incoming farmers and used the profits to build mills and furniture factories at the Chadokoin rapids. There the town of Jamestown grew up, and furniture replaced lumber in the holds of the westward-bound keelboats.[4]

Jamestown served as one of hundreds of way stations for America's journey from the farm to the city. Farmers' sons and daughters not attracted all the way to New York or Chicago, or even to Buffalo or Cleveland, could get a taste at Jamestown of community and commerce. One of the sons, arriving in 1859, was John Jay Whitney.

He had been born in 1834, the youngest of eight children in a family that had come to Watertown, Massachusetts, in the Puritan migration from England in 1635 and had worked its way west to Conesus, New York, thirty miles from Jamestown. His family were farmers, not rich, but established enough to send even their youngest son to high school. When John was seventeen, a local doctor shaped his career by diagnosing his breathing difficulties as consumption and prescribing an outdoor occupation. John chose to become a traveling peddler in the old Southwest, selling bibles, sachets, and writing paper to the people of Arkansas, Louisiana, and Texas.[5]

But before leaving for the West in 1852, he stopped at the village of Silver Creek, near Jamestown, to say goodbye to his sister Lucia, who was teaching music to the children of a wealthy family, the Tews. John Whitney was standing at the gate of the Tew vineyard when he first saw a small, slim young woman walk toward him, stop, take off her sunbonnet, and let down a shower of golden hair. They met and talked, and the memory of Agnes Reynolds Tew's golden hair and soft voice stayed with him through seven years on the frontier—seven eventful years that lived on in family tales of hostile Indians, a dramatic horseback rescue, a narrow escape from quicksand, and a meeting with Sam Houston. John's letters described another side, too: cholera, poverty, and dismal frontier towns with their fallen women.[6]

When he left for the West, he had promised that he would never marry until he had $3,000 and some prospects. In 1859, he returned with the $3,000 and asked George Washington Tew for the hand of his daughter Agnes. They settled in Jamestown, the site of the Tews' main business interests.

Two other important arrivals reached Jamestown at about the same time. The railroad came in August 1860, when the Chautauqua County government came up with the $200,000 needed to convince the Atlantic and Western to lay its tracks south of the divide, rather than hug the lake shore. And the stationary steam engine arrived, adding its power to the limited energy flow of the Chadokoin.[7]

John Whitney matured into a shrewd, bearded, likeable cigar smoker, skilled in cardplaying and business. Traces of his consumption kept him out of the Civil War. His choice of a father-in-law provided him with valuable business connections. George Washington Tew was "a man of great force of character," according to the county history, "whose sound judgment was proverbial." It had helped Tew rise from his origins as a tinsmith through creation and management of a tinware and sheet iron business. He then read the law, became county clerk, moved on to bank cashier, and finally founded banks of his own in Silver Creek and Jamestown.[8]

John Whitney brought to the Tew family a head more attuned to business than either of George's sons had and a fine tenor voice to complete the Tew quartet that sang each Sunday morning in the Presbyterian church at Silver Creek. In 1868, John and Agnes brought the family a son, Willis. Two years later, they added a daughter, Carrie.

The population of Jamestown had reached 5,000 by 1870, but the local leadership felt dissatisfied with the pace of growth. The town's newspaper compared Jamestown's growth unfavorably with that of Grand Rapids, Michigan. Starting in 1860 with the same population, the same type of forest resources, and the same furniture industries as its eastern rival, Grand Rapids had grown three times as fast.[9] To help the town catch up, Jamestown's leaders encouraged William Hall, a local lumberman, to team with British textile manufacturer Samuel Broadbent to bring to town in 1873 the first Alpaca mill west of Philadelphia. They housed it in a long, four-story brick building by the river, powered by 1,000 horsepower of steam engines: Jamestown's first modern factory. That same year, local subscriptions aided a group led by former New York governor Reuben Fenton to set up a factory to make cane seat chairs. And in the spring of 1873, John Whitney formed a partnership with the son of a lumberman and an experienced chairmaker. They invested $20,000 in setting up a fifty-employee factory for making wood seat chairs.[10]

These three ventures touched off a generation of rapid growth. More light manufacturing industries would later follow: tables, decorative metal, photographic paper, washing machines. The population of Jamestown doubled in each of the next two decades. The dirt roads running through town became paved streets, with water pipes under them and a horse-drawn railway down their middle. It was in this vigorous village swelling into a city that Willis Whitney grew up.[11]

We first glimpse him at about the age of seven or eight, after supper on a winter evening. Told to climb the stairs of his family's home and put himself to bed, he refused. He saw things in the dark, he explained. His sister Carrie, though two years younger, had to go with him and protect him.[12]

In the second glimpse, he is not quite ten years old but already caught up in the local spirit of enterprise. He organized his friends into a junk-collecting business: bones, scrap iron, worn-out pots and pans. He bought on credit from other boys, carefully entering the agreed-on terms into a homemade ledger. Seventy years later, he could still recall the delight he had felt when the price of scrap rose from forty cents to seventy cents a hundredweight "after I had collected tons of them at much lower rates, buying on credit and selling for cash—thus nearly doubling my profits."[13]

His father's Jamestown Wood Seat Chair Company prospered too. The fifty workmen became one hundred. Sales passed the $100,000 mark. John Whitney's company rebuilt from two serious fires, held its own in times of financial stringency, and grew with prosperity. "Specimens of their work can be seen in churches, school houses, and public buildings," the local newspaper observed, "while their large shipments are daily increasing."[14]

The owners of the new manufacturing plants along the creek built fine new homes in the 1870s on the hill south of the Chadokoin. John Whitney built a square, redbrick house with high, arched windows, located near those of the Halls and Broadheads of the Alpaca mills. The house had a windowed cupola on its shallow roof. It served Carrie as a doll house and Willis as a quiet place to go to escape from other people and read and think. "I was always one of the 'odd sort,' " he wrote many years later, "and so, lonesome or isolated mentally."[15]

Looking north from his cupola over the roof of the Broadhead house next door, he could see the factories along the creek. His father had to walk only fifteen minutes each morning to reach his factory office and only another five minutes to continue up the north side hill to the town hall or the Board of Trade. Home, work, and community were closely connected in the manufacturing republic. John Whitney participated in village government as an assessor, a member of the village corporation, and finally as the last president of the village in 1886, the year it became a city.

His son would recall John Whitney's integrity and carefulness with money. "I was early taught," Willis wrote later, "that a dollar a day was a fair wage and that frequently was unearned."[16] In 1895, awaiting a family visit while a graduate student in Germany, he predicted that his father would call the Germans "greenhorns" and wonder why nobody there spoke English.[17] In 1945, he described his father this way:

> A high principled man, father too set me a good example. He was practical in the New England fashion, and made me familiar with most of the so-called worldly maxims. I well remember how earnestly he tried to teach me the value of a dollar. It was hard enough for me to learn that essential thing, and it is doubtful if I have ever thoroughly learned it, although I've always had enough money for my needs, which are moderate.[18]

Here he characteristically underestimated how well he had learned those worldly maxims. He too would become careful with a dollar. "I never endorsed a note, and God willing I never will," he wrote in 1913.[19] He would look on money not as a treasure to be laid up but as a means of helping others; a score registered for services rendered to society by a businessman, a teacher, or a research director.

He would also follow his father in adopting conservative political views, based on a belief in natural differences among people. John Whitney had followed the Tews into the Republican party. He led the committee of village trustees that recommended a city charter in 1885. The growth of population that spurred this step stemmed from an influx of Swedish immigrants, mostly former farmers who had quickly become skilled woodworkers in the local factories. They had been loyal supporters of the Republican tickets made up of or chosen by the owners of those factories. But in 1885, the local Democrats thought up a way to break down the elite-immigrant alliance. They nominated three Swedish-Americans for local offices, confident that the Republicans would rather offend their political partners than offer the Swedes a proportionate share of local power. They guessed right. "To elect three of that nationality to the board of trustees would be a manifest absurdity," the Republican-leaning local newspaper proclaimed. "Our Scandanavian friends are by no means such unreasonable citizens as that." The Democrats made some headway by this tactic, but control remained vested in the hands of the "capitalists, manufacturers and lawyers—men who pay heavy taxes and who have had large experience in public affairs." John Whitney was a member of the inner circle of this ruling group.[20]

But the number of "Scandanavian friends" continued to grow. Willis Whitney could look eastward from his rooftop cupola and see more houses springing up on the already densely populated "Swede hill." While he carried on his bone and scrap metal business for amusement and extra spending money, the children of Swede Hill helped support their families by weaving cane seats for chairs at ten cents apiece. And while Carrie Whitney learned to play the piano, the twelve-year old daughters of those immigrant families painted chairs for eleven hours a day and took home a day's pay of forty cents. At least so the newspaper alleged, though it drew an angry denial from the management of the Cane Seat Chair Company: the girls worked only ten hours a day it claimed, and the pay was fifty cents. And besides, hours and pay made little difference, since the "painting girls are snatched up by the young Swedes as profitable wives."[21]

The newspapers contained no such exchanges regarding John Whitney's Wood Seat Chair Company, lending at least tacit support to the family's claim that his factory paid higher wages and demanded shorter hours. And concern for the welfare of the working girls moved Agnes Whitney to become a leader in the campaign of the local Womens' Christian Association to create a home for working girls. "It is a fact patent to all who have given the subject any consideration," the Association proclaimed in 1885, "that in many instances proper and healthful home influences do not surround these women." In 1887, after Willis and Carrie had left for school and the Whitneys no longer needed such a big house, they donated it to the Association, and it became the Agnes Home for working girls.[22]

The gift typified Agnes Whitney's religious and social concern. "Deeply religious" and "a woman of marked uprightness of character" were the descriptions her son would apply to her. "One thing she impressed upon me during my impressionable years was that integrity topped the list of qualities that a boy ought to value."[23] Her religious faith was of the unquestioning, serene kind that led her to write in a poem celebrating her eightieth birthday in 1919: "we cannot know, nor care to see the way/ The Father leads His children, day by day."[24]

Alongside religious values, she also filled the house with good books. And she insisted that her son work with his hands. So, in his teenage years, Willis spent his summer mornings working in the chair factory. He experienced industry as something still small in scale, involving dozens of people rather than thousands. Skill with simple hand tools—slash saws, molders, and shapers—still mattered more than machinery. But abundant power from a centralized source had begun to make itself felt. Seeking to explain the impact of electricity years later, he put it this way:

> having once worked in a chair factory where belts connected every machine to shafts that were obviously driven by the big belt of a powerful Corliss engine, I naturally still look for belts.[25]

So John and Agnes Whitney's worldly maxims and religious training stood against a background of steam-powered manufacturing and the exploitation of child and immigrant labor. Willis could see evidence of both from his rooftop cupola: to the north, the factories along the creek, to the east the houses on Swede Hill. But he could also look out to the south and west, and catch glimpses in the distance of wooded country.

He spent many afternoons and weekends there, hiking in the woods stretching down to and along Chautauqua Lake. Those walks remained his happiest memories of childhood: the long downhill road to the swimming hole with young beech trees peeking through the rail fences on either side; the full days of hiking, swimming, and exploring; and the happy weariness of the long uphill walk home. He began to observe and experiment in those woods. If you carve your initials on a tree and come back a year later, will the initials have been moved up by the tree's growth? (The answer, he observed, was no). His mother, who had earlier encouraged him to extend his reading from the stories of Jules Verne to the essays of Charles Lamb, now also encouraged this interest in experiment. She turned over to him a room on the first floor where he could put wood shavings on the floor to absorb the overflow from simple experiments in chemistry.

Formal education at the Jamestown Union School, the recently formed district public school, contributed less to his growing interests. He acquired an aversion to Greek and Latin and little instruction in science or mathematics. But in 1885, when he was sixteen, one of his neighbors brought a first glimpse of science to him.

William C. J. Hall was the son of a cofounder of the Alpaca Mills and was carrying on the business in 1885. But his real love was science. He made much use of his collection of fine microscopes and shared his findings with other members of the Chautauqua Society of History and Natural Science. He joined with other local scions, such as Whitney's uncle, George Tew, Jr., to found a local YMCA. He taught there a class in microscopy.

Whitney joined that class when he was sixteen. One night a week, a dozen boys would take seats around the rotating table in the Hall parlor and pass glimpses of a new world from eye to eye. Hall taught the boys how to prepare their own microscope slides, and Willis soon joined with his classmates to buy a microtome to cut the very thin slices needed for mounting on those slides. Next, he redirected his father's promised $75 gift from a bicycle to a microscope of his own. "I later procured one for $250," he wrote in 1921, "which throughout thirty-five years I have used almost daily."

> One of the first experiments I tried with the microscope was to precipitate metallic silver from silver nitrate solution onto a speck of copper filings. Anyone who has watched these beautiful crystals grow knows that they are surpassingly wonderful.[26]

Whitney's science would remain a visible thing, not a matter of mathematics or pointer readings. His doctoral project would involve observing the color changes of chemical solutions. His best chemistry work would make use of direct observations: the sudden reddening of a water solution as iron ions combined with dissolved oxygen, the clouding of a mixture as colloid particles settled out. This style would help him make direct, sensible attacks on practical problems. It would hamper him when a full explanation required theoretical models built of entities that could not be seen, such as atoms or electrons.

But in 1885 he was not yet apprenticed to science. He was simply a natural history and microscopy hobbyist headed toward a technical career by default. He was a studious yet lively and sociable teenager, with conventional middle-class views. His surviving high school essays include a description of Jamestown written in the best local booster style and a discussion of "Strikes" that concluded:

> It has always appeared to me to be a very unjust, unprofitable, and utterly foolish thing for a party of employees to band together and make threats to their employers. . . . Strikes are almost invariably led by someone who has a grudge against the employer.[27]

He kept a neat ledger detailing every receipt and expenditure of money. He put himself on a time budget, with at least four hours a day reserved for study. That schedule left room for an active social life, recorded in a diary in an elaborate code with symbols for parties, picnics, and visits. A special code symbol for "visits with microscope" suggested that he already considered science something to show and share, as well as study.[28]

He also actively accepted religion. He attended the Presbyterian Church, and judged from his youthful essays, he accepted that church's teachings in the same straightforward way that his mother did. "To be a Christian," he wrote, "open the door; accept God's gift; thank him." He chaired a YMCA committee that circulated invitations to church services to traveling salesmen staying at Jamestown's hotels. By the time he was seventeen, his religion had taken on a moralizing air. An 1886 letter to a friend, full of Polonius-like advice on the choice of companions and reading matter, concluded: "I would rather be an ignorant Christian than a learned infidel."[29]

The moralizing would soon fall away, having served as a scaffolding to support the construction of a morality that remained. Like his father's worldly maxims, his mother's religious piety would survive in spirit long after its letter had faded.

Willis graduated from high school in the spring of 1886 with no definite vocational plans and only one clear intention for the immediate future. He had made up his mind to marry Evelyn B. Jones. They first met when both were six years old, on the way to the first grade class of the Jamestown Free School, when he stopped to help her look for a nickel she had lost in the tall grass. Her name had been one of many appearing in his diary as young women who went with him on picnics or got visited with microscope. Her father was an easygoing traveling salesman, her mother a stern pillar of the Presbyterian church. She leaned more toward her mother's seriousness than her father's fun. As a graduation speaker at the Jamestown Union High School and Collegiate Institute, she had held forth on "Opportunity Now." To her mind, the newspaper reported, "none should ever stimulate Micawber or wait for a ship to come in. There are always opportunities to work for success."[30] She enrolled in the local normal school with the intention of becoming a teacher.

John Whitney, perhaps remembering his own seven-year wait before marriage, urged his son to wait at least through the four years of college. Willis was thinking this over in the summer of 1886, as the family spent its vacation at Prince Edward Island, Canada, and stopped in Boston on the way back. According to Willis' later account, he and his father were walking down Boylston Street near Copley Square when they saw an impressive example of classical architecture, with such names as Newton and Franklin carved into plaques on the walls. They "wandered into the Rogers Building, thinking it was another Natural History Museum." It was in fact the Massachusetts Institute of Technology. A young Institute staff member, James F. Munro, told the "story of technology" to father and son, and "the kid became interested and was marked or marred for life." Entrance exams were being given that week. Willis took them, passed, and got admitted into the Institute as a "special student"—that is, one not yet committed to a particular degree program.[31]

Willis' first encounter with MIT may actually have been more deliberate than that remembered account implies. MIT was a natural destination for a young man with scientific interests, a distaste for Greek and Latin, and an upper middle class background. And the idea fit in with family plans. A year earlier, Agnes Whitney learned that she was slowly going blind from failure of the optic nerve. John Whitney decided to retire from business to spend more time with his wife and family. "I figured out that life was for living," family tradition quotes him as saying. "I thought I had laid aside enough . . . I never saw any point in having so much that I had not time for life."[32] In 1887 he sold the chair company and invested the money in local real estate. He and Agnes fulfilled their earlier intention by donating their house as a home for working girls. John Whitney decided to move the family to Boston, where Willis could attend MIT and Carrie could study piano with a noted Boston teacher.

Willis Whitney would spend his summers in Jamestown for most of the next fifteen years and would return there to do one important technical job. But in 1886 he cut his ties with his boyhood home and with the habits he had formed there. He would never again keep the orderly ledgers and diaries that had helped him follow his father's worldly maxims. He would drift away from the simple and literal religion he had learned from his mother, though he underwent no dramatic loss of faith. During his freshman year at MIT he taught Sunday school in Boston's Chinatown and helped organize worship services for sailors in the harbor. But his skepticism grew, fed by, among other things, the antireligious essays of Mark Twain. Formal religion faded away. Science replaced it.[33]

And though his parents came to Boston, he drifted away from them too. He remained a dutiful son. For example, when his mother was approaching complete blindness in 1902, he interrupted his busy professional career to accompany her on a three-month tour of Europe for a final view of the sights there. But John and Agnes Whitney gradually came to have less and less to say to their son. Willis' niece Agnes recalls his visits many years later to mother in her Boston apartment. Mother and son would sit together in the drawing room. The conversation would begin, sputter along for a while, and finally flicker out. Willis would finally give up, and as his mother sat sightlessly across from him, he would read his newspaper until it was time to leave.[34]

Jamestown and his family became for Whitney, not a base to return to, but a basis for comparison. General Electric's works on the banks of New York's Mohawk River contrasted sharply with the factories on the Chadokoin. He would not find at Schenectady the close connections among home, work, and community that he had known in his youth. Most leaders of giant corporations avoided local responsibilities of the sort John Whitney had sought. But in place of paternalism and local control, those corporations offered rising wages and the beginnings of a system of pensions and benefits. And they did more than meet the needs of village, county, or region. To produce machines to power a nation, they drew, not just on local materials and skills, but on the world. General Electric brought together on the banks of a New York river steel from Pittsburgh, copper from Arizona, mica from Canada, tungsten from the mines of China, labor from the villages of Italy and Poland, and scientific knowledge from the laboratories of Germany.

But even in this new world, the influence of Jamestown would not be wholly lost. Whitney would capture in an industrial research laboratory some of the atmosphere of the Jamestown Wood Seat Chair Company. He would try to make that laboratory a happy family dedicated to a common task, not a machine built of human parts. But in 1886 both the opportunity to do this and the idea that he might ever want to remained hidden in an unglimpsed future as he traveled to Boston to gain an education that would prepare him for a profession.

3/

Technology

For a boy to come in off the street and gain admission to MIT on the spot was not unusual in the 1880s although it would be unheard of a century later. The school had not yet become a world-renowned university strongly supported by an endowment and government funds and spreading its research and academic departments over a Cambridge campus. Instead, "Technology" or "Boston Tech," as it was then labeled, was an engineering training school cramped into a small patch of land in Boston's Back Bay and paying five-sixths of its operating expenses with students' tuition.[1]

Those financial needs dictated a policy of growth: charge each student enough to make a profit and bring in as many students as possible. Under Technology's vigorous third president, economist Francis Amasa Walker, the size of the student body grew from 200 in 1881 to 1,200 in 1891. Walker achieved this growth by opening the doors to any applicant who could pass the semiannual entrance examination in arithmetic, algebra, plane geometry, english grammar and composition, history, literature, and geography and could pay the tuition. He then relied on a tough freshman curriculum to weed out the unfit. The institute, he declared, "is a place for men to work, not for boys to play."[2]

But two trends of the 1880s turned the institute into more than a workhouse or a playground. The United States was becoming a part of a world scientific community. And Americans were creating a new cluster of technology-based industries. MIT's graduates could take leading roles in either of these efforts. Under the guidance of his most influential teacher, Arthur A. Noyes, Whitney chose initially to take part in the first one. He turned his back temporarily on the predominantly industry-oriented MIT ethic and became a scientist.

Whitney and 197 other boys and girls entered MIT in 1886. He and 123 other men and women survived their freshman year. For Whitney, it was an uphill climb. The mechanical drawing courses left him with a distaste for drafting that ruled out a career in civil or mechanical engineering. He got only a minimum passing grade in seven of his sixteen freshman courses. The others, which he passed with credit, included both semesters of chemistry.[3] His main memory of that first year would be evenings alone in his nine dollar-a-week rented room on Tremont Street, studying hard until midnight. Then, he recalled,

> before taking up my French lessons, which were extra, I laid aside my other studies . . . and took a walk down Washington Street to a place opposite the Boston Globe office. There I got what was called Sennet's surpassing coffee and wheat cakes, so at 1 AM I could give my French the "once over" before going to bed.[4]

By entering as what MIT called a special student, Whitney postponed the choice of a major field. He later recalled making the decision at the end of his freshman year. But the MIT catalogue indicates that he remained a "special" through his second year. In any case, the choice came before he was ready for it. He could not decide whether to make the practical choice and enter the new field of electrical engineering or to follow his interest in microscopy and experiment by enrolling in biology or chemistry.

His indecision paralled a broader division that then confronted the institute. It would, as historian John Servos has shown, divide the MIT faculty for the next half century.[5] The two sides disagreed on whether MIT should become a research university or a center of applied science. The two pulls were personified by two of Whitney's teachers. Each offered him a sharply different career model as he stood on the verge of a career choice.

One of them, physicist Charles R. Cross, had established a scientific reputation for his studies in acoustics. But he turned to applied science. In 1882, he founded MIT's electrical engineering course. The other, chemist Arthur A. Noyes, a recent graduate of the institute and now instructor of qualitative analysis, already aimed at a career that combined research with teaching.

"Charlie" Cross has been described as a "dour, baldheaded individual dressed always in a black cutaway coat . . . a rigid disciplinarian with a sharp tongue, a terror to the dull witted."[6] Over a forty-year career, his view of education remained in line with the prevailing vocational emphasis that he found at the institute when he joined its faculty in the 1870s. "The institute is primarily a professional school. That is the only excuse for its being," he wrote to an MIT president in 1903:

> Professional schools cannot reasonably expect the fun and frolic and general good times which are found in a college. Days of play and evenings of conviviality are not compatible with the serious work of preparation for an onerous profession.[7]

Cross taught his view of professionalism in science and engineering by example, as well as in the classroom. He showed by his own career that one future for the emerging professions of physicist and electrical engineer lay in forming strong ties with the electrical industry. When Alexander Graham Bell needed help in understanding the acoustics of the ear in the mid-1870s, he came to Cross. The two collaborated on work that put Bell on the path to the telephone. When, in the 1880s, Thomas Edison needed a respected scientist to take the stand and testify that U.S. patent 791,080, the key to the Edison incandescent lamp, was original, unobvious, and practical, Edison's lawyers called on Cross.[8] The testimony proved crucial to Edison's victory. Forty years later the company that grew out of Edison's lamp, General Electric, still paid Cross a $500 annual retainer for legal services. "I should dislike to see a man of Professor Cross' authority used against us in litigation," GE's chief patent attorney explained.[9]

And when GE's other progenitor, inventor Elihu Thomson, wanted to draw on college-trained technical talent for his electrical manufacturing company, he too turned to Charlie Cross. Thomson's formal education had stopped at high school. But he had become an enthusiastic amateur scientist, as well as a prolific inventor. In the mid-1880s he allied with businessman Charles A. Coffin to form the Thomson-Houston Company (Houston was Thomson's first scientific colleague), located in Lynn, Massachusetts, just north of Boston. It made arc lighting systems, such as the one that lighted Whitney's midnight walks to Sennet's restaurant. In 1886, the year Whitney entered MIT, Cross invited Thomson to lecture to the MIT electrical engineering class. The inventor, whose scholarly demeanor had earned him the nickname "Professor," made a good impression at the Institute. And he came away with a new appreciation of the value of the college-trained engineer. The next year, Thomson-Houston began recruiting graduates of MIT and other engineering schools to form a cadre of experts to take over the job of designing, testing, and installing electrical equipment.[10]

So, to Charlie Cross, the job of MIT was to turn boys into professional engineers who put physics to work in industry. Cross' view of physics was exactly what colleague Henry A. Rowland of Johns Hopkins stood up to condemn and oppose in his famous address "A Plea for Pure Science." "What must be done to create a science of physics in this country," Rowland asked, "rather than to call telegraphs, electric lights, and such conveniences by the name of science."[11] As Whitney stood poised on the edge of entering Cross' electrical engineering curriculum, a few chemists at MIT, led by Noyes, were creating another conception of science education that came closer to Rowland's standard.

The son of a socially prominent but not wealthy Newburyport, Massachusetts, lawyer, Noyes had taught himself chemistry in his home workshop and had published a research paper even before graduating from MIT in 1887. He entered the profession of chemistry just as it was getting strongly on the path of true scientific professionalism. The American Chemical Society had been founded in 1876, and in the same year Daniel Coit Gilman began to create America's first research university, the Johns Hopkins, by hiring such champions of pure research as Henry Rowland and chemist Ira Remsen. In 1879, Remsen had founded the nation's first true journal of chemical research. When Noyes graduated from MIT and accepted a post as instructor of chemistry at the Institute, he and his colleagues, Henry P. Talbot, Augustus H. Gill, and Samuel Mulliken, formed a small pocket of support for the research ideal.[12]

Noyes' photographs show him as a lean man with the intense expression and fine hands ascribed, often wrongly, to violin players. His toothbrush mustache and refined features suggested a British nobleman or butler. His refinement and reserved manner did not, however, prevent him from becoming, in the words of a later student, Linus Pauling, "a *great* teacher of chemistry."[13]

Noyes devoted the best years of his teaching career to fighting the prevailing MIT educational idea of mass-producing skilled employees for industry. He championed independent thinking. He opposed the rote learning that Charlie Cross and most of his colleagues stressed. "It is power that counts, and not knowledge," Noyes later wrote.

> In the laboratory and drawing room, where students tend to work as if their whole purpose were to go through the mechanical operations as rapidly as possible, the successful instructor will be constantly on the alert to check this tendency. He will be with the student at his desk as much as possible, not telling him what to do, but seeing that he understands and plans out the work for himself.[14]

And this personal contact served to do more than merely impart power over scientific ideas. "We must also keep in view the moral end," he wrote,

> which is the cultivation of the spirit which will lead that power to be devoted to some high form of service . . . to accomplish

much in this direction, we must get into personal relations with the students.[15]

In 1887, as Whitney pondered his choice of a major field, MIT stood poised to go in either of two possible directions. It could follow Cross' lead and become the West Point of the industrial state or it could follow Noyes' lead and evolve into a true research university, turning out graduates with high scientific ideals, with power, as well as knowledge, and with the ability to think for themselves.

But I must not carry this picture too far, into a bad allegorical play pitting black-coated Charlie Cross, representing sordid materialism, against white-coated Arthur Noyes, representing the spirit of research, in a battle for the soul of young American science, personified by nineteen-year old Willis Whitney. There are a few things wrong with that picture.

First, Noyes liked Cross. "I am glad you like Prof. Cross so much," he wrote a friend in 1890. "I guess almost every one does who comes to know him. He is, I think, a thoroughly sincere man—always tells you just what he thinks and is ready to advise you."[16] Second, Noyes did not spurn applied chemistry and the money it could bring in. He devoted a portion of his most active research years before 1900 to the effort to invent and patent a new photographic developer and to a major consulting project for the photographic industry. In this, Noyes followed most of even the most research-minded of his colleagues. A few American scientists of the era, such as Harvard chemists Wolcott Gibbs and Josiah P. Cooke, refused industrial requests for consulting, arguing that "the commercial spirit is fatal."[17] But most of their colleagues disagreed. Even the high-principled Henry Rowland carried out efficiency tests on Thomas Edison's generator and lamp, advised on the Niagara Falls electric power project, and, when he felt underpaid for his consulting services, successfully sued to collect a fee of $10,000.[18]

So the line between pure and applied science was not so clearly drawn in the 1880s as an uncritical reading of "A Plea for Pure Science" might suggest. Nor did Whitney agonize long and deeply over the issue when it came time for him to choose his major. Rather than rely on the advice of either Cross or Noyes, he followed his father's suggestion and took the problem directly to the president of MIT, Francis Amasa Walker.

Walker's office stood on the left of the main entrance hall of the Rogers building. His door stayed open, and he encouraged both faculty and students to drop in. (Twenty-five years later, Willis Whitney would establish his office to the right of the main entrance hall of the GE Research Laboratory and put a sign reading "Come in, rain or shine" above its always-open door.)[19] Whitney told Walker that he was uncertain which course to choose, though he was leaning toward electrical engineering. Walker replied that the electrical engineering course was young, its laboratories were ill equipped, and its role was not yet established. He suggested instead the more established scientific courses and sent Whitney off to talk to William T. Sidgwick, head of the biology department.

Sidgwick noted that he had been a chemistry major and that, in any case, the choice of a major made little difference. According to Whitney's later recollections, he put Sidgwick's advice together with the advice of a friend who had already chosen a chemistry major and with the bad impression of the biology department he had got while arguing with a biology instructor over the merits of the binocular microscope. He chose chemistry. "If I were choosing again," he would say in the 1940s, "I would still choose chemistry. I would seek a broader understanding of basic principles . . . I would lean toward the biological side."[20]

Course V at MIT emphasized neither basic principles nor biology. "The course in Chemistry," proclaimed the Institute's 1886 catalogue,

> is primarily designed to prepare students for actual work in connection with manufactures based on chemical principles. It is also adapted to those who intend to become teachers of chemistry . . . of 61 living graduates of this course, there are now engaged 12% in dyeing and bleaching works, 5% as chem-

ists in iron works, 3% as railroad chemists, 7% as analytical chemists, 8% as metallurgists and assayers, 14% as chemical manufacturers, 25% as professors and instructors in chemistry, 3% in gas works, and 3% as students of chemistry.[21]

When he began this course in 1888, Whitney had no definite intention of entering any one of those careers. For the next two years, he regularly climbed the three flights of stairs to the chemistry classrooms in MIT's newest building. He completed a year of general laboratory practice, three years of analytical chemistry, and a year each of organic and theoretical chemistry. Then he descended to the basement of the building to take a year of industrial chemistry and to write a senior thesis on "A Study of the Methods Used in the Determination of Nitrates in Natural Waters."[22]

It was in the qualitative analysis course that Whitney made contact with the teaching skill and the high ideals of Noyes, who took a personal interest in Whitney and pulled him through the course at a time when Whitney's devotion to chemistry was wavering. "Up to the end of the course, the teacher should consider every student who is doing unsatisfactory work as one of the problems for which he must try to find a solution," Noyes wrote later.[23]

> There is, I believe, no better way of securing attention from a student who is neglecting his work or of bringing up to standard one who is having difficulty with the subject than by showing a personal interest in him.

A letter Noyes sent to Whitney at the end of the first semester of the 1887–88 academic year indicates that kind of personal interest. "I take great pleasure in sending you word that your mark in qualitative analysis for the term is a credit," Noyes wrote. "I hardly think it is necessary for you to change your course, do you?" This proved the first of two occasions, spaced twenty years apart, when Noyes steered his wavering colleague back onto the path of science.[24]

In the fall of 1888, Noyes took a logical step to further his

Whitney at 22 in the year of his graduation from MIT, 1890.

own progress toward a research career. He sailed for Germany, intending to study organic chemistry under the world's leader in that subject, Adolf von Baeyer of the University of Munich. Whitney retained the momentum Noyes had helped to give him and worked his way through his last two years at the Institute with increasing academic success. He chose on graduation in 1890 to begin his professional career as an assistant instructor of chemistry at MIT.

He became one of two among the thirteen chemistry graduates, and one of a dozen or so among the 102 graduates of the class of 1890, to choose a teaching post. Two-thirds of the class, and more than half of the chemistry majors, went directly into industrial jobs. The chemists became managers of chemical manufactories and dye works, consulting chemists, or employees of companies making acids, gunpowder, iron, and steel. The nation's rapidly growing chemical, electrical, and metallurgical industries offered these technically trained men and women many opportunities for rapid advancement. By 1925, no less than one-seventh of the class of 1890 had become company presidents or chairmen, and another 5 percent were chief engineers or treasurers. Many were leaders of technical or semitechnical professions. For example, Darragh de Lancey of Eastman Kodak, Edwin W. Raymond of GE, and Calvin W. Rice of the American Society of Mechanical Engineers stood at the top of the profession of mechanical engineering, and Charles Neave of Western Electric was one of the nation's leading patent attorneys. Four members of the class of 1890—Pierre S. DuPont of the Delaware dynasty, astronomer George Ellery Hale, Harvard economist William Z. Ripley, and Whitney—were national figures.[25]

So Whitney did not choose a teaching career because his MIT degree failed to open up other opportunities for achievement or advancement. He appears instead to have recognized that he had only begun his education in chemistry. Remaining at MIT allowed him to continue that education.

His family's comfortable financial circumstances enabled him to make this decision without passing up marriage. On June 26, 1890, he married Evelyn Jones at her home in Jamestown. After a honeymoon at Niagara Falls and the Thousand Islands, they moved into an apartment on Beacon Street in Boston. The next summer, Evelyn gave birth to a daughter, also named Evelyn but called almost from the first Ennin. Willis loved children and might have wanted more, but (according to their niece) Evelyn had had a difficult childbirth and refused to go through it again. Ennin remained an only child, and that became one of a number of growing strains on what appeared to outsiders as a happy marriage. Evelyn's reserve contrasted with Willis' enthusiasm. Her lack of interest in science made her a less than perfect audience for his monologues on chemistry, nature, and the meaning of life. She loved the city; he liked to get back to the country whenever he could. She preferred a decorous round of social calls and church attendance. He enjoyed spur-of-the-moment expeditions and Sunday mornings spent riding his bicycle. Within four years of their marriage, his career would begin to take him on more and more extended absences from the home. Unlike his father, Willis would find in work a substitute for, rather than a supplement to, a full family life.[26]

But if Whitney's personal life underwent a sharp transition in 1890, his education returned to the course he had chosen for it. For in that year his most important teacher, Noyes, returned from Germany. He brought back a new spirit, fermented in the liveliest chemistry laboratory in Germany.

When Noyes reached Europe in 1888, he learned that Baeyer's Munich laboratory was already overstocked with students. So he went instead to study organic chemistry under Wislencius at Leipzig. He began an *arbeit* (thesis project) on the effect of the structure of organic molecules on the properties of chemically identical substances. But by the end of the year, he reported to a friend, the *arbeit* looked hopeless. However, he had found a brighter prospect. He had begun attending lectures in theoretical and physical chemistry and "had become much interested in the subject, especially as it is one for the most part new to me." Physics, he learned—in an insight that would shape his scientific life, and Whitney's career path— is a tool for investigating chemistry, "just as astronomy calls optics to its aid." By February 1889, he had chosen a new *arbeit* in the field of physical chemistry, a study of the dissolving of salts. He was doing it under Leipzig's professor of physical chemistry, Wilhelm Ostwald. "My 'old man,' I mean Prof. Ostwald, is a very pleasant man," Noyes wrote home. "And he is a bear, I tell you, in knowledge. He has got not only chemistry, but physics, down cold."[27]

The old man was only forty years old and was bear-like only in his broad shoulders and full beard. Wilhelm Ostwald overflowed the boundaries of chemistry and physics into philosophy, literature, psychology, linguistics, and landscape painting. He was, above all an enthusiast and a reformer. His later causes would include energetics (a fundamental revision of the foundations of physics, basing them on the concept of energy rather than those of mass, length, and time); philosophical monism (the doctrine that reality is one, rather than divided into plural entities, such as mind and matter); and a universal language of his own invention. At one point he would even propose a mathematical formula for calculating happiness. But in 1889, his cause was still the rapidly emerging discipline of physical chemistry. Into it he poured his lucid and prolific writing, his charm and imagination, and his capacity for hard work. He had turned a former stable at 89 Bargstrasse in Leipzig into the greatest physical chemistry laboratory in the world.[28]

Noyes became Ostwald's second American student. He joined a group of researchers seeking to understand the forces governing chemical reactions by bringing physics to the aid of chemistry. Just then, they were concentrating on a specific issue: what happens to a substance when it dissolves in water? Does it combine chemically with the water particles, or does it only break up into pieces that mix with the water?

Ostwald did not answer these questions. Instead he served, as his American disciple Wilder D. Bancroft put it, as one of those "who do not make the great discovery but who see the bearing of it, and who preach the gospel to the heathen."[29] He claimed later to have first glimpsed that gospel on a day in 1886 that had brought him simultaneously a toothache, a daughter, and the doctoral thesis of a little-known Swedish chemist named Svante Arrhenius. That thesis contained the "bold and chemically implausible suggestion" that a large share of all the particles of a substance dissolved in a liquid permanently split up into smaller pieces.[30] Some of the pieces carried a positive electrical charge. The others carried a sufficiently large negative charge to make the sum of all the charges zero. In modern terms, the molecules of the solute split up into ions. A salt "molecule" (actually a sodium and a chloride atom next to each other in a crystal) split up to form a positively charged sodium ion and a negatively charged chloride ion with a charge equal in magnitude though opposite in sign. This claim dovetailed with the findings of the Dutch chemist Jacobus van't Hoff that small particles in solution behave like the particles of a dilute gas and can be described by the same theory, the theory of thermodynamics. Ostwald seized on the work of Arrhenius and van't Hoff, furthered it by showing how it explained earlier findings about the strength of acids, and helped inform the scientific world about it through the journal he founded in 1887, the *Zeitschrift fur Physikalische Chemie*. By 1889, Ostwald, Arrhenius, and van't Hoff were the three musketeers of physical chemistry, and Noyes was just one of many young chemists seeking to become their d'Artagnan.[31]

In 1890, Noyes came back to Boston with a Leipzig doctorate earned for his work on an extension of van't Hoff's theory and with a determination to continue vigorous research on physical chemistry, even in the not altogether friendly climate of MIT. He needed assistants and collaborators. Whitney, though busy with his teaching, had the time and the inclination to help. He became a convert to the Ostwald school.

In this conversion, the influence of Noyes seems to have played a larger role than the intellectual appeal of physical chemistry. That discipline, with its emphasis on physics and its dependence on mathematics, seems far removed from Whitney's inclination toward the microscope, the direct experiment, and the simple model. But the physical chemists' program did involve intriguing experiments. It did offer a road to professional status in chemistry. And it did enable him to continue his fruitful association with Arthur A. Noyes. Summing up Noyes' influence, Whitney put it this way:

> He let me work with him on some physical chemical researches, and this work was responsible for my later spending 2 years with Ostwald in Leipzig, and a summer with Friedel in Paris. Work with these men gave me a feeling of surety in chemistry that no mere talk could have done.[32]

He later particularly recalled a Saturday morning in the fall of 1891. He and Noyes had conceived an idea about the lowering of the freezing point of sodium aluminate solutions and a way to use that idea in an experiment testing one of the implications of Arrhenius' theory. They also had in their pockets tickets to that afternoon's Harvard-Princeton football game. But "it looked as though a few days' work on freezing point determinations and electrical conductivities would answer the question. We could not wait, so we gave up the game and stayed in the laboratory." The small chance that Whitney might turn into a sports fan diminished; his growing commitment to a career in chemistry increased.[33]

That Saturday's work led to Whitney's first scientific publication, a joint paper with Noyes that appeared in Ostwald's journal in 1892.[34] The results disclosed in the paper provided further support to the still controversial views of Arrhenius and van't Hoff. The presence of Whitney's name indicated that the process of building physical chemistry into a discipline had both leaped the Atlantic and entered a second generation. Noyes and two other "Ostwald boys," Theodore W. Richards of Harvard and W. Lash Miller of Toronto, had already begun steering their most promising students into Ostwald's specialty. They would stimulate the flow of some forty North Americans to Leipzig. By 1905, those first two generations of Ostwald boys would have established physical chemistry courses at thirty-nine institutions, teaching more than 550 students. Holders of Leipzig doctorates, such as Noyes, Richards, and Bancroft, would be rated as leading shapers of the American chemical profession.[35]

So the main result of Whitney's MIT education was his apprenticeship to the field of physical chemistry. Like a cook or a chemist, he had already blended several ingredients into the compound of his life: the memory of small-town intimacy and paternalism, seasoned by a desire to transcend the manufacturing republic's parochial vision; moral standards and an appreciation of the value of money, imbued by his parents' training; and a taste for the straightforward scientific questions that could be answered by a look through the microscope or by a simple experiment. By 1891, he had added three more ingredients: the prestige and employability of an MIT diploma; a marriage formally happy enough but offering little distraction from a career; and, most important, the guidance and example of Arthur A. Noyes. In the 1890s, he would mix in four more constituents: teaching experience, a doctoral degree, an idealized vision of German science obtained while getting that degree, and a first glimpse of the possible rewards of industrial chemistry.

4/

And Note the Glow

Whitney's favorite classroom experiment during the years he taught chemistry at MIT was one he borrowed from a book by Charles W. Eliot of Harvard. The student began with a length of a particularly heat resistant glass tubing. He used a gas-blast lamp and careful glass blowing techniques to shape it into a type of reaction vessel called a matrass. Into it went sulfur and finely divided particles of iron, in the ratio of the two elements' atomic weights, 32 to 56. Whitney told the student to heat the mixture gradually with a bunsen burner and note what he saw. A bright glow would suddenly appear and spread throughout the mixture. That glow signaled the combination of the iron and the sulfur to form iron sulfide. That reaction liberated far more heat than the bunsen flame had provided—enough heat, usually, to crack the matrass.

But in writing up the experiment, most students merely reported that the two elements had reacted. "Thousands of times," Whitney recalled later, "I wrote after that particular experiment these words: 'repeat and note the glow.' "[1] To the student this may have seemed a nuisance, repeating the laborious construction of a matrass and the experiment merely to note a glow that he had seen but had not seen fit to remark on. To Whitney, however, noting the glow was essential. To him, the core of chemistry was "truthful observation." And observation was an active process. He saw students as seekers of knowledge, rather than as mere vessels into which knowledge was to be poured.

Between 1890 and 1900 Whitney himself began to note a new glow. MIT failed to fill his expectations of what a career in chemistry should be. Instead, it opened for him doors to richer opportunities. He encountered them in Germany, at professional society meetings, and on temporary forays into industry. By 1900, he would be ready to add a major new element to the compound of his life.

In teaching chemistry at MIT, Whitney followed Noyes' example and developed teaching methods based on experiment and thought, rather than on repetition and memorization. "It is particularly true in chemistry," he would write later, "that an excess of school training, characterized by repeated and lengthy analyses, is apt to spoil the interest of an otherwise good man."[2] On another occasion he echoed Noyes: "I have laid special emphasis on the individual mental effort of the student."[3]

In the laboratory, he would assign the student a problem of chemical analysis that was not in the textbook. The student had to consult the literature, decide on a method for himself, carry it out in his own way, and write it out in a paper to be read to the class.[4] Such a procedure taught a student to think like a researcher. It clashed with the prevailing emphasis then dominant at MIT, where Cross' aim of producing industrial employees had won out, at least temporarily, over Noyes' spirit of research. Even Noyes' own department had spun off a course in chemical engineering in 1888. "The demands made upon the Institute for chemists of industrial works—in the lines of dyeing, metallurgy, fertilizers, etc.—is greater than we can supply," MIT's president reported in the next year.[5] The corps of young instructors that Whitney joined had been recruited, not to create researchers, but to give chemists headed for industry, and engineers satisfying their science requirement, a grounding in chemistry's practical side. Whitney's first assignment was to teach sanitary chemistry—the chemistry of sewage cleanup. Only in 1898 would he move on to teach theoretical chemistry.

MIT's policies mirrored those of most American universities. As Servos has noted, U.S. chemistry faculties recruited a growing number of physical chemists from 1890 to 1910 mainly because physical chemistry provided a good background for a teacher of general chemistry.[6] Such a teacher got reminded frequently that he had not been called to the university to pursue his own research or to turn his students into a new generation of Ostwald boys. Instead, his job was to provide elementary knowledge of chemistry to a future engineer or executive who would never again lift a retort or light a bunsen burner. The students who passed through MIT while Willis Whitney was teaching there included such future leaders of American industry as Irinee du Pont, Alfred Sloan of General Motors, Paul Litchfield of Goodyear Rubber, and the Whitney student who would later become his superior at General Electric, Gerard Swope. Such students noted a different kind of glow than the one that warmed Whitney and Noyes.

The Institute's rapid growth slowed in the 1890s. Enrollment stayed at about 1,200 for a decade. Instructors such as Whitney could not expect to advance to an assistant professor's rank as fast after 1891 as they would have if the rapid growth of the previous decade had continued. And since most of the professors were relatively young, few opportunities for advancement would open due to death or retirement. Even for an instructor who demonstrated excellence in teaching, advancement would be slow.

In his first three years at MIT, Whitney did not even gain promotion from assistant to full instructor. His life was pleasant enough, with colleagues such as Noyes and Henry Talbot back from Europe to give intellectual stimulation, with new hobbies such as bicycling to fill his weekends, and with the companionship of his wife and growing daughter in their Beacon Street apartment. But he may have sensed that he needed something more to advance more rapidly in his chosen profession, for in 1894, he decided to follow Noyes' path to Leipzig and Ostwald.

He chose to go to Germany alone, to get settled and well started on a Ph.D. program, and only then to bring over his wife and daughter. That decision allowed him to enjoy for a year the bachelor's life that he had passed up by marrying immediately after graduation from college. So, in May 1894, he was sitting alone in a deck chair on the transatlantic liner *Au-*

gusta Victoria when two young girls walked by arm-in-arm and stopped to talk. Hannah and Mimi Schulze soon introduced him to their family. A shipboard friendship sprung up. For the rest of the voyage, Whitney spent much of his time in the company of the Schulzes, a German-American family with homes in Hoboken, New Jersey, and Hesse-Cassel, Germany. He found himself especially drawn to the oldest daughter seventeen-year-old Ida Schulze.

By the time the ship reached port, he had gained a lasting friend and correspondent. The letters between him and Ida spanned the next forty years, ending only when Ida, who eventually became an enthusiastic Nazi, disappeared into the inferno of wartime Germany. But the letters were most frequent during the next decade. They contain the most open and unrestrained expression extant of Whitney's thoughts and feelings. The feelings appear not to have extended beyond friendship. "It is no secret between us that I have a high opinion and almost improper regard for you," Whitney wrote in 1898. The key word is "almost." They rarely met. But even by letter, Ida offered him a warm, spontaneous companionship that Evelyn could not supply. Ida was enthusiastic, emotional, and interested in art and ideas. She regarded Whitney as she would an older brother. He confided things in her that he kept from his wife.[7]

As he described it in those letters to Ida, his year of freedom in Germany allowed him to live the life of a cosmopolitan, sampling the best of science and culture. His father had provided him with enough extra money that he could begin his visit with a summer of traveling, rather than set right to work. He took a steamer up the Rhine, visited Weimar and Eisenach, toured Cologne and Munich, and spent nine days in Switzerland. This "most pleasant and valuable summer" of his life left him impressed with "the terrible minuteness of my corner of the universe." He decided to immerse himself in German culture, as well as in physical chemistry. He developed an interest in the paintings in Munich's gallery, the medieval implements on display in Nuremberg's tower, and even for the Kaiser ("What he says goes, and that's the stuff to make Konigs of.")[8]

In the fall he returned to Leipzig and moved into a "real German home," renting two attic rooms 100 steps above street level in the house of a Leipzig widow. He lived cheaply, dining on sauerkraut and single-dish dinners, and skimping on coal to heat his rooms, even in midwinter. He used the money he saved to enjoy evenings on the town, such as the one he described to Ida in February 1895: dinner at the hotel de Prusse with a new Hungarian friend; seats at the opera ("I've never heard such music before"); some good wine and conversation at the Cafe Bauer; and finally back to his rooms to write his uplifting thoughts into a letter to Ida before the echo of the music, the taste of the wine, and the glow of the "Great old talks" had faded. "I'll simply try now," he wrote,

> to be whiter than I ever was before. Life is so short, its true purpose and ziel so concealed by everyday scrambles for bread, the natural tendency of the mind is naturally downward, and it's refreshing once in a while to stop and think what we're here for.

Then, in midletter, a sudden shift from inspiration to curiosity, from the meaning of life to the mechanics of death:

> We ought to realize that it's something to be alive, we're going to be dead for an awful long time, and it isn't so very long now to the beginning of our deadness. . . . Did you ever stop and think what you'd do first if you knew just when your machinery was going to stop? Mighty interesting thought that.[9]

On the mornings after such nights, his attention had to shift back from the span of his life to a nearer deadline. He had allotted himself two years in Germany to earn his doctorate. He had taken on a thesis project in Ostwald's laboratory, a study of color changes during chemical reactions. And he had accepted the additional task of translating into English an electrochemistry textbook written by Ostwald's colleague Max Le

Blanc.[10] So his attention turned from good talk at the Cafe Bauer to hard work in the laboratory at 89 Bargstrasse.

By 1895, the former stable had become one of the world's most honored and overcrowded centers of scientific research. The flood of students came largely from abroad, especially from the United States.

To some of the purists in the German chemical community, the "ionen"—the adherents of the Arrhenius dissociation theory—were mere descriptive chemists. They were inferior to the organic chemists, who sought and gained the true prize of chemistry: discovery and identification of the chemical formula for a new substance. But physical chemistry's very emphasis on processes, with its practical value in improving the yield of chemical reactions, appealed to Americans. "A good training in physical chemistry is the best possible training for the technical chemist," wrote Bancroft, who had been at Leipzig two years before Whitney. "The ideals of the organic chemist are not the ideals of the manufacturer."[11]

Bancroft would have been in Leipzig at the right time to encounter personally the inspirational Ostwald, "walking quickly from table to table," showing an active interest in each student's work and leaving the door of his personal laboratory open to everyone.[12] By the time Whitney got there, Ostwald had begun to change. The enthusiast was turning into a bit of a crank. Most of his scientific colleagues rejected the principle of energetics that he so stubbornly advocated. And while some physical chemists, such as his colleague van't Hoff and his student Walther Nernst, could entertain the idea that matter was built up of actual, though submicroscopically tiny, particles called atoms and molecules, Ostwald kept up a stubborn and sometimes bitter defense against that atomic hypothesis. The strain of these controversies, combined with the effort of moving into a new laboratory to replace the overcrowded former stable, seem to have brought on a period of mental and physical exhaustion in Ostwald during the mid-1890s.[13]

So it is not surprising that Whitney found the great man less pleasant and helpful than he had hoped. He settled down to the experimental work for his doctorate and to the slow job of translating the electrochemistry textbook. His evenings were still brightened by good talk, with new friends such as Charles Davenport, a volatile fellow student from the United States, and two men who would later become world leaders in physical chemistry, Frederick Donnan of England and W. Lash Miller of Canada. But the initial euphoria of freedom in Europe wore off. Late winter's dark, rainy days confined Whitney to the attic flat. The magnitude of the job that he had given himself only two years to accomplish became evident. The tone of his letters to Ida changed. It was now a "painfully blue" Whitney who wrote longingly of the home and family he had begun to miss. "Let me see," he reassured himself. "I've got the best wife in the world, that's something." [14]

The best wife in the world arrived in Leipzig in April 1895, accompanied by her daughter and her husband's parents. The family enjoyed a short vacation in Switzerland. Then illness struck John and Agnes Whitney, and especially Evelyn, who was left "practically an invalid." Willis spent much of that summer and fall of 1895 nursing a sick family, while pushing forward his experimental work and "that infernal translation." His second year in Germany became as much of a struggle as his first had been a pleasure. [15]

But he carried that struggle to a successful conclusion. In the winter he completed his laboratory work and earned his doctoral degree. He finished the translation. And in the spring of 1896 he celebrated his success by taking the family to Paris. There Evelyn completed her recovery while he attended lectures at the Sorbonne by organic chemist Jules Friedel. He also visited the Paris laboratory of Henri Moissan. There he heard that electrochemist explain how he put bits of graphite into his high-temperature electric furnace and subjected them to enough heat and pressure to turn them into what he thought was diamond. Whitney had already translated a chapter of Le Blanc's book entitled "The Electric Furnace and Its Industrial Importance." Seeing Moissan use such a furnace may have impressed its value even more firmly on his mind, for eight years later, after Moissan's diamonds had turned out to be merely bits of silicon carbide, Whitney used an electric furnace to transform carbon into a less glamorous but highly useful form, a tough graphite coating on the filament of an electric light bulb. This would lead to the most important invention of his research career.[16]

But the transformation that impressed Whitney most during his two years in Europe had nothing to do with either diamonds or light bulbs. It happened on the day in Leipzig when he successfully defended his thesis and completed the transformation of an assistant instructor of chemistry into a doctor of philosophy. He now belonged to a worldwide chemical fraternity with achievements and traditions far more prestigious than those of American chemistry. "When I 'made my doctor' in Germany," he said twenty years later, "a laurel wreath was put at my place at table. In America I should have had to buy a bunch of cigars for the boys."[17] As that comparison suggests, Whitney brought back an idealized picture of German science with him when he returned in 1896 to confront American reality.

As historian Hugh Hawkins has noted, "what Americans thought they had witnessed in Germany"—the devotion of university teachers to research, the freedom of choice of research topics, the graduate seminars, free electives, and other educational innovations—often had a deeper impact on those Americans than the facets of the German educational system they actually experienced.[18] Whitney would later place little emphasis on the aloofness of Ostwald, the overcrowded laboratory conditions, the drudgery of doing his translation, and the other difficulties of his time in Germany. Instead, just as his view of German culture would remain what he had glimpsed in Munich museums or from the deck of a Rhine steamer, his view of German science would remain the ideal system he thought he had glimpsed beyond the limits of his lab bench and his attic rooms. "In almost every little town of the Empire," he would write there is a university. In almost every university there are several high professors, and in almost every professor there is a research man of high order. . . . every one of these professors delved patiently in his university laboratory using his own and his students' hands, and his lectures were far the lesser part of his work . . . a doctor who has shown great productivity and originality becomes "professor" and that means "wie ein Gott"— only a little lower than a Kaiser.[19]

He would then complete the comparison with another slighting reference to the American parallel: "A professor with us is a conscientious alumnus little older than his assistants. He is stunting his mental growth on a salary no chauffeur would accept."

The contrast contained a good deal of truth, but not the whole truth. Certainly Germany's chemistry profession contained a far larger percentage of researchers of a high order than America's did. The roughly four thousand chemists in Germany in 1897 included perhaps as many as 1,000 researchers. The United States had more people who called themselves chemists—perhaps 5,000 in all—but only about 150 of them did real research and published the results. Germany had a dozen strong universities with research-oriented chemistry departments. In the United States, only the Johns Hopkins, Harvard, Chicago, and a few other schools had serious graduate programs in chemistry. Germany's collection of Technische Hochschulen had far more distinguished faculties and insisted on a far more rigorous application of scientific principles than America's only near educational equivalent, MIT, did.[20]

But Whitney's idealized picture left out some important points. In Germany, only a small fraction of new Ph.D.s could hope ever to ascend to the 'wie ein Gott' level of a professorship. For most of them, the choice lay among the "scandalously poor" pay and conditions of an assistant (a Ph.D. who had not yet taken the 'habilitation,' or license to teach); the only slightly better status of Privatdozent (a holder of the habilitation who had not found a permanent faculty position); or a job in industry. By 1910, some 60 percent of Germany's Ph.D. chemists woud be working for chemical firms. Many of them reached high management positions. But very few did real research or published their results. And a wide gap in prestige and professional status separated them from their academic colleagues.[21]

"In national mental development we might be wise to learn to do as well as Germany," Whitney would argue.[22] He would exert a major, though unsuccessful, effort to secure a form of government patronage for science modeled on the German system. But while proclaiming the superiority of what he thought he had seen in Germany, he would be achieving a compound career impossible in that country. He would become both a professor and a business executive, both an influential industrial leader and an honored member of the inner circle of the profession of American chemistry. And his efforts and example would help create a permanent type of institution, the industrial research laboratory, that would make it easier for those who followed him to bridge the gap between science and industry that loomed so wide in Germany.

But before he could help shape the American scientific community, Whitney had to solidify his place in it. Within a year after his return from Leipzig, he had taken an important step in this direction by adding to his Leipzig olive wreath a membership in the American Chemical Society. That society, like the profession it represented, had existed in the United States for some time but was only beginning to rise to world prominence. Whitney climbed aboard at just the right time to take a good place on that rising wave.

In 1897, the 5,000 Americans who called themselves chemists formed a professional community about the same size as that of the dentists and slightly smaller than that of the undertakers. But unlike such professions, chemists filled strategic positions in a wide range of industries. Some ran manufacturing plants that produced acids or alkalis at sites where abundant materials and energy were available, such as the brine pools

Willis R. Whitney in his 20s, while a young faculty member at MIT in the mid 1890s.

of Michigan or the water power of Niagara Falls. Others processed these raw materials into more complex industrial chemicals in such major industrial regions, such as northern New Jersey. Still others served industries such as steel, railroads, munitions, leather, foodstuffs, and textiles as experts, testers, or consultants. A few had found positions in national, state, or local government, helping clean up wastes or doing research or testing for agriculture.[23]

Perhaps 500 of these American chemists had any academic credentials beyond that of a bachelor's degree. And only a couple hundred specialized in the discipline's major research areas, organic, inorganic, or physical chemistry. The great majority worked as chemical analysts, engineers, pharmacists, medical chemists, sanitary chemists, or agricultural chemists. But the minority of degree holders was growing rapidly. Graduates of MIT's four-year programs found a high demand for their services in industry. Graduates of advanced degree programs found positions teaching chemistry to undergraduates. These degree holders formed the core of an organizing movement stirring within American chemistry.[24]

The leaders of that profession had formed the American Chemical Society twenty years earlier, in the glow of the nation's centennial. But in the 1880s that society had faded into a New York City-based "Gentlemen's club." Then, in 1891, a group of dynamic younger leaders, headed by Harvey W. Wiley of the University of Wisconsin and Frank Clarke of Cincinnati, took over. They proclaimed a policy of creating a society truly national in scope and bringing it to a professional level rivaling its counterparts in Europe. The organization quickly absorbed rival chemical societies, grew to a membership of more than one thousand by 1900, and began a course of further expansion that would see its membership double roughly every ten years until the 1950s, when growth slowed down.[25]

Chemists interested principally in research formed a minority of the American Chemical Society. But that minority firmly controlled the top positions. For example, while fewer than 10 percent of the society's membership had studied in Europe, more than half of its first twenty-five presidents had.[26] Like Whitney, many of them had brought back personal visions of the great tradition of Wohler, Bunsen, Leibig, and Ostwald. They sought to turn those visions into American realities. A Leipzig graduate whose research had already appeared in a German journal could expect in 1897 not only to be welcomed into the American Chemical Society but also to be groomed for a place alongside its minority of research-oriented leaders—individuals such as Wiley, Clarke, Ira Remsen, Charles A. Chandler, and Noyes.

Whitney took advantage of this chance for instant status. When the society's leadership called for the organization of local sections, he became one of the founders of the northeastern section, headquartered in Boston. Joining him in this organizational effort was Elihu Thomson, whom we had met earlier as the self-trained inventor-entrepreneur who addressed Cross' electrical engineering class and who had since become wealthy, semiretired, and an adviser to the young General Electric Company. And when Noyes created, in 1897, the first journal of abstracts of American chemical research publications—the parent of today's *Chemical Abstracts*—Whitney prepared the section on biological chemistry.[27]

So Whitney could see before him a clear path to leadership in the profession of chemistry. At the same time, he faced the prospect of slow advancement at MIT. Even after his return from Germany with his Ph.D., he would spend four more years as an instructor before promotion. Why did he not strike out on his own and get a position as an assistant professor at another university? Certainly such positions became available in the 1890s. Whitney's personality and demonstrated teaching ability would have impressed a search committee. At another school, he could have created his own physical chemistry laboratory and probably have advanced rapidly to full professor. To explore why he did not take this step, I compare him to two slightly senior colleagues who did: Noyes and Bancroft. Noyes created two of the world's leading centers of academic physical chemistry research, first at MIT and later at Caltech. Bancroft created a third at Cornell. Both resembled Whitney in their training, teaching ability, and dedication to research. But there were important differences, too.

Noyes and Whitney differed in their personalities and in their approaches to science. The reserved and sensitive Noyes worked quietly behind the scenes. He counseled students privately, in warm letters or on sailing trips, rather than dominating the laboratory with enthusiasm and a booming voice. And he understood far better than Whitney—indeed, better than Wilhelm Ostwald himself—that the future of physical chemistry lay in an ever closer union with physics. Whitney hated to lay aside his microscope; Noyes would embrace the opportunities opened up by such advances as X-ray diffraction. And while Whitney would continue to press unsuccessfully for government support of science on the German model, Noyes would learn to work effectively with a new and distinctly American source of funding, the private foundation.

Bancroft, like Whitney, had a Leipzig Ph.D. an exothermic style, and a broad ranging interest in science and its applications. He traveled the path not taken by Whitney, leaving an instructor's position at Harvard to take an assistant professorship at Cornell. There he produced a steady stream of papers and five books. He pioneered in the application and extension of the phase rule discovered by physicist J. Willard Gibbs, and his work eventually broadened to take in alloys, colloids, and medical chemistry. He founded his own laboratory and his own journal. His outgoing, extravagant personality featured a lively sense of humor, at times a bit too sharp to be funny, and an impressive personal magnetism, at times a bit too theatrical to be taken seriously. He was a generalist and a superb lecturer but neither an accomplished experimenter nor a first-rate theorist. Unlike Noyes, he seized on the qualitative rather than the quantitative, took his hints from the practical need rather than the physicist's discoveries, and relied on an intuition and an enthusiasm that would sometimes lead him down some embarrassingly wrong paths.[28]

Here were two models set up by slightly senior colleagues for Whitney to emulate. In personality, he fit a professor's post even better than either of them. He could inspire and subtly direct the work of students and subordinates, as a generation of later colleagues such as Arthur D. Little, Irving Langmuir, William D. Coolidge, and Albert W. Hull would testify. He could display a magnetism and enthusiasm like Bancroft's but without the extravagance. In his ability to champion others with more originality than himself, he resembled Wilhelm Ostwald.

Indeed, on the score of personality and leadership, Whitney could have taken a place as a sort of American Ostwald. He did not do so. He did grow a full professorial beard resembling Ostwald's though it failed to hide the still boyish handsomeness of his face. But he did not move into an assistant professor's post to suit the beard. Many explanations are possible. He may have tried and failed, though no letters survive to suggest that this happened. He and Evelyn liked Boston and may have been reluctant to leave. His devotion to the academic life was not total; his letters reveal an alloyed enthusiasm. "I am kept pretty busy by my work," he wrote Ida Schulze in March 1897, "and part of it I like very well."[29] In September of that year, after a summer of camping by the shore of Chautauqua Lake, he added:

> My work, always uninteresting to anyone but myself, is starting along slowly. I rise a very little every year, at least in my estimation, and my pay is slowly getting worth working for. I do hate giving up nice summer fun for hard work though.[30]

But Whitney's attachment to Boston and his reluctance to work hard in the summer should not be exaggerated. When the General Electric opportunity came along a few years later he gave up both Boston and his vacations. The more important reason that Whitney did not move to an independent academic position seems to be not a lack of ambition or industry but an unwillingness to focus his efforts within the narrow bounds of an academic career. Noyes had come back from Germany with a clear scientific strategy: to extend the ionic theory and to search out its limitations. Bancroft came back equally committed to extending the application of Gibbs' phase rule. Whitney came back with no such intellectual focus for his work. In experiments on solutions, he followed Noyes' lead. Regarding the seminal work of Gibbs, he later admitted: "I studied his papers in the Connecticut *Transactions,* but could not grasp their significance."[31] Noyes carried out his program in a steady stream of research papers in the 1890s and published a textbook besides. Bancroft wrote a book on the phase rule and founded a journal. Whitney's publication list was modest, with only eight titles by 1900, and included no books or review articles.

So Whitney's rise in academic science appears limited not by his temperament but by his intellect. He remained a generalist in an age of growing specialization. Owing either to lack of understanding or lack of interest, he did not dedicate his efforts to a definite research program in physical chemistry, as Noyes and Bancroft did. His limitations as a pure scientist—that is, as a research strategist and producer of influential papers—show up clearly in a contrast between his joint work with Noyes and the independent scientific work he did while still at MIT.

Begin the contrast with a look at a joint paper that Noyes and Whitney published in 1897 on the dissolution of substances in their own solutions. It follows perfectly the model for a modern research paper. It begins with a clearly delimited question: how fast will a block of salt or metal dissolve when placed in a liquid that already holds in solution a given amount of that salt or metal? It presents a simple hypothesis: that at the surface of the block, the liquid will always remain exactly saturated. That is, it will hold as much of the dissolved substance as a liquid normally can at its particular temperature and pressure without any crystallizing out. This saturation condition will govern the rate of further dissolution. More specifically the rate of further dissolution will be proportional to the difference between that saturation concentration and the concentration of dissolved material in the surrounding, unsaturated liquid. It describes a straightforward set of experiments designed to test the hypothesis. It presents a table of data and a graph illustrating the conclusion that those data do confirm the hypothesis. The results are published compactly and promptly: a small step forward for physical chemistry, soon to be followed by more from Noyes' laboratory.[32]

Now contrast that paper with one published by Whitney alone, "On the Corrosion of Iron." It describes work that Whitney began just after completing that joint paper with Noyes, work usually described in Whitney's biographical sketches as the most important science of his career. But its author seems to have felt little compulsion to publish it rapidly. An effort apparently completed before the turn of the century does not appear in the *Journal of the American Chemical Society* until 1903. And even then, it appears as a descriptive review, rather than as a report of quantitative results.[33]

It addresses a long-standing question: why does iron rust when wet? To answer that question, Whitney applied the ionic hypothesis of physical chemistry to the field of electrochemistry: the study of the relations between chemical change and the movement of electric charge. Electrochemistry had been put on a modern footing by Michael Faraday more than half a century earlier when he showed that chemically equivalent amounts of a substance (that is, a mass of any substance in grams numerically equal to its molecular weight) released identical amounts of electric charge in an electrochemical reaction. A contemporary of Faraday's, the French chemist De la Rive, had seized on this hint to explain the rusting of iron as an electrochemical process. Small regions of impurity on a piece of iron, De la Rive suggested, entered into electrochemical reactions with the liquid to provide one route for transfer of electric charge according to Faraday's law. The iron and the liquid underwent a reaction that completed the circuit of charge transfer. The whole thing worked like a tiny electric battery. The rusting process really represented the discharge of that tiny battery.

By the late 1890s, at least two competing theories had arisen. One held that oxygen and hydrogen in contact with the iron formed a reactive but short-lived layer of the chemical hydrogen peroxide on the surface of the iron, and it caused the rusting. So iron would dissolve only into water if oxygen was present. Another theory held that the dissolving of iron and subsequent forming of rust would occur only if carbonic acid was present.

Whitney had been drawn into this controversy while carrying out a consulting assignment at a Boston area hospital troubled by rusting pipes. He had found that carbonic acid had indeed been present in the hospital's pipes. Water treatment to eliminate the acid solved the problem. But was carbonic acid always necessary for rusting? Whitney aimed to apply the ionic theory to show that it was not.[34]

To do this, he expanded the mechanism De la Rive had suggested into a physical chemistry model of the corrosion of iron. The physical chemistry of a battery had recently been explained by Nernst. A battery typically consists of pieces of two different metals (the electrodes) separated by a layer of liquid (the electrolyte). At one electrode, called the cathode, the electrode metal dissolves slightly into ions that enter the electrolyte and into electrons that remain in the electrode.* That dissolving reaction is called oxidation. The ions then travel through the electrolyte, representing a transfer of positive charge. Meanwhile, at the other electrode, called the anode, a reaction called reduction is occurring. That means the combination of dissolved particles of the anode's material with the anode itself. This reaction represents a transfer of positive charge and requires electrons for its completion. So if you connect a wire from the cathode to the anode, those excess electrons that were produced at the cathode can flow through the wire and meet the anode's need. On the way, they can supply energy for an external need—to start a car or light a lamp, for example.

Applying this theory to the corrosion of iron meant assigning to the chemical players present during rusting their appropriate parts in Nernst's little drama described above. The iron takes the part of the cathode. The water can serve as the electrolyte, thanks to the ionic theory; an electrolyte has to contain its own ions, and Arrhenius' theory had argued that water did indeed dissociate slightly into positive and negative ions. But where was the anode? Here the physical chemists filled in a blank in De la Rive's theory. The anode consisted of regions of metal (either a different metal or part of the iron it-

---

*Elecrons, the fundamental particles of negative charge, had not yet been discovered at the time Nernst introduced his theory. Indeed, some electrochemists would deny their physical existence. The terminology used here is a modern paraphrase of the language Whitney would actually have encountered or used.

self) electrically in contact with the iron but coated with hydrogen ions. The reduction reaction consisted of the recombination of those hydrogen ions into hydrogen atoms, with the aid of electrons that moved through the metal to the reaction site. So this circle of reactions had two net effects. At the anode, hydrogen evolved. And at the iron cathode, iron dissolved. If oxygen had dissolved into the water near the cathode, that oxygen would chemically combine with the dissolved iron to form the characteristic red flakes of rust. The key point of the theory was its argument that neither air nor acid was required to make the iron enter the electrolyte. The mere presence of dissociated hydrogen ions in the electrolyte and the proper electrical contact between anode and cathode sufficed.

So to test the theory, Whitney had to find out if the iron would in fact dissove in water that had been carefully purified to remove all traces of air and acid. He placed pieces of iron in sealed bottles of water that had been carefully treated to remove all traces of oxygen and carbonic acid. He left the bottles on the shelf for weeks. Then he took them down, opened them, and shook them. Clouds of reddish rust immediately formed and settled to the bottom of each bottle. This rapid and copious rust formation indicated that iron had been steadily dissolving in the water while the sealed bottle stood on the shelf. For such a large amount of iron could not have dissolved in the short time between opening the bottle and shaking it to provide the oxygen needed to form the rust particles. This demonstration that iron would dissolve in the absence of carbonic acid and oxygen provided strong evidence against the carbonic acid and hydrogen peroxide theories but fit the prediction of the electrochemical theory.

Whitney had arrived at his conclusions and performed the key experiment before 1900. He had sent his undergraduate students out to gather further evidence in the electrochemical theory's favor. For example, the theory predicted that hydrogen would be produced during electrochemical rusting of pipes. A Whitney student opened up rusty radiators in Boston apartments, lit a match, and verfied that hydrogen was indeed present. Other students carried out variations of the bottle experiment.

But Whitney published none of this until 1903. And even then, his paper provided a general review of the subject, not a series of experimental results. He described the key experiment with the acid-free, oxygen-free bottles loosely in one paragraph set in the middle of several pages of discussion. He provided no supporting data, tables, or graphs. The article contained only two citations of previous work. If Whitney had searched the literature even as far as Ostwald's *Zeitschrift fur Physikalische Chemie,* physical chemistry's leading journal, he would have found that he had been beaten to the punch. Wilhelm Palmaer, a student of Arrhenius in Sweden, had published an article in 1901 that presented arguments and described experiments similar to his in support of the electrochemical theory of the corrosion of iron.[35] Whitney's readable paper can be credited with introducing that theory to a wide American audience. But it cannot be put forward as evidence that Whitney "discovered" or "proved" the theory.

This episode sums up Whitney's career as an academic scientist. He kept his pure research in close touch with applied problems. He had no trouble choosing interesting questions, in arriving at good answers to them, or in designing simple, effective experiments to test those answers. But he did not publish his results regularly in the short, specific, footnoted, quantitative research papers that are the mark of a modern scientist.

At the same time as he was diverging from the model of a pure scentist, his interest in applied science was growing. Starting in 1897, he began to spend an increasing share of his time consulting for industry. The investigation of the rusting hospital pipes would be followed up by other projects that offered bigger opportunities for making money.

This activity did not mark a turning away from the path marked out by Noyes. Opposition to the trade school emphasis of MIT education did not require, in Noyes' view, a rejection of personal opportunities to profit from chemical research. While turning out the stream of research papers that established his place among the ionists in the 1890s, Noyes also found time to follow up some of his ideas for making money in the photography business. "I have discovered a new developer," he wrote to a student in 1891. "I think there may be money in it." He went on to explain his motives:

> I can imagine the look of scorn which has been gradually deepening on your face as you have read through these pages—scorn at my turning my attention to industrial work. But I have told you the cause of it—der Liebe—and besides, think of the assistants I can have to work on ions—one for each ion—if it succeeds.[36]

It did not succeed. Noyes learned in 1893 that a German inventor had already patented the developer. But he continued to take on other occasional projects in applied chemistry, such as consulting work for a manufacturer of water filtration equipment and for a mining concern. Then, in 1898, he and Whitney were offered another opportunity by a manufacturer of photographic paper, the American Aristotype Company. They accepted and embarked on a project that would change both their lives. Noyes would get from it the money he needed to establish a laboratory for doing pure research in physical chemistry. Whitney would use it as a stepping stone to a new career.

The opportunity concerned a glue-like substance called collodion, a reconstituted form of cotton or other natural fiber that can be dissolved in a mixture of ether and alcohol. The solution can be spread out on plates, where it will dry into flat, smooth, hard sheets. A coating of silver emulsion can be bonded to the sheets to make the light-sensitive "paper" on which photographs can be printed from negatives. One of the most important types of this printing-out paper used an emulsion of silver chloride that could be made especially sensitive to light by heating it. In the 1890s, America's biggest plant for making this collodion chloride printing-out paper was located in

Jamestown, New York, on Southside Hill, just a block from the Whitney family home.

A Dane named Charles Christiansen had brought the process to Jamstown in 1889. The group of local businessmen who financed his factory included Whitney's uncle, George Tew. They installed a New York advertising man, Charles Abbot, as president of the company. He made the venture an instant success. But the depression of 1893 caused prices to fall sharply. Abbot lowered prices in response and found it very difficult to get those prices up again when recovery came. He faced too much competition. On one side stood the dominant force in the industry, George Eastman, whose company produced the rival gelatine bromide paper. On the other side stood a talented newcomer, a Belgian-born holder of an Sc.D. in chemistry, Leo Baekeland. He had invented a new kind of paper that would bring out a good image under precisely controllable artificial light, rather than require natural daylight as the rival types did.[37]

By 1898, Abbot had adopted a two-pronged response to these threats. He sought to combine with his rivals and stabilize prices. And he tried to cut the costs of his own production process. This cost-cutting effort brought Whitney and Noyes into the picture. The ether and alcohol solvents that nitrocellulose was dissolved in to make collodion accounted for a major part of the production costs of the paper. When these solvents evaporated into the air as the paper dried, that money evaporated away. At some point between 1896 and 1898, some representative of American Aristotype came to Whitney and Noyes and asked them to devise a process for recovering the solvents.[38]

The approach may have come from Whitney's family connections or through former Jamestown neighbors such as the American Aristotype plant manager Harry Sheldon. Perhaps George Eastman served as a go-between. By the later 1890s, he was developing close ties to MIT and was deeply into merger talks with Abbot.

However they got the problem, by mid-1898 Whitney and Noyes had solved it. They kept the details of their method of solvent recovery secret. But it appears to have involved collecting the air above the collodion with fans and passing it over a specially prepared solution that contained a petroleum-based chemical. That solution absorbed the ether and alcohol, and the two solvents were then separated out by distillation.[39]

In July 1899, Whitney and Noyes signed a contract with the American Aristotype Company to govern use of the process they invented. That contract presents a revealing picture of relations between academic scientists and businessmen in the period that has aptly been named the "putting out era" of industrial research.[40] The two academics agreed to grant the company exclusive use of their process. The company in turn agreed to pay half the cost of a small chemical plant on the grounds of the Aristotype Works. Whitney and Noyes would put up the other half of the money and hire a competent superintendent "who will not seek to inquire into trade secrets and processes" at the Aristotype plant while running the solvent recovery unit. Abbot and his associates had chosen to protect the technology base of their company by trade secrecy rather than patents. They required Whitney and Noyes to take the same route. "The contract shall continue," both parties agreed, "as long as said process shall remain a trade secret and unknown to and not used by any other manufacturer of collodion photographic materials." As long as the contract remained in force, Whitney and Noyes would be entitled to "one fourth of the net earnings of said recovery process."[41]

In other words, the academics had achieved the comfortable position of being asked to operate a small chemical business with no cost for raw materials, half of their capital supplied by their customer, and a guaranteed market for their product. However careful with his money Whitney had been made by his father's maxims, this gamble looked good to him. "I have invested all that I can lay hands on in a small chemical manufactory," he wrote Ida Schulze in the fall of 1898. The investment brought rapid returns. Within a short time Whitney and Noyes were each collecting more than $1000 a month. By early 1901, Whitney alone had taken in more than $20,000.[42]

The secrecy of the process held up well enough for the partners to build an enlarged plant in 1900 and to renegotiate the agreement in 1904 to receive a continuing payment for the next five years of $150 a month plus 5 percent of profits. By then, Abbot had succeeded in merging the Aristotype Company with George Eastman's company on favorable terms. The influence of the solvent process on the merger was probably not decisive. In his thoroughly researched history of this phase of the photographic industry, historian Reese Jenkins does not mention it. But it may have helped, especially since it could be used with Eastman's other collodion manufacturing processes, including the making of roll film. The merged companies rewarded Whitney and Noyes by purchasing the solvent recovery plant with Eastman Kodak stock. The proceeds from the sale of Whitney's share of that stock eventually paid for his first house in Schenectady.[43]

So Whitney's first major venture into industrial chemistry brought him gratifying returns and valuable lessons. It showed him that he did not have to invent a new product to make money. Industries would pay well for process innovations that lowered their costs of production. An academic chemist could put his training to work designing these money-saving processes without leaving the university.

These lessons did not suffice to detach Whitney immediately from an academic career. Arthur D. Little, founder of a rapidly growing chemical consulting firm, claimed later that in the late 1890s he had offered Whitney a job that would have paid twice the salary he was getting from MIT. Whitney had turned him down, Little said, with the words "I'd rather teach than be president."[44]

That answer should not be taken to imply an indifference to money. Whitney could afford to pass up a bigger salary. His father's aid would have allowed him to live comfortably on whatever MIT paid him. He valued his MIT salary, not as a necessity, but as a mark of his independence and a measure of his professional success. At about the time Little made his offer, Whitney tried to get a reading on that success measure.

He went to the president of MIT and asked for a raise of $75 in his annual pay. This probably occurred after the 1897 death of president Amasa Walker, through whose open door Whitney had walked as a freshman. His successor, Charles R. Craft, was less approachable, but as a chemist himself, more directly familiar with Whitney's work and promise. He flatly turned down the request. The memory of that rebuff long rankled.[45]

So the last years of the nineteenth century brought Whitney sharp reminders of the slow pace of academic advancement and of the rapid growth of industry's interest in chemists. The decade since his graduation from MIT had seen him advance only a single step on the academic ladder, from assistant to full instructor. Industry, in the form of the Aristotype opportunity and the Little offer, seemed more interested in noting the glow of this exothermic young chemist. And by the end of the decade, industry had recovered completely from the depression of 1893. The distraction of the Spanish-American War was over. Industrial opportunities could only increase.

Picture then, in 1900, a handsome thirty-two-year-old man of medium height and build, still in the process of finding a career for himself. His face has filled out in the four years since his return from Germany but retains the questioning eyes and the outthrust chin beneath a professor's beard. He has an outgoing personality and sound habits; he does not smoke or drink, and he spends as much time out of doors as his teaching job allows.

His family life remains outwardly happy enough. But his trip to Germany has begun a stretch of fifteen years of frequent and lengthy absences from the home. Evelyn has begun to spend more and more of her time with her sister Harriet, whom her husband has never liked, or on vacation in Jamestown. "You see, I'm a widower again," Whitney writes to Ida Schulze in May 1897, describing Evelyn and Ennin's latest departure for a summer vacation. "It's always thus. I'm always leaving them or they are leaving me."[46]

The long stretches of his life without his family could be "rather lonesome of course," he admitted. But the weekends could be filled by bicycle trips to visit friends in the suburbs and the weeks by evenings at the theatre. He went twice in one week to see Sol Smith Russell's *Bachelor's Romance*, finding it "one of the sweetest, most homelike, cleanest things I've seen in a long time." Part of its appeal may have stemmed from happy memories of his own bachelor's romance. Writing to congratulate Ida on her betrothal in October 1898, he told her: "there's no better state for the living mortal. Married people are much worse off."[47]

A six-week family vacation on the shores of Chautauqua Lake in 1897 only emphasized the growing differences within the family. Willis remained enthusiastic, healthy, and vigorously active. In an effort that would become a local legend, he even set out to build his own island in the lake, transporting tons of rock and dirt out to an offshore shoal to build it up into a permanent landmark. Meanwhile, he reported to Ida that all was not well with his wife. "She doesn't have any appetite and is rather nervous. The doctor says months of rest will be necessary to work a change in her external economy." He went on the make one of the few even indirect references to his marriage that he was ever to write down.

> You are right about the people who complain about the way the world uses them. It is the very essence of living to see, find, or make the best of everything. I'm sorry for those whose burdens seem great and can only conjecture what I would do in their place, but you and I, kid, are not loaded down with cares and worries and the sun shines on us every day of the year. We are in luck. Let's wiggle about in the light we've got. The proper thing to do with enjoyable things is to enjoy them and this properly done must constitute the best method of appreciation.[48]

He also began to drift apart from his daughter. He doted on her when they were together. But over her first sixteen years, his absences grew more frequent. She grew healthy and independent. She shared his love of animals and the outdoors. But her independence tended to express itself in headstrong moodiness. Her pets became the center of her life. And she never extended her love of nature into an interest in the microscope or the concepts of science that her father tried to share with her.[49]

So by 1900, Whitney's professional life had become active enough to keep him away from his family for long stretches. He had explored some promising career paths in teaching, research, and consulting. But he had not committed himself to a program that would widen one of those paths into a road. He continued to put his life together out of diverse elements drawn from university duties, the chemical profession, industrial projects, and his responsibilities as a husband and father.

On October 10, 1900, Whitney got an opportunity to develop this compound further by altering the proportions of the elements that went into it. The opportunity came in the form of a letter from Elihu Thomson. That inventor's interest in education had helped cement ties between MIT and the electrical industry. His interest in science had led him to become one of the founders of the local section of the American Chemical Society. At the General Electric Company, which he had helped create, he remained active as a consultant, with an office at the company's Lynn, Massachusetts, plant. Most recently, in 1899, he had been named one of MIT's first two nonresident professors.

The note from Thomson showed he had got involved in a new effort to combine industry and science. It read:

> I am requested to arrange to have an interview with you in regard to the possibility of your taking up electro-chemical and similar work with the General Electric Company in Schenectady. If you could call at my office at the works of the General Electric Company in Lynn, say Friday afternoon this week, I could talk the matter over with you, or, if more convenient, the matter could rest.[50]

5/

Industrial Research Experiment

At that Friday afternoon meeting, Whitney got an offer that would change his life. But he was not quite ready to make the change. Even when, a few weeks later, he accepted the offer, he accepted it as an experiment. For the next two years, he continued the varied scientific and personal activities he had begun before receiving Thomson's letter. He undertook a research program at MIT in colloid science, a field only indirectly related to General Electric's interests. He helped launch a new academic laboratory devoted to pure research in physical chemistry. He participated as a founding member and officer in a new specialized scientific society, the American Electrochemical Society. And he tried to continue his teaching.

But during those two years, the experiment proved less reversible than he thought it would. His responsibilities to General Electric steadily crowded out those other activities. His intention to create a compound, rather than an elemental, life remained. But his research experiment at General Electric forced him to find a new way to carry out that intention.

On that October day in 1900, the office at the Lynn plant held two other General Electric representatives besides Elihu Thomson. Like him, and unlike most of the other leaders of their company, they looked and talked more like professors than businessmen. Albert G. Davis' studious look came from the early balding of the broad dome of his head, leaving only a fringe of curls surrounding it. He combined a technical degree from MIT with training in the law. In only five years with GE, he had become its leading patent attorney.[1] Edwin W. Rice, the fourth participant in the meeting, looked more like one of GE's bookkeepers than one of its vice presidents. Grey already flecked his receding brown hair, his toothbrush mustache, and the goatee that failed to hide his weak chin. His soft voice and tactful manner owed more to the influence of his father, a minister and Sunday-school organizer, than to his eighteen years of association with businessmen, foremen, and inventors. In 1882, he had rejected his father's offer of an MIT education in favor of following his Philadelphia Technical High School teacher Elihu Thomson to New England for a flier in the new electrical industry. While Thomson invented improved types of arc lights, generators, regulators, and systems, Rice hired workmen, supervised the preparation of drawings, bought machine tools, and organized manufacturing processes. The complementary skills of "E.W." and his professor, supplemented by the business talents of their associate Charles A. Coffin, carried their company to success. In 1892, it merged with Thomas Edison's companies to form General Electric. By 1900, Rice had risen to the post of GE's third vice president of engineering and manufacturing.[2]

A quarter century later, Davis tried to recall the discussion he and Rice had on the train down to Boston about the approach they should take to Whitney. He remembered emphasizing that they should assure him that "although we were businessmen, we too possessed scientific ideals."[3] They were, and they did. But their business needs and scientific ideals had met in a problem that involved a thread of carbon slender as a hair and a few inches long: the filament of an incandescent lamp.

Enclosed in an evacuated glass bulb, that filament remained the heart of General Electric's most profitable product. In the twenty-one years since Edison had perfected his carbon filament lamp, its use had grown until, by 1900, 23 million light bulbs were sold in the United States. But that was slightly less than one for every three Americans, so a giant market remained to be tapped. (By 1979, 1.5 billion light bulbs would be sold in the United States, or nearly seven for each person.)[4] GE's strong position in carbon filament lamps offered it no assurance that it would capture the big emerging market for the people's lamp. For a stream of inventions originating in Europe around the turn of the century threatened to make the Edison-type lamp obsolete.

How had General Electric got into this vulnerable position? Rice and Davis knew that the threatening inventions had been made mainly by Europeans with advanced training in science. And they knew that their own company had failed to make effective use of either advanced science or of trained scientists.

The failure could be traced back to Thomas Edison. He had called on some chemists and physicists, a few of them with postgraduate training in German laboratories, to help him develop his lamp in 1879. But he made sure that their interest in chemistry and physics did not get in the way of invention. "We've got to keep coming up with something useful," an associate later recalled him saying.

> We can't be like those old German professors who, as long as they can get their black bread and beer, are content to spend their whole lives studying the fuzz on a bee.[5]

The wording of that quote probably improved over the years, but its spirit reflects the authentic Edison. Edison enjoyed science, and when he put his hand to it he could make valuable contributions. For example, in 1878 he developed the tasimeter, a heat-detecting device of unprecedented sensitivity, and used it on a scientific expedition to measure the temperature of the sun's corona during an eclipse.[6] And in 1882, he observed in one of his light bulbs the "Edison effect," a current of electricity passing not through wires but through the evacuated space within the lamp. It would later become a basis for modern electronics.

But Edison chose not to follow up on these discoveries unless they promised an immediate payoff. When the tasimeter proved impractical as a heat detector, and when the Edison effect showed no signs of commercial value, he dropped both. "I have little room for the purely aesthetic side of my work," he explained.[7]

His use of trained scientists was as limited and selective as his use of science. He hired Francis Upton, who had studied physics with Barker at Princeton and Helmholz in Germany. But he turned Upton first into a mathematical assistant and then into a lamp factory manager. He hired chemists with Ph.D.s to become insulation specialists or literature searchers. They did not carry out scientific investigations or write scientific papers.[8] For a brief period in the late 1870s, Edison courted the endorsement of leaders of academic science for his inventions. He visited a meeting of the National Academy of Sciences to demonstrate his phonograph and put his name to a paper that Francis Upton delivered to the American Association for the Advancement of Science. He contracted with two of the nation's leading physicists, Henry A. Rowland and George Barker, to have them do tests that supported his claims about the efficiency of his system of electric lighting. But his romance with the scientists quickly cooled when Barker began to praise the work of rival lighting inventor Hiram Maxim, and Rowland began to resent the suggestion that Edison's supporters could buy his good opinion.[9]

After Edison left the electrical industry in the late 1880s, his successors not only continued his policy of neglect for pure science but even extended it to a neglect for the advanced development work in which Edison had excelled. Neither the Edison General Electric Company nor its successor, General Electric, maintained a laboratory at all comparable to Edison's Menlo Park. Instead, those companies imitated the sharply different technological strategy of their rival, the Westinghouse Electric and Manufacturing Company: they purchased patents and short-term consulting services from independent inventors.

Westinghouse had used this strategy effectively from 1885 on to gain a foothold in the new field of alternating current. This technology, pioneered in Europe, offered company founder George Westinghouse a way to supply electric power at lower cost than Edison's direct current system. To exploit this opportunity in the late 1880s, Westingouse purchased the patents of Briton William Gibbs and Frenchman Lucien Gaulard on the transformer, the invention that held the key to supplying alternating current. And to secure rights to the best method of using alternating current to power factories, he purchased the patents of Serbian-born inventor Nikola Tesla on the induction motor. Westinghouse then provided inventor William Stanley with funds to establish a laboratory at Great Barrington, Massachusetts, to develop the transformer further for American use. And he hired Tesla as a consultant to aid the Westinghouse engineers at Pittsburgh in perfecting the induction motor. But neither effort became a permanent research operation. Both Tesla and Stanley had severed their connections with Westinghouse by 1890.[10]

After their work had created a competitive advantage for the Westinghouse company by the early 1890s, General Electric responded in kind. It purchased the patents and consulting services of inventor Charles Bradley, who held the rights to a key device for changing alternating to direct current, the rotary converter. And to design an induction motor to match Tesla's, GE purchased the consulting services of the Swedish engineer Ernst Danielson and of physicist Louis Bell, who held a Ph.D. from Johns Hopkins. By 1897, GE secured technological parity with Westinghouse and entered into a mutually beneficial patent exchange with its rival by swapping rights to its patents in lighting, traction, and the rotary converter for Westinghouse's on the transformer and inducton motor. By then Bradley had left for the electrochemical industry, Danielson was back in Sweden, and Bell had returned to teaching.[11]

In the last two decades of the nineteenth century, that policy of leasing rather than purchasing technical talent appeared not only sufficient but also necessary. For corporations then had no solid legal basis for believing that they could own the entire technical output of an employee. An inventor under contract to a company had legal grounds for claiming that the company owned only those inventions that he made in the narrow field that the contract might specify. For example, in 1885 William Stanley had agreed to run a laboratory for Westinghouse, supported by $1,200 a month from that company, to develop the transformer. By December 1886, he was claiming that a discovery he made in that laboratory in a closely related but separate field—a new electric lighting concept called "molecular light"—belonged to him alone.[12]

And even full-time employees could claim ownership of their own inventions. In 1890, the manager of the Edison Machine Works in Schenectady wrote to the company's lawyers to complain that employees were securing parents and refusing to turn them over to the company. He received a discouraging answer. "The invention," the lawyers explained,

> belongs wholly to the person who first receives the idea and reduces it to a practical form. It makes no difference that at the time he may be in the employ of another man who is paying him for devoting his time to the very subject in connection with which the invention is made.

But, the lawyers suggested, there was some hope:

> The only way that occurs to us by which the Machine Works can avoid the constant recurrence of the annoyance mentioned is to enter into a contract with each of their employees to the effect that all inventions made in matters connected with the work which they are engaged to perform during their connection with the company shall belong to the company. This, while it would doubtless cause considerable trouble for the company, seems to be the best way in which the difficulty can be avoided. Whether it is practicable for you to make such contracts is of course a question for you to decide. We fear our suggestion is somewhat impracticable.[13]

For most companies in 1890, that suggestion would indeed have been impracticable, as the lawyers feared. Owners of small manufacturing plants lacked the legal skills to write such a contract. And even if they hired lawyers to do the writing, enforcing the contract might require too much of the time of the owner and his few assistants.

But by the 1890s, a few companies had begun to look upon the whole nation as their market and were beginning to develop the internal organization needed to serve that market efficiently. That meant centralized, formalized management hierarchies, with layers of middle management organized by function into departments: manufacturing, advertising, engineering, and legal. The trend had begun with the railroads at midcentury. In the following decades it had accelerated to take in industries such as meat packing, oil production, sewing machines, steel, and electrical manufacturing.[14]

For such integrated corporations, technology stood as a key raw material to be controlled in much the same way as iron ore reserves, rights of way, or underground oil pools. Technology rights had to be secured, by purchase, by merger, or by internal development. That suggestion of the lawyers to have all employees sign comprehensive contracts handing over in advance to the company any inventions they might make did not appear at all impractical.

In 1892, Edison's companies, including the Schenectady machine works, merged with the Thomson Houston companies of Lynn, Massachusetts, to form the General Electric Company. GE's management quickly established the kind of centralized structure needed to control technology and other key resources. By 1900, engineers joining GE signed a printed contract turning over in advance to the company any inventions they might make while in the company's employ.

So a social invention, the contract assigning future patent rights to an employer, made practical for companies the kind of employment offer that Thomson, Davis, and Rice made to Whitney on that October day in 1900. That mechanism for controlling technology fit in with two mechanisms for controlling markets: the merger and the trust. The market for steel and cigarettes, lubricants and locomotives, typewriters and transformers, and dozens of other goods had grown to encompass the whole nation by 1900. But the capability to satisfy the demands of that market had grown even faster. The return of prosperity after the depression of 1893 brought the threat of ruinous competition, excess manufacturing capacity, and decreasing profits. Industry's answer came in the form of a great wave of mergers: in 1899, 340 companies disappeared into the new combinations, versus only 36 three years earlier. In 1900, the number of merged companies rose to more than 1,200. The new giant companies could shut down their inefficient plants, control production and prices, and maintain profits high. But what would prevent new competitors from springing up, entering the once-again attractive market, and setting off another round of overproduction, falling prices, and vanishing profits? The control of technology provided one possible answer.[15]

No industry illustrated this logic more clearly than the manufacture of incandescent lamps. After Edison proved the practicality of the carbon-filament lamp, a cluster of companies sprang up to share his market and his profits. The creation of General Electric in 1892 had coincided with the final legal decision affirming Edison's key lamp patent. For two years, GE wielded that patent like a sword to cut down the independent lamp makers. But with the expiration of Edison's patent in 1894, they began to spring up again. For a while, the purchase of new patents sufficed to block these new rivals. For example, in 1898, GE's chief lamp engineer John W. Howell interrupted his honeymoon to sail to Italy and buy up the patents of inventor Arturo Maligniani on a new way to improve the vacuum inside an incandescent lamp. GE put that patent to work to close down a number of competitors.[16]

Meanwhile, Howell and his colleagues were mechanizing the process of lamp manufacture by inventing the unit system of production, a sort of automatic assembly line that reduced the labor content of a lamp and allowed GE to produce lamps at lower cost than its rivals. These technical strengths in patents and manufacturing served as powerful arguments when GE president Charles A. Coffin sought to bring the remaining independents within the GE fold. He persuaded two of the most capable independent lamp executives, Burton Tremaine and Franklin Terry, to form a federation of independent manufacturers under the name National Electric Lamp. Though ostensibly a rival, it was in fact controlled by GE, which owned 60 percent of its stock.[17]

This strategy of controlling the market by purchasing patents, lowering manufacturing costs, and absorbing rivals succeeded. By 1900, the GE-National combination controlled more than 90 percent of lamp sales. And the strategy required little spending for the internal development of advanced technology. Annual GE expenditures for research on and development of incandescent lamps fell to a low of only $4,878 in the depression year of 1895 and came back up to only about $25,000 a year by the end of the decade—less than half the sum Edison alone had spent in 1879.[18]

But the coming of a new century revealed a weakness in this parsimonious policy. GE's control of the technology encompassed only the carbon-filament high-vacuum incandescent lamp, the type Edison had pioneered. In the 1880s and 1890s, trained electrochemists and electrophysicists, mainly in Germany, had come up with new types of lamps that bypassed the Edison-type technology.

Ph.D. chemist Carl Auer Von Welsbach had invented and perfected an incandescent mantle for the gas lamp that sharply improved the efficiency of the incandescent electric lamp's rival. And chemist Walther Nernst, who had taken a doctorate under Ostwald, and whose contributions to physical chemistry would later earn him a Nobel Prize, discovered the electrical analogue to the Welsbach burner. He found that a stick of the right kind of ceramic, when heated by an electric current passing through it, converted part of the energy of the electricity into light. He used that discovery to build a lamp that required no vacuum for its operation yet was longer lived and 50 percent more efficient than the best carbon-filament incandescent lamp.[19]

And in Berlin, professor of physics Leo Arons carried out a thorough experimental study of another long-known light source, the mercury vapor lamp. Put a mist of mercury vapor at low pressure in a glass tube, put a high voltage across it, and it gives off light. The ghostly green glow that Arons' lamps gave off was not suitable for lighting a living room. But the efficiency of his lamps was even higher than Nernst's.

Meanwhile, researchers in a number of European laboratories sought a metal lamp filament with a higher melting point than carbon, another route to a more efficient lamp. Von Welsbach had achieved some success with the metal osmium. Though it was too rare for commercial use, osmium's performance as a filament suggested that other metals with similar properties might be worth a look.

Some of these new lamps and new ideas had become more than laboratory curiosities by 1900. For example, Nernst had sold the patent rights to his invention to Germany's largest electrical manufacturing company, AEG, for a million dollars. (Later in life, Nernst would tell his students of his meeting with Edison at the St. Louis World's Fair of 1903. Edison complained of the difficulties he had faced in selling his lamp ideas to the capitalists, and the relatively small reward he had earned. "That's the trouble with you, Edison," Nernst claims to have replied. "You're no businessman.") Nernst proved again that he was a businessman in 1894 by negotiating a second lucrative sale of his lamp rights, this one for the United States market. The buyer, and the creator of a new company to introduce the Nernst lamp in America, was George Westinghouse.[20]

And General Electric's most dangerous competitor was preparing another possible end run around the incandescent lamp. Westinghouse had also placed his financial support behind the work of Peter Cooper Hewitt, an inventor who was seeking to turn the mercury vapor lamp into a practical light source.[21]

So by September 1900, General Electric faced a clear competitive threat to its electric lighting business. That threat was largely based on the work of trained scientists. This sharply increased the receptivity of the leaders of the company to the concept of a research laboratory when that concept was proposed to them by GE's chief consulting engineer, Charles Proteus Steinmetz.

Steinmetz had actually proposed the laboratory idea at least twice before, in 1897 and 1899. Those times, he took a different approach. He had noted that electrochemistry—the use of electrical energy to promote useful chemical reactions such as the reduction of aluminum from its ore—had become one of the nation's fastest growing industries. Perhaps there were opportunities here for the nation's biggest electrical manufacturing company. He suggested that GE set up an electrochemical research laboratory at its Schenectady Works, power it with electricity from a nearby hydroelectric project the company had built, and see if researchers could discover any potentially profitable new electrochemical processes.[22] In making this suggestion, Steinmetz may have been inspired by the creation a year earlier at Niagara Falls of the Ampere Electrochemical Company. That organization, founded by former GE consultant Charles S. Bradley, was essentially a privately financed development laboratory aimed at finding new processes and licensing or selling them to electrochemical manufacturers.[23]

GE did not act on these proposals. So a year later, on September 21, 1900, Steinmetz rephrased his suggestion in terms the company would find harder to ignore: as a solution to the competitive threat to GE's lighting business. Steinmetz's letter to Edwin W. Rice on that date emphasized that an electrochemical research laboratory could invent new types of lamps for GE. Steinmetz proposed four main targets for initial work: mercury vapor lamps, Nernst-type lamps, new filaments, and new materials for arc lamp electrodes. He next listed general chemical research as something to be done "in spare time." But even while focusing the laboratory on the lighting problem, Steinmetz argued that it should not become a mere appendage of the production line. "Absolutely essential to the success of this proposition," he wrote, "appears to be that the experimental laboratory is entirely separate from the factory."[24]

He sent copies of the letter to Albert G. Davis and Elihu Thomson. Both immediately endorsed the idea. "It seems to me therefore that it would be wise for a considerable sum of money to be spent in the active development of the mercury lamp," Davis wrote to Rice. "If someone gets ahead of us in this development, we will have to spend large sums in buying patent rights, whereas if we do the work ourselves this necessity will be avoided."[25]

Thomson took a broader view in his letter to Rice. "It does seem to me," he wrote

> that a Company as large as the General Electric Company should not fail to continue investigating and developing in new fields: there should, in fact, be a research laboratory for commercial applications of new principles, and even for the discovery of those principles.[26]

Rice took Steinmetz's proposal and the two endorsements to GE president Charles A. Coffin and asked for permission to try out the idea. Coffin agreed, and Rice took on executive responsibility for the experiment in research.

How original an experiment was it? Elihu Thomson's endorsement describes the idea of a research laboratory in terms of two missions: "the commercial applications of new principles" and the "discovery of those principles." Founding a laboratory to do the first of these jobs was not a new idea in 1900. But creating an industrial laboartory to do the second job was.

Laboratories for the application of new scientific principles had been established in the German chemical industry in the middle of the nineteenth century. They had proved highly successful in generating new products such as synthetic dyes.[27] In the United States, Edison's Menlo Park laboratory also met the first half of Thomson's description. Edison and his colleagues kept a close watch on the scientific literature and put both the ideas and the tools of science to work.

By 1900 several American companies had established laboratories run by trained scientists. In the 1870s, the Pennsylvania Railroad had hired Charles Dudley, a chemist with a Ph.D. from Yale, to set up procedures for testing the quality of the varied materials, from soap to steel, that the railroad purchased. In 1889, Standard Oil created a laboratory run by William Burton, who had earned his doctorate in chemistry under Remsen at Johns Hopkins. In 1885, American Telephone and Telegraph had chosen Hammond V. Hayes, a Ph.D. physicist from Harvard, to run its mechanical department. Du Pont had set up its first laboratory, on the banks of the Brandywine River in Delaware, in 1881. And as the historian of industrial chemistry Williams Haynes notes, "before the last quarter of the century most U.S. chemical plants had a chemist or two on the premises." These chemists handled a variety of jobs that might collectively be labeled industrial research: analyzing raw materials, testing finished products, improving apparatus, and finding new uses for chemicals and by-products. At least one of the chemical industry's laboratories, the Ampere Electrochemical Company, was dedicated entirely to developing new chemical processes. The most nearly comprehensive effort to add up all these research efforts concludes that at least thirty-nine industrial research laboratories had been founded in the United States by 1900.[28]

So the idea of a research laboratory for "the commercial application of new principles" was nothing new in 1900. The novelty of GE's proposal came with Thomson's second aim: contributing to the "discovery of those principles." Those thirty-nine American laboratories and their counterparts in Europe did little if any research aimed at scientific discovery. The scientists at Germany's pioneering industrial chemistry laboratories, as historian John J. Beer points out, "felt that fundamental research was the province of the academic institutions" and "did little in the line of purely speculative inquiry."[29] Edison's decision not to follow up on such pure science opportunities as the tasimeter and the Edison effect has already been noted. Charles Dudley's work for the Pennsylvania Railroad earned him sufficient esteem in the chemical profession for him to become the first industrial chemist elected president of the American Chemical Society. But as he admitted in his 1899 presidential address to that society, his laboratory aimed at putting chemistry to use, not at exploring and publishing data on the "new and unknown reactions" often encountered in the course of that work.[30]

At Standard Oil, William Burton's laboratory existed, not to make discoveries, but to prepare academically trained chemists for management positions. Burton tried to move his men as quickly as possible into the Company's operating departments, where "almost without exception the scientific men have become excellent executives."[31] At AT&T, Hammond V. Hayes had initiated work on the fundamental problems of telephone transmission in his laboratory. But he soon gave up the effort, concluding:

> I have determined for the future to abandon theoretical work for this department, devoting all of our attention to practical development of instruments and apparatus . . . I think the theoretical work can be accomplished quite as well and more economically by collaboration with the students of the Massachusetts Institute of Technology and . . . Harvard College.[32]

Williams Haynes notes that the laboratories of the late nineteenth century chemical industry stayed within the same bounds: "they did not often carry on research for its own sake."[33]

In contrast to these predecessors, Steinmetz, Davis, Thomson, and Rice proposed to devote the new General Electric laboratory at least secondarily to scientific discovery. Meeting the threat to the incandescent lamp would have first priority. Chemical investigations would have to be carried out "in spare time," as Steinmetz put it in his initial proposal. But science would be a legitimate mission. Looking back thirty-three years later on that October 1900 meeting, Rice recalled: "we all agreed it was to be a real scientific laboratory."[34]

One need not accept this retrospective claim at full value or assume that when a vice president of the General Electric Company used the words "real scientific laboratory" he meant the same thing by them as Whitney, Noyes, or Ostwald would have. But the General Electric leaders had practical, as well as aesthetic, reasons for making at least a nod in the direction of pure science. One of the new and promising lighting methods, the Nernst lamp, had been invented in a real scientific laboratory. Three others, the Welsbach mantle, the mercury vapor lamp, and the osmium lamp, had been invented or improved by people trained in such laboratories. Other industrialists had sensed the social value of pure science: Nobel had established his prizes in a will that had taken effect not long ago; Carnegie was shaping the first of the major U.S. private foundations to support purely scientific work on a major scale. The spirit of research had become highly respectable. Recognizing it might help GE attract creative researchers.

Steinmetz had discussed the need for at least one first-rate researcher in his original letter. "The laboratory," he wrote

> would require a good, well-paid practical chemist of considerable originality, able to follow and work out independently any suggestions that might be made. He should have a fair knowledge of electricity and general physics, be well familiar with glass blowing, and posses somewhat pronounced administrative ability.[35]

This position could have been filled by recruiting within the chemical industry. Perhaps, for example, Rice could have lured away one of the chemists in William Burton's Standard Oil laboratory. But Rice went instead to a university. He asked Thomson to suggest a candidate, but Thomson could not think of anyone. So Rice inquired next of a man whose connections with both industry and academe were even more extensive than Thomson's: physicist Cross of MIT. Cross suggested Whitney.[36]

So trends in the organization of giant corporations, a social invention enabling companies to control the key resource of technology, a business threat to one giant corporation's most important product, a suggestion by that company's chief consulting engineer, and a recommendation by one of that company's academic consultants had converged to bring Rice, Davis, Thomson, and Whitney together at Lynn, Massachusetts, on an October day in 1900. The GE leaders offered Whitney the job of directing a new "electro-chemical laboratory." Whitney hesitated. "When I was first tempted to leave a teaching position at Boston Tech," he said later, "I thought I was deciding between working for myself and others by teaching and research, or burying my possible individuality in a large soulless industry."[37] He quickly made it clear that if he took the job at all he would do so only on a part-time basis that would allow him to retain his MIT position. On that basis, he was definitely interested. But before making a final decision, he would have to see the setting and meet the GE leader with whom he would work most closely. So within a month he was on a train traveling westward to find out more about Schenectady and Steinmetz.

Before 1886, Schenectady had resembled Jamestown, though on a larger scale. It prospered owing to its favorable location on the Erie Canal and the New York Central Railroad. Its manufacturing enterprises produced locomotives, railway cars, and farm machinery. In 1886, Thomas Edison had become cramped by a lack of space and annoyed by a strike at his machine works on Goerck Street in New York City. So he had moved that machine works into an abandoned locomotive factory on the flood plain of the Mohawk River, within a mile of downtown Schenectady. After the Edison and Thomson-Houston companies had combined to form GE, that Schenectady site, surrounded by room for expansion, had been chosen as the main manufacturing works and administrative center of the new company.

As Whitney's train pulled into Schenectady, he could see the manufacturing republic giving way to the industrial state. GE had recently seized control of the city's street railway system and was using it to open up new neighborhoods to hold the growing force of workers, engineers, and managers. The descendants of Schenectady's earliest Dutch settlers, and other members of the old social elite, were left undisturbed in the downtown "stockade" section. GE was developing a new section, on a tree-shaded plateau a mile west of downtown, as a preserve for company executives. Just farther to the west, contractors were building family housing for engineers, clerks, accountants, and lesser managers. On hills rising from the river to the south went the workers' housing: row on row of "Schenectady flats," long, narrow two-or three-family houses with each floor consisting of a living room and kitchen connected by a narrow hall off which opened four small rooms. And on Liberty Street, along the dirty, smelly Erie Canal that bisected the city's business district, stood boarding houses for the bachelor engineers. One such house, nicknamed "Liberty Hall," held the cluttered, overdecorated Victorian nightmare of an apartment occupied by the man Whitney had come to see, Charles Proteus Steinmetz.[38]

Although only three years older than Whitney, Steinmetz had firmly established himself in the top rank of the American technical community. He had been born in Breslau, Germany, the hunchbacked son of a minor railway official. He studied at the university of Breslau, working toward a doctorate in mathematics, but leaving suddenly just before earning that degree. He later attributed his sudden departure to the threat of arrest by Bismarck's police, due to his active participation in the local socialist movement. But it may also have been apparent, in 1889, that a young man with technical training could make his fortune faster in the United States than in Germany. Steinmetz picked up a bit more of that technical training in Switzerland, then went back to Germany just long enough to catch a boat for New York. He arrived nearly penniless but with a letter of introduction to an exile of the earlier revolutionary era of 1848, Rudolf Eickemeyer of Yonkers. Eickemeyer had already made two fortunes, first by inventing and manufacturing new types of hat-making machinery, and then by producing revolvers during the Civil War. When Steinmetz arrived in 1899, he was trying to turn an avocation into a third business by inventing new types of electric motors. He gladly took Steinmetz on as a one-man experimental laboratory and calculating department.[39]

Eickmeyer suggested to Steinmetz an important problem, predicting the energy losses caused in the steel electromagnets in electric motors by the use of alternating currents. He provided Steinmetz with experimental equipment to measure those losses. Steinmetz used that equipment to score his first technical triumph. In 1891, he read a paper to the American Institute of Electrical Engineers in New York City describing the results of these experiments. It concluded with a useful empirical finding. The losses in question, the so-called hysteresis losses, became 2.8 times as large every time the magnetizing force causing them was doubled.[40]

Most of Steinmetz's findings had been anticipated by British physicist Alfred Ewing, and the main conclusion of that 1891 paper turned out to be an empirical approximation, not a law of science. But the scientific style of Steinmetz's presentation fit perfectly with the aims of the society to which he read the paper. The electrical engineers, like Whitney's Chemical Society colleagues, were seeking to upgrade their image as scientific professionals. This German-trained mathematician, with his scholarly and self-confident air, his quick pen (he would publish more than a dozen books and two hundred papers), and his command of physical theory, fit the new image perfectly. Here, one of his listeners remarked, is a paper that could have been given to the Royal Society, or the Physical Society of London.[41]

Steinmetz's next major paper, a theoretical one given in 1893 on the use of imaginary numbers in electrical engineering calculations, provided his colleagues an even better example of modernity and sophistication. Its main results had again been anticipated, this time by Professor Arthur Kennelly of Harvard. But the paper served to eduate engineers in an important new class of methods.[42]

By this time General Electric had acquired Eickmyer's company (not, as legend has it, to obtain Steinmetz, but because Eickmyer had made important inventions on electric railway motors). Rice first put Steinmetz in charge of GE's calculating department, the group that predicted the expected characteristics of the new alternating current devices. Within a few years Rice created for Steinmetz the new post of chief consulting engineer. The job involved Steinmetz in troubleshooting on major company technical problems and in advising GE's top management about technical issues and opportunities. It left him plenty of time to write, lecture, and teach.

Left to right: Charles P. Steinmetz, John T. H. Dempster, first employee of the GE Research Laboratory, and Willis R. Whitney. The combination of snow and Whitney's beard suggest this picture was taken during the winter of 1900–1901, Whitney's first as GE's Director of Research.

By the time Whitney met him in Schenectady in 1900, Steinmetz had proved that his greatness lay, not in discovering and inventing, but in teaching and inspiring. He not only expressed but embodied the idea that scientific principles could be put to work in industry. Many members of the electrical engineering generation that came of age after 1900 (Harold Black, the inventor of the negative feedback amplifier, for example) would never forget the sight of Steinmetz on the lecture platform, gesturing with his cigar, tangling his argument into a thicket of unfamiliar ideas and blackboard symbols, but somehow implanting the unshakeable conviction that theory could be used to solve practical problems and make inventions.[43]

Steinmetz also appreciated the value of experiment. He began some experiments in new lighting methods in the 1890s before he finally sold GE's management on his proposal for an electrochemical laboratory. He appears not to have sought the post of director of that laboratory for himself. But he undoubtedly intended to exert great influence on the director.

He and Whitney could hardly have been more different personally. It was a cigar-smoking socialist meeting a non-smoking Republican; an abrasive practical joker meeting a natural diplomat; a theoretician meeting an experimenter. But they shared a determination to put science to work without "burying my possible individuality in a large soulless industry." That must have sufficed to convince each of them that the two could work together. For Whitney agreed to take the job. He would keep his MIT post. But he would also devote two days a week to industrial research. (Within a few months that commitment had been increased to three days a week.) He would begin on December 15. His first headquarters would be a carriage barn behind Steinmetz's Liberty Hall boarding house, on the banks of the Erie Canal. General Electric would later label it the barn where industrial research was born.

Why did Whitney accept? The closest thing to an explanation that he wrote at the time appears in a letter to Ida Schulze the following March.

> A few months ago the General Electric Company offered me the position as director of an experimental electro chemical research laboratory which they wished established here at Schenectady, New York, and I accepted with the idea of trying my hand at discovery until next October, when, on the opening of the Institute, I can make new plans desirable for all concerned.[44]

He must also have been attracted by the initial salary. For two days' work a week he would get $2,400 a year, well over three times the average annual income of an American family in 1900.[45] He did not really need the money. He already had his MIT salary, the thousands of dollars a year starting to come in from the Aristotype project, and his father's wealth to draw on. But the new salary represented a substantial vote of confidence in his abilities. And it comitted him to nothing permanent. His motive in taking the job seems to be contained in one of the phrases he used in that letter to Ida: "trying my hand." He was experimenting at mixing another new element into the compound of his life.

Under the new arrangement, he told Ida,

> I spend four days each week at the Institute and three days in my new laboratory here. Two nights a week I sleep on the railroad between my two offices. It's all very fine, but somewhat wearing, for it looks to me as if there was a week's worth of work each week at both ends of the line.[46]

At the Schenectady end, he had inherited from Steinmetz a laboratory assistant. Tall, thin, horse-faced Tom Dempster had no scientific training. But he possessed a lively sense of humor, and wide-ranging interests. He might, a co-worker remarked later, be seen knitting a scarf one day and playing a trombone the next.[47]

Whitney and Dempster began by attacking the problem at the top of Steinmetz's list, the mercury vapor lamp. Dempster would make and evacuate glass tubes containing a small pool of mercury, and electrodes that could be attached by means of wires penetrating through the glass to a source of electricity. Applying the electric current would vaporize some of the mercury and cause the interior of the tube to give off a green glow. Whitney's job was to turn that glow into a more daylight-like hue, somehow shifting much of the light output from green over to yellow and red. And he also sought to find a more convenient way of turning on the lamp than tilting it at just the right angle to cause a trickle of mercury to connect the two electrodes and start the electric current flowing. As a secondary problem, he began to look for new uses for magnetite, a form of iron ore. GE had access to large quantities of it at low cost. It had an unusual combination of high electrical conductivity and good heat resistance that gave it promise for use in current collectors for motors or electrodes in arc lamps.

Steinmetz also attacked the magnetite problem. Whitney came to appreciate that the theorist was also a tenacious experimen-

"The barn where industrial research was born." In this carriage house behind the home of Charles Proteus Steinmetz in Schenectady, Whitney began doing research for GE in the winter of 1900–1901.

ter. But he and Steinmetz never became close friends. He attended without enthusiasm a few sessions of Steinmetz's poker club, "the society for the equalization of income." But mostly he stayed away from Liberty Hall.[48]

In the spring of 1901, a fire damaged the barn. In June, Whitney secured Rice's permission to reestablish the laboratory in a one-story wooden building at the Schenectady Works and to bring in four new men from MIT. Two of them, physicist Ezekiel Weintraub and chemist Julius Ober, were European-trained Ph.D.s. The others, William Arsem and Howard Wood, had just earned bachelors' degrees. Whitney failed, however, to land the candidate he wanted most. William D. Coolidge, a former student of his and presently his colleague, a holder of a Leipzig Ph.D. in physics, told Whitney that he preferred to work for Noyes on the chemistry of solutions.[49]

With the MIT term over, Whitney could stop his commuting. He sent Evelyn and Ennin off to Jamestown and settled down for a comfortable bachelor's summer in Schenectady. Each morning he would get up before 6 A.M. and spend an hour riding his bicycle through the quiet streets. Then he would breakfast and put in a day at the laboratory. The work went slowly. "These men of mine are all at work," he wrote his parents, "but what they do is just fail, fail, fail." The mercury lamp was proving intractable. That did not discourage him. "I don't care for money, not a snap," he added. "If only I could succeed I'll hold down this job if I had to pay what I get paid."[50]

Two months earlier he had expressed similar sentiments to Ida Schulze. "The only thing I really want now," he wrote,

> is to accomplish some great thing for the 'General Electric.' They are giving me free hand here to spend and experiment as well as I am able, and I shall die with a ten-ton shadow on my opinion of Whitney if I don't do some good work here.[51]

But was that great thing for the General Electric really the only thing Whitney wanted to accomplish in 1901? He may have said so, but his actions suggest otherwise. For back at MIT he was undertaking a whole range of other experiments. They suggest he had not yet settled fully into the identity of the corporation's chemist. He still sought to build a compound life out of varied elements.

He had continued teaching in the spring of 1901, and in February MIT had finally promoted him to assistant professor. If that had happened six months earlier, it might have convinced him to turn down the GE offer. But now he was committed to a year's trial at Schenectady.[52]

He had also begun to establish himself in a new specialty within physical chemistry, the study of colloids. That name *colloid,* taken from the Greek word for glue, had first been attached in the mid-nineteenth century to a class of solutions too thick and sticky to pass through certain membranes. By the time Whitney entered the field at the turn of the century, chemists accepted that this behavior was due to the colloid's structure.

It was made up of clumps of matter thousands of times as large as the structural units of matter, though still too small to be seen under a microscope.

The field appealed to Whitney because it combined physical chemistry, useful applications, and his old love, biology.[53] In 1894, physical chemist Jacques Loeb had demonstrated a chemical method for causing sea urchin eggs to hatch without being fertilized. That experiment seemed to point the way to a strictly chemical explanation of life processes and struck another blow against the doctrine that some mysterious vital spark was needed to produce or reproduce life. Whitney hoped to be able to show that processes of colloid formation played an intimate part in this chemistry of life, especially in the growth of living things. And he had plenty of more immediate reasons for studying colloids. Understanding how colloid particles stuck together could lead to a better understanding of the sticking of glues, the dyeing of textiles, the coloring of glass, the settling of slimes, and many other useful processes.

Whitney concentrated on explaining why colloid particles reach a certain size and then stop growing and remain suspended in a liquid. Why do the clumps not continue to grow until the coalesce into pieces heavy enough to settle out as easily visible lumps? For example, why does a correctly made sauce Bernaise come out as a smooth colloidal solution rather than a lumpy failure? Electrochemists believed that both the growth and the cessation of growth of colloidal particles could be explained by the competing influences of chemical combining forces and electrical charge. Charged particles in solution would meet and chemically combine, building up into colloidal particles. But as they built, their charge would increase. That increasing charge would mean increasing electrical repulsion between pairs of particles. That repulsion would eventually keep them too far apart for the shorter range chemical forces to act. To enable the particles to grow further, one had to partly discharge the particles by adding oppositely charged ions that would be attracted to the particles, stick to them owing to that electrical attraction, and neutralize some of their charge.

Whitney tested this idea on the colloid arsenious sulfide. To 200 cubic centimeters (cc) of the colloid, he added varying amounts of a 1 percent solution of the salt barium chloride. If less than 30 cc of the barium chloride solution was added, nothing happened. But shortly after the addition of 30 cc or more, clumps of arsenious sulfide large enough to be visible began to appear. Whitney interpreted these results as supporting the electrostatic repulsion theory. The 30-cc dose provided just enough ions to discharge the particles sufficiently to allow them to come close enough together to chemically combine into the visible clumps.

Chemists still accept this explanation for many colloids, including sauce Bernaise, though it must be qualified by considerations of particle shape and layering of atoms within the particle. The careful experiments that Whitney and his MIT student Julius Ober carried out to test this electrostatic repulsion theory were described in a 1901 article in the *Journal of the American Chemical Society.*[54] Results described in that article continued to be cited by colloid chemists for thirty years, representing Whitney's longest lived and most substantial contribution to the scientific literature.

His colloid science research indicates that Whitney still sought a compound life, with industrial research linked to teaching and academic science by a railroad line. But that possibility had begun to slip away. On August 6, 1901, he wrote to MIT president Henry S. Pritchett requesting a leave of absence for a year to devote full time to the GE laboartory. "At the time I accepted this position," he told Pritchett

I did not feel I could decide on my future plans. I had always hoped to be an investigating teacher pure and simple, and it seemed as though I was commencing to enjoy that pleasure when the company tempted me to come here. I had hoped that I might be able to retain my position at the Institute as well as to control the work of the laboratory because of the very great value such work is to anyone teaching in a technical school. This is probably possible, but there are several reasons why I ought not to attempt it in the coming year.[55]

The details of the growing effort at Schenectady—moving into a new laboratory building, and laying out a research program for his enlarged staff—would require his full attention in the months ahead. "I yet feel the responsibility of the position to such a degree," he wrote to Prichett

> that I do not consider money a recompense, and if I were choosing for personal satisfaction I would to-day prefer my position at the institute at no salary to this with twice what it can properly pay. As I think I told you, I do not mean to let the amount of salary influence me so long as I have an independent income as I at present have.

He went on to reflect on the compatibility of an industrial job with a scientist's ideals. "The only objection I can possibly find to my work here," he wrote,

> is the feeling which anyone else in my place would also experience. This is the desirability of tangibile and negotiable results. There is no evidence, on the part of the officers of the company, of impatience or a wish to interfere at all in my work—in fact, I might complain of a lack of suggestion on their part; but I know I was put here for a purpose, that the Laboratory is not primarily a philanthropic asylum for indigent chemists, and I must not let it become one even secondarily.

But this 1901 letter should not be viewed as a final break with academic science. For at the same time as Whitney was proclaiming his determination not to found a philanthropic asylum for indigent chemists in Schenectady, he was on the verge of preparing an application to a philanthropic foundation for the support of pure chemistry research in Boston.

The foundation was Andrew Carnegie's. The occasion was the continuing resistance by Noyes, with Whitney's support, against the prevailing vocational school emphasis at MIT. By July 1901, Noyes was telling friends that he would remain at MIT only if he was provided with a research laboratory independent of the chemistry department. Otherwise, he would go to the Johns Hopkins, or perhaps to a small private laboratory out in the suburbs like the one his friend Hale had founded near Chicago to do astronomy.[56]

The money Noyes and Whitney earned on the Aristotype project made possible a new approach to MIT. If the Institute would establish a department of chemical research, Noyes proposed in 1901, he would contribute $5,000 a year to support it. MIT's executive committee considered this bold request for a research-oriented graduate program and turned it down.[57]

Noyes turned next to the Carnegie Institution in Washington, and Whitney also turned in that direction. That institution had just recently got its program of support for research underway. In 1902, Noyes asked for $5,900 to support his work on the physical chemistry of solutions. He got the money. Whitney applied for a smaller grant to support his colloid work. His application reflected his personal mixture of interests in pure and in applied research. Colloid studies might unlock the secret of life, he proposed. And even if they did not, they were bound to prove useful for improving the tanning of leather or the mordanting of dyes.[58]

The Institution turned down Whitney's request for funds. He continued, however, to keep in close touch with Noyes and his work, and in 1903, he stood ready to support Noyes in a new approach to the MIT executive committee. Noyes would divert $3,000 a year from his Aristotype earnings, and Whitney would divert $1,500 a year from his, to the support of an MIT Physical Chemistry Laboratory. This time the Institute accepted. Whitney moved into Noyes' new laboratory as a principal researcher. Under Noyes' leadership the laboratory moved rapidly to a position alongside Harvard, the Johns Hopkins, Columbia, Cornell, Illinois, and Chicago at the summit of American chemical research. And it educated dozens of the next generation of American chemists, including leaders such as Gilbert N. Lewis and Richard C. Tolman in pure chemistry, and William A. Washburn and William D. Coolidge in applied science.[59]

Whitney's place in that laboratory gave him a new Boston

base at the end of the railroad line that, for him, connected pure and applied science. And in 1902, he participated actively in the forging of another link between the knowledge-oriented and results-oriented branches of the American chemistry community when he became a founding member and officer of the American Electrochemical Society.

Like so much of American chemistry, this new organization followed a German model. The German Electrochemical Society, founded in 1892, had recognized that electrochemistry presented an intersection of science and industry. Its board of directors included both Wilhelm Ostwald and his student Walther Rathenau, scion of the founder and president of Germany's largest electrical manufacturing company.[60]

That society lasted only a decade in Germany. But the idea behind it suited American conditions much better. At its founding in 1902, the American Electrochemical Society proclaimed its purpose as "the advancement of the theory and practice of electrochemistry." Its initial slate of officers included two men whose roles shadowed those of Ostwald and Rathenau: Bancroft of Cornell, and the research director of America's largest electrical manufacturing company, Whitney.[61]

The American society took root and flourished. At its meetings, academic leaders such as Louis Kahlenberg of Wisconsin and Joseph Richards of Lehigh would exchange ideas with industrial chemists such as Leo Baekeland and Edward Acheson. Papers on the electron and dissociation theories would appear on the program alongside papers on iron production, graphite electrodes, and storage batteries. Whitney would discuss the results of research on alloys with Bancroft and invite him to visit the GE Research Laboratory and address the staff.

The Electrochemical Society illustrated an emerging strength of American science. The bonds between its pure and applied wings started off strong and kept being strengthened. In chemistry, leading academics such as Remsen and Noyes might assert the primacy of research in allocating space within professional journals and in electing officers to the American

Chemical Society. But they received too many reminders of the dependence of pure research on the results of applied research to allow the erection of a barrier between the two. The funds to support their work might come directly from the profits of a consulting venture, such as the Whitney-Noyes Aristotype project. Or those funds might come from the stored wealth produced by a technology-based industry, such as Carnegie's steel or Rockefeller's oil. Students and teachers from the best research universities, such as William Burton and Whitney, had gone to industry and set up chemical laboratories. Perhaps eventually some of those laboratories would make true contributions to research. Similar opportunities were opening in government laboratories, such as the Agriculture Department's experiment stations or the new National Bureau of Standards.

So American science was becoming a compound of mutually supporting activities in pure and applied research. And Whitney was trying to become an individual compound of the same range of mutually supporting diverse elements. The profession created its compound by recognizing the contributions of a range of individuals: of industry-oriented William Burton, of inventive Leo Baekeland, of a great teacher such as Wilder D. Bancroft, and a great discipline builder such as Arthur A. Noyes. But could one individual combine in himself all those individual elements? Whitney's industrial research experiment had begun in 1900 as part of a personal effort to put together just such a compound. But by 1901, the element of teaching had already been crowded out. Over the next eight years, the whole experiment would have to be radically redesigned.

6/

Burnt-Out Bulb

"Ginger" Adams would later become the head of the GE Research Laboratory machine shop and a formidable figure in his own right. But in 1903, he was a resistor maker at the two-year-old electrochemical laboratory at GE's Schenectady Works, "young and green and simply scared stiff." He would not have dared to approach the Laboratory's director, Dr. Whitney, whom he assumed to be a bearded, dignified professor. So Whitney instead came to him one day at lunch—and turned out to be clean shaven and informal, "a young fellow with his sleeves rolled up." That day Adams' mother had put in his lunch a big piece of homemade fruitcake. "I'm surprised at your mother, giving you so much rich food," Whitney said, and "instantly sacrificed himself by devouring every crumb."[1]

The incident captures Whitney's way of running a laboratory: to appear at the employee's desk, bench, or work station, informal, enthusiastic, and forward, trying to say or do something to shock the employee into action, whether by suggesting a new line of experiments or simply by stealing a fruitcake. He was a leader, not an administrator. He thought in terms of people and experiments, not in terms of projects, budgets, and organization charts. This emphasis on ideas and individuals led him to an early success at General Electric that helped convince him in 1904 to make industrial research his career. But failure and frustration followed, of the kind that an individualist might well attribute to failures in his own leadership. By 1908, Whitney would be seriously questioning that career choice. The lamp that had flared so brightly would nearly burn out.

The Laboratory's budget and total employment were each doubling annually, standing at more than $60,000 and forty people by 1904. The first staff pictures show that almost everyone was at least as young as the 35-year-old director. Whitney sits in the middle, shorn of his professor's beard, his face radiating confidence. The Laboratory belonged to him. Steinmetz had challenged his leadership at first, hoping to expand his initial patronage of the Laboratory into a permanent advisor's role. Tom Dempster later recalled the frequent arguments between the two. "Their methods were different," he noted. "Steinmetz liked to start at the end of a problem and work back. Dr. Whitney liked to start at the beginning and work forward." Whitney's approach prevailed. Steinmetz repaired to his home laboratory. "Then we didn't often see him," Dempster notes.[2]

Whitney went on to modify an important specification Steinmetz had laid down in designing the Laboratory: "Absolutely essential to the success of this proposition appears to be that the experimental laboratory is entirely separate from the factory."[3] Organizationally, this idea persisted. Whitney reported directly to the vice president of engineering throughout his career, rather than to the manager of the Schenectady Works. But the "entirely" in Steinmetz's sentence came to look to Whitney too extreme. Taken literally, it could destroy the Laboratory.

For it soon became apparent to Whitney that the lab would not offer the Company any immediate payoffs from its major research projects. The quest for a daylight-colored mercury vapor lamp would be long. Whitney and Dempster tried again and again to salt the mercury vapor or coat the bulb with fluorescent materials that would shift some of the green or blue light into the red and yellow regions. They did not stumble onto any practical answers. The magnetite arc lamp looked more promising, but Steinmetz took it with him to his home laboratory. Some early efforts on the ceramic glower lamp did not lead to any improvement on Nernst's invention. How could the Laboratory prove its worth during the long and risky search for the light source of the future?

The answer, Whitney quickly decided, was to take on short-range problems brought to him by the leading engineers at the

Works. "Mr. Emmet's man commenced work on a condenser built up of varnished paper," he noted on July 9, 1901. The irascible William LeRoy Emmet was one of GE's outstanding electrical engineers and a valuable ally. "Mr. Eveleth and Mr. Hewlett brought problem of lightning arrestors," Whitney wrote in his notebook on the next day.[4] The popular and diplomatic Charles Eveleth would rise to vice president of GE manufacturing; Edward Hewlett was one of the Company's most productive inventors. The problem they brought was not pure research. They asked Whitney to bake them some resistors that would not decrease in resistance when heated. Whitney not only accepted the assignment but tackled it himself.

This new emphasis must be taken into account when interpreting the first public reference to the new Laboratory. On page 13 of the 1902 Annual Report of General Electric, near the end of his third vice president's report, Edwin W. Rice described it this way:

> Although our engineers have always been liberally supplied with every facility for the development of new and original designs and improvements of existing standards, it has been deemed wise during the past year to establish a laboratory to be devoted exclusively to original research. It is hoped by this means that many profitable fields may be discovered.[5]

This short and apparently clear statement raises more questions than it answers. Distinctions among research, development, and engineering remain difficult to make even today. The meaning of that term "original research" must have been even less clear in 1902. And although it was "hoped by this means that many profitable fields would be discovered," what if the time to discovery, or the time between discovery and profitability was long?

Whitney quickly came up with his answer: do not insist on "exclusively" devoting the laboratory to the type of original research that might be carried out at Noyes' laboratory of physical chemistry. While trying to do some great thing for the

General Electric, do a lot of small things, too, in order to keep up the Company's interest.

To understand this strategy better, let's look at the work of the Laboratory as Whitney saw it in 1901–1904: as a collection of individuals or small teams, each taking on a different problem. The problems covered the whole range from original research on new light sources to routine assistance on the production problems of the Works.

Despite initial difficulties, Whitney did not abandon the mercury lamp. Instead, he handed the project over to physicist Ezekiel Weintraub. A short, precise looking man with a Van Dyke beard, Weintraub had been born in Mogilev, Russia, and was educated in Germany. He had been serving as a research assistant at MIT when Whitney took him on. Dr. Weintraub arrived from Boston with "a very remarkable improvement in starting the (mercury) lamp," Whitney wrote in his lab notebook in October 1901, and from then on most of the Laboratory's new ideas about mercury lamps came from Weintraub and his assistants. His work also appeared in the first scientific publication of the Laboratory, an article on mercury lamps in the *Philosophical Magazine* of London, one of the world's leading scientific journals, in 1904.[6]

Weintraub's ability was matched by an independence that offered Whitney his first big managerial challenge. The engineer or scientist of the early twentith century signed over his services to an industrial corporation in a limited-duration "engineer's contract" typically committing him to one or two years. This engineer's contract would then be renegotiated, and if agreement could not be reached, the technical person would play out the option and become a free agent. Weintraub's engineer's contract suggests the lengths to which Whitney would go to get and keep a good researcher. The salary of $3,000 a year matched that of a full professor and was about four times that earned by a skilled machinist at the Schenectady Works. (The starting salary for even a highly regarded Ph.D. scientist today is less than twice a machinist's salary.) But money alone apparently was not sufficient to bring Weintraub to Schenectady. He also secured the right to spend his summers with pay doing research in Europe. And he inserted in his contract terms that Whitney paraphrased in his notebook as follows: "Conditions effecting [sic] the position he now holds should not be changed so as to make it exceedingly distasteful or intolerable for him."[7]

Weintraub's productivity justified the special treatment. In 1902, he invented a better way of starting the mercury lamp, using a jolt of high voltage instead of tilting the tube as his predecessors had done. And he discovered how to use the mercury arc, not only as a light source, but also as a rectifier— that is, a method of changing alternating current (AC) to direct current (DC) and vice versa. By 1900, AC had established itself as the most convenient way of transmitting electricity in large amounts. But cities such as New York and Boston still possessed the extensive DC lighting systems installed by Edison, and most cities had DC trolley systems. A simple and effective method of converting AC to DC that dispensed with the moving parts of the mechanical system then in use offered obvious commercial promise.[8]

Weintraub was not the first to discover the rectifying properties of the mercury arc. Independent inventor Peter Cooper Hewitt had beaten GE to the punch again. But here an advantage of the big company intervenes. It can play the game of patents like horseshoes and score points by being close. A delay intervenes between the filing for and the issuing of a patent. If a second patent application covering the same ground arrives during that delay, a state called an interference is created. Both claimants are called on to bring their notebooks, witnesses, and other evidence to the patent office, and the one who can prove the earliest date of conceiving the idea and reducing it to practice gets the patent.[9] This process can take years.

This delay favors the side with more money. Its lawyers can drag out the interference until its weaker opponent finds it necessary to settle the case, rather than pursue it to an expensive and doubtful conclusion. Inventor William Stanley—no enemy of GE but rather a man who had made hundreds of thousands of dollars selling his own company to GE and who remained on the GE payroll as a consultant—described in 1903 "the present methods adopted by the industrial trusts in dealing with the inventor." Upon hearing of an important new invention, Stanley claimed, the trust would send its lawyers to the inventor and tell him that "one of the trust's inventors had worked out the same result some years before." If the inventor did not sell his rights immediately, the trust put in a new application and caused an interference and a lengthy investigation. "In 99 cases out of 100," Stanley claimed, (the inventor) "sells for a trifle and finds himself impoverished and unknown."[10]

The Hewitt-Weintraub interference on the mercury and rectifier illustrates how effectively a large company could combine this tactic with the output of its Research Laboratory. The interference stretched out until 1911, when Hewitt finally prevailed. But by then Hewitt's lamp and rectifier business had been badly weakened by the expense of the suit and by the loss of the backing of George Westinghouse, who had gone bankrupt in the crash of 1907. Within two years of the settlement, GE had negotiated a patent license, and within eight more, Hewitt had sold his company to GE.[11]

So Weintraub's work would have a payoff. But it would never hit its main target, the commercial, daylight-colored mercury lamp. The understanding of phosphors and electronics needed to create the modern fluorescent lamp would not become available until the 1930s. And Weintraub ran into additional difficulties and hazards. Sealing in the mercury vapor proved difficult. Intense ultraviolet light from one experimental lamp temporarily blinded one GE researcher who was not careful to shield his eyes.[12]

By 1904, Whitney was indicating in his notebook that Weintraub was going off on his own to adopt the mercury arc to other fields besides lighting: relaying and amplifying telephone signals, and methods of receiving wireless telegraphy.

Even if successful, these projects would not help GE much. Whitney let this work proceed, but it did not represent the kind of team spirit he wanted to establish in the Research Laboratory. Whitney later told historian Kendall Birr that the excessive independence of foreign-born scientists threatened the Laboratory's existence. In the early years, Whitney stated, he hired foreign-born scientists "imbued with the German idea of individualistic, secretive research." Disputes among these men led patent attorney A. G. Davis to call the Laboratory the "menagerie" or the "bear pit." But "gradually the troublemakers were replaced."[13]

It is difficult to tell the depth of Whitney's feelings about "troublemakers" with foreign background who carried out "individualistic secretive research." But the policies he followed indicate that while he wanted to draw on German ideas, he wanted them extended and applied by American minds. In the Research Laboratory's library, German-language periodicals outnumbered English-language ones 10 to 8. But at the bench, an American-born Ph.D. commanded a salary 50 percent higher than a Ph.D. of European descent. Weintraub, the sole exception, left the Laboratory by 1910 to head up his own GE research group at Lynn, Massachusetts. By then his colleagues Ossian Kruh, Erland Zell, Isidor Ladoff, John Harden, and other foreign-born Ph.D.s had also departed.[14]

One of Whitney's first American-born employees with a Ph.D., chemist William Weedon, proved more congenial. Whitney collaborated with him on the Laboratory's second major lighting project, the development of an arc lamp with an electrode made of the heat-resistant alloy titanium carbide.[15] The approach Whitney and Weedon took aimed at understanding the scientific principles of electric arcs, as well as testing titanium carbide electrodes. This dual approach embodied the spirit Whitney had hoped to bring to Schenectady and differentiated the new Laboratory from those of Edison, Charles Dudley, and William Burton. But it presented Whitney with two problems. Exactly how do you make practical use of scientific knowledge? And if you discover facts that are both of scientific interest and of commercial value, when, if ever, do you publish them in the open scientific literature?

The first question is rarely answered in the simple, straightforward manner of the textbooks. An industrial researcher can rarely use a scientific theory to make precise quantitative predictions that will permit the design of a new device or process from first principles. Instead, the theory usually provides hints or narrows the field of search by ruling out some possibilities. Theory provides the inventor with a helpful analogy, model, or viewpoint, not with a recipe.

In looking at the science of the electric arc in 1902, Whitney and Weedon could have taken either of two theoretical viewpoints: the electrochemist's or the physicist's. To an electrochemist, an arc can be compared by analogy to the pair of electrochemical reactions that run an electric battery: an oxidation at one electrode and a reduction at another electrode physically separated from the first.

In a battery one can actually weigh the amount of material that the ions carry through the electrolyte from one electrode to another. For a given amount of electric charge transferred between electrodes, each element, when used as a negative electrode, transfers a constant and characteristic amount of mass via ions. Double the charge transferred and one doubles the mass transferred. This linear and constant relation between electrical and mass transfer had been discovered by Michael Faraday nearly sixty years earlier.

In basing their description of an electric arc on an analogy with this battery process, electrochemists considered the air between the two electrodes of the arc as the electrolyte. They assumed that the current of the arc would be carried through the electrolyte by negative ions. In an arc lamp, Whitney proposed, the oxidation reaction was the formation of these ions at the surface of the mercury pool, which served as cathode. The reduction was the combination of these ions with charges at an iron electrode to yield mercury atoms that fell back into the pool. The passage of a given current would be accompanied by the transfer of a constant and characteristic amount of matter, just as Faraday had found for the electrochemical cell.[16]

The physicists of 1902 were beginning to look at things a little bit differently. In the late nineteenth century, they had applied voltages to separated electrodes within evacuated glass bulbs and found that under the right conditions, invisible "rays" carried current between the two electrodes. Just before 1900, Hittorf of Germany, Zeeman and Lorentz of Holland, and especially the British physicist J. J. Thomson, showed that the properties of these rays—the way they were bent by electric and magnetic fields, for examples—could best be explained by assuming that they were actually streams of negatively charged particles, each less than one-thousandth the mass of the smallest charged particle previously found, the positive ion of hydrogen. Physicists applied to this particle the previously suggested name "electron." They then proposed that the electric arc, despite its air gap rather than vacuum, and its emission of light and heat rather than invisible rays, worked essentially like the vacuum tube. Most of the current was carried by those almost unimaginably tiny electrons, and the mass transferred by that electron current would be far too small to detect. The mercury ions were actually positive and served to neutralize the negative charge in the air gap.[17]

Whitney and Weedon understood this physicists' analogy, but they rejected it. They adopted instead the one proposed by their own discipline of electrochemistry. After all, that analogy had served Whitney well in his work on corrosion. They set out to run arcs, to weigh the electrodes, to determine the amount of mass transferred with the electric charge, and thereby become the Faradays of the electric arc. They rejected the physicists' view, even though they were fully aware of it. In fact, they had often discussed it at the Laboratory's colloquium.

The colloquium had been one of Whitney's first administrative innovations. It symbolized his determination to bring at least some of the university's research tradition to industry. Once a week—though not on Company time—the Laboratory staff came together to discuss the latest discoveries and research programs in science, as presented by an outside speaker or one of the GE staff members. The colloquium began on Thursday evening, September 29, 1901, with Ezekiel Weintraub and William Arsem giving talks on the electron theory. Subsequent subjects included the work of J. J. Thomson, radioactivity, and the ionic theory.[18]

Whitney listened to the talks on J. J. Thomson and the electron, took part in the discussions, but was not converted. He wrote in his notebook in 1901:

> In the mercury arc it has been shown that a magnet deflects the cathode (negative) end of the arc *very much* more strongly than the anode . . . it seems quite probable that the mercury ions travel as negative particles across the gap only.[19]

But he refused to equate these negative particles with Thomson's electrons. Instead, he set Weedon to work trying to weigh "the amount of material which is transported during the running of the arc," and looking for a "law for arcs corresponding to Faraday's law for solutions." The basic experiment was to weigh the arc's electrodes, run an electric current through them, then weigh them again. Arcs with carbon electrodes acting across an air gap gave varying results that were hard to interpret, since, in addition to any mass transfered by the arc, the electrodes also lost weight by burning. Use less combustible arc materials, Whitney suggested. Weedon ran copper arcs in air, with no better results. Next, to try the experiment in an atmosphere that would not support burning, Weedon ran copper and iron arcs in hydrogen and under water. Still, he got inconsistent results. If a given charge transfer carried a constant amount of mass, that mass was too small to be measured by weighing.[20]

This series of disappointments shook Whitney's and Weedon's confidence in the electrochemist's theory of the electric arc. They became more receptive to the physicist's theory; Weedon's paper describing his experiments quotes J. J. Thomson's "The Conduction of Electricity Through Gases."[21]

But the conversion lacked conviction. As late as 1910, Whitney would write: "I enjoy what I can understand of the electron theory, and I once went through the indexes of the Bieblatter (a chemical reference work) to determine the enormous difference between the description of negative ions and of positive. I thought then that as for positive ions, there wasn't any such animal."[22] As we shall see, when Whitney later got an opportunity in 1910 to make an important discovery by interpreting some of his experimental results on lamp vacua in terms of the electron theory, he failed to grasp it.

But this episode shows more than Whitney's limitations as a scientist. It shows that at least some of the work of General Electric's Laboratory was devoted to truly original research. The confrontation of the electrochemical and the electron theories of conduction stood as one of the forefront problems of physics and physical chemistry in 1904. Whitney and Weedon had attacked that problem in the hope of both contributing to knowledge and bringing back knowledge that would contribute to the invention of better electric lights. In this project, the corporation's chemists sought to serve the corporation by being real chemists.

The results of their joint work included not only the outcome of these experiments but also a more practical finding. However arcs worked, titanium carbide, one of the alloys Weedon had experimented with, looked as though it would make a very long-lasting arc lamp electrode. How should this new knowledge be released to the world? Here Whitney established a policy that would remain in place through his whole tenure as research director and remains the policy in virtually all industrial laboratories today. The contribution to knowledge that lacked commercial value could be published immediately. Weedon's article on the unsuccessful search for a Faraday's law of arcs appeared in the *Transactions of the American Electrochemical Society* in 1904.[23] But the commercially valuable news about titanium carbide had to be withheld from publication until patents could be secured and General Electric could be given a sufficient head start in their use. When Weedon finally presented this finding to the Electrochemical Society in 1907, Whitney led off the discussion:

> I rise not to discuss the subject matter presented in the paper, but to apologize for the delay in the publication of the experiments. It is difficult for a company like the General Electric Company, as I believe you will understand, to permit the early publication of the results of work of this class, obtained by men operating in the Laboratory, and I think I am right in saying that Dr. Weedon had this paper written as early as 1904. He kindly held the paper in abeyance until its publication could be permitted. Our Research Laboratory would like to be able to publish rapidly and immediately of its experiments, but the commercial conditions do not always permit this.[24]

Whitney went on to give a reason for the publication delay: "If the Laboratory published articles such as this one," he explained,

> at the time the experiments were carried out, the commercial conditions might be something as follows: The people would say: "Well, that new lamp is coming out now, and we want that lamp and will not buy any other."

But that reasoning could hardly have convinced many members of his audience. The more important reason for delaying publication was patents. Industrial researchers delay publication of knowledge mainly to convert that knowledge into private property through the patent system. By this delay they violate two principal tenets of the scientist's unwritten code: knowledge should be made available to fellow scientists as soon as possible and knowledge should remain public property. In this respect, the corporation's chemists allowed their loyalty to the corporation to block the carrying out of part of their duty to the community of chemists. Delaying knowledge that titanium carbide would make a good arc lamp could hardly be expected to seriously set back the pursuit of knowledge. But what would happen later when a discovery would loom as important both to science and to knowledge?

Whitney was too busy in those first five years to worry much about this question. "I never saw time go so fast in my life," he wrote his parents in 1903.

> I dread going back to Boston now, it's such fun here, but I suppose it's fun anywhere when you're busy. I imagine I'd soon forget and lose all track of chemistry if I staid [sic] here all the time, and that is one reason I don't want to do so ($10,000 [annual salary] would tempt me a lot though). I find I've got $2,500 now here in bank thanks to recent Aristo checks and absence in Europe.* Got any use for it?[25]

The breezy talk of money seems more for his father's benefit than as an indication that an idealist chemist-teacher has changed completely into a man of business. Personal relations remained more important to him than dollars. Within the industrial "bear pit" Whitney was assembling around him a congenial team of confidants, the nucleus of a happy family that he could rule over as paternally as any Jamestown mill owner. The growing paperwork of the Laboratory by 1903 had forced him to hire a typist. The young woman who took the post, Mary Christie, quickly became a full-fledged secretary, and it was not long before she assumed the unofficial role of confidant, adviser, and setter of the Laboratory's social and moral tone. She would retain that role for the next thirty-seven years.

Other members of the Laboratory's inner circle were drawn from MIT. Howard Wood set out to develop some of the mercury lamp and rectifier ideas Weintraub had come up with. William Arsem took up a parallel approach to the light of the future, investigating hard-to-melt metals as possible incandescent lamp filaments. In the process, he built and operated one of the first vacuum furnaces in American industry. Emory Gilson, an MIT mechanical engineer, took on some of the practical problems sent down from the Works, such as casting magnetitite and designing better current interrupters. Fred Sexton was hired from the Institute to assist Steinmetz's Lib-

---

*Whitney took his mother on a sightseeing trip to Europe in 1902, just before the final loss of her remaining eyesight.

erty Hall roommate, engineer Eskil Berg, in the study of hysteresis in electric motors.[26] His classmate Edna May Best joined the staff, as one of America's first women industrial scientists, to study improved conduits for electrical conductors. "Freddy Sexton had despised her when they were at Tech," Ginger Adams recalled later

> and he was disgusted when he learned she was coming to Schenectady. May was never one to overlook a challenge like that . . . it was only a matter of weeks when Freddy was looking at engagement rings.[27]

When Fred Sexton decided he belonged in a university, Whitney helped him find a teaching job in Canada. He loaned Fred equipment and supplemented his salary by forwarding consulting work to him. May Sexton's cheery letters, addressed to "dear old boss," testify to the continuing warm relationship among the three. The Sexton's had their first child in 1906 and named him Whitney.[28]

In a small laboratory of only forty or so people, including only a dozen or so trained scientists and engineers, Whitney could establish this kind of personal relationship with any staff member willing to return it. He could also carry the administrative and paperwork burdens of laboratory management lightly enough to continue to carry on research himself. And this proved fortunate. For once he had opened the Laboratory's door to the problems of the Works, his list of potential projects grew even faster than his staff. His notebook entry in September 20, 1902, followed a list of the work of the Laboratory's thirteen principal researchers with a list of twenty-nine possible subjects in addition to the ones they were already working on. The projects ranged from improved trolley wire to electrolytic ore refining. He needed all the hands he could get, including his own.[29]

By then he had put Weintraub in charge of the mercury arc work, and Weedon was carrying out the basic research experiments on arcs. So Whitney took up one of the most mundane of the remaining problems, the improved resistance rods for

1 Julius E Ober
2 Wm Weedon
3 Lawrence E Barringer
4 Chas F Lindsay
5 Edna May Best (1st Woman Chemist)
6 Chas P Steinmetz
7 Willis R Whitney
8 Ralph C Robinson
9 Rob't S Russell

10 Alex M Jackson
11 Emery G Gilson
12 Samuel Ferguson (Hartford Ins Corp)
13 ?
14 Otto Kank
15 ? Harden
16 Wm C Arsem
17 Howard Wood
18 Ezekiel Weintraub

Research Lab
about 1904

Staff of the GE Research Laboratory, about 1904.

meters and lightning arrestors that Works engineers Charles Eveleth and Edward Hewlett had requested.

The problem had two parts: first, make small electrical circuit elements, whose resistance measured one million ohms, for use in meters; then, for a lightning arrestor, make circuit elements that increased in resistance when heated by a rush of electric current. Tackling the first part, Whitney learned that resistors were convenionally made of a mixture of carbon and clay rolled into a cylinder an inch or so long and perhaps a quarter of an inch in diameter and then baked to hardness in a kiln. To raise the resistance, put in more clay; to lower it, put in more carbon. General Electric had brought from New York City a family of ceramic craftsmen originally from Bohemia, named Cermak, to set up a porcelain plant at the Schenectady Works, and the Cermaks had taken on the job of making the million-ohm resistors in their conventional kilns. Whitney, viewing the process and talking to the ceramicists, learned that they could not control the baking process precisely enough to turn out rods of uniformly high resistance.[30]

For Whitney, the answer sprang easily from the electro-chemistry he had translated in LeBlanc's textbook and had seen in operation in Henri Moisson's laboratory in Paris. "Carbon rods," he noted on September 11, 1901, "might be baked in an electric oven fed with or filled with carbon dioxide to pre-vent burning of carbon." Within four weeks he had demon-strated that such a furnace could precisely control a ceramic cylinder's resistance. A mixture containing between 10.1 per-cent and 11.1 percent carbon, formed into cylinders exactly one inch long, and baked with precise timing in the extremely uni-form conditions of the electric oven, gave exactly the desired million ohms.[31]

The result of the process met the need of the meter depart-ment so well that its management asked Whitney to manufac-ture the resistors. He agreed, and the Laboratory, which had been set up "entirely separate from the manufacturing oper-ations," became itself a small manufacturing operation. This established what would be another of Whitney's major poli-cies. For the rest of his tenure as director, the Laboratory would manufacture specialty products and sell them—mainly within GE, but occasionally outside—to pay for part of its budget. At times, the proceeds from these sales were large; in 1914, they paid more than two-thirds of the Laboratory's annual ex-penses (see figure 3).

Whitney proceeded in 1902 to develop his electric oven in the form of a long carbon tube loosely filled with carbon gran-ules. Electric contacts at each end of the tube supplied the heating current. The object to be baked was pulled through at a precisely timed rate. By this means he controlled the dura-tion and temperature of firing far more precisely than was possible in a conventional kiln. He made the resistors with sil-icon carbide mixed with carbon and clay. He learned that bak-ing them hot enough removed a thin conducting layer from the surface and gave them a very uniform resistance. Heating them less, and leaving the layer on, gave the rods the desired characteristic of increasing resistance when heated that the lightning arrestor people wanted. (Conventional resistance rods, by contrast, decrease in resistance as they get hotter.) This gave the Laboratory a second product.[32]

He was soon at work on a third. General Electric made meter and lightning resistor rods annually by the thousands. But the Company produced another resistance annually by the millions—the filament of the incandescent lamp. Could the electric furnace do anything important for the light bulb? If it could, Whitney might be able to make a big contribution to solving the lighting problem that the Laboratory had been established to attack. He worked on various approaches through 1903, and by December he had found the answer. Make a carbon filament by the then-standard method of squirting a cellulose solution through a small hole into a special curing solution. Then take that filament and run it through the carefully controlled inferno of the electric furnace. This heat treatment, far hotter than those to which any previous inventor had subjected a lamp filament, turned the surface of the filament into a special structure of graphite with properties resembling that of metal. The surface layer conducted almost all the filament's electric current. The resistance of this surface layer increased with rising temperature, like that of a metal, and it could be run far hotter than a conventional carbon filament. This meant the lamp had 50 percent higher efficiency than a conventional filament of the same 800-hour life. The resulting product, the General Electric Metallized, or GEM, lamp, turned out to indeed be a "great thing for General Electric"—the most valuable individual invention Whitney was to make in his career.[33]

This success confirmed the wisdom of his policy of taking on the problems of the factory. The invention grew mainly and logically from the work he had been doing on resistance rods in answer to requests by the Schenectady Works engineers. And because he had already established contact with the GE Lamp Factory in Harrison, New Jersey, the transfer of the idea from the Laboratory to the operating department went smoothly. By mid-December 1903, John W. Howell, manager of the Harrison plant, had visited the Laboratory to view the new process. By early January, 1904, the patent applications had been filed, and Whitney was cautioning his staff not to say anything about this new electric furnace work. He would soon be making the researcher's perennial complaint that the operating people were not proceeding fast enough with his invention. But in January he was still basking in the glow of success.[34]

It was in this state that he took up in early 1904 a personal question that he had been putting off for too long. Where should he make his home—in Boston or Schenectady? He had hoped to divide his time between industrial research in Schenectady and physical chemistry research in Boston and perhaps even get back into teaching. But as early as September 1902, when he referred in his notebook to "the service of two masters," he surely remembered his Bible well enough to recognize the impossibility of such divided allegiance. By May 1904, he had made his choice. The notebook entry describing it displays a touch of residual doubt: "Moved my family to Schenectady for good—or evil."[35]

The move to Schenectady allowed him to regain some of the rural flavor of Jamestown. For while nearly all of GE's executives and engineering leaders chose homes in the downtown "GE plot" set aside for Company dignitaries, Whitney chose to live in the suburb of Alplaus, separated by a four-mile drive and a river from Schenectady and the Works. The house he bought with the Aristotype earnings had a small farm attached and a woods nearby.

The Alplaus home also offered the first chance in nearly ten years to keep his family together, and especially to get to know his daughter. Ennin was already twelve years old. Their life together so far had been made up mainly of separations—his departures for Germany or Schenectady, or hers for summers in Jamestown. She continued to grow up bright, vigorous, and temperamental. The center of her life had become her pets—mainly the stray cats she could persuade her parents to take into the Boston apartment. Now at the farm she could have the horse she had always dreamed of.

This new chance to both have a farm and get to know his

daughter exhilarated Whitney nearly as much as his big invention. "I feel I should never grow beyond 10 years old on a farm," he wrote his parents the next winter.[36] He and Ennin improvised a dog sled to ride along the snow-covered roads and skate-sailed on the frozen river. They joined in the theatricals, parties, and "stunts" at the corner schoolhouse and went along on a "straw ride" to nearby Vischer's Ferry for a dinner of oyster stew.[37] A photo of Whitney and Ennin from those Alplaus days survived. She is sitting on a gate, for once in a dress rather than her usual farm outfit, a wise but innocent look on her face. He is standing beside her, handsome and confident in his well-cut three-piece suit, legs crossed, with one hand on the gate and the other on his hip. They're looking into each other's eyes, the half smile on each face suggesting a shared joke or a secret.[38]

Evelyn Whitney did not share completely in this rural idyll. She had come to love the convenience and culture of Boston. She was not ready to settle down into a country life. She made no open revolt, and outwardly her marriage appeared a happy one. But to maintain this equilibrium she exacted concessions. She would take frequent trips to Boston, eventually spending most of her winters there. And in the summers she invited her sister Harriet for long visits. Whitney came to thoroughly dislike Harriet, telling his friend Coolidge a few years later that "he'd rather spend his life in hell than shut up in the same house with her."[39]

Evelyn's rural home also hampered her in securing the place in Schenectady society that her position entitled her to. Her husband the professor (MIT allowed him to retain the rank in absentia) was now also a rising young corporate executive. He had traded his bicycle for an automobile, still a luxury item in Schenectady in 1905. He joined the Mohawk Club, the social meeting place for the Company and city elite. He was earning notice as an inventor of important new products for GE.

The most important of his inventions, the GEM lamp, was moving toward success. Whitney meant to hurry it along, even if that meant butting in on the jobs of GE's engineers. "I went over to Harrison to see how they were getting along with the new filament work," he wrote in July, 1904.

> I was a little surprised to see that they were not very far along on this work but altogether I was a little glad for they are doing just the kind of work that I can do better in the laboratory I think, and I will go ahead very soon now to try to beat them to the ultimate goal, i.e., the commercial production of the stuff and its exact control.[40]

He enjoyed the confidence of GE's management. "I notice," he wrote in the same letter, "that although hard times are the cause of very marked reductions in the departments of the factory, there has been no real call on me for greater economies."[41]

Once a month he now met with an advisory council of GE's technical leaders: Thomson, Rice, Steinmetz, Stanley, John W. Howell, and three others. That council had been created in September 1903, when Rice suggested that the Laboratory had become too big for responsibility for its work to rest exclusively on one man. The members of the council suggested new projects and commented on the progress of ongoing ones. They served as a sort of board of directors, leaving executive responsibilities in Whitney's hands.

The advisory council meetings also gave Whitney a chance to see more of Thomson. As long as Whitney still lived in Boston, the two would travel back from Schenectady together on the train. As Thomson's biographer David O. Woodbury tells it, each trip would invariably begin with a dinner of Manhattan cocktails and mushroom omelet at Keeler's Restaurant in Albany and would continue with conversation deep into the night on the Boston-bound train. "While the waiter hovered over them affectionately," Woodbury reports, "they would fly away into the future to survey unknown lands."[42]

Advisory committees were central to the management style of the General Electric Company at this time. President Charles A. Coffin set Company strategy from his office in New York

City. In carrying out that strategy, the Company's functional empires—manufacturing, engineering, purchasing, finance and sales—often clashed, and committees had to be established to settle the disputes.[43] Rice had wisely set up a committee for research in advance, before Whitney stepped on anyone's toes.

Coffin did not take much direct interest in the Research Laboratory, but he created an ideal growing climate for it by the three-part strategy he established for GE: centralize, improve manufacturing efficiency, diversify. Centralization justified the establishment of a central research laboratory at the Company's main works. The need to increase manufacturing efficiency brought Works engineers to that laboratory with requests for improvements, and that work gave Whitney a way to keep the pot boiling until longer range work paid off. Rice recognized this strategy and encouraged it; "Mr. Rice wants account kept of the 'potboilers' we succeed in doing together with their estimated value to the company," Whitney noted in early 1904.[44]

But the most promising of the three strategies for the Laboratory's future was diversification. Perhaps Coffin was frightened by the new teeth that President Theodore Roosevelt and the Supreme Court's Northern Securities Decision had put into the Sherman Antitrust Law. For he chose to make GE's profits grow, not by crowding competitors such as Westinghouse out of business and establishing a monopoly over established electrical manufacturing products, but by seeking new and profitable product lines.

So as Roosevelt carried on his predecessors' policy of strengthening the U.S. Navy, GE was there, working with the inventive Naval officer Bradley A. Fiske on new ways to use electricity on warships—to hoist ammunition, power searchlights, and turn gun turrets. By mid-1904, GE had about $2 million in outstanding orders to supply equipment for Navy ships under construction.[45] (In those days, $2 million was real money, about one-tenth of GE's annual sales.) As cities grew, and electric propulsion replaced the horse and the cable for pulling trolley cars, street railway motors grew in importance as a company product, rivaling light bulbs and generators. Since GE's street railway motors ran on direct current, but its generators produced alternating current, this field offered a promising opportunity for the mercury vapor AC-to-DC converter that Weintraub and Hewitt had discovered. "The thing I am most interested in now," Whitney wrote his parents in January 1905, "is a rectifier to take the place of the motor generator sets used along the trolley lines."[46]

So by early 1905, it appeared that Whitney had created the situation in life he so long had sought. He was attacking problems in technology that possessed both scientific and commercial importance. He retained his standing in the chemical community as a researcher in both electrochemistry and colloids. He kept his connection with MIT and Noyes' Laboratory and his leading roles in the American Chemical Society and the Electrochemical Society. He had recaptured a bit of Jamestown in his Alplaus farm and had brought his family back together after years of recurrent separations. But before he could settle down and enjoy this compound life, a problem emerged that almost shattered it.

It had begun in late 1904, as a small shadow flitting across the pages of his Laboratory notebook: "25 Aug. 1904: Get Dr. Weintraub to start on metal filaments again . . . 1 Sept. 1904: In PM spent two hours in Mr. Davis' office on Tantalum filament . . . 6–7 Sept. 1904: Trip to NY & Harrison re tantalum lamps (two watts per c.p.) . . . 9 Sept. 04: Gave Weintraub tantalum lamp to dissect."[47]

The tantalum lamp, invented by chemist Werner Von Bolton at the laboratory of the Siemens and Halske Company in Berlin, was not the first metal filament lamp ever made. But it was the first one made of a metal with a higher melting point than carbon that offered the prospect of production at commercially attractive prices. And that higher melting point meant an efficacy of 4.8 lumens per watt, 15 percent better than even Whitney's new GEM lamp.[48] ("Efficacy" is the term used by lighting engineers for the amount of light, measured in lumens, produced by a lamp for every watt of energy consumed.) In accordance with an agreement between the two companies, Siemens and Halske offered the new lamp to GE in 1904 at a stiff price. Acceptance of the offer might not only doom the GEM lamp to instant obsolescence but also indicate that the new Research Laboratory had failed in its most important mission. Recall Albert G. Davis' justification for support of the Laboratory. "If someone gets ahead of us," he wrote referring to the development of new light sources, "we will have to spend large sums in buying patent reights, whereas if we do the work ourselves this necessity will be avoided."

As this prospect began to appear serious, Whitney had to reconsider the idea of moving the Laboratory's research into new projects outside the lighting field. Coffin's GE strategy might emphasize diversification, but a large centralized company whose most profitable product had been attacked had to put defense before diversification. Whitney began to redeploy his troops on the lighting front. "Started Dr. Weintraub and Carl Krueger on tungsten for filament," he wrote in October 1904, "and asked Arsem to choose the metal which most interested him among the promising lot."[49]

The assignments represented a counterattack on the tantalum threat. On the periodic chart of the chemical elements, molybdenum, uranium, thorium, and tungsten surround tantalum. The scientific literature indicated that they shared or exceeded tantalum's high melting point. But could any of them be shaped economically into filaments? Researchers dating back to Edison had tried the most promising of the lot, tungsten, but had found it too brittle for use.[50]

To cover all bets, Whitney assigned each of the promising squares on the periodic chart to one of his researchers and began to ititiate experiments of his own. He wrote up patent applications on work he had done earlier on squashing red-hot blobs of tungsten with a hammer in hopes of eliminating its brittleness.[51] But the program over the next six months brought no immediate results. By mid-1905 he found it necessary to concentrate the Laboratory's work, and his own, even more completely on the metal filament.

This new mood of urgency brought out a side of his management style that had always coexisted with his enthusiastic informality. As his treatment of Steinmetz indicated, he allowed no questioning about who ran the Laboratory. He made sure that all incoming proposals and outgoing inventions and ideas would be funneled through him. Back in mid-1903, he had addressed a general notice to all departments at the Schenectady Works declaring that all requests for help from the Laboratory must be sent to him, not taken directly to individual researchers.[52] And because Laboratory notebooks could become vital evidence in later patent suits, he insisted that all researchers make regular entries in theirs. "Write *something* in your notebook every day," Whitney would later tell new staff members, "even if it's only 'I didn't do a damn thing today.' "[53] Once a month a "report of work" summing up the month's notebook entries had to be written, signed, witnessed, and submitted to Whitney. In addition, patentable ideas had to be described in special letters addressed to him. He would decide if they were promising enough to be forwarded to Company patent attorneys.[54]

He enforced these reporting requirements. "Second talk with Jackson on salary," he noted in 1903. "Told him to wait two weeks to see if I could satisfy myself as to his willingness to do right about reports." In another case, he found it necessary to deliver a verbal reminder to a staff member about the "Co.'s right to all inventions & c."[55]

As the filament race became more urgent, the need for this kind of discipline and focus became more pressing. The choice of the most promising metal quickly centered on tantalum versus tungsten, although work continued on the others. Whitney dropped his own other research schemes in June 1905 and resolved to "attempt new schemes to improve the tungsten filament." The next day he described a "scheme for making on a scientific exact basis pure metal filaments such as tungsten." He proposed to overcome tungsten's brittleness by grinding it into a fine powder, mixing it with a binder made of sugar, alcohol, or wax, squirting the resulting paste through a small hole to extrude a thin short piece of wire, and baking that wire to drive off the carbon and hydrogen of the binder, leaving grains of tungsten sintered together into a thin, hard, brittle filament. He probably did not yet know that this idea had already been conceived, reduced to practice, and patented by two Austrians, Alexander Just and Franz Hanaman.[56]

In the summer of 1905, Whitney had organized the filament effort around three main projects. Chemist E. N. Beckwith and three assistants were working on the squirted filament approach. William Arsem was trying to purify tungsten in his vacuum furnace, in the hope that the metal's brittleness was due solely to impurities and could be removed with them. And Ezekiel Weintraub was supposed to be leading a general study of the causes of brittleness in tungsten and thorium. But Weintraub refused to be diverted from his work on the adaptation of the mercury arc to telephony and wireless telegraphy.[57]

Whitney had already recognized that he needed another outstanding scientist on his staff, one as talented as Weintraub but less of a lone wolf. In 1902, he had failed to land one very promising Leipzig electrochemistry graduate when Frank Cottrell had turned down the post of assistant director of the Laboratory to take a much lower paying academic position at Berkeley. (Cottrell's outstanding achievement there would be not in science but in technology. He would invent a new electrostatic precipitator for cleaning up factory smoke and dedicate the proceedings from the invention to establishing the Research Corporation, a venture capital source aimed at supporting science and helping university researchers exploit their own inventions by driving hard bargains with established corporations.)[58] In 1905, Whitney turned again to the man who had turned down his initial offer, his MIT colleague, Coolidge.

Since his days as a student in one of Whitney's first chemistry classes at MIT, Coolidge had earned a bachelor's degree in electrical engineering and a doctorate in physics in 1900 under Leipzig's Gustav Wiedemann and had spent five years with

Noyes as a researcher in physical chemistry. He impressed all who worked with him by his skill at designing apparatus and getting experiments to work. Wiedemann had chosen Coolidge as his special assistant, and Noyes had entrusted him with the most difficult experimental tasks at the new Physical Chemistry Laboratory. Coolidge designed a metal chamber capable of withstanding the extreme pressures and temperatures needed to test the properties of solutions under the extreme conditions where deviations from the simple ionic theories of Arrhenius might be expected to show up most dramatically. He might show little interest in theory and engage in little speculation about the fundamental questions of physics and chemistry. But when Will Coolidge identified, or was presented with, an experimental problem, he fought his way to its solution.[59]

His reserved personality; precise voice; thin, tight-lipped face; and careful manner—qualities that would become more familiar to the American public twenty years later in his distant cousin Calvin—embodied the Yankee traditions of the small Massachusetts town where he had grown up. Whitney knew that Coolidge would be a team player. On June 15, 1905, Rice gave permission to offer Coolidge the position of assistant director of the Laboratory, a salary about twice Coolidge's MIT pay, and an extremely tempting promise. Coolidge could bring to Schenectady the pressure vessel he had designed at Noyes' laboratory and spend one-third of his time carrying out the physical chemistry experiments that were beginning to earn him a scientific reputation.[60]

Coolidge accepted and immediately threw himself into the struggle to perfect the tungsten filament. The exact way he got involved in that effort comes down to us in two versions, both given under oath in a 1920 patent case. "Upon entering the employment of the General Electric Company," Coolidge explained, "I was asked by Dr. Whitney to consider myself a free lance and take up any line of work which interested me."[61] But questioning of Whitney elicited a slightly different picture.

Q. 49. When Dr. Coolidge entered the Laboratory, did you have anything to do with the signing of his duties?
A. Yes . . .
Q. 50. Did you tell him what line of work or investigation to pursue . . . ?
A. We probably agreed on it.
Q. 51. What was that line of work?
A. It soon became the tungsten work.[62]

One can bring the two statements into accord by assuming that Whitney did negotiate an agreement with Coolidge to get him to concentrate on the tungsten project but did so tactfully enough that Coolidge retained his sense of being a "free lance." Assigning work by negotiation—"peddling" problems rather than directing research—became an essential element of Whitney's management style.

Free lance or not, Coolidge did not wait to get to Schenectady to start work on tungsten. He borrowed equipment from the MIT physics department and spent six weeks in Boston trying to deform tungsten without cracking it. He would melt a piece of tungsten into a blob under an electric discharge in a vacuum, remove it, and hit it with a hammer. By February 1906, he was able to bring Whitney some tungsten pieces that had "hammered quite well." But when he tried to pull or press them into rods they cracked.[63]

Meanwhile, the wax process gave more promising results. The Laboratory built a few experimental tungsten filament bulbs, including one Whitney unveiled dramatically at a dinner party for GE executives. By April 1906, the Company was considering plans to build a demonstration circuit in New Jersey using lamps made with the binder process.[64]

But by then Rice knew that the Europeans were far ahead of his own researchers. So he told Whitney and John W. Howell to travel to Europe and come back with the best agreements they could negotiate to allow GE to use the technology and get into the business of making metal filament lamps. They arrived in Berlin to find that the European lead was even greater than they had thought. The lobby of their hotel was already lighted with metal filament lamps, produced by the Auer Gesellschaft, a branch of the company led by Count Auer von Welsbach that had earlier introduced the incandescent mantle for gas lights. The lamp's name, Osram, hinted at its composition: a mixture of *Os*mium and Wolf*ram* (tungsten). Auer had invented a way to make the osmium lamp by a binder process a few years earlier but found it too expensive to produce. He had more recently learned that the less expensive tungsten could be mixed with the costly osmium and finally substituted for it altogether.[65]

Whitney and Howell toured the Auer factory and came away impressed with the high degree of mechanization involved. They also learned the details of a pair of rival processes patented by Just and Hanaman, employing binders to make the tungsten hold together. One of their methods was already in use in Hungary, but it appeared complex and unreliable. Whitney and Howell recommended that GE ignore Just and Hanaman for now and instead purchase the rights to the Siemens & Halske tantalum lamp—the one that had started all the metal filament fuss—and the Auer tungsten process.[66]

Their negotiating position for acquiring these rights was strengthened by good news from Schenectady. In June 1906, Coolidge observed that mercury in contact with hot tungsten seemed to be absorbed by it. He quickly tried the effect for a variety of metals and found that tungsten would take up enough cadmium and bismuth to form a flexible amalgam that could be squeezed through a die to make a long, fine, and flexible wire. This represented an advance over the previous carbon-tungsten binder mixtures, which could be squeezed out only into short lengths. The new process had along way to go to reach commercial application, but it served a useful bargaining purpose. Howell, who had made a return trip to America, brought back to Germany some of the Coolidge wire, and by showing it in the right places, he and Whitney obtained somewhat better terms than might otherwise have resulted.[67]

But in all, the trip represented a defeat for the Laboratory.

It had failed to anticipate key innovations in the lighting field. Now GE was going to have to pay $250,000 for only the right to purchase tantalum wire from Siemens & Halske and make it into lamps. It agreed not to make the wire in America or even to learn the details of the process. And it paid another $100,000 for the right to try to adapt the Auer process to American conditions. These were expenses that the Laboratory had been founded with the purpose of preventing.[68]

The business consequences of failing to tie down patent control of the metal filament lamp loomed even larger. GE's lamp people put a brave face on and declared that "it will probably find its own place and will not take the place of the carbon filament lamp."[69] But in fact, when the metal filament appeared in 1907, the carbon lamp ceased its annual sales growth of 30 percent a year, peaked at a total sales of 65 million lamps in 1907, and began to decline. The tungsten lamp took off immediately at a growth rate of more than 40 percent a year, on its way to sales of more than 100 million lamps by 1914, and more than 200 million by 1920. Metal filaments would turn the light bulb into a mass consumption product. In 1906, GE bought rights to only two metal filament processes; others remained outside its grasp. If GE lost its patent control, it would have to share this mass market with many rivals, and prices might fall disastrously. One solution was further expensive purchases. Already, in May 1906, an Austrian inventor named Kuzel had offered his promising tungsten patent to GE for another $500,000. However, the race had not been lost. Only the first lap had been run. Whitney could redeem himself and the Laboratory by developing major improvements in tungsten lamp manufacture that would reestablish GE's dominance.[70]

Whitney got back to Schenectady on September 6, 1906, to begin a year of mounting tension. He had put his technical judgment behind the Auer process; now it was up to him to make it work in America. At the same time, it was too early in the race to unsaddle the other two promising horses, Coolidge's new amalgam process and William Arsem's vacuum-melted tungsten. Whitney took on the job of adapting the Auer process himself, and this put him in a difficult position. He was directing the work of Arsem and Coolidge at the same time as he competed with them to be the first to come up with a practical manufacturing process.[71]

Coolidge did not hold GE to the promise of one-third time for pure research. His pressure vessel lay discarded in a corner until he sent it back to Noyes. The work became "strenuous," and Mr. Rice "wanted things pushed," Coolidge reported.[72] "I am fully satisfied that this work is not so much to my taste as investigation in pure science in connection with some college," he had written his mother in March 1906. But the work also had its consolations.

> It pays well and I can save money on it. Later, after I get some money ahead, I can do as I want to. And I am having an experience here which is fitting me all the time for a still bigger salary either here or somewhere else as director perhaps of a laboratory.
>
> I am fortunate now in being in on the most important problem the lab has ever had, and our success on that problem would make the Company give the lab anything that Whitney sees fit to ask for. If we can get the metal, tungsten, in such shape that it can be drawn into wire, it means millions of dollars to the Company. Whitney and I both feel sure of ultimate success and think that although other people are at work on it, our chances of getting there first are good.[73]

But with Whitney's return from Europe in September, he and Coolidge were no longer just working together in competition with the world. They were also competing with each other. And as Coolidge's experimental skills brought his amalgam process steadily forward toward practicality, Whitney experienced one frustration after another with the cranky Auer process. "First good batch of Auer filaments were spoiled by placing them in an iron tube furnace which had rusted a lot," he noted on October 30, 1906. As disappointments within the Laboratory accumulated, pressures from the outside mounted.

GE's European agents sent clipping after clipping of new filament developments on the continent, and Whitney's alphabetically arranged clipping book of filament candidates filled: colloidal metals, cadmium, chromium, indium, manganese, molybdenum, osmium, niobium, platinum, tantalum, tungsten, titanium, zircon, and zinc were all subjects of optimistic European claims. And the Nernst lamp remained a major competitor, too. George Westinghouse was completing negotiations that would result in 1907 in a $250,000 contract to light New York's Pennsylvania Station with the efficient ceramic glowers. "A succession of competing new illuminating schemes gave me some temporary heartaches," Whitney wrote later. "They scared me because I might possibly see the institution that I served lose its high place in the lighting field through some negligence or careless action of mine."[74]

Through the winter of 1906, Whitney bore his triple burden: assessing the value of competing lamp schemes and advising the Company; managing the work of Coolidge, Arsem, and the rest of the Laboratory's researchers; and competing with them by seeking to bring the Auer process into successful production. "I am almost sorry that Whitney ever took hold of the German method in the Laboratory, because he's having an awful time with it," Coolidge wrote. "But having started it of course, he's got to make a success of it."[75]

Whitney tried to maintain a spirit of teamwork in the midst of the competition. On February 10, 1907, he brought the Laboratory's staff, now swollen to one-hundred-fifty, together at a party. He read original poems, and others put on a musical parody of the weekly colloquium, with protagonists based on his idiosyncrasies and those of Coolidge. But the tension was beginning to tell even on the enthusiastic and even-tempered Coolidge. The previous August he had expressed his frustration at the pressure put on him ("life is much too short for a man to do what I have been forced to do for the last few months") in a demand for a higher salary ("if the Co. doesn't want to pay me 4000 next year, I don't care for the job.")[76] Through the winter, the salary dispute dragged on, and only in March 1907 was Whitney able to secure the raise. But by then, Coolidge wanted more. "Mr. Rice wanted me to sign a contract for two years, beginning with last September at $4000. But I am demurring," he wrote his mother, "I . . . am worth to them anything that I'll ever have the nerve to ask them."[77] But Whitney persuaded Coolidge to sign and made his position more attractive by hiring another Leipzig-trained electrochemist, Colin G. Fink, to aid him on his tungsten work.[78]

Despite their competition, Whitney never stinted in his support of Coolidge. But while he settled Coolidge's salary, his own remained unsettled. He generously made his resources available to those in need. By the summer of 1907, Coolidge estimated that Whitney had about $1,500 in loans outstanding to younger staff members. He had ceased doing research in pure science. His latest scientific paper, appearing that year in the *Journal of the American Chemical Society*, represented work done years earlier. It would be five years before he published another covering new work.[79]

The compound that seemed so nearly completed when he had moved to Schenectady in 1904 was decomposing. The GEM lamp, which he had hoped would become his great contribution to General Electric, had proved only a temporary stopgap preceding the metal filament lamp. His chance for continuing to be a major contributor to the development of physical chemistry had passed, crowded out of his life by a busy schedule of meetings in GE executive offices, long days on the train to the Harrison lamp plant or to the Black Hills of North Dakota to look over a promising deposit of tantalum ore, and service on the witness stand in patent suits. His wish to create a happy family life on the farm also began to vanish, as the pattern of separation from his family resumed, owing first to the long European trip in 1906 and then to the late nights and weekends spent struggling with the Auer process. His remaining hopes for family happiness centered more and more on his daughter. "Remember that you are the whole show for me and mama," he wrote her from Berlin in 1906. "I am glad that you learn easily, but that imposes an additional obligation on

Staff of the GE Research Laboratory, 1906. Whitney is in the second row, third from right. To his left is Ezekiel Weintraub. Behind Weintraub is Mary Christie.

you, you must learn much."[80] But she refused to share his interest in learning, instead devoting more and more of her life to her horses and her cats.

In mid-1907, the filament race between Whitney and Coolidge came to an anticlimactic conclusion. Another German process—one of the two invented by Just and Hanaman that Whitney and Howell had turned down in 1906—now began to look clearly superior to either the Coolidge or the Auer processes. The General Electric and National Electric Lamp Association factories set out to adopt it. They would continue developing Coolidge's method too, while dropping the Auer method altogether. This meant a personal defeat for Whitney, although it did create a much needed breathing spell. In August, Coolidge left on vacation for the Grand Canyon, and Whitney accepted an invitation from Arthur A. Noyes to sail the coast of Maine. "Whitney does not look at all well," Coolidge wrote on August 3, "and I'm awfully glad he leaves tonight to join Noyes for their boat cruise."[81]

The relief proved only temporary. Whitney came back to

learn that the panic of 1907 was blowing through Wall Street. General Electric's president Coffin had ballasted the Company with cash reserves but still thought it prudent to order the sails reefed. Rice's assistant Francis C. Pratt, a tough New Englander who was taking over more and more of the direction of the Company's engineering and manufacturing, passed the word to Whitney: prepare contingency plans to cut lab expenses by 10, 20, and 30 percent.[82]

"Spent Friday and Saturday working on a scheme to cut lab expenses," he wrote in his notebook on September 13, 1907.[83] The next Tuesday Caroline Whitney Barret received an emergency call in Boston: her brother Willis was lying in Schenectady's Ellis Hospital, close to death. She rushed to Schenectady and spent an anxious night of waiting and walking with Coolidge along Schenectady's deserted streets before the doctors could assure them that Willis was out of danger.[84]

The cause of the crisis, according to Whitney's family, was appendictis left too long untreated. But it climaxed three years of growing mental and physical strain that may have contributed both to the timing and severity of the attack. As early as 1905, he had been confiding to his friend and former employee May Best Sexton that he was tormented by thoughts whose secret nature he could not reveal. "I'm not a bit curious any more as to what the awful thing is," she wrote him. *"Think* of the relief it would be to drop the strain of hiding the fact that something troubles you."[85] And looking back in 1909 on those 1905 troubles, Whitney wrote in a diary:

> It is interesting to note how little one can change himself. I find that just four years ago I passed such a day as today when I wanted to do something that I prevented myself from doing. A feeling of sourness and internal absorption makes me anything but a pleasure to others.[86]

He never revealed either to May Best or to his notebook the source of the sourness or the temptation he needed to resist. But the Laboratory's troubles with the metal filament increased the strain. During Whitney's illness, Coolidge took over as Laboratory director, and he was soon telling his parents that "I begin to wonder about my own mental condition." Three years of such pressures had undermined Whitney's. "Whitney stays out in Alplaus to keep toubles away from him," Coolidge wrote in December.[87]

Whatever the combination of mental and physical factors involved, Whitney was at a low point as he lay in Ellis Hospital and subsequently when he returned to the Alplaus farm and then went to St. Petersburg, Florida, for a three-month convalescence. He knew the Laboratory staff had been cut back 30 percent in accordance with the most extreme of the plans Pratt had requested. The filament race appeared lost with the decision to use the foreign patents. The effort for which he had sacrificed teaching, his personal research, and his family life seemed to have ended in failure. He had come to question his choice of a career at General Electric. That winter, he wrote to Noyes that he was seriously considering resigning the post of research director, leaving science, and embarking on a new vocation as a surgeon.[88]

7/

Redesigning the Experiment

Noyes emphatically disagreed with Whitney's new intention to change careers. "I do not think you should follow up your idea of becoming a surgeon," he wrote on February 1, 1908, to the still convalescing Whitney in St. Petersburg. Surgery, Noyes explained, would benefit only a few people. And it required mainly manipulative skill, "rather than the qualities of originality, practical execution, and effective dealing with men which you possess in so high a degree."[1] Those talents ought not, perhaps, be harnessed only to a profit-seeking corporation. Whitney might better serve "the interests of humanity" by directing a university applied science laboratory. But wherever he practiced it, continuing his present role offered Whitney his greatest opportunity for service. "With respect to yourself," Noyes argued:

> I think first of all you should give great weight to the fact that in your present position you are "the right man in the right place." It isn't jollying when I say that I don't believe there is a man in the country who has so fully the combination of qualities as you have, for the direction of a technical research laboratory.

Buoyed by this advice, by similarly supportive words from Rice, and by his rest in Florida, Whitney gradually regained his equilibrium. He decided to return to the Research Laboratory and carry his experiment in industrial research through to success. But that meant redesigning the experiment. He would have to drop still more elements from his personal compound at the same time as he broadened and deepened the efforts of his laboratory.

On the personal side, he never again assumed primary research responsiblity for a laboratory project crucial to General Electric, as he had done with the Auer filament process. He would peddle such problems to subordinates. He would stick to newer areas less central to immediate business interests—to the study of lamp vacua, for example, or the design of electric heaters. If one of these projects looked promising, he would turn it over to others.

He also gave up any remaining pretensions of being an important contributor to science, even in his specialties of electrochemistry and colloids. Increasingly, he would discharge his urge to do original research into his hobbies: into the study of the life cycle of turtles, or the search for Indian arrowheads, or agricultural experiments on his farm.

He would redirect the energy that had formerly gone into doing a great thing individually for General Electric or for science. Now he would seek to energize individuals or teams that were more capable or in a better position to do those great things than he was. He would try to turn the laboratory into a happy family, with himself as the father. His most famous mannerisms as a research director would originate in this period of recovery from his 1908 illness. The "Come in, rain or shine" sign would appear above his always open office door. The cheery greeting "are you having fun?" would begin to echo in the Laboratory halls. Behind these gestures lay much new thinking about the right role for industrial research and the right way to direct it.

Under his leadership, the laboratory would succeed in providing General Electric with the technology that assured it continued dominance of the electric lighting business. General Electric, in return, would support Whitney in diversifying the laboratory. Never again would its survival depend on a single project. It would never become exclusively, or even mainly, devoted to fundamental research. It would span the entire range from product improvement to basic science. In one room, engineers would be modifying the carbon content of motor brushes. In a second, physicists would be applying recent findings in electron physics to radio. In a third, a chemist would be carrying out experiments unrelated to GE's business interests that would win him a Nobel Prize. All of those efforts would fit within Whitney's definition of industrial research.

And because of the success and diversity of the laboratory he ran, Whitney would give a new meaning to the role of the corporation's chemist. He would become a keeper of the bridge between basic science and its applications for the entire American chemical community. He would help that community heal a breach between its pure and applied branches. He would help reinforce the cooperation between academic and industrial chemists that represented then, and still represents today, one of American chemistry's greatest strengths.

But before he could do all this, the filament problem had to be solved. Fortunately, as Whitney rode the train north from Florida in the spring of 1908, that problem was on its way to solution. The answer had begun to emerge a full year earlier, when Coolidge had made a surprising discovery. If he heated a tungsten wire made by his amalgam process to a comparatively low temperature, less than 400 degrees C., it bent without cracking. In March 1907, Coolidge rolled heated amalgam filaments down to only 3½ thousandths of an inch in diameter without a crack. "It makes the problem of drawing tungsten hot seem very promising to me," he wrote to Whitney. "It might well be that tungsten at three or four hundred degrees centigrade is as easy to draw as iron."[2]

Whitney made sure Coolidge's work got recognized. "I am also pleased to see that I am getting the credit for my recent discovery that tungsten is a ductile metal below red heat," Coolidge wrote to his parents. "I might have been forgotten, but Whitney looked after that all right."[3] But before the discovery could be put to use, GE's management decided in mid-1907 to concentrate development work on the new "German process," the one invented by Just and Hanaman. By the end of 1907, Coolidge was preparing to drop work on tungsten. "I think I'd like to take up some new and big problem that hasn't been touched at all in the Lab," he told his parents, probably something on which I could publish my results. When my process is relegated to the scrap heap I shall feel all right, but that as the nett [sic] result of the two years of hard work is a bit unsatisfactory to me. No matter how you look at it, the scrap heap is a poor place to look for memorial tablets.[4]

In the spring of 1908, when Whitney got back from Florida, the work on filaments had eased. But it had not stopped completely. Coolidge was studying tungsten oxide powders. Colin G. Fink was attacking a problem Whitney had given him a year earlier, the production of wire from the metal molybdenum. But the filament work lacked focus and direction. It got them, as it had before, from Europe.

In May 1908, Rice sent Coolidge on a trip to help GE's British affiliates adopt his amalgam process, and to visit the best lamp research laboratories on the continent. In early June, he wired Whitney from Berlin. At the Osram laboratory there, he had seen a molybdenum filament that had been subjected to a special heat treatment that allowed it to be bent without cracking, even after having been cooled to room temperature. Since molybdenum shared tungsten's tendency to assume a brittle form when drawn into a wire and cooled, this represented a major advance on Coolidge's earlier discovery that tungsten could remain nonbrittle, or ductile, down to 300 degrees C. On June 6, Whitney asked researchers Chester Moore and William Arsem to try to duplicate the German result. Meanwhile, Fink took one of the molybdenum filaments he had already made, stuck it in a vise, and tried to bend it without heating it. To his surprise, it bent cold without cracking.[5]

This molybdenum clue revitalized the laboratory's filament effort. Molybdenum and tungsten were neighbors on the periodic table and shared many properties. What worked for one ought to work, with suitable modifications, for the other. Coolidge believed that mechanical working of the two metals would remove the brittleness more effectively than the chemical process the Germans used. That process remained Osram's secret when Coolidge departed for America in July. Back in Schenectady, Fink was trying to improve on it with new chemical and heat treatments. Coolidge took up the problem of hammering hot sintered blocks of molybdenum and tungsten to achieve the cold working property by mechanical means alone.

In October, when Whitney emerged from a brief return visit to Schenectady's Ellis Hospital, Coolidge had not yet met with success. He had shown that small wires of tungsten, made by the amalgam process and then subjected to a hot rolling process, lost some of their brittleness, even after cooling to room temperature. But could tungsten be thinned from crumbly blocks of pressed powder to those small wires without the addition of another metal to make it easier to bend?

Convinced that mechanical working alone could provide the most practical method, Coolidge tried hammering heated blocks of tungsten and molybdenum. They invariably shattered. Perhaps success required a more skillful hammerer. He brought in Mr. Still, a blacksmith from the Works. He achieved no better results, and a power hammer also failed. Rather than give up, Coolidge looked around for a better method of even and gradual application of mechanical force while gradually cooling the metal from red heat to room temperature. In late 1908 he found it. He had embarked on a tour of wire- and needle-making factories, and at the Eddy Machine Company in Rhode Island, and the Excelsior Needle Company in Connecticut, he heard about swaging: hitting a piece of metal with repeated rapid blows of specially shaped pairs of hammers and dies to reduce its thickness gradually. He ordered a swaging machine and tried it out. In its original form, it worked little better than the previous unsuccessful methods. But Coolidge radically redesigned the swaging dies and devised a way of heating them while they were working. The combination of swaging and gradual cooling enabled him, in May 1909, to transform for the first time ever a brittle block of molybdenum into a fine and ductile wire by mechanical means alone.[6]

"What is true of molybdenum will, I believe, be true of tungsten," he wrote Whitney on May 31, 1909. But he questioned whether the results of his hard work represented an invention original enough to qualify for a patent. "It seems now very probable to me," he said, "that almost the entire novelty in our final process for manufacturing drawn tungsten will be in the hot swaging. . . . I think that in the hot swaging methods and devices which we have tried and are trying, the field has been pretty thoroughly covered."[7]

But Whitney was not about to let this opportunity slip off the hook. Here was a way to reassert GE's hold on the technology of electric lighting. To pay off, it had to be patented. "I do not recall of this principle for the production of ductile metal having been used in the art before," he answered Coolidge. He forwarded Coolidge's letter and a description of his results to the GE patent department. By mid-June 1909, the attorneys there had agreed with Whitney. They urged Coolidge to apply his molybdenum hot swaging method to tungsten without delay.[8]

Whitney and the attorneys proved right. The Coolidge hot swaging process for the production of ductile tungsten would prove patentable. It would be sustained by the courts against many challengers (though GE's additional claim that Coolidge had invented not only a process but also a new form of tungsten would be overthrown in 1925). Combined with purchase of the Just and Hanaman patents on the use of tungsten in lamp filaments, Coolidge's patent would help give GE as iron-clad a control over the making of tungsten filaments as it had enjoyed over the making of carbon filaments when the Edison patent had been in force. Because of this, the Coolidge patent would become one of the most valuable ones GE owned and a vindication of the establishment of the Research Laboratory.[9]

Using the process on tungsten would not prove as easy as patenting it. Coolidge soon found that filaments produced by hot swaging and drawing pure tungsten had disappointingly short lifetimes in lamps. He put the failed filaments under a microscope and discovered the reason. The hot swaged and drawn filaments had been ductile because the process had converted the blocky tungsten crystals originally present into thin, overlapping fibrous structures that could yield to bend-ing. But the heating of the filament in the lamp turned those fibrous structures back into big blocky crystals. Eventually, a boundary between two of the crystals would extend across the entire diameter of the filament. The filament would slip, or offset, along this boundary until it finally broke.[10]

How did you prevent the blocky crystals from reforming? In May 1909, Coolidge had already thought of an analogy that suggested an answer. He thought of another process that required retaining a small grain size: the solidifying of flavored milk as fine-grained ice cream instead of coarse-grained ice. In that case, glycerine had been added to prevent grain growth. What could be added to tungsten to achieve the same end? It had to be a very heat resistant substance that would spread out evenly within the material. This suggested to Coolidge that "the colloidal suspension of some substance, such as thorium oxide, in the tungsten" might be the answer. It took a year's hard work to prove it, but Coolidge was right.[11]

By the end of 1910, the decade-long quest for the twentieth century's incandescent lamp was nearing its conclusion. That lamp would use a ductile tungsten filament made by the Coolidge process. To begin that process, a lampmaker crushed tungsten oxide ore into a fine powder and then reduced the powder to pure tungsten by heating it in a hydrogen atmosphere. He then doped it with a pinch of thorium oxide to prevent later embrittling. Next he pressed the powder into a block and sintered it—that is, heated it until the grains of powder stuck together. He then passed the block through a series of heated swaging machines of Coolidge's special design. The first machines were at red heat, the others successively cooler. Swaging, the key to the entire process, stretched out the grains without breaking the block. When the block had been elongated and thinned sufficiently, it could be passed through heated rolls, again at gradually decreasing temperatures. Finally, the lampmaker drew the thin cylinder of tungsten that came out of the rolls through diamond dies to make a wire. The brittle block of tungsten had been transformed into a fine,

During a visit by Thomas A. Edison to the General Electric Research Laboratory in Schenectady, N.Y., in 1914, Dr. William D. Coolidge, assistant director, explains how tungsten is made ductile by means of the apparatus in the foreground. The tungsten enters the furnace in front, is heated to swaging temperature, and then reduced in cross section by the swager, rotated by the electric motor. Dr. Coolidge, who later served as director of the Research Laboratory from 1932 to 1945, died on February 3, 1975 at the age of 101.

flexible wire that could be shaped into a filament on a high-speed machine without breaking.[12]

General Electric's lamp factories adopted the Coolidge process in 1911. This meant scrapping hundreds of thousands of dollars worth of still relatively new equipment for making Just-Hanaman-type filaments. But the combined lower manufacturing cost and higher quality of the Coolidge filament made the switch a profitable one. The patents were issued in 1913. Their arrival proved timely, for in 1912, the Justice Department agreed to a consent decree for General Electric settling an antitrust case concerning incandescent lamps. The department had charged GE with operating the ostensibly competing National Electric Lamp Company as a secret partner and thereby gaining a near monopoly of the lamp business. The consent decree forced GE to drop this tactic of monopolization by merger. But at the same time the court affirmed the legality of competitive advantage gained by patents. Control of the technology of the tungsten filament lamp through patents became GE's main defense of its continued dominance of the incandescent lamp business. The Coolidge patent took its place as a key fortification in that defense line.[13]

The main credit for this timely technical triumph belonged to Coolidge. But there was plenty of credit to share. It had been a team effort involving some 40 people, 20 of them trained scientists. About three-fourths of the entire staff of the laboratory, which had grown from 40 in 1904 to 106 in 1910, worked on some phase of the lamp filament problem. More than a dozen of the people who worked alongside Coolidge held technical degrees in science or engineering. The most important of them had been Colin G. Fink. His efforts had paralleled and supported Coolidge's. After leaving GE a few years later, he would insist in print and in the courts that he had been the true inventor of the ductile tungsten process.[14]

The man who had assembled the team, obtained support for it, and kept it focused on the target deserved a share of the credit too. Whitney had brought Coolidge to General Electric. He had kept Coolidge there in 1907, when salary troubles had

The GE Research Lab's weekly colloquium featured talks by both staff members and visitors. This speaker at this colloquium, in about 1910, was William Walker, an MIT chemical engineer whose specialty was corrosion.

almost sent him looking for another position. Whitney had appreciated the patentability of the hot swaging process better than Coolidge had. And he had established the regular two-way communication between the Research Laboratory and the GE lamp department that made possible the swift movement of the new process from laboratory to assembly line.

The entire filament campaign served as Whitney's education in industrial research. He had learned that an industrial laboratory had to be far more than a citadel of fundamental science. It had to take on the problems of urgent importance to GE's businesses, such as developing resistors for lightning arrestors or metal filaments for incandescent lamps. More fundamental issues, like a Faraday's law for arcs, and more basic inventions, like a daylight-colored mercury vapor lamp, would have to wait. Defense had to come before diversification. And patents had to come before publication. Patantability considerations had to shape the entire innovative process, rather than be tacked on as an afterthought.

Whitney also learned that teamwork did not spring up automatically among a group of individualistic scientists. It had to be actively promoted. He learned that a research director who personally leads a project addressing the laboratory's most important technical challenge (as he had done with the Auer process) risks competing with his own subordinates and sacrificing his effectiveness as their leader. And finally, he learned, or at least convinced himself, that Noyes was correct. He was indeed the "right man in the right place." He should make directing research at General Electric his life's work.

As he learned these lessons, he reshaped the research laboratory experiment he had begun in 1900. He took a first step in February 1908 by changing the role of the laboratory colloquium. Until then, the colloquium had been a way to get a staff member to explain to colleagues a discovery recently written up in the scientific literature. It had also provided a forum for visitors. Whitney now proposed to require each staff member to discuss his own work in colloquium. This new procedure, he noted, would not just educate and instruct but also would "raise the efficiency of the lab." It would encourage teamwork. As Whitney put it: "it affects the personnel by effecting closer and more friendly intercourse (not one against the other but we against the world)."

He recognized that the new procedure had a major drawback, too. "In new and fertile fields, morally the property for a while of an individual, is it fair to ask him to open the field?" He decided that it was fair. In the long run, each researcher would gain more from the disclosures of others than he gave up by his own. The total productivity of the lab would rise: "contributions are thus more apt to be made and used."[15]

In mid-1908, Whitney noted a second change in his research experiment. The laboratory would have to concentrate more on short-term targets than he had thought a few years earlier. "The times are so hard," he wrote his parents in May 1908,

that I don't dare take a long road. That is, I don't dare to try one of those long shots which may turn out good in a few years but is not good now. I see how hard the rest of our organization is pushed to hang on to the value of a dollar.[16]

But the main target of his redesigning efforts was not the colloquium or the list of projects. It was himself. He decided that he had to work even harder than before at learning the individual strengths and weaknesses of the men and women of the laboratory. He had to find new ways to bring out the best in each of them.

In a personal diary he began in December 1908, he thought over this process of developing people. He started by considering the case of two "very flexible men" whom he had nicknamed "No" and "Ne." Each needed a slightly different form of help and encouragement, and Whitney carefully tailored his treatment to these different needs. "I know that discouragement makes for poor work in No's case," Whitney wrote. "I will encourage him to excess. . . . I give No the idea that as fast as his experiments are capable of being even tried by help, he [should] use such assistance."[17]

By contrast, the tougher minded Ne required constructive criticism, rather than encouragement. "His probably greater interest and faith will sooner yield returns," Whitney wrote.

> With Ne I will try more rope, more liberty, but I must force myself here into greater interest in detailed calculations and schemes. I must wisely criticize. I must show that I expect the goods, but also that I expect to see him deliver them easily.

Taking the time to give each researcher this kind of personal treatment meant spending much of each day walking the laboratory, with a question, a challenge, or a word of encouragement at each stop. It meant an office with an always open door, with that "Come in, Rain or Shine" sign above it. In 1908, that office was only a walled-off corner of the laboratory's main workroom. The manager's roll-top desk piled high with administrative paperwork shared space with the chemist's bench, the racks of chemicals, the mazes of wiring looping down from porcelain insulators nailed to the wall, and the glass vacuum system held in place by metal clamps.[18]

To get the administrative paperwork off the rolltop desk, Whitney and Rice created in 1908 a new position, the executive engineer of the Research Laboratory. He would serve as the day-to-day administrator. They agreed on an excellent choice for the post, a straw-haired, diplomatic minister's son turned electrical engineer named Samuel Ferguson. He kept track of expenditures, prepared summary reports of the state of the laboratory's many projects for the advisory council, negotiated technology transfers to GE's operating departments, and generally lifted the administrative load from Whitney's shoulders. In the process he honed the management skills that he would take with him in 1912 to an executive position with the Hartford Electric Power Company. He there became a leading statesman of the American electric power industry.[19]

Ferguson's taking over of the day-to-day management chores made it easier for Whitney to revive another element in his personal compound of activities: active participation in his profession. In 1908 the American Chemical Society was facing the threat of a split between its pure and applied wings. No person was in a better position to help prevent that split than Whitney.

Applied chemists—independent consultants, operators of chemical manufactories and dye works, food and agricultural chemists, and the rest—still made up a large majority of the society in 1908. But their colleagues occupying chairs of chemistry at Harvard, Columbia, MIT, the Johns Hopkins, Chicago, Michigan, and a few other top research institutions now controlled the society's highest offices and dictated the contents of its journal. This elite had no intention of turning the republic of chemistry into a democracy. "Those engaged in industrial pursuits," wrote W. F. Hillebrand, a member of this professoriat, in his 1906 presidential address,

> must always remember that although they equal in number the educators and their students, or may even form a majority of the society, it is none the less true that the former are and will no doubt continue to be the greater producers of the new and original matter, and hence be deserving of greater considera-

Whitney's office, in 1909, was also his laboratory, as these two views show.

tion in proportion to their numbers than those who are less productive.[20]

Those engaged in industrial pursuits began to look into the possibility of forming their own technical organizations. In June 1907, a committee of fifty chemists "prominent in applied chemistry" met to discuss a proposal from Richard K. Meade of Nazareth, Pennsylvania, to create a society to "raise the standards of chemists among manufacturers." Whitney was on the committee. It voted, with only seven in opposition and seven abstainers (including Whitney), to create a new technical organization, the American Institute of Chemical Engineers.[21]

Whitney did not join the new organization that the committee had created. He preferred to maintain the unity of the chemical profession under the umbrella of the American Chemical Society, while working within that society to give applied chemists a larger role. His redesigned research director's role gave him the opportunity to do this. His background of work in both the pure and the applied camps made his participation effective. In 1908 he served on another committee of fifty, this one aiming at unity rather than schism. The committee recommended the creation of a new American Chemical Society journal, *Industrial and Engineering Chemistry*. Whitney became a member of a committee of ten that launched the new journal. He retained a close connection with it during its early years, submitting articles and editorials, helping choose an editor, and guiding him through a difficult teething period. By the middle of the next decade, the journal had emerged as an effective voice for and outlet for the ideas of applied chemists.[22]

As another symbol of the unity of the profession, Whitney was elected to serve as president of the American Chemical Society in 1909. The honor meant a great deal to him. He became only the second industrial chemist to gain the post. (Charles Dudley of the Pennsylvania Railroad had been the first.) He devoted a lot of his time to that job in 1909, working mainly through personal contact and at the lecture podium.

The office force of the GE Research Lab, in about 1910. Left to right:
L. M. Willey, accountant; Samuel Ferguson, executive engineer;
Mary Christie, secretary to Dr. Whitney; unidentified.

His addresses to the society's annual meeting and to local groups
stressed the lesson of his own experience: the corporation's
chemist could remain the kind of chemist that the American
Chemical Society had been organized to represent.

Two of the addresses he gave in 1909 and 1910 stand as the
best summaries of his views on managing industrial research.
Anyone wanting to learn quickly what Whitney meant by the
title "research director" should read those talks on "Organization of Industrial Research" and "Research as a Financial
Asset."[23]

And reading between the lines of those papers suggests that
a specific experience lay behind each general pronouncement.
"The personal," he began, "comes first, relatively and chronologically, and the mental precedes the material."[24] Here he
was perhaps thinking of his efforts to appease the personal side
of the stubbornly independent Ezekiel Weintraub, or perhaps
the day two of his proud and sensitive subordinates, Colin G.
Fink and Harold Frodsham, had nearly fought a duel on the

laboratory floor. The first job of a research director, he explained, was to neutralize those potentials for sparking discord.

The laboratory director must make concessions to the personality of each worker. But he may make no concessions about the ownership of the resulting work. "Whatever invention results from his work becomes the property of the company," Whitney stated. "I believe that no other way is practicable." Here he may have been thinking of the need to take away from William Weedon the right to publish his work on arc lamp electrodes, or the day he had found it necessary to remind chemist Israel Ladoff of the "Co.'s right to all inventions &c." [25]

Along with the personal and the proprietary, a research director had a third job: setting the right tone for technical work. Here the rule was optimism. "Anything which to the fair mind seems possible," he proclaimed, "is to the trained persistence permissible." Here he may have been looking back over the lamp filament campaign. When he had pushed ahead optimistically, as he had done with the GEM lamp, he had been rewarded with success. When he had paused to doubt his mission, as he had done in the dark days late in 1907, the doubts had almost borne him down. A bit more optimism at that low point would have carried him through unscathed to the triumphs of 1910. "With active optimism," he argued, "even in the absence of more than average knowledge, useful discoveries are almost sure to be made." [26]

The speech went on to deal with the more concrete responsibilities of a research director's job. He had to make sure that his staff members reported their work in writing, both in daily entries in a laboratory notebook and weekly letters to the research director. He had to provide the staff with the needed equipment and with a library of scientific journals. He ended with a burst of prophecy. Silicon, he proclaimed, would find major uses in the years ahead. The solid state revolution of the 1950s would make this guess look prophetic.

But, prediction aside, Whitney's main emphasis remained on the three most important jobs of a research director. He had to bring out the individual strengths of each researcher while blending diverse personalities into a team. He had to make sure that the results of all technical work done by the employee got turned over to the company, and, where possible, patented. And he had to induce an optimisti, try-anything spirit of research and problem-solving.

If those were the main elements of a research director's job, they were not the basis used by the company to judge his success. That measure he alluded to in the title of his other influential address of 1909–10: "Research as a Financial Asset." Here he defined a research laboratory as "a place where men are occupied with new problems, presumably not too far in advance of technical application."[27] The procedure a company ought to follow was simple. Put together a collection of scientists and engineers with complementary skills. Give them "apparatus especially designed for experimental work," allow them "access to all parts of a large manufacturing plant," and support them with a budget of more than a hundred thousand dollars a year. (His laboratory's budget when he wrote those words was $160,000 for 1910.) Then give the laboratory a decade or so to work. Take a look at the end of that decade to see if the products the lab turned out had given the company an acceptable return on its investment in research.

This criterion gave Whitney a chance to brag a little. For he had begun to keep track of the sales of his laboratory's inventions, and the results looked very good indeed. The GEM lamp, although by now certain to be superseded by tungsten, still accounted for more than a million dollars a year in sales in 1910. The mercury rectifier, based on Weintraub's work, represented another $500,000 annually. The magnetite arc lamp (a dubious inclusion on the list, since it actually resulted from Steinmetz's work at his home laboratory) now lit Schenectady and a score of other American cities and added another half million. Arc lamp tubes and electrodes and molded insulating materials each brought in more than $100,000. Another dozen or so potboilers, including Whitney's resistance rods and lightning arrestor components, summed to another $150,000.

Adding it all up gave a total of more than $2.4 million in easily identifiable annual sales. And that did not even count the laboratory's big winner, the drawn tungsten process Coolidge had just invented but had not yet put into production. One needed to credit only 7 percent of those sales to the Research Laboratory to demonstrate that it paid for itself. Anything more represented profit.[28]

Whitney detailed this economic case to an MIT audience in 1910. He coupled it with a plea for American universities to emulate their German counterparts and engage in the "apparent overproduction" of researchers with Ph.Ds. American industry could offer the surplus doctors jobs that would allow them to retain their identities as professional scientists. In an industrial reserach laboratory, a person attracted to the content of the physical sciences, the identity of a researcher, the wish to attack practical problems, and the desire to share in the financial rewards of industry could choose a career that would satisfy all these desires.

So the industrial research laboratory, in Whitney's view, would prove good for the individual and good for industry. But did it offer anything for science? Did such a laboratory make deposits in the bank of knowledge or only withdrawals?

In 1909 and 1910, Whitney did not do much bragging about his laboratory's scientific accomplishments. They were, in fact, unimpressive, compared to those of an academic science department of a top university. The GE Research Laboratory's professional scientists had produced an average of less than one technical paper per man-year of effort during the lab's first decade. As a bench mark for comparison, a 1976 study by Paul Forman et al. reports that U.S. academic physics laboratories produced an average of three papers per man-year of scientific effort.[29] Whitney's own record of eleven papers during those ten years was one of the laboratory's best. Coolidge produced no papers at all during his first five years at GE.

Paper counting alone is an imperfect measure of scientific achievement. And papers were not GE research's most important product. The laboratory had been set up as a defensive business weapon. Looked at in perspective, the remarkable thing about that laboratory's performance was not that its scientists published so little but that they published at all. Whitney had stuck to his aim of making scientific publication an actual, if secondary, characteristic of an industrial research laboratory. Publication had been sometimes delayed, as in the case of Weedon but rarely if ever suppressed. Freedom to do fundamental research and to publish the results had attracted scientists of the caliber of Coolidge and Fink. But once on board, they had concentrated on applied science. Could the laboratory retain the services of an individual who wanted to become and remain a fundamental scientist of the first rank? In 1910, a twenty-nine-year-old chemist named Irving Langmuir began to give Whitney the chance to find out.

None of the scores of surviving photos of Langmuir shows him smiling. But beneath the cold austerity of a boy brought up in a family clinging tenaciously to a slipping upper middle class status burned a fire of ambition. The desire for material success may have fueled that ambition, but the oxygen of a pure love of science sustained it. When he had been an engineering student at the Columbia School of Mines, a professor had asked him what he wanted out of life. To be "free to do research as I wish," he had answered.[30]

His mother, the widow of an insurance executive, encouraged him. He went to the University of Göttingen in Germany to take a Ph.D. in chemistry under Walther Nernst. Accepting the advice of his brother, an industrial chemist, that "for further progress it will be necessary to have experience in teaching," he took a position at Stevens Tech in New Jersey. He soon found that teaching job to offer neither freedom to do research as he wished nor the opportunity for further progress his brother had spoken of. The eight teaching hours a day he faced in the fall term of 1907 nearly crowded out research altogether. And his salary reached a temporary plateau at a level that seemed to him too low in 1909 when his new department chairman flatly turned down his latest request for a raise.[31]

By then he had prepared an escape route. At a chemical society meeting, his Columbia classmate Colin G. Fink had told him about the General Electric Research Laboratory and about its director's policy of hiring promising young academic chemists for summer work. Langmuir wrote to Whitney in January 1909. After noting that "the opportunities for efficient research are greater in your laboratory than in any other in the country," he asked for one of those summer jobs. Whitney at first turned him down. The last remaining opening had already been promised to George Forbes of Harvard. But Forbes canceled out, and on July 16, Langmuir could write to his mother:

> On Monday I go to Schenectady and in all probability will do good enough work so that Whitney will offer me a salary anywhere from $1200 to $1400 for the next year. If I like the work I shall accept this . . . while at Schenectady I will be looking around for a really good position in a university.[32]

Langmuir's confidence proved justified, but his predictions were probably not confirmed. The salary offer almost certainly was higher than the $1400 he had sought. (The records that might confirm this have not survived.) And if he looked at all for a better university position, he did not find one. His post at General Electric became not a stepping-stone to, but a substitute for, the kind of academic position he had sought.

He brought Whitney the challenge of managing a researcher with outstanding talent, great ambition, the desire to do real science, and a far from total commitment to the ideals of industry. "Conditions in America are so rotten at present that I doubt if anything short of socialism can improve them," Langmuir wrote to a friend in 1908. "All railways and large corporations should be owned by the government."[33]

This budding socialist needed careful handling. When Langmuir arrived in the laboratory, Whitney told him to take some time to look around and find a project that interested him. As in the case of Coolidge four years earlier, Langmuir got the feeling (or at least so he recalled it years later) that he was to be a free lance. But like Coolidge, he soon agreed that he would spend his time improving the light bulb. Coolidge's early drawn tungsten filaments had proved brittle, and Coolidge suggested that this might be due to gas trapped within them. Langmuir agreed to find out. Taking up this problem allowed him to build on the thesis work he had done at Göttingen on the behavior of gases near a hot wire.[34]

Whitney soon saw that, as in the case of the man named Ne in his 1908 diary, he had a researcher loaded with ideas and capable of pursuing them independently. As with Ne, the management recipe called for "more rope, more liberty," combined with "greater interest in detailed calculations and schemes," wise criticism, and a clear show "that I expect the goods but also that I expect to see him deliver them easily."

Langmuir was a proud and sensitive man. He had found Nernst "rather hard to get along with" and had left Stevens partly over resentment of a newly appointed department chairman. But in Whitney he at last found a superior who treated him as a valued colleague. "I see a good deal of Dr. Whitney now," he wrote his mother in October 1909. "He talks over a good deal of his work with me." In January 1910, he added:

> I am seeing a great deal of Dr. Whitney again, this time not because he is so much interested in the work I am doing as talking over with me the work of others. The other day I happened to make a suggestion as to a new experiment which will probably enable us to get rid of gases in the glass bulb . . . more rapidly. I so pleased Dr. Whitney that he has been keeping me fully posted as to the results of all experiments on lamps so that we can talk them over and he may thus possibly get more useful suggestions.[35]

At Stevens, Langmuir had no assistant. He had built his own research apparatus and had squeezed a little time to use it between his long hours of teaching and the consulting jobs he had taken on to supplement his salary. At General Electric, by the end of his first year on the job, he had three assistants, and little else to do but research. One of the assistants, Samuel

Sweetser, was a skilled toolmaker who had left GE to buy a farm. Whitney had brought him back to become Langmuir's personal technician. For twenty-four years he served as Langmuir's hands, building the delicate and complex vacuum systems and gas analysis devices needed to make precise measurements of gas pressures and compositions, electron currents, surface properties, and plasma conductivities.

In December 1909, Langmuir described how he and Sweetser had finished building "an apparatus which is wonderful in its complexity and I hope its efficiency."[36] It consisted essentially of a pressure measurement and gas analysis system, an arrangement for obtaining as high a vacuum as possible, and, as the reaction vessel, an ordinary light bulb. Since Coolidge had solved the brittle filament problem by adding thoria to the tungsten, Langmuir had switched to another problem: understanding why lamps blackened in use. A black coating that accumulated on the inner surface of a light bulb gradually reduced its light output until after six hundred hours of use it supplied less than half the light it had given off when new. The problem did not present the pressing urgency of the filament challenge. But lessening bulb blackening offered yet another way for the new Research Laboratory to strengthen GE's competitive position in the lamp business.

Whitney himself had taken on the problem in 1908. Earlier, when he and Coolidge had competed on metal filament processes, the unity of the laboratory had been at risk. He had learned from that experience. As Langmuir's lamp blackening studies picked up steam, Whitney gracefully stepped aside.

It was good that he did. For the same narrow focus on the electrochemical theory that had prevented him and Weedon from correctly interpreting the action of the mercury arc helped block him from understanding the chemical reactions that went on in a light bulb's "vacuum." Once again Whitney read the publications by British and German physicists about molecules, atoms, and electrons. By 1912, he was willing to concede that " 'Ions' and electrons are not the personal property of a small group of pure physicists, but are rapidly becoming the *alpha, beta,* and *gamma* of electrochemistry in general."[37] But he was unwilling, or unable, to apply this insight, and to interpret the data he took on the life and properties of light bulbs in terms of the motion of ions, electrons, and molecules. Instead he merely described his findings in a 1912 paper, concluding that beyond a certain point further improvements in the vacuum of a lamp ceased to bring corresponding improvements in its lifetime. He left the interpretation of his findings to others.[38]

Langmuir took on this job of interpretation. Like his teacher Nernst, and unlike Whitney and his teacher Ostwald, he was able both to accept the physical reality of ions, electrons, atoms, and molecules and to incorporate them into his scientific work. He had learned to think vividly in atomic terms.

Langmuir's biographer Albert Rosenfeld gives an intriguing suggestion about Langmuir's ability to envision matter in this new way. At age eleven, his family belatedly discovered that he had poor eyesight and gave him his first pair of spectacles. "He was amazed," Rosenfeld relates

> to discover that the blurred greenery on trees was made up of thousands of individual leaves, each with its own distinct shape and structure. Thereafter he never tired of examining the myriad tiny details of the natural world.[39]

Seventeen years later he put on a pair of atomic spectacles: the apparatus "wonderful in its complexity" that he had built with Sweetser. It enabled him to resolve mentally a bulb full of gas into individual atoms and molecules, just as those first spectacles had enabled him to resolve visually a tree full of greenery into individual leaves.

His strategy differed sharply from Whitney's. Rather than seek a still more perfect vacuum inside the bulb, he would deliberately introduce controlled doses of gas. He had done this sort of experiment with Nernst, studying the reactions of nitrogen near a hot Nernst glower. Now, thanks to his new apparatus and Coolidge's tungsten filament, he could extend that work to far lower pressures and higher temperatures. His basic reaction chamber would be a tungsten filament light bulb. Out of it he would bring inventions worth millions of dollars to General Electric and discoveries worth a Nobel Prize.

He began, in early 1910, by putting small doses of hydrogen into the bulb. It disappeared, and this "clean up" of hydrogen coincided with a steep drop in the filament's temperature. He explained this in terms of a ballet of atoms within the bulb. The hot filament, he suggested, broke each hydrogen molecule into a pair of atoms. This molecule-breaking reaction drew heat from the filament, causing the temperature drop he had seen. The hydrogen atoms then flew to the glass bulb, paired up again into molecules on its cooler survace, and stuck there. This explanation did more than explain the cleanup of hydrogen. It also suggested a new way to prepare and study a rarely observed entity, the free atom of hydrogen. For the paper describing this work, Langmuir won his first scientific honor, the Nichols Prize.[40]

Oxygen put into the bulb also disappeared. Langmuir studied oxygen cleanup in 1910 and 1911 and concluded that the gas somehow stuck to the filament. For the moment, a description of the process in atomic terms eluded him.[41] But he was able to paint a convincing atomic picture of the behavior of the next gas he introduced into the bulb, water vapor. He observed that small traces of water vapor enormously accelerated lamp blackening. He proposed that the molecules served as a sort of continuously circulating atomic ferryboat. Near the hot filament, water vapor molecules broke up into hydrogen and oxygen, and the oxygen atoms would combine with atoms of tungsten evaporated off the filament. Those newly formed tungsten oxide molecules would fly to the glass surface and stick there. At the cooler glass surface, the oxygen atoms gave up their tungsten partners, hooked up with hydrogen again, and, as part of a water vapor molecule, circulated back to the filament to start the process again. The tungsten left behind would stick to the glass and blacken the lamp. Without this water vapor ferry, the atmosphere near the hot filament would quickly saturate with tungsten, limiting the rate of evaporation of the filament. With the water vapor ferryboat carrying off tungsten, the evaporation proceeded much faster.[42]

This excellent bit of scientific detective work did not revolutionize lampmaking. Veteran lampmakers already knew from experience that the presence of water vapor made for bad lamps. But what others had observed Langmuir explained. He published the result, adding to his growing scientific reputation. And he moved on to an area with growing potential for invention in 1912 by introducing small quantities of nitrogen into lamps.[43]

The nitrogen cleaned up very, very slowly. This confimed the findings of the handful of inventors, dating back to Edison, who had already experimented with or even patented nitrogen-filled light bulbs by 1912. The nitrogen atmosphere protected the filament from oxidation as well as a vacuum did. But, unlike a vacuum, the pressure of nitrogen molecules on the filament retarded evaporation of tungsten, thereby slowing down the blackening of the lamp. The nitrogen molecules also, however, carried off heat from the filament to the glass surface by convection—that is, by the relatively long range motion of atoms and molecules. This heat loss had, so far, doomed the efforts of would-be inventors of a practical nitrogen-filled lamp by reducing the efficiency of such a lamp to a level far below its vacuum competitor.[44]

Here Langmuir could reach into his scientific arsenal and pull out a weapon those previous inventors lacked: a thorough understanding of heat transfer. He had begun his study of this subject at Göttingen. But he had deepened his knowledge by taking on one of the potboiler projects that Whitney had accepted for the laboratory. In 1911 and 1912 Langmuir had traveled once a week from Schenectady to nearby Pittsfield, Massachusetts, to help veteran inventor and GE consultant William Stanley with his efforts to invent better thermos bottles and electric stoves. Characteristically, Langmuir turned this prosaic assignment into a scientific opportunity. He wrote and published a pair of detailed studies on the transfer of energy from a hot surface to a stream of gas flowing past it. One thing he learned while doing this work provided the crucial clue to a practical gas-filled lamp.[45]

Gas moving near a surface gets slowed down by friction and forms a stationary blanket that covers the surface. The blanket of still gas can have a big effect on heat transfer from the surface. For heat from the surface has to pass through the blanket by the relatively slow process of conduction before it can be removed from the blanket's outer edge by the much faster process of convection. Langmuir was not the first person to observe this phenomenon. But he was the first one to recognize that it applied to light bulb filaments. The thickness of that blanket could be much thicker than the thickness of a filament. So the slow conduction process, rather than the fast convection process, could govern the rate of heat loss through the gas. Langmuir found that increasing the diameter of the filament would sharply increase its light output (since light output goes up proportional to the diameter squared) while scarcely increasing conduction losses at all. So a short, thick filament—or better yet, a filament coiled into a tight helix—could burn hotter in nitrogen than in vacuum, be protected by the inert nitrogen gas from filament evaporation and subsequent blackening, yet avoid excessive heat loss through the gas. He now knew how to make a practical gas-filled lamp.[46]

This gas-filled lamp became known as the "Mazda C," through the GE lamp department's campaign to enlist the ancient Persian god of light into its advertising efforts. Argon would replace nitrogen as the inert gas. The Mazda C and its successors would eventually displace vacuum lamps in all sizes down through 60 watts. It completed a revolution in lamp efficiency. Lamps made by the Coolidge process to last for 600 hours and consume 400 watts of power gave off 10 lumens of light for each watt of power consumed—twice as much light output per unit of energy input than the carbon filament lamp. Gradual introduction of the gas-filled lamp in the smaller sizes led to a 60-watt lamp with a lifetime of 750 hours that produced 15 lumens per watt, a further increase of 50 percent in efficiency.[47]

These dry statistics came to life in a small ceremony repeated more and more often from 1910 on: an American family turning on at dusk, for the first time, its houseful of electric light. For although the cost of the tungsten lamp was higher than that of its carbon predecessor, its higher efficiency, coupled with comparable efficiency improvements in the generation of electricity, caused the cost of electric light to the consumer to drop by 1930 to only one-fourth the 1910 level. This drop in costs drove to completion the revolution Edison had begun. In 1910, America burned one light bulb for each four of its inhabitants. By 1925, it would burn four bulbs for each inhabitant.[48]

For General Electric, the lighting of a nation meant growing profits. Through the Just and Hanaman, Coolidge, and Langmuir patents, the company controlled the modern incandescent lamp until the 1930s. Its manufacturing engineers, such as William R. Burrows at Harrison, devised automated production methods that doubled the number of lamps produced by each person-hour of labor. GE held the enviable position of being able to reduce steadily the price of its Mazda lamps while increasing the profits from their sale. In the 1920s, those profits reached more than $30 million a year, a 30 percent return on the capital invested in the lamp business.[49]

If anyone in General Electric had questioned the value of research as clearly scientific as Langmuir's (and in spite of widely quoted allegations, there is no evidence that anyone ever did), the business potential of the gas-filled lamp silenced the doubters.[50] Langmuir would, from 1912 on, be free "to do research as I wish" and to turn the clues he had uncovered during his study of cleanup in lamps into fundamental scientific discoveries.

There was that mystery about oxygen cleanup, for example. Langmuir could now relate the disappearance of oxygen molecules in the bulb to new ideas about chemical bonding that were beginning to appear in the scientific literature. A major debate concerned the nature of the forces that held the atoms of a gas to a metal surface. Were they the same forces that linked atoms together into molecules, or were they different ones? Armed with the data from his oxygen cleanup experiments and with further studies carried out from 1913 through 1915, Langmuir made a convincing case for the first alternative. Oxygen molecules disappeared in a lamp because the surface atoms of the tungsten filament, having tungsten neighbors only on one side, had not exhausted their capacity to combine chemically with other atoms. This unused combining power, or "unsaturated valence," extended tentacle-like above the surface, caught oxygen molecules that hit the surface, and held them tight, forming a single layer of oxygen on the tungsten surface. Langmuir drew a picture of gas molecules striking the surface, a fraction of them sticking at each instant, a fraction of them bouncing off, and another fraction of the already stuck ones coming undone. At equilibrium, the number leaving had to equal the number arriving. Expressed mathmatically, this insight became the "Langmuir isotherm," a simple, effective way of characterizing the building up of a layer of atoms or molecules on a surface. It threw light on fundamental mechanisms of chemical reactions at surfaces. For this and further contributions to the chemistry of surfaces, Langmuir won the 1932 Nobel Prize for chemistry.[51]

He was quick to express his appreciation for Whitney's encouragement, especially at the beginning. "During those first few years," he later wrote,

> while I was thus having such a good time satisfying my curiosity, and publishing various scientific papers on chemical reactions at low pressures, I frequently wondered whether it was quite fair that I should spend my whole time in an industrial organization on such purely scientific work, for I confess I didn't see what applications could be made of it, nor did I ever have any applications in mind. Several times I talked the matter over with Dr. Whitney, saying that I could not tell where this work was going to lead us. He replied, however, that it was not necessary, as far as he was concerned, that it should lead anywhere. He would like to see me continue working along any fundamental lines that would give us more information in regard to the phenomena taking place in incandescent lamps, and

that I should feel perfectly free to go ahead on many such lines that seemed of interest to me. For nearly three years I worked in this way with several assistants before any application was made of any of the work that I had done.

In adopting this broad-minded attitude, Dr. Whitney, I believe, showed himself to be a real pioneer in the new type of modern industrial research.[52]

This description of a sheltered scientist doing "purely scientific work" is oversimplified. Langmuir's laboratory notebooks, reports of work, and letters to his mother give a fuller picture of those first three years: of competition with Coolidge on developing a better form of tungsten wire; of applying for a patent on an improvement in the exhausting of lamps (and even for one on the use of tungsten in pen points); of hopes, expressed in 1909, of coming up with lamps "better than anything yet made" in three weeks, not three years; of those journeys to Pittsfield to help Stanley with his stoves and thermos bottles; and of many more examples of the mixing of pure and applied science. But the picture of Whitney encouraging Langmuir to continue "working along any fundamental lines that would give us more information in regard to the phenomena taking place in incandescent lamps" does ring true. Whitney did not encourage work done in silent isolation, whether it was pure or applied science. But once a scientist had proved himself a contributing member of the team, as Langmuir had done in 1909 and 1910, and had showed himself to possess the spark of creative research ability, as Langmuir had done almost immediately, Whitney was ready to apply that management recipe from his 1908 diary: "more rope, more liberty."

Whitney never recruited another scientist of the caliber of Langmuir, whose ability to combine practical results with fundamental contributions to science remains unmatched. Langmuir represents the creative limit of industrial research. As such, he attracted others determined to do real science in industry. Saul Dushman of the University of Toronto came to General Electric in 1912 to give a thirty-minute colloquium on his re-

In about 1920, Irving Langmuir (l.) shows Whitney one of his inventions, the Pliotron tube, an improved form of three-element thermionic vacuum tube used for amplifying electrical and radio signals.

search in physical chemistry. As he listened to Langmuir answer it with an incisive thirty-minute critique, he learned that an industrial laboratory could apply the same high critical standards to scientific work that he was used to in a university. He accepted a job at the Research Laboratory and became one of the world's leading experts in high vacuum research.[53] Albert Hull of Worcester Poly took a summer job at the laboratory in 1912. The combination of Langmuir's example and Whitney's encouragement powerfully impressed him. "Work along the lines in which you were interested in last summer," Whitney wrote Hull in 1913

> has continued so attractive that I am sure we ought to tempt you now to agree to come here next summer and to stay if possible.[54]

Hull came to stay and went on to become a pioneer in X-ray diffraction studies and electron physics, a president of the American Physical Society, a member of the National Academy of Sciences, and a prolific inventor of new types of vacuum tubes. Over the next two decades, a small group of scientists determined to use the GE Research Laboratory as a real scientific laboratory would follow Langmuir, Dushman, and Hull to General Electric. The group included such individuals as Kenneth Kingdon, Lewi Tonks, Wheeler P. Davey, and Katharine Blodgett. They joined a nucleus of scientific strength created by Coolidge, Weedon, Fink, and Weintraub. This core of individuals determined to remain contributing scientists never represented more than a dozen or so out of a staff that would grow into the hundreds. Not all of them stayed. Weedon left GE to join Du Pont. Weintraub had left the Research Laboratory by 1910 to head his own GE lab at Lynn, Massachusetts. Fink, embittered by what he viewed as an overemphasis on Coolidge's role in the tungsten success, also moved on to another GE lab, and from there to private consulting and a distinguished academic career at Columbia. Davey left for Penn State.[55]

But enough good people came and stayed for General Electric and Whitney to fulfill their aim of creating a real scientific laboratory. The General Electric Research Laboratory, under Whitney's leadership, demonstrated once and for all that professional scientists could build scientific careers in industry.

In opening up such a career to others, Whitney knew by 1912 that he had denied it to himself. He was now a research director, not a scientist. He relinquished any claims to forefront expertise, even in his specialties of electrochemistry and colloid studies. His 1912 paper on vacua disclosed the results of his last sustained effort to make a contribution to a major research area of physical science. By the time he had published the paper, Langmuir's work was going far beyond his own. Far from resenting this, he spurred Langmuir on.

But at the same time he transferred more and more of his own energy into his hobbies. The turtle studies began in 1912. The log of dates, locations, and descriptions of turtle encounters replaced the colloid theory of cell growth and the search for a Faraday's law of arcs in Whitney's research program. The substitution suited him. Turtle studies could be leisurely, empirical, and unpublished. No theory of turtles existed. No colleague competed with him to compile more and better turtle data. Following turtles, hunting for arrowheads, understanding the life cycle of the oak borer, and tracing the life cycle of the plant gall became his relief valves. Without them, the mere cheering from the sidelines while others did chemistry might have generated unbearable frustrations.[56]

The hobbies also served as a relief valve for an increasingly frustrating family life. Evelyn still took her regular trips to Boston. Ennin never caught the interest in science her father tried to pass on to her. When she reached college age, she spurned his offer of an education at Vassar. She wanted instead to marry a local farmer, Von Alstyne Schermerhorn, a taciturn man of modest means descended from a family of Schenectady's earliest Dutch settlers, and to live with him on a farm. Whitney objected to her marrying at eighteen. His father had waited seven years on the frontier before marrying. He had waited four years at MIT. Surely Ennin too could wait a while. Father and daughter finally compromised. Ennin and Van would go to Cornell and take the agricultural course before coming home to marry. In December 1911, Ennin was in Ithaca, and Evelyn was in Boston. "It seems pretty lonesome with both you and Mama away," Whitney wrote in one of his daily letters to his daughter, "but so long as you are both doing things which are more enjoyable now or ensure more pleasure later, I guess I can get along."[57]

By then he had a new project. He had decided to move from his house in Alplaus to a real farm in the Schenectady suburb of Niskayuna. Off the main road between Schenectady and Troy, down a winding hill and across a bridge that spanned a stream called Lisha Kill, his new stone house was going up in the winter of 1911. Between his work at the laboratory and his frequent business trips, he spent his spare time out at the farm. "Got back from Washington yesterday PM just in time to go over and see the new place," he wrote to Ennin on December 8. A trip a week later gives the flavor of his schedule: a full day at the Harrison lamp works; dinner at the Chemists' Club in New York City; a night aboard the train from New York to Albany, arriving at 7 in the morning; a drive to the lab, getting there in time to start the day at 8; work until noon, "and then run for the farm," to tramp the fields in overalls and boots to inspect and direct construction. "I'm mighty tired, been running about all day, and I'm terribly hungry," he ended.[58]

The farm became the rural sanctuary he had sought. He lived there for the rest of his life. But it did not heal the splits in his family. His farming efforts may have been partly an effort to find something in common with his daughter. But she did not respond. His daily letters mixed news items, such as mention of the 250 cakes of ice he had stored for Ennin's hens, with advocacy. First came advice (December 11, 1911: "you inherit from your old man a hell of an impatience. It won't do to go too far on that tack . . . think over some of your steps before you make them."), then reassurance (February 6, 1913: "you have never been a disappointment to us [as you say]), and finally an undisguised plea (March 30, 1913: "don't imagine your most pressing call in life is to get immediately married so you can shift for yourself . . . Mama and I need you here.") The plea succeeded in convincing her to complete the Cornell course. But immediately on graduation she married Van, and they set up their own farm in Charlton, New York, ten miles away from the new Whitney home.[59]

Although Whitney made the gesture of having his Niskayuna farmhouse designed by his architect brother-in-law, Evelyn never became reconciled to it. "Mama isn't very well," Whitney wrote to Ennin in November 1912.

> She thinks life is pretty hard here on the farm, and she longs for Alplaus. I wish she could have exactly what she wants, but I don't know how to get it for her. I suppose I'll have to build a house in town some day, for I can see there's too much loneliness here for her.[60]

He never built that house in town. Instead, his family life settled down into an uneasy equilibrium. His real happy family was down at the laboratory. There he had Mary Christie for an aide and confidant (I have found no evidence that their forty-five-year relationship ever went further than that). Ferguson served as a capable and affable administrator. A building full of young scientists, engineers, technicians, and shop people welcomed him on his daily tours, each person with a different story of success or failure at the bench. Each day he could look in on at least one great inventor, Coolidge, and at least one great scientist, Langmuir. Each was at the peak of his career. The research director supplied most of the warmth to these encounters. Coolidge's nickname "Cool" fit him, while Langmuir's concentration on his work deepened into a glacial absentmindedness that became legendary. But at least the three leaders of GE research formed a loyal team: "not one against the other, but we against the world."

Between 1908 and 1912 Whitney put together a professional identity and a personal life that he would be able to sustain for the next two decades. The professional identity was that of a research director. He would do no more formal teaching, concentrating instead on suggestion and inspiration. He would continue to do research in the laboratory, but it would not be forefront research, and it would not address General Electric's most pressing technical problems. Instead it would open up new areas or explore intriguing byways. He would publish little of a technical nature, make no effort to retain his reputation as a working scientist, and avoid competing with his subordinates. In order to enable others to become the corporation's chemists, Whitney would sacrifice his role as one.

The identity of an industrial research director that Whitney was doing so much to create differed sharply from that of a director of an academic laboratory. The leaders of academic laboratories around the world—such individuals as Ostwald, Rutherford, Noyes, Millikan, and, later in the twentieth century, Enrico Fermi, Gilbert N. Lewis, and Ernest O. Lawrence—typically reached the summit of eminence in pure science by their individual contributions before taking over a laboratory. The most eminent industrial research directors— such as Whitney, Frank Jewett of Bell, C. E. K. Mees of Eastman Kodak, and E. C. Sullivan of Corning—achieved far less in pure, or even applied, science. They did enough individual work to gain the respect of their colleagues but not much more. Individuals rose to the post of director of industrial research, owing not to scientific eminence, but to apparent or demonstrated ability to inspire or direct the work of others.

Whitney did not begin the line of modern industrial research directors. He had outstanding predecessors: Carl Duisberg in the German dye industry, Charles Dudley on the Pennsylvania Railroad, and William Burton at Standard Oil, for example. They too had built careers on the boundary of science and industry. Whitney differed from these predecessors in creating a broader concept of industrial research. Where Duisberg left pure research to the universities, Whitney created an atmosphere where Langmuir, Hull, and Dushman could combine science with invention. Where Dudley stated that "the principal difference between the pure and applied chemist is that the latter withholds the results of his work from the world for a period of time,"[61] Whitney encouraged the immediate publication of purely scientific results by the members of his staff, withholding temporarily only those papers of clear commercial significance. Where Burton designed his laboratory as a training ground for executives, Whitney designed his as a place for a career.

The personal identity Whitney created, like his professional identity, also combined practicality and personal fulfillment. This identity had many sides. He was an enthusiastic cheerleader of research, touring the laboratory to spread encouragement; a sound businessman, making good his father's New England maxims by showing how science could be made to pay; a private man, retreating to a farmhouse isolated in the countryside, yet within easy reach of the GE Works; a professional scientist, occupying the presidential chair of the American Chemical Society; and a scientific hobbyist, writing up his research findings, not in the *Journal of the American Chemical Society*, but in a turtle log. He had tried to synthesize a more ambitious personal compound in the years 1900 to 1907, one that also included teaching, doing a great thing technically for General Electric, using colloid science to solve the mysteries of life, and creating an actual happy family, rather than just a metaphorical one at his laboratory. He had failed to keep that compound together. The more sustainable one he created from 1908 to 1912 would hold. It would permit him during the next decade to emerge from the narrow bounds of Schenectady, chemistry, and light bulbs and take a place on a wider national and technical stage.

8/

On a Wider Stage

Sixteen years later, Arthur H. Compton would receive a Nobel Prize for physics. But in 1914, he was a graduate student at Princeton and unsure that physics could be made into a life-time career. The search for knowledge might challenge the mind, but did it offer great enough opportunities for salary and service? One of Compton's professors knew a good way to convince him that it did. "Mr. Compton . . . has asked me for my opinion as to the possibilities of a career in research apart from teaching," he wrote to Whitney. "I told him I would write to you to ask whether you thought that the possibilities of such a career were favorable."

"If I were Mr. Compton I should want to run around and make a few visits to some of the laboratories of the country," Whitney replied. "We should be glad to give him personal help in any way possible." Compton came to Schenectady and went away both impressed and strengthened in his commitment to the vocation of physics. "As I saw the different kinds of work going on," he wrote Whitney, "any doubt that remained in my mind as to what work I wished to take up rapidly disap-peared." He completed his doctoral work and took a position as an industrial physicist—at Westinghouse, not at GE. ("A very bright fellow," Whitney remarked a few years later, "but for some reason or other I did not tempt him to come with us here.")[1]

As the incident indicates, Whitney's influence had reached beyond the General Electric Company and the chemistry profession by 1914. He had stepped onto the stage of national scientific leadership. Individuals such as Compton, and rep-resentatives of corporations such as Eastman Kodak, General Motors, and Du Pont, came to him to learn how to organize research laboratories. The nation called on him in a time of peril to help organize an unprecedented effort to put science to work in war. And after that war he would take a place in an emerging national scientific leadership trying to sustain the government's role in supporting science.

That new national scientific leadership remained a small world for the next two decades. Whitney stood near the center of it and touched the lives of many of its members. Compton would make his career in universities but would retain ties with Whitney and his laboratory. He would become a GE consultant and provide the company with a key hint that helped stimulate the development of the fluorescent lamp. His brother Karl also became a physicist, a leader of the national science establishment, and a GE consultant. When he came under consideration for the post of president of MIT, two backers who helped him get the job were a pair of prominent alumni, Whitney and GE president Swope.

Robert A. Millikan, another important shaper of American science and the nation's second Nobel laureate in physics, also got to know Whitney. They both served as advisers to the government on antisubmarine problems during the war, directing complementary (and competing) research attacks on the submarine threat. After the war Millikan went to the California Institute of Technology to help turn that university into one of the world's leading scientific centers. Two of his collaborators in that effort were Whitney's teacher Noyes and Whitney's MIT classmate George Ellery Hale. When Hale took the lead in organizing the National Research Council during the war, he called on leaders of industrial research such as Whitney and Frank Jewett of Western Electric to join with the academic scientists. Meanwhile, at Harvard in 1915, a chemistry graduate student named James B. Conant attended a lecture by Whitney and came away charged with the conviction that there could be real science in industry. Like the Comptons and Millikan, he made his career in a university, but he consulted for DuPont while he rose to the presidency of Harvard.[2]

Whitney's role on this wider stage both helped initiate and

serves to illustrate a change that America's science leadership was undergoing. It was finding the self-confidence it needed to establish American science as a powerful, autonomous, and self-renewing producer of knowledge and participant in the councils of the nation. In the previous generation, American scientific leaders had sensed their disciplines' weaknesses compared with German and British rivals. Their frustration at lack of support and prestige occasionally surfaced in elitist rhetoric. Henry Rowland pleaded for pure science, and Albert A. Michelson, America's first Nobel laureate for physics, told graduate student Jewett that to take a job with Western Electric would be to prostitute his scientific ideals.[3] But behind that rhetoric, the great majority of U.S. scientists had no objection to serving industry or government as consultants when it paid to do so.

The new generation of scientific leaders, the one that came of age around the time of the First World War, spoke more politely of industry than Rowland and Michelson had done. But they came to industry and to government, not for consulting crumbs, but for endowments and legislation that would put science on a permanent and independent footing. Behind the polite language of leaders such as Hale and Millikan stood an elitism as complete as Rowland's. To them, industrial science would remain a useful, but definitely second-class, citizen of the republic of science. Whitney helped this new leadership emerge and served it as an object lesson of the national value of science. But he would find that the trends he had helped to create—American science's growing professionalism and its increasing ability to gain larger scale financial support—would eventually pass him by.

Whitney's emergence onto a wider stage took place in three phases. First came technological diversification. The GE Research Laboratory went beyond the light bulb and took on new fields ranging from consumer appliances to radio to X-rays. Second came national service. As a member of the Naval Consulting Board during World War I, Whitney participated in scientific and technological strategy making at the highest national levels. And third came active participation in an effort to ensure that government support for science did not end when the war did.

The first phase served as a foundation for the other two. With Langmuir's invention of the gas-filled lamp in 1913, the laboratory had erected the main towers of a legal fortification that would defend the GE lamp business from competitive attack. Whitney still had to help fill in the fortification, by long hours in court testifying about the Coolidge patent, for example, and by complicated negotiations with the chemical companies to secure acceptable prices for the argon used to fill Langmuir's lamp. But Whitney's attention turned to new areas: electric appliances, electron devices, and X-ray tubes. He no longer depended for guidance on the advisory council that had, back in 1905, warned him about the threat of metal filaments or told him to push full speed ahead toward the goal of a practical mercury lamp. The council still existed in 1913, but now its members mainly listened as Whitney described the wide range of new projects, from fabricating heaters to fixing nitrogen, that he was considering launching. The council members did not really understand what Langmuir was up to, Albert G. Davis confessed later. But if Whitney said it was important, that was good enough for them. The council that had been founded back in 1904 to avoid putting too much decision-making strain on one man would fade away by 1920 because that one man had proved himself equal to the strain.[4]

Whitney still made those decisions in a small, unpretentious office rigged up with laboratory equipment that he still used daily. To avoid competing with his subordinates and to lead the laboratory's new thrust to diversify, he had picked a new project in 1911 that pointed toward a new field. He was working with metallurgist Chester Moore to develop a safe, reliable electric heating unit for General Electric's new line of irons, stoves, and industrial heaters. GE had entered those fields in a tentative way in 1906, exhibiting some flat irons, percolators, and frying pans at the Chicago Electrical Exhibit, and then adding them to its electrical supplies catalog alongside the transformers, lamps, and switches. But electrical appliances remained expensive curiosities in 1911. They were slow to warm up, quick to break down, and often unsafe owing to the dangers posed by the resistance wire that turned the electricity into heat.[5]

Since no conventional wire insulation could withstand cooking or water-boiling temperatures, those early heating units used heating coils made of uninsulated wire. The challenge of devising a safer solution, of surrounding the wire with a substance that would tolerate high temperatures, let heat out, but keep electricity in and that would be inexpensive enough to use in manufacturing, suited Whitney's empirical approach. He kept Moore busy with suggestions of new ideas. By 1912, they had found a promising candidate. They devised a way of putting resistance wire in a metal sheath and then packing magnesium oxide between the wire and the sheath. This "sheath wire" held up so well under intense heat that it could be immersed in molten iron and cast into a primitive version of today's electric hot plate. Making the first demonstration hot plate in 1912 was Whitney's idea. He always believed that the best way to sell a Research Laboratory invention to a GE "customer" was to embody that invention in hardware that the customer could get his hands on and try out.

Sheath wire went into production for GE heating devices by 1915. By then, an engineer at GE's Pittsfield, Massachusetts, plant, Charles G. Abbot, had taken up the idea and suggested a major improvment. He proposed to coil the wire before putting it in the sheath. This greatly increased the heat each unit could generate but proved very difficult to embody in an assembly that could be manufactured reliably. Abbot took on and met this challenge. The product he developed, Calrod wire, became the standard form of electrical heating wire. It was the main technical asset that GE brought to the 1917 merger that joined the company's domestic heating lines with those of two other appliance companies to create the Edison Electric Appliance Company. By the mid 1920s that GE-owned firm's trade name Hotpoint had become well known, and the flat, round,

"Are you having fun?" The cast of the laboratory's minstrel show in 1914 provides one answer to Whitney's perennial question.

black coils of Calrod units were on their way to becoming a familiar sight in American kitchens.[6]

So Whitney's invention of sheath wire played an important role in General Electric's diversification into a company that sold a broad line of consumer products. His laboratory's next major technical effort would support another broadening of GE's product line, into the entirely new technology and business of electronics.

The mercury vapor rectifier pioneered by Peter Cooper Hewitt and Ezekiel Weintraub might be labeled an electronic device. Other roots of the technology go well back into the nineteenth century. But the modern age of electronics is usually dated from the invention by Lee De Forest in 1906 of a three-element vacuum tube he called the audion and today's electrical engineers call the vacuum triode. It offered for the first time a way to use a weak electrical signal to control the flow of a much stronger one, much as the light touch of a hand on a faucet might control a strong flow of water.

The first audions looked like light bulbs, and many of the things that happened inside them also happened inside the blackening light bulbs that both Whitney and Langmuir were studying between 1910 and 1913. In particular, both GE scientists bumped into what was, although De Forest did not know it in 1906, the phenomenon that made the audion work. It went by the name "Edison effect," since Edison had discovered it in the 1880s, and consisted of the flow of an electric current from a hot, negatively charged surface in a vacuum to another neutral or positively charged surface nearby.

The differing reactions of Whitney and Langmuir to that Edison effect demonstrate both Whitney's limitations as a scientist and his good judgment in turning problems over to scientists who surmounted those limitations. Whitney knew by 1910 of the work by British physicist Owen Richardson, who had shown the Edison effect to consist of the evaporation of electrons from a heated conductor in a vacuum and the flow of the electrons through the vacuum to another conductor nearby. But once again, he rejected this idea in favor of an electrochemical explanation. Chemist Frederick Soddy had tried to explain Richardson's results in terms of chemical reactions among the impurities in Richardson's evacuated tubes. Whitney believed him. Across the bottom of his typed-up 1909 notes on the work of a German scientist that explained the Edison effect by a theory like Richardson's, Whitney wrote "disproved by Soddy."[7]

But at the same time, he kept the door open for those willing to venture further than he could. In 1909 he met regularly with Coolidge, Langmuir, lighting researcher Gorton Fonda, and a few others one night a week to discuss recent developments in electron theory.[8] And he provided Langmuir with enough assistants that one of them, Howard Barnes, could look in 1911 at the Edison effect in lamps, to see if it helped cause blackening. It did not appear to, and if Langmuir had been interested only in light bulbs, that would have been the end of it.[9]

But Langmuir, virtually alone among GE scientists in 1912, also had ambitions of creating a scientific reputation based on publication. He had published two papers in 1910, five in 1911, and two by the middle of 1912, when he seized on the Edison effect (or, as Richardson labeled it, thermionic emission) as a promising topic for another scientific study. In August 1912 he asked his assistant Samuel Sweetser to measure the thermionic currents in some specially modified, highly evacuated light bulbs. The measured currents turned out to be far lower than Richardson's theory predicted. This supported Soddy's view that if you made the vacuum nearly perfect enough, the alleged thermionic currents would vanish. Experiments carried out by Coolidge in October 1912 also seemed to refute Richardson and support Soddy. "Talking with Langmuir this morning," GE chemist George McKay reported on October 2, "on various problems in connection with discharge in vacuum tubes. Dr. Coolidge has what is comparitively conclusive proof that Richardson's theory on emission of ions from hot bodies is not true."[10]

So the GE scientists seemed to have uncoverd important evidence bearing on—perhaps even settling—a major scientific controversy. Publication of those results would especially enhance Langmuir's reputation in American science, since Richardson was now one of America's most prominent physicists, having accepted a professorship at Princeton in 1909. But before publishing, Langmuir took the opportunity to discuss his results with Richardson himself, at the October 12, 1912, meeting of the American Physical Society. "Had long talk with Richardson. He cannot adequately defend his theory," Langmuir noted triumphantly in his diary after that meeting.[11] He invited Richardson to come up to Schenectady in November and look at the experimental results that refuted thermionic emission.

In preparation for that visit, Langmuir went back to the laboratory to verify those results and found out that he had misinterpreted them. Richardson's theory, he suddenly realized, did provide the foundation for a correct prediction of the magnitude of the current of electrons emitted by a hot filament. The currents Langmiur and Coolidge observed were small, not because Richardson's boiling-off mechanism was not happening, but because another phenomenon was happening too. The electrons were encountering a sort of subatomic traffic jam just outside the filament surface. This traffic jam, called the space charge effect, had been observed before for positive ions by C. M. Child, a physicist at Colgate University. But it had never before been related to electron emission. Langmuir now showed that some simple calculations based on a theory using both Richardson's idea and space charge yielded a very good prediction of the experimental results he had obtained. The theory also indicated how redesigning the tube or changing its operating conditions—putting the electrodes closer together or increasing the voltage, for example—could reduce the traffic jam and increase the current. And once he understood space charge, Langmuir could understand another curious observation he had made about his experimental tubes. A relatively small electric charge placed on the bulb, or on a third electrode within it, could control the electron current. Though he had not initially intended to, Langmiur had learned how to build an improved De Forest audion.[12]

By the time Richardson came for his visit in November 1912, Langmuir had all this ready to show him. He was also ready to write a paper that, though it did not refute Richardson's results, extended them significantly enough to become just the kind of eye-opener that Langmuir had hoped to spring upon the scientific community.[13]

That paper would have to stay on the shelf for about six months, for thanks to the way Whitney had organized the laboratory, Langmuir's research could quickly be translated into useful and perhaps patentable technology. Whitney had set up a lamp vacuum committee in 1912 that met monthly to ponder the value of just such work as Langmuir was doing. One member of the committee was Laurence A. Hawkins, who had just succeeded Samuel Ferguson in the post of executive engineer. Hawkins heard about Langmuir's work at the November and December committee meetings and realized its implications for the field of wireless telegraphy, a field in which

General Electric had already become interested. In January 1913 he introduced Langmuir to GE's leading wireless telegraphy expert, Ernst Alexanderson.[14]

Not long before, Alexanderson had learned that other wireless telegraphy inventors, such as John Hays Hammond, Jr., and De Forest, were at work on improved versions of the De Forest audion to be used to detect or to amplify radio signals. Langmuir's discoveries put GE into the middle of this race, and soon it was in the lead. By March 1913 GE had a strong interdisciplinary team at work, with Langmuir nailing down the science, his cousin William White putting the science to work to design improved detecting amd amplifying tubes, and Alexanderson putting the tubes into improved transmitting and receiving systems. By the end of 1913, GE had only one major American rival in the brand new field of putting electronics into wireless telegraphy. That rival was American Telephone and Telegraph (AT&T), which was in the process of creating in its Western Electric manufacturing arm the research organization that would eventually become Bell Laboratories. On October 30, 1912, just eighteen days after Langmuir confronted Richardson at the Physical Society meeting, De Forest showed the AT&T researchers how the audion could be used to amplify telephone signals. An AT&T team under Harold D. Arnold, a physicist who had been hired specifically to develop such an amplifier for use in a coast-to-coast long-distance telephone line, then went ahead to improve the audion in just the same way Langmuir was doing.[15]

Meanwhile, Langmuir had convinced colleague Coolidge that the combination of Richardson's theory and space charge explained Coolidge's inability to get large electron currents in his experimental X-ray tube. Coolidge used this knowledge to redesign his tube, to get the large currents, and use them to make more penetrating X-rays in a more reliable manner than had ever before been possible. His "Coolidge tube" marked a revolutionary advance in X-ray technology.[16]

Whitney saw in 1913 that Langmuir's electron tubes and Coolidge's X-ray tube offered two opportunities to move from defense of GE's established businesses to diversification into new areas. In wireless telegraphy, GE was building an occasional model of Alexanderson's radio wave generator, the alternator, in 1913 and was wondering whether to enter seriously into the wireless equipment supply business. In X-rays, GE had withdrawn from the production of tubes in 1911 because the market appeared small and fragmented, and the early X-ray tube was a technically simple product that small firms could produce cheaper than GE could. The new Coolidge tube, like the new type of electron tube, represented a sophisticated technology that could be protected by patents and by the research and manufacturing skills of a large corporation.

This move from defense to diversification marks a new epoch in American industrial research. Before 1913, research aimed at new products had mainly been done at independent laboratories on the model of Edison's Menlo Park or the Ampere Electrochemical Company. The few giant corporations that founded research labs did so to protect their established products: GE's light bulbs, AT&T's telephone service, Kodak's film and cameras. But Whitney, with the support of the founding fathers of GE research, Steinmetz, Rice, Thomson and Davis, had always looked beyond defense. Now Langmuir's work gave him the opportunity to follow through.

In wireless, this did not prove difficult. World War I awakened military interest in improved communication. As he had done with sheath wire, Whitney urged the electronics team to put its new technology into hardware that could be demonstrated to potential customers. In 1915, he asked White to build two all-vacuum-tube radio transmitters that were "more or less portable" (each weighed about 100 pounds) and made contact with the Navy to get the GE equipment a trial on the *U.S.S. Wyoming* and *U.S.S. Virginia*. By the spring of 1916, the Navy had got interested enough for Whitney to set up a pilot plant at the Research Laboratory for vacuum tube production. GE was in the electronics business to stay.[17]

The X-ray opportunity required more careful handling. After Coolidge's demonstration of his tube's promise, Hawkins studied commercial possibilities and recommended that GE stay out of X-ray tube manufacture. The manager of GE's lighting department agreed. But when Coolidge showed the tube to leading radiologists in the fall of 1913, they became "exceedingly enthusiastic," asserting that it had potential not only for improved diagnostics but perhaps also for cancer treatment. Coolidge recommended that to make sure the full potential of the tube would be realized, GE should control its manufacture at least until development work was completed.

Top management recognized the unique nature of the opportunity. "Mr. Coffin and Mr. Rice have expressed the opinion very strongly," Albert G. Davis reported,

> that the tube should be exploited in such a way as to confer a public benefit, feeling that it is a device which is useful to humanity and that we cannot afford to take an arbitrary, or even perhaps any ordinary commercial position with regard to it.[18]

By early 1914, the Research Laboratory was making one or two tubes a week and selling them to doctors. Rice soon became a management champion of the tube. In January 1914 he told Hawkins that the Company "should not hesitate about undertaking to manufacture and sell them." Later that same year, Coolidge hired a physician to serve as GE's field representative, educating doctors about the new tube's features and advantages. Production remained on a small scale through 1916, when Whitney asked Rice for permission to set up a manufacturing plant in Schenectady. "I think we could make something like $100,000 a year without any trouble," Whitney reported, "if we had 100 square feet of floor space."[19]

A few problems remained. Other companies might infringe Coolidge's patent or try to get around it by citing the work of German researcher Julius Lilienfeld, who made a very similar improvement to the X-ray tube at just about the same time Coolidge did. In fact, however, those rival firms largely ignored the new technology. They found it easier, and apparently more profitable, to continue to build the simpler gas-filled tubes than to acquire the expertise in vacuum techniques needed to build the Coolidge tube. And though the leading radiologists enthusiastically went over to the new tube, the majority of their less progressive colleagues stuck stubbornly to the established type. So the market needed to justify the development of standardized Coolidge tubes and techniques for their production did not immediately develop.

The U.S. entry into World War I helped solve this problem. General Electric obtained a contract to use the Coolidge tube in a portable X-ray apparatus for military use. This spurred development. After the war, in 1920, Rice, now GE's president, decided that the only way the company could achieve both the benefit to humanity and the high profitability that making the Coolidge tube offered was to become a full-line X-ray equipment supplier. So GE bought the Victor X-ray Company, the biggest of the U.S. X-ray equipment manufacturers, and converted it into a producer of Coolidge tubes. The move made GE a world leader in the supply of medical diagnostic equipment, a role it retains today.[20]

Within General Electric, then, the laboratory began to lead efforts at diversication, moving beyond its previous role of defense. And outside the company, it and Whitney began by 1910 to serve as models of an industrial research lab and its direction. For example, when Eastman Kodak proposed to set up a laboratory in 1912, Frank W. Lovejoy, an executive of that company, wrote to Whitney for advice. Whitney answered with a detailed description of his policies. He emphasized the importance of keeping organizationally separate from the factory "for the purpose of permitting rather remote experimental work, which the pressure on a factory organization might sidetrack"; of relying on an advisory council's help in determining the "magnitude and direction of the work"; of charging each factory for the work done directly for it, while making up the difference between the total of those direct charges and the lab's annual budget with a "general fund" contributed by company headquarters; of finding out about problems to work on in "all conceivable ways" from department heads, engineers, and even foremen; and of holding weekly meetings of researchers doing related work (such as the members of the Lamp Vacuum committee). He concluded with two more general comments. "I dread organization and system so much," he noted, "that I want to warn others from spending too much time and effort on it." And an industrial research organization, however successful, must avoid overconfidence. "It is not safe to assume," he warned, "that we are indispensable to the Company."[21]

When Lovejoy and his superior, George Eastman, found a director for their new laboratory, a British chemist named C. E. K. Mees, they made sure he visited Whitney in Schenectady to see first hand the application of these principles. Mees would later assert that he patterned some, though by no means all, of his research management methods on Whitney's. He followed Whitney in encouraging scientists to maintain their professional status and standards and to publish the results of their work when company interests permitted. He agreed with Whitney that research direction was best done by suggestion and negotiation, not by order, and that the researcher himself was the best judge of the methods to use.[22]

Charles Kettering, the outstanding inventor and engineer who founded Delco and later became General Motors' first research director, also became a visitor to Schenectady and an admirer of Whitney's methods. Other companies that sent people to Schenectady to tour the laboratory or corresponded with Whitney to learn more about organizing research included Du Pont, Eli Lilly, Curtiss, and Hyatt Roller Bearings.[23]

So by 1914, Whitney had slipped comfortably into the role of the model director of a model research laboratory. He showed little desire to trade on his growing prominence to move up the corporate ladder, back into academic life, or into public affairs. The few excursions he took into politics suggest a blend of progressivism, nationalism, and elitism something like that of Theodore Roosevelt, the only politician for whom he ever expressed admiration.[24] When conservative chemists tried to use the editorial columns of the journal *Industrial and Engi-*

Meeting of the Lamp Vacuum Committee of the GE Research Lab in about 1915. Whitney is third from the left. To his left is Laurence Hawkins. Irving Langmuir is at the far right.

neering Chemistry to attack the recently enacted Pure Food and Drug Act, Whitney opposed them. "I lean myself toward an attitude of supporting any proper attempt to protect the quality of the food of the country," he told that journal's editor in 1911. And concerning the support of science, in 1911 he favored self-help rather than government intervention. "Let us raise an endowment fund to help young chemists to advance themselves and their science," he wrote to a colleague in 1911.

> A few seem to fear what they call paternalism, but this name less perfectly fits the case than fraternalism, against which fewer could scoff.[25]

He paid little attention to the issue of national defense, though he did add his name to a 1913 Navy League petition asking for a "Council of National Defense to decide on a continuing and consistent program of naval construction."[26] But Whitney had little use for councils, or committees, or indeed, for the democratic process at all. He admitted to an elitism based, not on assumptions of class or hereditary superiority, but simply on the belief that only individuals could accomplish anything. "A democracy does not appeal to me where high quality is the aim," he wrote J. M. Cattell in 1911. "Certainly in the matter of discovery and experimental work we find that committees cannot invent, and responsibility divided is as good as shifted."[27]

The events that would test these views began in 1914, as war broke out in Europe, and then hopes for its rapid end sank into the mud of Flanders. The prospect of a long war brought chemistry into strategic prominence. Cut off from the nitrate supplies of Chile, Germany literally pulled that key ingredient in explosives from the air, using a process invented by physical chemist Fritz Haber and engineer Carl Bosch. Faced with a deadlock on the Western Front, German chemists led by Nernst instructed the army in the use of chlorine gas to sear the lungs of unprotected enemy soldiers and to open a gaping, though unexploited, hole in the enemy line.

Chemistry may have helped shape the war on land, but Americans experienced most directly the war at sea, and another new technology. On May 1, 1915, a German torpedo sent the British liner *Lusitania* and 1,134 of its passengers, including 124 Americans, to the bottom of the Irish Channel. Within a month, another U-boat attack sank the *Essex,* and more Americans died. The submarine menace had suddenly become an immediate danger. The Wilson administration agonized over the right political response. But the technical response seemed obvious. America's most honored inventor expressed it for the nation on June 30, 1915. The time had come, Edison told a *New York Times* reporter, for a mobilization of ingenuity.

The next day Secretary of the Navy Josephus Daniels set plans underway to mobilize Edison himself. By September 1915, Daniels and Edison had put together a new "department of invention and development," soon to be officially named the Naval Consulting Board (NCB). It was to consist of Edison, his chief engineer Miller R. Hutchinson, and two representatives from each of eleven technical societies. One of them, the American Chemical Society, polled some 150 prominent members to select its representatives and came up with Baekeland and Whitney.[28]

Whitney accepted this call to national service but did not welcome it. His responses to newspaper inquiries were polite but brief. He particularly objected to requests for photographs. "The reason isn't clear to me," he told journalist H. H. McClure, "but I have just an instinctive dislike to having my face published."[29]

But he showed no reluctance to immerse himself in the activities of the NCB with all the energies he had applied to his own laboratory. Historians now recognize that Board as a pioneering effort to mobilize technology for defense on a national scale. But recent scholarship also echoes historian Richard Hewlett's view that the effort failed in its mission. Hewlett attributes the failure mainly to the inability of Edison and his staff to organize the Board effectively. Historian Daniel Kevles indicts the Board for sticking to Edisonian trial-and-error invention and excluding the scientists. Only when the physicists got on the job, in a separate effort organized by the National Research Council, says Kevles, things began to move. Let us see what light a look at Whitney's role in the defense effort can cast on these views and on our understanding of the development of Whitney as a national scientific statesman.[30]

Certainly the Board's composition was narrow. The American Physical Society and the National Academy of Sciences were both left off. Representation favored the professional inventor-entrepreneurs of the Edison type, such as Hudson Maxim, Peter Cooper Hewitt, Frank J. Sprague, and Elmer Sperry, and people who, like Whitney, had signed at least one prewar petition urging increased armament. But this narrowness was not so much a cause of the Board's problems as it was a symptom of a deeper failing. The Board members misunderstood the nature of American technological strength.

That misunderstanding took the form of an implicit assumption that America's legions of dispersed inventors would respond effectively to the challenges of war, just as they responded effectively to the opportunities of peace. The same inspiration that brought forth the telephone and light bulb would bring forth ideas for fighting the submarine menace, making nitrogen, or building better war planes. All the NCB needed to do was to act as a sort of patent office for national defense. It should organize itself into committees and make surveys. But it did not need to tell the inventors what to invent.

It is true that, in addition to this patent office role, Daniels and Edison also initially proposed a $5 million Naval research laboratory where civilian researchers could work under the Navy's direct supervision. But this proposal bogged down in arguments over where it should be located and whether it should be a scientific laboratory or, as Edison proposed, an inventive workshop in the Menlo Park mold with "no system . . . no rules . . . and a big scrap heap." No laboratory was created until the 1920s. The main accomplishment of the NCB in late 1915 was to organize itself into fifteen committees and to sit back and wait for the ideas to come in.

Whitney, who became chairman of the committee on chemistry and physics, must take part of the blame for this policy of inaction that kept the Board from accomplishing much between late 1915 and the beginning of 1917. No Board member should have known better than he did that technology did not mobilize itself. Inventors and scientists had to be directed to attack the problems of submarine detection in productive ways, just as they needed to be directed in their attacks on the metal lamp filament problem. It was not a question of whether the Edisonian cut-and-try method was superior to the physicist's more scientific approach. Edison's actual method was not cut-and-try. A physicist such as Coolidge could use methods just as "Edisonian" as the master's. The reason the patent office approach failed was the difference between the market for military inventions and their civilian counterparts. In the military market, the inventor had one customer with a narrowly defined mission in mind. To suit the customer and carry out the mission, that customer had to be involved in every step of the inventive process. The NCB eventually recognized the need to serve as an active agent in marrying military needs and inventive skill. But it did not recognize this until early 1917.

And with hindsight, we can see that the delay was decisive and nearly disastrous. It turned out to take roughly two years to develop each of the major technical innovations that America came up with for World War I: for example, submarine detection apparatus, nitrogen fixation plants, and aircraft engines. If focused development programs had got going promptly in early 1916, the technologies might have been ready in early 1918. Instead, owing to the delay, they were not really ready until the end of the war. American-made fixed nitrogen and aircraft engines never entered the war at all. The submarine detectors got into it so late that although they represented a notable achievement, they had only a small effect on combating the U-boats. When the battle of the Atlantic reached its crisis in late 1917, the detectors were only entering the advanced development stage. The convoy system, not technology, won that battle.[31]

What were the members of the NCB doing during 1916, that year of lost opportunities? Why were they not putting together technical teams to attack the major defense problems? A look at Whitney's 1916 activities suggests some answers. He was trying to do a job of education. The United States was not in the war in 1916 and had no intention of getting into it. The submarine menace was subsiding. It was by no means clear that America would ever fight anyone or where such a fight might take place. Certainly a wholesale movement of American troops to Europe seemed far from the most likely possibility.

Whitney and his colleagues put immediate priority, not on crash programs of research or development, but on lecturing or demonstrating to the American people about the need for a stepped-up defense effort. Whitney gave more speeches in late 1915 and 1916 than in any other period of his career, and some of the titles suggest the educational job he was trying to do: "Preparedness"; "Water Power and Defense"; "Research as a National Duty."[32] His speaking efforts were driven by the same impulse that led Howard E. Coffin of the Naval Consulting Board's Production Committee to organize a massive parade through New York City in May 1916 that sent 125,000 people, joined by Edison, the Board, and 200 bands into the streets of Manhattan. In the Board's view, education by means of speeches and articles, and dramatization by means of parades, had to precede true mobilization.

In Schenectady, a city with a substantial German-American population and with a socialist party that had twice in the decade won control of the city government, Whitney encountered a lot of antiwar and proneutrality sentiment. In May 1915, in fact, he had turned down a request to serve as vice-president of a meeting featuring a speech by his GE colleague Steinmetz "under the auspices of the American Truth Society in the interests of strict American neutrality." Skeptical though he was about democracy, Whitney spent much of 1916 trying democratically to sell the public the idea of an enlarged defense effort.[33]

And Whitney had another idea to sell the public in 1916, one that was shared by many of his colleagues in science. In May 1916, one of those colleagues, George Ellery Hale, an MIT classmate of Whitney's and now a prominent astronomer, wrote that the national defense emergency offered "the greatest chance we ever had to advance research in America."[34] During that crucial year of 1916, Whitney and Hale spent as much as or more time discussing how to get the government permanently committed to supporting science than they spent considering how to find submarines or fix nitrogen. (The words "defense," "preparedness," and "duty" appear in the titles of three of Whitney's 1916 speeches; the word "research" appears in eight titles.)

The differing approaches taken by Whitney and Hale in their efforts to promote research will be considered later. The important point here is that support of those efforts distracted American scientists from the job of mobilizing science for defense in 1916. During World War II, scientific statesmen such as Vannevar Bush, Arthur Compton, and James Conant organized science for war first, well before Pearl Harbor, and then waited until victory was in sight before pushing for a National Science Foundation. Whitney and his contemporaries put the job of promoting science first, with nearly fatal consequences to the defense technology effort.

It took Germany's threat to resume unrestricted submarine warfare in early 1917 to get national science and the NCB focused on the immediate job at hand. In January the Board finally set up a "Special Problems Committee" under the chairmanship of engineer Laurence Addicks to set real work underway on methods of fighting submarines. Its seven subcommittees each addressed a specific technical topic. Whitney chaired the subcommittee attacking perhaps the most critical and challenging of the problems, detection of submarines by sound.[35]

Before the war, Boston entrepreneur Henry J. W. Fay had purchased some inventions made by Reginald A. Fessenden, the man who a decade earlier had broadcast words and music by means of radio waves for the first time ever and created the Submarine Signal Company. Its aim was to develop Fessenden's system for sending messages through water by sound waves into a commercial system for signaling between ships. Back in 1906 General Electric had worked with Fessenden on building equipment for that first radio broadcast. Now, in January 1917, Fay approached GE with another offer of collaboration, this time on the use of Fessenden's methods for the detection of submarines. Whitney immediately brought the matter before the NCB. By the early spring of 1917, the NCB had established an experimental station at Nahant, Massachusetts, a small peninsula north of Boston. It was funded by the Navy's Bureau of Steam Engineering.[36]

Whitney immediately sent a contingent of General Electric researchers to begin work. They were soon joined by a delegation from AT&T. The caliber of the members of the Nahant group is suggested by their later achievements. On the GE side, one of them, Langmuir, would go on to win a Nobel

Prize, and another, Eveleth, would become the Company's vice-president for manufacturing. The AT&T contingent included two future presidents of Bell Laboratories, Harold D. Arnold and Oliver E. Buckley. Whitney "directed" this industrial all-star team in his usual manner of combining frequent visits, suggestions, and encouragement with an understanding that good people should be allowed to choose their own path to the goal.

That goal, at first, was adapting the Fessenden oscillator, a mechanical system for amplifying a narrow band of frequencies of sound waves, to the detection of submarines. By May 14, the Nahant group reported some initial success. From their shore station, they could hear the propellor noises from a moving submarine ten miles away, as long as no other shipping was nearby to drown out the signal. But the clumsy oscillator would be difficult to install on a ship, and the ship's own noises would likely reduce detection range to one mile.[37]

As the team grew to understand the submarine detection problem, the unsuitability of the Fessenden system became apparent. Compare its performance with the specification of an ideal detection system, written a year later:

> The general requirements of a listening apparatus which embodies all that could be desired may be stated as follows: it must be adapted to detect a submarine at a considerable distance without interference from noise produced by other shipping, or wave noise, or by noise due to motion of the boat on which it is installed; it should be able to give the direction and distance of a submarine accurately; it should be seaworthy, of robust mechanical construction, convenient, and rapid in operation.[38]

The oscillator failed on most of these counts, and if the Nahant researchers had simply pushed ahead with it, their project would have failed too. But fortunately other ideas soon arose. Credit for bringing them to the Nahant team's attention belongs largely to the energetic Millikan. He had made the original suggestion that GE and AT&T join forces. He had also proposed that university physicists join the team. This suggestion had been turned down by the admiral heading the Navy's Bureau of Steam Engineering, on the grounds, Millikan alleges, that university participation would complicate an already difficult patent situation.[39]

But Millikan had another avenue of influence. Edison's NCB had pointedly avoided calling on the services of the National Academy of Sciences, America's premier scientific organization—and one that had been founded in the Civil War era precisely for the purpose of mobilizing scientific advice. The Academy had actually become more of an elderly gentlemen's social club, but by 1916 a young inductee, Hale, was ready to change that. He led the formation of a new scientific advisory body, the National Research Council. (NRC). Its membership included both the leaders of the National Academy of Sciences and prominent industrial scientists who had not yet in 1916 been admitted to the Academy, such as Whitney, and John J. Carty of Western Electric. The NRC's stated purpose was to put America's scientific and technological strength at the service of the government in the war emergency. But its 1916 activities, like those of the NCB, consisted mainly of the creation of committees and the promotion of the general cause of preparedness and research. Mention of real effort on the antisubmarine problem, for example, does not appear in the published minutes of the NRC until May 1917, when physicist Michael Pupin spoke of the "urgent necessity" of finding a way to detect submarines and introduced Carty, who described the activities at Nahant.[40]

Before that, in February 1917, Whitney had met with Millikan at the Chemists' Club in New York. The imminence of U.S. entry into the war made temporary allies of these two strong-minded scientists. At the very same time they met to discuss cooperation, they were preparing to go to court on opposite sides of a battle over the basic patent rights to the high vacuum tube. Whitney backed Langmuir; Millikan would testify on behalf of his former student, Harold D. Arnold. But they did not let this rivalry carry over into war work. Millikan told

Whitney of his desire to put the physicists to work on the submarine problem and of the cool reception he had got from the Navy. Whitney, in Millikan's words "urged me to go ahead with the presenting of our plans to the Navy."[41]

Millikan proceeded to put a few physicists to work under NRC auspices in New York City on the problem. And the NRC sent a scientific mission to Europe to look first hand at the problem and at Allied research efforts. In June 1917, a return delegation led by eminent scientists such as Max Abraham of France and Ernest Rutherford of Britain came to America to take part in a conference on submarine detection. On June 14, Rutherford described to the Americans his colleagues' work on Broca tubes, which are essentially forms of stethescopes in which each ear is connected to a separate microphone. The difference of sound intensity in each ear indicates the direction of the sound.[42]

Whitney, attending the conference and aware by now of the deficiencies of the Fessenden oscillator seized on this clue. He went back to Schenectady and put Coolidge to work on Broca tube or stethescope-type devices. Coolidge set up experiments on a leaky barge on the Mohawk River. He quickly came up with a major improvement by making the sound-sensing elements and connector tubes of an underwater stethescope out of hard rubber instead of metal. This enabled him to gather a wider spectrum of the sound frequencies emitted by a moving submarine. Low sensitivity over a broad frequency range, rather than the high sensitivity over a narrow frequency range that Fessenden had sought, proved to be the key to a practical submarine detector.

Whitney immediately moved the new idea from Schenectady to Nahant for further development. By August the research team used this simple underwater stethescope to detect moving submerged submarines from the deck of an anchored ship. This new device (named the "C tube" after Coolidge), was clearly only a beginning. Langmuir, Arnold, and Buckley set to work on an electronic version that could be lowered deeper into the water to avoid surface noises. But the entire team knew that their job was not to invent the best of all possible submarine detectors but, in the words of a subsequent Navy report, "to turn out in the shortest possible time an instrument which should be of actual use in detecting submarines." So, by the fall of 1917, Whitney and Eveleth already had arranged for the manufacture of C tubes by General Electric and for moving them overseas.

Meanwhile, Millikan had urged that a new submarine detection laboratory be set up at New London, Connecticut, to be run by academic scientists. Whitney might well have resented this suggestion to duplicate or compete with the Nahant laboratory. But if he did, he put such feelings aside. The NRC scientists felt "aggrieved," he wrote Navy Secretary Daniels in July 1917, and it would not cost much to mollify them by giving them their own research station where they could try out their own ideas. "If a little of the energy which, I fear, may otherwise develop into hard feeling could be utilized in the submarine work," he concluded, "time could be saved."[43] Daniels approved the establishment of the New London station.

Time was crucial in 1917. A memo issued to Whitney and his colleagues described how the continuation of 1917 trends in submarine warfare could cause allied shipping capacity to fall to only 5.1 million tons by January 1919, compared to 9 million in January 1918 and 13 million in January 1917.[44] But by now the dual efforts at Nahant and New London were working with an effectiveness that would match anything displayed in World War II. The NRC scientists, led by physicist Max Mason, invented a Broca tube device with multiple listening tubes that promised to outperform the C tube. But since its added complexity implied a longer development time the Nahant group redoubled its efforts to put the C tube into immediate service.

Early in December, the battleship *Delaware* docked at Nahant. Four Nahant staff members moved fifteen tons of their equipment on board and sailed off to England. By Christmas, Eveleth was in London, trying to persuade the British Admiralty to give the C tube a sea trial. The British were only in the trial stage with their own antisubmarine devices. In just eight months of work, Nahant had caught up with a British effort that had been underway for three years. The British had not been delayed by a lack of good ideas. Their problem, in Eveleth's words, was

> the fact that it has not been the custom in this country to co-ordinate the efforts of scientists and manufacturers and they do not understand each other's language or methods, and it is frankly stated to us by both sides that we could take the ideas that they have here, go to America, develop and complete finished apparatus, and return quicker than the work can be done here.[45]

Eveleth and his American colleague Charles F. Scott agreed on the main source of the American success at coordinating research, development, and manufacturing. As Eveleth put it to Whitney:

> Mr. Scott and I certainly realize now, more than ever before, the reasons why we at Nahant have been able to make headway. It is due to your method of organization in combining ideas with accomplishment such as is done every day in the research laboratory.[46]

But the headway Nahant had made in 1917 could not entirely overcome the effects of the delayed start on the problem. The achievements of 1917 made it possible to begin learning how to use the C tube in warfare, but actual effective operational use of the tube was still months away.

In the first week in January, Eveleth and Scott boarded a 100 ton trawler to accompany a British and American naval team taking the C tube out on its first experimental submarine patrol. Three of the trawlers chugged out into the English Channel at the slow speed of ten knots, spaced a mile or two apart in a line. They would run for half an hour, then cut their engines, lower the C tubes over the side, and listen. Almost immediately the operators reported contacts: sounds in the earphones that might come from submarines. But then came frustration, for the trawlers were too slow to chase down anything that they heard. What sub hunters really needed, reported the chief U.S. representative at the trials, R. H. Leigh, were bigger boats capable of speeds of 20 knots or more.[47]

Back in the United States, Thomas Robins, the secretary of the NCB, had been campaigning since October to convince the Navy to build just this kind of boat. Whitney enthusiastically supported him. But the Navy insisted that there were not enough riveters in the shipbuilding industry to carry out the program of destroyer building the Navy was already committed to and also take on this new job.

Millikan managed to get something moving, convincing Henry Ford to convert one of his automobile plants to the building of rivetless submarine chasers. But the Ford "Eagle boats" never really proved satisfactory, and they reached Europe too late to get into much action.[48]

Owing to the lack of proper ships and tactics, the 1918 service of the submarine detectors consisted of a learning period, not a record of submarine sinkings. More than 1,000 C tubes were built by war's end, and hundreds of boats were equipped with them. No doubt the stepped-up patrolling of the channel by detector-equipped boats inconvenienced enemy submarines. And occasionally it did more. On September 6, 1918, for example, the U.S. Navy's Ashley Adams reported on his thirty-hour chase of a C tube contact. That chase, Adams believed, brought the enemy to bay. The last thing he heard through his earphones was "sounds like rifle or revolver shots. . . . Three first, followed by twenty-two. After this, nothing."[49]

But Adams could not confirm his suspected kill. Nor did any other subchaser in the channel. Usually, the combination of a slow boat and the hunter's inexperience allowed the quarry to slip away. As Admiral William Sims, commander of U.S. Naval forces operating in European waters, concluded on September 18, 1918:

Frequent occasions have occurred where the use of sound detection devices has offered our forces excellent opportunities to deliver strong attacks. In some of these cases the operation has been excellent, but in many the inexperience of the personnel in the use of the new ideas involved has prevented the attainment of any definite results.[50]

In action in the Gulf of Otranto, on the Adriatic Sea, against Italian submarines, the subchasers fared far better. The narrower waters and the less skilled enemy allowed attacks to be pressed home and kills recorded. But back on the key battle front, in the Atlantic, victory over the submarine came from effective use of the convoy system, not from new technology.[51]

The antisubmarine effort had taught many lessons. Physicists had proved their value. The Mason type of multiple Broca tube proved the best antisubmarine device built during the war. Its late arrival limited its use in action, but the achievement it and other New London work represented established that station as the main center of U.S. underwater sound detection research. The C tube that Whitney's team developed at Nahant was inferior to the Mason device. But it could be developed, manufactured, and put to work fast. Far more C tubes saw war service than any other device.

The most important lesson of the technological war, however, went beyond any transient rivalries among academic physicists, industrial researchers, and Edisonian inventors. The scientists and engineers learned that they could not wait until war was declared to begin developing weapons for defense, nor rely on the spontaneous initiative of the nation's independent inventors and researchers to produce those weapons. Development had to begin in peacetime and had to be directed from the top. The lesson was not lost on Vannevar Bush, who served in World War I as a young engineer in the submarine detection effort and who would serve in World War II as America's science czar.

Whitney got a second reminder of this lesson in the fall of 1918, when he moved to a second wartime job. He accepted the post of director of research on nitrogen fixation for the Ordnance Department. Like submarine detection, the need for a reliable supply of fixed nitrogen for explosives and fertilizer had been recognized as a crucial defense necessity in 1915. The chemistry and physics committee of the NCB, which Whitney headed, had as one of its main responsibilities the search for a chemical process to produce nitrates from domestic raw materials and supplement the precarious supply imported from Chile. But, as with submarines, Whitney spent 1916 educating, not directing research. His main contribution, a paper entitled "Water Power and National Defense," urged the development of hydroelectric power and its application to nitrate production but presented the problem as one of long-range preparedness, not immediate danger. The Army's Ordnance Department had taken a more active role and had secured a $20 million appropriation in 1916 for the design of a nitrate plant.

But an argument among chemists had delayed the effort. Several ways of making nitrates were possible, none of which had yet been put on a sound commercial footing in the United States. Two looked most attractive: the Haber process, a relatively efficient method of uniting nitrogen from the air with manufactured hydrogen to make ammonia that would be technically difficult to implement; and the cyanamid process, a method that made less efficient use of energy but would be easier to implement. After listening to the advocates of each method debate for about a year, the heads of the Ordnance Department decided in 1917 to try the risky Haber process. This proved to be the wrong choice. American chemists and chemical engineers, lacking the detailed knowledge of the engineering tricks and catalysts that the German inventors of the process had developed, could not get the experimental American Haber process plant to work. Only in mid-1918 were plans approved to build a back-up cyanamid plant. It was just going into production on Armistice day and survived to become a technological white elephant. (In fact, the government's efforts to get rid of it in the 1920s sparked the Muscle Shoals debate over private versus public use of the nation's water power that led eventually to the creation of the Tennessee Valley authority.)[52]

The naming of Whitney as research director represented a

tardy recognition of the need for understanding of the chemistry behind nitrogen fixation. He arrived on the scene too late to direct any major research that would impact the war effort. "I could not see any way of starting and running a research laboratory in Washington myself," he wrote to colleague Charles Herty in November 1918, "but am very sure it ought to be done."[53] He proposed the creation of such a laboratory and arranged for it to be turned over to the Agriculture Department when peace came. That laboratory eventually made valuable contributions to American application of the Haber process.

But the wartime nitrogen problem, like the submarine threat, yielded to tactics, not to technology. A team headed by lawyer Chandler P. Anderson, under the direction of financier Bernard Baruch, outmaneuvered Germany and bought up the Chilean nitrate supply on behalf of the U.S. War Industries Board. This ensured adequate supplies for the duration of the war. By contrast, the chemists' efforts produced only, in the words of chemist and historian L. F. Haber, "delays, unusual muddle, and vast expense that yielded negligible results."[54]

One should not judge the failure of the chemists too harshly. America was only in the war for some eighteen months, far too short a time to produce new technology from scratch. America's scientists and engineers performed well once they got started. They developed submarine detectors, built a cyanimid plant, produced optical glass and gas masks, and implemented artillery ranging methods and ground-to-air radio. But since they did not get started until war had been declared, the fruits of their effort did not ripen until after the war had ended.

And the NCB's original picture of the United States as a dispersed reserve of national ingenuity had been the biggest disappointment of the war years. Of some 100,000 inventions sent to the Board by patriotic citizens, exactly one made it into use by the war's end. Technology for modern war had to be produced to order by research and development teams organized for specific purposes, assembled at well-equipped laboratories, and given adequate resources. Their work had to be meshed with the plans of the military and coupled with tactical doctrines for using new weapons. The best submarine-detecting device would be useless without a doctrine accepted by the Navy for its use, a crew trained to use it, a boat fast enough to chase down the submarines it detected, and weapons to kill the sub that had been cornered. To have all this ready in time for war meant starting, not on the day war was declared, but on the day war clouds first appeared on the horizon—or earlier.

An immediate acknowledgment of this lesson came after the war. Whitney and his colleagues on the NCB got together and recommended a site for the Naval Research Laboratory that Edison and Daniels had first proposed back in 1915 and Congress had authorized in 1916 and 1917. Formally commissioned in 1923, that laboratory succeeded in carrying out sustained research and development in peacetime, most notably on radar, that helped prepare the nation to fight World War II.[55]

But Whitney, along with academic colleagues such as Hale, Millikan, and Noyes, used the war experience as evidence for a broader argument. They sought to convert the mood of wartime urgency into a permanent mobilization of scientific talent for peaceful research. They had long believed that the United States did not spend enough public or private money on scientific research. They had begun by 1916 to try to build permanent mechanisms for national research funding.

Whitney, Hale, Millikan, and Noyes all agreed that more money should go to science. But each one's views on the shape that support ought to take was colored by that individual's personality and past experiences. Whitney still carried in his mind an idealized picture of prewar German science, supported by the government, based on research-minded professors, and producing an overflow of talented Ph.D.'s sufficient to fill the laboratories of industry, as well as those of the universities. Hale, the son of a wealthy elevator manufacturer, had been able to pass up doctoral work in Germany and a teaching career and to raise enough money from private sources to pursue an independent career of research in astronomy. In Daniel Kevles' apt words, "he had the skyscraper drive of his father. He walked with a quick nervous step; nothing but frequent illness ever dissipated his energetic ambition."[56] Millikan, a man whose aristocratic bearing bordered on arrogance, was embarking on a third career after the war. He had first earned a reputation at the University of Chicago as an excellent physics teacher and textbook writer. He next turned himself into an experimental physicist skilled enough to do work that would win the Nobel Prize. But his wartime experience, traveling the country in an Army captain's uniform, getting the ear of industry leaders and public officials, successfully promoting the New London scientific station and the Eagle boat, had unveiled perhaps his greatest talent: selling science. He looked and sounded like a corporation president himself and could make science sound like a solid investment. And he enjoyed attention. "Men like Whitney and like myself have been pulled out of the ruts in which our lives had been running and have been thrown into completely new surroundings," he wrote in 1918.[57] Unlike Whitney, he found those new surroundings wholly to his liking. Noyes did not try to share the limelight with Hale and Millikan. But he supported them as an extremely effective behind-the-scenes organizer. His experience at MIT, where ambitious promoters of chemical engineering were eclipsing his purely scientific chemical laboratory, had confirmed his view that science needed stronger support than a university alone could give.[58]

The four men illustrate the diversity of the leadership of a national scientific community that faced two main questions in 1918 in its efforts to promote national science: Who should put up the money? Who should decide how the money should be spent? Here Whitney separated from Hale, Millikan, and Noyes. He sought funding direct from the Federal government. They placed greater reliance on private sources: direct endowments from industries or individuals or grants from philanthropic foundations. Whitney would give the money to the best universities around the nation and let them decide how to use it.

Hale, Millikan, and Noyes would concentrate control of research funds in the hands of the National Academy of Science's elite.

Whitney and Hale had not kept in close touch since their days as classmates at MIT. Only in 1915, as Hale was launching his campaign to increase public support for science, did they begin to correspond. Hale's first letter set the tone for what would come to be a growing contrast between two different views toward science policy. "I am anxious to see a closer connection between pure science and its applications in the industries," he began.

> Your extraordinary success in research, and the judicial attitude I know you bear toward both phases of scientific work, lend very exceptional weight to your influence. We have now reached a point in the development of the academy where it should soon be possible to give proper recognition to the practical applications of science, and I should like to have your advice and aid.[59]

For all its compliments, this letter already hints at the differences that would divide Hale and Whitney. Hale worked from a model that always made a sharp separation between "pure science," produced in universities and independent laboratories by the scientific elite, and its "applications in the industries." His somewhat condescending remark that it would "soon be possible" for the National Academy to recognize the importance of applied science suggested that Whitney's achievements of the past fifteen years at GE somehow lacked legitimacy until given the imprimatur of an elite that Whitney was still two years away from being asked to join. Hale was far from the most elitist of the members of the National Academy in regard to applied science. He was taking the initiative to bring it in. Some of his older colleagues at the Academy would resist its inclusion altogether, denying membership to Thomas Edison until 1926. But though Hale was generous by comparison to those conservatives, he shared some of their elitist views.[60]

Hale had spelled out his program for revitalizing the National Academy in his 1915 publication *National Academies and*

The staff of the GE Research Laboratory in 1918.

the Progress of Research. He had called for selling business on the value of science, promoting interdisciplinary work in larger groups, and organizing all this under the Academy's aegis. The idea of increased support of science by industry was in the air by this time, thanks at least in part to the example created by Whitney at General Electric. At the University of Pittsburgh, chemist Robert Kennedy Duncan had set up a Department of Industrial Research, supported in 1913 by a $500,000 grant from the Mellon family and aimed at attacking industrial problems in a university setting. In 1916, the American Association for the Advancement of Science would set up a Committee of one hundred to promote further cooperation between industry and the universities.

In 1916, the year of waiting and propaganda for preparedness, Hale and Whitney stepped up their efforts. Hale focused his on the National Research Council and its potential role as the general staff of American research. He gained the support of national scientific leaders such as Millikan, Noyes, and the director of research of Western Electric, Jewett.

Whitney was a member of the NRC but not one of its real

leaders. Instead, he put his influence behind a proposal that arose in the hinterlands of science. It came from a former student of his, Andrey A. Potter, now a professor of electrical engineering at Kansas University. Potter had worked with Senator Francis Newlands of Nevada to draw up a bill extending the government's support of research from agriculture to engineering and science. Earlier legislation had set up agricultural research stations at American land grant colleges. Under this bill, the government would designate the land grant college or university in each state as an engineering research station and grant it $15,000 a year in Federal funds.[61]

In support of this bill, Whitney undertook one of his few campaigns to convert his influence with American scientists into backing for a specific piece of legislation. In April 1916 he wrote to Hale, describing the Newlands Bill as "the most promising effort actually well under way to bring about conditions of research in this country at all approaching what we ought to have."[62] The $15,000 per state was only a beginning. As the new research stations proved their value, funding would rise. The important thing now was to enact the principle of government support for science.

But Hale did not respond to the Newlands bill with the same enthusiasm shown by Whitney. He objected to the bill's placing the national control of the distribution of funds under a political appointee, the Secretary of the Interior. And Whitney began to hear from scientists at institutions other than the land grant colleges. They objected to a program that would use public funds to strengthen their rivals.[63] Hale proposed that the National Academy set up a small comittee to suggest changes in the details of the bill to make it more acceptable. Millikan became the chairman of this committee, and Whitney and Michael Pupin, professor of physics at Columbia, became its members.

Whitney began to become impatient with the quibbling. "I think we all ought to recognize," he wrote to Noyes in June 1916 that it is exceedingly important to do something definite and with decent rapidity, and I have felt that most academically trained people are apt to be so deliberate that the results are not commensurate with the efforts.[64]

In 1916, to any audience that would listen, he presented his diagnosis of the problems of American research and his prescription for their cure. He would begin by showing a lantern slide of a group of serious young men stiffly posed for a formal portrait: the chemist Wohler's research group at Göttingen in 1856. Three or four of the young men were Americans, he would explain. From 1856 to the outbreak of the current war, America had learned its chemistry in Germany. He would then paint with words the idealized picture of German science that he had brought back on the *H.M.S. Teutonic* in 1896: in each town a university; in each university several professors dedicated to pure research, each one treated "wie ein Gott" by his community; from each professor's laboratory a stream of trained men pouring forth to swell the ranks of research or to serve science-based industries. Against this nation of investigators stood America, a nation of inventors, occasionally flashing forth with the genius of Edison but more often producing quacks who claimed they could produce perpetual motion or turn water into gasoline. That contrast, Whitney argued, must not continue. "One of the best methods for insuring strength in times of war and of peace as well lies in the extended and continual discovery of new laws of nature and properties of materials." To ensure that strength in wartime, the nation needed a Naval Research Laboratory. To ensure it in peacetime, the nation needed the Newlands bill.[65]

Whitney wanted action in 1916. With Millikan and Pupin, he worked out a compromise on the Newlands Bill. It would have given the National Academy of Sciences a larger role in the distribution of funds and would have aimed the bill more at fundamental research. But this made the land grant college leadership angry. Whitney called for another conference to settle the differences among the embattled factions. But the science and engineering community never united behind any version of the bill, and it died in committee.[66]

By early 1917, Whitney's feelings toward his pure science colleagues were beginning to sour. "I want you to think a moment on the Newlands Bill," he wrote Hale. The scientific community had to unite behind some version of the bill. "The only alternative I see is some long drawn out work on the part of committees," he concluded.

> After attending the recent meeting in New York of the Committee on Scientific Research, I made up my mind that when the number of scientists gathered together is more than two or three, the Lord is certainly in some other place. Twelve year old children can do more constructive work in an hour than a committee of 100 scientists could do in a year, as our American scientists are actually constructed.[67]

After setting aside the campaign for the rest of 1917 in favor of wartime work on submarine detection, Whitney resumed the effort to secure government support for research in 1918. A new congressional vehicle, the Smith-Howard Bill, emerged. But the split between the land-grant schools and their rivals remained. The new legislation met the same fate as the Newlands Bill.

The episode convinced Hale to drop temporarily the effort to get government to pay for science. "To tell the truth," he wrote Whitney,

> I am not at all sure that governmental funds would offer any real advantage. Do you think, for instance, that any great good would result if all our educational institutions were run by the government and supported by the tax payers? I believe some of the greatest advantages we ever had have come through the freedom or initiative in the absence of bureaucratic control, which our present system has so greatly encouraged.[68]

Hale wanted to shift the campaign and tap private and industrial sources of wealth instead of government ones. Whitney disagreed. "I believe that while it is a good plan to continue to encourage people of wealth to support the sciences as we do in America," he had written Hale in June 1918, "it would be better if the democracy could be brought to pay its own expenses in this line, just as in lower schooling and as Germany did."[69]

Why did Whitney continue to press for government support? The best historical account of post World War I science policy presents him as a spokesman for a self-serving industrial establishment, eager to get the government to pay for research results that industry could then use for free.[70] But this interpretation ignores the reasons Whitney himself gives for his position. He did not want the government to pay for research as much as he wanted it to pay for the *education* of researchers. This emphasis comes through again and again. In remarks to the Advisory Committee on Industrial Research in May 1918, "Dr. Whitney urged the more generous support of our universities in the education of research men, and emphasized the present great need for more trained men to conduct research along many lines." Later in the same meeting, "Dr. Whitney strenuously reiterated the need for more trained men." In that June 1918 letter to Hale, he had explained his continuing support for Federal funding this way:

> I am interested primarily in the production of the type of men in quantity which I know we sorely lack, and in the product of their work in American science and industry. While I therefore will gladly help any plan for research such as the one which you gave us in outline (Hale's plan for going after private wealth), I want to have you see that the country owes it to itself to arrange for the facilities which advanced students need.[71]

In a December 1918 address, Whitney dismissed the suggestion that the industrial laboratories "could supply the country's deficiency in scientific research and in teaching." He, on the contrary, agreed with the directors of other major laboratories, such as Skinner of Westinghouse and Carty and Jewett of AT&T, that "there does not seem to be the slightest possibility of this meeting the real need of the country." The United

States must apply the method Germany used so successfully: application of government funding to college and graduate education, aimed at "the highest possible training on the part of a selected few."[72]

Whitney's continued advocacy of government support seems to stem from a continuing belief in the idealized model of the German experience and its benefits to the nation. Narrower economic considerations do not seem to have shaped his view. That view would not prevail in the 1920s. Private, not public, funds would become the main support of pure science in that decade, thanks largely to the work of Hale, Millikan, Noyes, and the other leaders of the NRC. Major philanthropic foundations would establish postdoctoral fellowships to provide aid to a new generation of American researchers.

Whitney himself largely withdrew in the 1920s from the lobbying role he had taken on between 1914 and 1920. He would continue to serve the government when called on, becoming, for example, a member of a Navy board that investigated the safety of submarines. But he would rarely seek to influence legislation. On the lecture platform in the 1920s he would make general proclamations of the value of research rather than offering the specific prescriptions for strengthening it that he had put forward in the previous decade. He continued to exert his influence through private discussions at the Cosmos Club in Washington or the Chemists' Club in New York. But he did not become a force at the increasingly important centers of science policy growing up at the NRC and the offices of the Rockefeller and Carnegie foundations.

Control of the strategy of American science belonged increasingly to others who had emerged with Whitney onto that wider stage of national renown in the second decade of the century. Hale alternated between bouts with illness and forays of successful fund raising to support fellowships and to pay for giant telescopes. Millikan became a familiar figure in corporate board rooms, extolling the virtues of science, though seldom coming away with the full funding commitment he asked for. Noyes worked with Millikan to build a great scientific institution at the California Institute of Technology, while continuing to launch the careers of outstanding young chemists.

Thanks to the work of such leaders, the next generation of scientists had a wider range of choices open to them than Whitney had. Arthur A. Crompton, for example, did not find himself locked into his first industrial job, at Westinghouse, when that company began to question the wisdom of its support of basic research. He took advantage of one of the new NRC fellowships to travel to Cambridge and work with Rutherford at the Cavendish Laboratory. Then he returned to America to take an academic post.

Whitney turned back to his General Electric Laboratory. When asked in 1923 to take a high position with the NRC, he declined, saying:

> I still have the feeling pretty strong that the Research Laboratory would die at once but for me (I know that's not so but I like it), and I have declined for the past twenty-three years to consider any other calling. I know that if I can grow anywhere in the world, I can grow there.[73]

Those opportunities for growth had emerged during a decade when Whitney had stepped out onto a wider national stage than GE or Schenectady. The laboratory he ran had grown from a defender of a giant company's most profitable business to a pioneer in new technologies such as radio, X-rays, and electronics. Whitney had helped educate other corporations about the organization of industrial research. He had helped lead a national effort to use science and technology for national defense. He had waged an unsuccessful campaign to transfer the German model of government support for research to the United States.

Those activities had made him a national figure. His public prestige would continue to grow in the following decade. But the real leadership of U.S. science was passing to a group and a generation that would largely leave him behind.

9/

Peak of Authority

At eight o'clock in the morning of a working day in the early 1920s, Whitney would swing his Model T Ford into a parking place next to Building 5 at the Schenectady Works. The man who stepped out bore little resemblance to the bearded professor who, two decades earlier, had begun each day with a spin on his bicycle before walking down the bank of the Erie Canal to work. The receding hairline and emerging jowls on the now clean-shaven face made him look more like a bank president than a scientist. The metal-rimmed glasses and the conservative three-piece blue suit heightened the impression. The round outthrust chin, the questioning eyes, and the vertical furrows between the eyebrows were still there, but one had to look harder to find them.

The new look suited a man who was no longer experimenting in industrial research. He now guided an ongoing institution. As a brief postwar recession gave way to the prosperity of the 1920s, industrial research began to become a familiar word in the press and on Wall Street. And the most familiar of all industrial research laboratories was the one run by Whitney for General Electric. In the nineteenth century, Samuel Smiles had captured the public image of British technology in his published lives of the great inventors and engineers. In the 1920s, the director of the Division of Engineering and Industrial Research of the National Research Council, (NRC), Maurice Holland, tried to capture the public image of American technology in his collection *Industrial Explorers*. It was a series of admiring sketches of the directors of research of the nation's high-technology companies, including AT&T, DuPont, Eastman Kodak, Corning Glass, and Curtiss Aeroplane. But the name of General Electric's research director led all the rest.

Willis R. Whitney at about age 60, about 1928.

"Willis R. Whitney," Holland proclaimed, "is undoubtedly the best beloved of all the remarkable men who are the crowned heads of research."[1]

The adjective "beloved" is well chosen. Whitney's open approach earned personal regard that went far beyond professional respect. This contrasted with the cooler, managerial approach of most research directors. GE metallurgist Truman Fuller later recalled the incredulity with which visiting Bell Laboratory researchers greeted Whitney's open door and "come in rain or shine" sign.

Whitney used this uniquely personal approach to answer a

critical problem of industrial research: how do you achieve productivity without stifling innovation? A bureaucratic laboratory might be highly productive in solving routine problems but might discourage new ideas. A laboratory modeled on a university science department might produce first-rate research publications, but those papers would probably not do much for General Electric's profits. Some historical studies of industrial research suggest that one of these extremes must prevail. A research laboratory in that view, must become either a bureaucratic science assembly line or a "university-in-exile." But recent, more detailed findings indicate more variety and complexity. At General Motors, the inspiring and hard-driving Charles Kettering kept researchers focused on immediate needs, while Company president Alfred Sloan intervened personally to ensure wider freedom for at least one creative researcher.[2] AT&T institutionalized the special status of its research organization by founding a separate entity, the Bell Laboratories.[3] At GE, Whitney sought to bring out both teamwork and individuality by treating his laboratory staff like a family, rather than like a business organization or a band of independent professionals. As he had done with "No" and "Ne" back in 1908, he worked through suggestion and inspiration, applied on an individual basis.

In the 1920s, this personal approach brought Whitney to the peak of his authority as a public figure. Popular accounts depicted him as the "molder of genius" and "dean of industrial research."[4] But they concentrated on his opinions and his turtles and gave little real insight into the way he ran the Laboratory. One way to get a better understanding of his methods is to follow him through a hypothetical day on that job. This composite photograph will blur together the specific features of individual days in an effort to give a true general picture of the work of the corporation's chemist.

Driving in to begin that day's work, Whitney could see daily signs of the vigorous growth of the city of Schenectady. Like Jamestown forty years earlier, new manufacturing jobs had drawn sons and daughters from the surrounding farms and

Home of the GE Research Laboratory at the Schenectady Works of
General Electric, 1902–1914. Work done in this building by Whitney,
William D. Coolidge, Irving Langmuir, and others proved the business value
of industrial research.

had attracted craftsmen and laborers from across the ocean.
But this was a different kind of urban growth, attuned not to
a manufacturing republic but to an industrial state. In Jamestown, the local business leadership had been the local government. Schenectady's two major employers, General Electric and
American Locomotive, kept hands off city politics.[5] Schenectady remained the official headquarters of General Electric and
the site of its largest works. But for the more than thirty years
since the company had been founded, its major decisions had
been made in the New York City offices of its president and
board chairman. In Jamestown, the character of work had de-

Location of the GE Research lab at the head of the main street of GE's Schenectady Works in 1923 (indicated by arrow). Whitney would later say he chose this site "so that people will see us when they come to work in the morning, and will know we're there to help them."

pended directly on the character of an individual employer: the workers at the cane seat chair factory faced far harsher conditions than their counterparts did at John Whitney's wood seat chair works down the street. In Schenectady, paternalistic treatment of labor was becoming institutionalized and uniform. The GE management first broke the craft unions at Schenectady, then replaced them with a system of piece rates, annual bonuses, workers' councils, and a wide range of amenities ranging from athletic fields to Americanization classes.[6] Some of the new houses Whitney saw as he drove to work were being financed by low-interest loans obtained for workers by the company.[7] At Jamestown, growth had been achieved by

In 1925, the GE Research Laboratory added a development building, shown
on the right to supplement the research building, shown on the left, that
the laboratory had occupied since 1914. Both buildings are still used by
the GE Research and Development Center.

luring in new companies such as American Aristotype. In
Schenectady diversification was carried out within a giant corporation. It was turning swollen wartime sales levels into postwar prosperity and new businesses. As General Electric's sales
tripled to $300 million in the decade 1914 to 1924, it added
dozens of new product lines. Its Schenectady work force surged
past the 20,000 mark.

That work force rose and fell with international business tides,
not with local conditions. Schenectady proudly proclaimed itself "the city that lights and hauls the world." As he swung his
car into the Works, Whitney saw evidence of this new worldwide thrust. A six-story office building had been built in 1919
just outside the main gate to house GE's newly established International subsidiary and its new manager, Swope. Whitney
knew him as his former chemistry student at MIT. The Schenectady Works bureaucracy knew him as an upstart brought
into the Company after the World War and groomed to suc-

GE's giants of technology, in 1923. Left to right, in front row: William D.
Coolidge, Willis R. Whitney, Thomas A. Edison, Charles Proteus
Steinmetz, Irving Langmuir. In the second row, second from right, is
the president of General Electric, Gerard Swope.

ceed to the Company's presidency, a post he would assume in
1923.[8]

The next building Whitney came to was his own, a rectan-
gular red brick structure seven stories high. The succession of
temporary quarters that began with the barn had finally given
way in 1914 to a specially designed 65,000-square-foot laboratory building. He would claim later to have personally selected its site at the head of the main avenue of the Works, "so
that people will see us when they come to work in the morning, and will know that we're there to help them."[9] And many
of the people who streamed down that avenue past Whitney
as he emerged from his car did owe their jobs to the laboratory. The fastest growing activity at the Works was radio set
manufacture, which depended on technology pioneered in the
Research Lab. The laboratory's own work force of more than

300 already filled its new building, and work had begun on a second one next door, designed to house development activities to make new products out of the next round of inventions.

Not only on Works Avenue, but on main streets across America, the words "industrial research" and "science" were becoming identified with new products and new prosperity. When people tuned their radio sets to KDKA in Pittsburgh or WGY in Schenectady, they were operating vacuum tubes relying on scientific theories and techniques that a decade earlier were confined to a few physics laboratories. The refrigerator cooling their beer in the kitchen was a triumph of modern engineering that had been virtually unknown in the home of 1915. Science got credit for these conveniences. "The 20s were a golden age of scientific faith," one historian has remarked, "not only among scientists and industrialists but also for the public at large." [10] For industrialists and the public, science meant, not such technical topics as catalysis or the nature of the electron, but growth businesses such as automobiles, aviation, movies, and radio. This identification was fostered by both industry and science. At GE, a skilled publicity man named Clyde Wagoner kept constantly before the public names such as Whitney, Langmuir, and above all, Steinmetz. (Steinmetz had died in 1923, but that only made him a more valuable property. Now he could no longer spoil his image with advocacy of socialism and eccentric pronouncements.) [11] Radio announcer Floyd Gibbons gave Wagoner a big assist in 1925 when he coined for the Research Laboratory the name "House of Magic." By 1922, student newspapers at 325 colleges and universities carried monthly messages describing GE Research to some 400,000 undergraduates, under headlines such as "From a Faint Blue Glow to Modern Miracles." "We have nothing to sell and are not trying to attract them into the organization," the director of that ad campaign told Whitney. Advertising about GE research, he explained, was intended to instill in tomorrow's national leaders "a wholesome natural feeling of appreciation of the service of the General Electric Company." [12]

Meanwhile, Maurice Holland of the NRC carried another

message to the leaders of American industry. His mission was to sell the idea of research, and to carry it out he sought advice from friends in the advertising business. As he recounted it in 1976:

"How can we create an image comparative to General Electric, or DuPont where research is the "royal road to riches," I asked. Their answer was "scare them! Make them realize that if they don't use research, their business will lose its markets . . ." With some modifications of format and subject matter, I used the "scare 'em" technique as well as the "success image" in our selling and promotion campaigns.[13]

But the growth in the number of U.S. industrial research laboratories from fewer than 100 before World War I to more than 1,000 by 1929 sprang not just from "scare 'em" or "success image" tactics. It also reflected solid achievements. "Defensive" research—research aimed at protecting established businesses—had helped save the light bulb business for General Electric and the long distance telephone business for AT&T. "Offensive" research—using science to find new product areas for the profitable investment of corporate money and skill—had put GE into the radio business, would help turn Du Pont into a chemistry company instead of a gunpowder company, and would help extend General Motors into fields such as refrigerators, coolants and tetraethyl lead. The exact contribution of industrial research may have been misunderstood. Industrial scientists did not invent light bulbs, long distance telephony, cellophane, radio, or the refrigerator. But they did invent the crucial improvements, such as a ductile tungsten process, wave filters, waterproof cellophane, better vacuum tube amplifiers, and freon refrigerants. These key improvements became the basis for commercial dominance. Industrialists as demanding as Swope of GE and Sloan of GM could understand this truth about industrial research and still maintain their faith in its value.[14]

Whitney himself tried to work closely with those tough, cool industrialists without becoming one of them. His new office in the new laboratory still stood near the entrance on the first floor and still carried the "Come in, rain or shine" sign over the open door. It still adjoined an "unpretentious and business like" work room where he could retreat to carry out an occasional experiment.[15] But the office he entered to begin our hypothetical day's work now held a real executive's desk and real executive's trappings. According to the laboratory's oral tradition, engineer Laurence A. Hawkins had pushed through the redecoration of the office while Whitney was touring Europe in 1923. He had entrusted the details to the laboratory's bookkeeper, L. M. Willey. When Hawkins saw the outcome of Willey's effort, he was appalled. "This looks like a French whorehouse," he is alleged to have remarked. "I'm sure I wouldn't know about that," Willey answered stiffly. "Take my word for it," Hawkins responded.[16]

Whether true or not, the story catches the personalities of two of the laboratory's chief administrators and two of the first people Whitney would talk to in his day's work. Hawkins was a gruff, salty, frank, one-of-the-boys type. His boyish grin, sharp nose, and lank, sandy hair gave him the look of a grown-up Huckleberry Finn. In fact, he held degrees in engineering and law and had a reputation as an excellent bargainer and manager. He not only handled the laboratory's day-to-day administration but also served as its ambassador to the rest of General Electric. Willey's attributes were more limited, and so was his job. He kept the laboratory's books and made most of the decisions on expenditure requests. He had the pursed long face, thinning hair, and suspicious nature expected in an accountant.

The third key administrator of the laboratory held the official title "secretary to Dr. Whitney." But Mary Christie's ability and close relationship to Whitney made her much more than that. Whitney still ran the laboratory according to his 1910 dictum that "the personal comes first, relatively and chronologically," and his 1909 assertion that "the one thing most needful is character, which means integrity, individuality, push, etc." In judging whether his associates possessed those qualities, he relied heavily on her advice. More than one member of the laboratory staff would later credit his promotions to her intervention. Words used to describe her tended toward the superlative: "tremendous efficiency . . . a crack mind . . . tremendous character . . . grit . . . willpower." She ran the office with efficiency and with a sense of humor. The other secretaries of the lab, whose work she supervised, admired her as much as the scientists and engineers did. In a later era, she might have held a title commensurate with the responsibilities she exercised.[17]

Whitney dealt continuously with Hawkins and Christie during the day, but his dealings with Willey were likely to be briefer. The laboratory's bookkeeping method was simple. Each laboratory project had a four-digit number called a shop order attached to it. The shop order served as a record of the expenditures to date on each project. Rough budgeting was done annually to set the expected annual expenditure for each of the shop orders. Willey used them to keep track of whether each was on budget. Upon completion of the project, he determined its total expenditures.

The job of liquidating those expenditures rested mainly with Hawkins. Each year he would visit GE operations and propose that each support research work at the laboratory. That support might come in the form of a general appropriation. A department such as incandescent lamp, which recalled the laboratory's strong past record of achievement, would have confidence that Whitney would do something useful with its money. So the lamp business' contribution would not be dependent on detailed instructions about its use. Other departments, such as turbine, would be more likely to appropriate money for a specific project. Others would listen to Hawkins' request and contribute nothing. A department that did so was taking a gamble. Suppose, to borrow an example from a 1925 letter describing this funding system, that the laboratory proposed that the rectifier department contribute $10,000 toward the development of a tungar (tungsten-argon) rectifier. If the department refused, the laboratory might go ahead and develop the new product anyway. When Hawkins came back to the department with the perfected tungar rectifier, he would now have a completed product rather than a prospect to offer, but the price tag would be higher. Company headquarters would instruct the department to accept and pay for the new product. And company management permitted the laboratory to charge off project development costs to the department that benefited from them. In the tactful words of that 1925 description:

> it will be understood that the laboratory, having shouldered the responsibility, is careful to insure that they do not make any loss over the transaction.[18]

To put it more bluntly, the lab inflated the cost of the successful development by stuffing it with the cost of other less successful ones—the "dead horses," as a later GE research director would describe them. By this tactic, by advance payments, development charges, and by the direct sales of such laboratory products as specialty metals and chemicals, the laboratory met between 75 percent and 95 percent of its annual cost. The rest was made up by a special allocation at the corporate level.[19]

Surviving records do not tell when this system was adopted, but it was in place by the mid 1920s and lasted until 1945. It had the advantage of clear accountability: the portions of the company that benefited most from the laboratory paid its bills. But it had the disadvantage of turning the relationship of the laboratory and the business operation into that of buyer and seller, rather than members of the same team. That disadvantage would later lead to serious development delays while Hawkins and a department manager quibbled over the price tag. But in the 1920s, it appears to have worked. Aided by Hawkins' fund-raising talents, the research laboratory's budget grew from $1.1 million in 1920 to $3.1 million in 1929.[20]

Whitney's discussions with Hawkins on our hypothetical morning would probably concern the broad outlines of research planning. Tactics were Hawkins' job; Whitney dealt with strategy. And probably one of the major strategic issues they would discuss at their morning meeting would be the radio problem.

Langmuir's discoveries, and the circuit and systems work of White and Alexanderson, had led under Whitney's encouragement to a GE business selling vacuum tubes to the Navy during World War I. But when peace came, GE found its hopes to extend the business blocked by patents on the three-element vacuum tube held by AT&T. A complex series of negotiations led in 1919 to the creation of the Radio Corporation of America to hold the pooled GE and AT&T radio patents, to purchase radio equipment from GE, and to sell it to customers. At that time, Whitney and his colleagues thought those customers would mainly be the military and ship owners. But the Westinghouse Electric Company, led by engineer Frank Conrad, appreciated the possibilities of a bigger market: broadcasting. Westinghouse successfully established a pioneering broadcasting station, KDKA in Pittsburgh, and bought up some important patents not yet included in the RCA pool. Using these as leverage, it forced its way into that pool, securing in July 1920, a share of RCA and an agreement that the manufacturing of RCA's radio sets would be split 60 percent to GE and 40 percent to Westinghouse.[21]

The creation of a mass radio receiver market took GE by surprise. As William C. White put it:

It is only natural that many of us in GE at the time feel that we "missed the boat." We knew our electronics but not human nature.[22]

Someone else who knew little about human nature must have designed the 60-40 split in radio receiving manufacturing, for it proved immediately impractical and drew the Research Laboratory deeper into radio set design. The sets were initially produced with GE and Westinghouse trademarks, but they did not sell in the desired proportions. So the companies agreed to design and build a uniform set under the RCA label. Competition in the marketplace vanished, replaced by technical competition between the GE and Westinghouse laboratories over the details of the RCA set. By 1922, standardization was being achieved, with the technical director of RCA, Alfred Goldsmith, assuming the position of arbitrator between the competitors.[23]

Whitney and Hawkins found the radio problem a different, and in some ways a more difficult, challenge than light bulbs. It encompassed not just technology but also consumer tastes, patents, business policies, and organizational changes. On one level, in 1922, GE and the Western Electric arm of AT&T were battling in court on the validity of Langmuir's patents on the high-vacuum tube. On another level, in that same year, leaders of the same companies were negotiating about cooperation between their respective laboratories on future developments. In 1920, GE and AT&T had combined to try to freeze Westinghouse out of radio. By 1923, Hawkins was reporting to Whitney that GE and Westinghouse were working together to circumvent the dominating influence imposed by RCA on radio design. On paper, the GE-RCA-Westinghouse combination might look like a formidable radio patent monopoly. In practice, its weaknesses became evident early. "It seems to be agreed outside that we have the best men and the poorest apparatus of anybody in the radio business," Hawkins wrote to Whitney in November 1922.[24] Aggressive independents such as Philco and Zenith were soon exploiting these weaknesses and claiming growing shares of the market.

In the 1920s Whitney and his superiors learned that research could create a place for GE in the new radio market. It could provide RCA with valuable patents that would bring in large royalties from licensees. But superiority in research alone—"the best men"—was not enough to create a monopoly.

Whitney continued to keep the laboratory's biggest effort aimed at electronics through the 1920s. That effort led to two inventions of major importance. Langmuir found that a filament of tungsten coated with thorium served as an excellent and long-lived source of electrons in a vacuum tube, and these thoriated cathodes achieved wide use in radio transmitters. Albert Hull had been using a specially made vacuum tube with an extra grid in his laboratory work when an alert patent attorney noticed it and suggested that it might be novel, nonobvious, and useful enough to merit patent protection. The resulting invention, the screen grid tube, went into wide use in radio receivers.

A major element of radio business strategy came out of the laboratory's earlier work. General Electric pushed the Langmuir patents on a high-vacuum tube through a twelve-year battle that went all the way to the Supreme Court. GE eventually lost—the court ruled Langmuir's work to be science, not invention. But, as with Weintraub's mercury arc patent applications twenty years earlier, winning was not everything. A temporary victory GE and Langmuir won in the courts in 1925, just as AT&T was about to come back into the radio business, helped convince that company to reverse its policy and stay out. So beside their major value in opening up vacuum tubes for technological development, Langmuir's electronic discoveries also served as a business weapon.[25]

The radio situation bogged down in bureaucratic infighting that eventually saw RCA achieve its complete independence from GE and Westinghouse in 1930 and take over its own manufacturing and research. By then, Whitney and Hawkins shifted the laboratory's effort in another direction. They had long hoped to apply electronics to the transmission and control of electric power, as well as of electrical signals. In 1922 the goal had seemed far off. But in September of that year, Research Laboratory physicist Kenneth Kingdon made a surprising discovery. He learned that a tube filled with cesium vapor at low pressure would carry currents hundreds of times as great as a vacuum tube, at a voltage low enough to be useful in industry. Langmuir immediately analyzed the findings and began to generalize them. "If it all works out as Langmuir now hopes," Hawkins wrote to Whitney, "it does make vacuum tubes an immediate possibility for power purposes, an event which I did not expect for five years at least."[26] It did not work out quite as well as Langmuir had hoped; for technical reasons, cesium tubes never turned out to be practical. But the more general findings that the GE researchers came up with in their subsequent research helped create the new technology of industrial electronics.

Setting priorities for work in this area of radio and electronics would likely be one of the important matters Whitney and Hawkins would discuss together on a typical morning at the laboratory. Whitney might next turn to his mail. His circle of correspondence was wide, and within it his breezy, personalized notes were famous. No General Electric executive was imposing enough to force Whitney to address him in bureaucratese. The manager of the Schenectady Works, George Emmons, ruled his domain with a quiet but formidable authority that rarely brought out the whimsical in subordinates or associates. But when he wrote to Emmons in 1919 to request some groundskeeping improvements, here's the way Whitney put it:

> It is difficult even for me. It might not reduce cost at all. But as prospective purchasers, physicians, Government officials, etc., often visit us for X-ray help and advice, and to see our facilities, they may be somewhat affected by the care and attention we give our general appearance. That is why I shave daily, pay laundry bills for collars (which I hate to wear) and wash my face in the morning. I cannot approximately estimate the saving in cost; though I think some economy exists. In this particular case, you now have in front of a very good looking set of office and plant buildings, a bad looking collection of old trucks which might all take on a look of respectability if the foremost and worst of them were slicked up. It is like removing a wart from an otherwise beautiful face. I intend to live on without this improvement if it is necessary, so that I may kick later about something else.[27]

That excerpt catches the tone of the Whitney correspondence: highly personal, expressed in the first person, full of colloquial terms and figures of speech. But Whitney's advice was serious, and his colleagues in GE management learned to listen to it. The manager of the GE refrigerator department, Theodore Quinn, recalled a letter he got from Whitney in 1925, just as GE's first mass-marketed domestic refrigerator was about to go on sale. "Dr. Whitney's breezy letter to me started something like this," Quinn recalled: 'Dear Ted, here's telling you how to run your business.' He went on to say that he knew nothing about manufacturing or selling, but 'damn it,' he had seen many a 'perfect product' prove 'imperfect'." Whitney suggested that the product be test marketed in the Schenectady area. That way, if its technologically sophisticated cooling system met with problems, the units could be brought back to the Schenectady plant "to admire them." Quinn followed Whitney's advice. A high proportion of the initial models did break down. The engineers at Schenectady who admired them learned how to improve their reliability enough that the eventual product (on which Quinn placed one of the first warranties in the history of the appliance business) proved a spectacular commercial success.[28]

Further correspondence might be addressed to one of his physical chemistry colleagues, such as Frederick G. Donnan in London or Lash Miller in Toronto. Whitney still kept in touch with other alumni of Leipzig, even though he no longer carried out research in their field. His current technical interests merged with his hobbies. Topics of letters in the early 1920s included entomology, oak tree galls, the role of oxygen in disease, and a request for the latest book on proteins. He rarely wrote to or heard from his Jamestown friends. A visit with one of them left Whitney with "the thought that I had dropped out of life about 20 years ago."[29] His mail was now full of requests for advice, either from professional colleagues seeking to fill positions or promote new organizations or from members of the public seeking his endorsement for their ideas on vivisection or spiritualism. There were requests for money too. At any time in the mid-1920s, Whitney was likely to be supporting the college education of two or three young engineers or scientists, either with loans or outright gifts. And as a trustee of Schenectady's Union College, he would be sending out appeals for money to upgrade that school's science and engineering curricula.[30]

Whitney treated his correspondence seriously and tried to give each letter a personal touch. But he was not the kind of executive who could spend all day in his office writing letters, holding meetings, and talking over strategy with his closest associates. The part of his day he most valued came when he got out of the office for his daily tour of the laboratory.

Getting around and talking personally with every researcher was getting to be a bigger effort. In 1920, the total employment of the laboratory passed the 300 mark, and after a brief setback in the 1921 recession, it began to climb again: to 392 by 1927, and then, in the economic boom, all the way to 535 in 1929. Just under half the employees were salaried workers. Most of the rest were laborers in the shops or on some of the small prototype assembly lines the lab maintained. Visiting even the 180 salaried staff members regularly in 1925 would have been a formidable undertaking. But talking with all of them was not necessary. The salaried staff included many people who had been promoted because of valued services to the laboratory in areas such as glass blowing or chemical analysis but who were not carrying out research. There were actually some 70 research scientists and engineers on the laboratory staff in 1925. Of them, about 20 would hold the degree of Ph.D. About the same number (though not exactly the same list of people) would actually be planning and carried out independent research. Whitney made a point of talking regularly with people on all levels of the laboratory, especially the highly valued craftsmen in the machine and glass shops. But the 20 or so real researchers were the main target of his daily tours.[31]

So, by late in the morning of a typical work day, Whitney's "are you having fun" would echo down the halls of the laboratory building. Ceramist Louis Navais remembered how he could hear Dr. Whitney coming a long way off and how much bigger he seemed than his average stature (5' 10'') and weight (165 pounds). Electrical engineer Willem Westendorp recalls

Whitney stopping him in a corridor or on the stairs for long conversations on wide-ranging topics. The sound of the director coming was a signal to look busy and put out cigarettes. Whitney hated the sight of anyone reading a newspaper, and he forbade smoking. He also made sure that all the laboratory followed his open-door policy by a simple tactic. He ordered a carpenter to remove all doors from the laboratory rooms.[32]

The laboratory's scientific reputation rested on the fundamental discoveries and inventions of its chemists and physicists. But most of the people Whitney visited on his daily tour worked on more immediate problems and represented other disciplines. For example, mechanical engineers Al Kimball and John Newkirk were helping Wilfrid Campbell of the turbine department explain why the metal disks at the heart of GE's largest turbines were breaking with alarming frequency. Chemist George M. J. McKay would probably have a new wire insulation compound under test. Electrical engineer Chester W. Rice, the son of laboratory cofounder E. W. Rice, was carrying out experiments to try out an idea of Whitney's that appeared to have great promise for large electrical generators. In 1921, Whitney had asked Rice to try a "fool stunt" of operating a generator in an atmosphere of hydrogen rather than air. The lighter molecules of hydrogen, he expected, would turn out to be far more effective in carrying off heat. Rice's careful experiments would prove the value of the idea—which, it turned out was already being perfected in Germany. By the 1930s, it would become an important innovation in electric power equipment.[33]

Most of the projects Whitney looked in on were of this direct, down-to-earth nature. Chemist Charles Van Brunt was developing a method of reclaiming engine oil. Metallurgist William Ruder was empirically testing levels of addition of silicon to steel to get the best "soft" magnetic material for use in transformers and motors. Mechanical engineer Emory Gilson was perfecting a new bearing material called Genelite. Most of the researchers working on these projects used empirical methods that Whitney himself favored. The microscope remained a major research tool for them. Ceramist Louis Navais, for example, relied heavily on it for his work on electrically insulating ceramics. Metallurgist Samuel Hoyt claims that Whitney hired him away from the GE lamp department not so much for his skills but for his beautiful Bausch and Lomb metallographic microscope.[34] Another metallurgist, Truman Fuller, carried on microscope studies of the corrosion of iron and used them to coauthor one of Whitney's few scientific papers of the 1920s.

Fuller typified the type of staff member Whitney liked to hire. His education had ended with a bachelor's degree in chemistry, but he had taught himself metallurgy at the GE Lamp Works. He willingly tackled any of the troubleshooting problems that came his way, relying more on inventiveness and persistence than on advanced theories. His cherubic appearance and outgoing good humor made him a natural end man for the laboratory's minstrel show. And, like Whitney, he disliked pretense, snobbishness, and sloth. Fuller loved to tell the story of an office-mate in the laboratory in the early 1920s, a stuffy, fastidious Englishman from MIT, who insisted on taking a regular afternoon nap. One afternoon, Fuller made sure that Whitney's visit to their office came at nap time; Whitney observed the sleeping scientist but said nothing. Unfortunately, when he awoke, the man chose that day to go down to see Whitney about a raise. Instead, Fuller recounts, he returned from Whitney's office with his dismissal notice.[35]

Whitney kept track of these people and projects using only the crudest handwritten organization charts. A surviving example from 1927 breaks the lab down into two main categories. On one side is "engineering research," and under it is a list of experts, each matched up with his specialty: "White responsible for radio tubes," "Mackay responsible for insulation," and so on. On the other side is a category called "general research," divided into two parts. One list of names, headed by Langmuir, includes most of the lab's physicists. The other, headed by Coolidge, is a collection of physicists, engineers, and chemists attacking problems ranging from refrigerators to cathode rays.[36]

Like his organization chart, Whitney's methods of managing research remained informal and unsystematized. As he had proposed to do in 1908, he mainly sought to provide the stimulus that would help a researcher plan his own work and solve his own problems. Whitney might come in, rest his elbows on the lab bench, watch the work for a while, and then bet the researcher a nickel that some different idea might work. If the researcher seemed bogged down, Whitney would try to get him to start talking to explain exactly what he had been trying and to detail exactly where the procedure seemed to go wrong. As Whitney explained years later:

> I've tried this experiment many times. I ask a fellow in the lab "what fun are you having now" I know by the look I get that he is swamped in the gloom of uncertainty mixed with tiny spots of hope. What good can I do listening to his last month's successes? It is the current wall of impenetrable fog which is painfully in his mind. So I have found (by his teaching me) that he is apt to "come out of it" if any ignorant cuss makes him slowly and *completely* tell his troubles. That's me. He begins often like this—"I was fine last week, then suddenly (or gradually) things got bad. Couldn't repeat it at all. Tried fresh stock, new materials, different technique. Did exactly what my notes say I did before, but there's some bug somewhere." This goes on until suddenly I am sure I see an interruption (maybe I hear it, as I do during my soap-radio program, when the cook turns on some light in the remote kitchen). In neurology you can't expect complete remoteness in a man. It may occur to him that he forgot to "spit on the bait." About then I go away.[37]

Whitney would emphasize that a research director is far too "external" to the actual scientific work to supply any useful detailed advice. "All I could supply was a listener, a sort of homeopathic surgeon," he concluded.

> I am growing certain that what research men who are stuck at the moment (or for a month) need is someone not only willing

to listen but actually to *start* a conversation and steer it into paths favorable for auto-catalysis.

This active element in Whitney's method should be stressed. He came not just to listen but also to start a conversation and steer it into productive directions. His role as "homeopathic surgeon" was not a passive one. Nor did it preclude him from other more traditional management jobs, however subtly and diplomatically he carried them out. The researcher may have had nearly complete control over how he conducted his work. But Whitney had decisive influence on both the target of the project and its pace. As he toured the laboratory, he was reviewing the state of the laboratory's sixty or so projects and deciding on their fate. Each year about ten of them would be terminated and about ten new ones begun.[38]

High turnover among new projects became an important part of his management method. Since the laboratory had to absorb the cost of its failures, Whitney wanted to find out quickly and inexpensively if a new idea showed promise. That meant beginning a lot of projects and terminating most of them within a few years of inception. "I am accustomed to buying and selling wholesale," he wrote in 1928:

> We may grow a peach and sell it with the gooper feathers on it, but sometimes we grow a green lemon that we "sour" fully and quietly digest . . . I can get exact figures to match my estimates, but they are entirely misleading unless they include ten lemons to each peach.[39]

The exact figures do match Whitney's estimates, though his emphasis is slightly misleading. Only one in ten may have been a peach, but most of the other nine were probably "potboilers," not lemons. In the year 1923, for example, the laboratory launched nine new projects. Most began on a small scale, less that $5,000 in expenses for the first year's work. They ranged from less than $100 on tungsten contacts to $34,000 on bearings and lubrication. Within two years, only four remained on the lab's list. In some cases, such as a project on aluminum castings, the job had been only temporary. In others, such as an idea for making phosphoric acid, a new proposal had been tried briefly and inexpensively and then dropped. Over the next five years, two more of the projects, both involving assistance to GE operations, were terminated. That left only two ongoing efforts by 1929. One of them was a continuing project of assistance to GE's power transmission department on high-tension cables. The other was the "peach": the invention of methods for making vacuum tubes out of metal instead of glass. The metal tubes were eventually introduced as a product in 1934 and enjoyed enormous success.[40]

Funding on that metal vacuum tube project had grown rapidly. When the first year's investigation showed promise, the budget rose from $1,500 to more than $60,000 for the second year and then averaged to more than $100,000 a year for the next five years. To bet that much money on a likely winner required taking some away from the apparent losers and not tying up too much of the lab's resources on potboilers. As Whitney toured the laboratory, serving as homeopathic surgeon and making sure people were having fun, he gathered the information needed to make these decisions.

He did not delegate the decisions to his subordinates. "Coolidge and Langmuir are assistant directors," Whitney wrote in 1923, "but the office boy does more nearly what the so-called director does."[41] With Hawkins' administrative help, Whitney clearly and decisively ran the laboratory.

His daily tour almost always included visits to the four scientists who had emerged as leaders of the laboratory, Saul Dushman, Albert Hull, Langmuir, and Coolidge. Dushman, with his bald head, round-rimmed glasses, and ever-present pipe in defiance of Whitney's smoking ban, looked the absent-minded theorist. He fancied becoming one too but actually enjoyed more success as an experimenter. When he had come to the laboratory, he was completely under the sway of the antiatomic ionist viewpoint that his teacher W. Lash Miller of Toronto had learned from Ostwald at Leipzig. But under Langmuir's guidance he had come to believe in electrons. And by the 1920s, he was even taking a step beyond Langmuir and working with the quantum theory. Whitney, who had some interest in but little understanding of these new ideas, was steering Dushman back to the more practical areas of lamps and vacuum tubes where he could make a solider experimental contribution.[42]

Hull had also briefly made a sortie into pure physics. In 1916, inspired by a remark made at a Research Lab colloquium by visiting British physicist William H. Bragg, he had independently discovered a method of determining the crystal structure of powdered material by X-rays. After the war, he proposed to continue this X-ray crystallography work. But when he discussed the idea with Whitney and Langmuir, neither was enthusiastic. They suggested that simply perfecting and extending an experimental technique would be unlikely to lead to anything new and important. Hull took the hint and turned back to his other specialty, the invention of new vacuum tubes. When Whitney came by on his daily round, he would likely find Hull's spare frame sprawled in an office chair rather than at the laboratory bench, sketching new ideas for vacuum tubes to be built by an assistant.[43]

Langmuir had also toyed with fundamental issues of the structure of matter before 1920 but like Hull had turned back to get his feet on the more familiar ground of surface chemistry and the physics of discharge tubes. His self-confidence had been reinforced by a decade of triumphs: invention of the gas-filled lamp and the high-vacuum tube, major discoveries in surface chemistry, and contributions to the octet theory of valence (the explanation of chemical bonding as the tendency of atoms and molecules to seek a stable outer shell of eight electrons). He had continued his surface studies using films of oil on water to study layers only one molecule thick. But he remained involved in the practical problems of the laboratory and subject to Whitney's managerial decisions. In 1920 he had undertaken fundamental work on the ways mixtures of ions and electrons behave at low pressures (transferring in the process the word "plasma" from biology to physics to refer to such mixtures). This work supported the laboratory's efforts to develop electronic devices capable of handling large amounts of power. He worked on this problem for eight years and produced important knowledge of the way the operation of such devices was controlled by the formation of a sheath of positive ions around a negative electrode. But his assistant recalls that Langmuir's eminence did not deter Whitney from taking the project away from him and turning it over to Hull, who was more likely to perfect a useful invention. Hull did, in fact, build on Langmuir's ideas and help GE introduce its version of the thyratron, one of the first electronic tubes suitable for high-power industrial uses.[44]

When Whitney reached Langmuir's office on his daily rounds, he would probably meet Samuel Sweetser, who still built apparatus and carried out experiments at Langmuir's direction. Sweetser had been joined by two young physicists. Harold Mott-Smith performed detailed calculations to flesh out Langmuir's theories on plasmas. Katharine Blodgett, who had recently returned from Britain's Cavendish Laboratory with the first doctorate in physics ever earned by a woman there, collaborated with Langmuir on surface chemistry. Langmuir came and went when he pleased, and at the time Whitney arrived at his laboratory room in the morning he would as likely be at his second home up at Lake George as at the desk or lab bench analyzing the latest experiments or calculations. Toward most colleagues, Langmuir continued to exhibit an icy indifference, representing not dislike but simply absorbtion in his own work. Only with one of the few whose intelligence he respected—such as Whitney—would the warmth of his enthusiasm occasionally break through the frozen surface.[45]

Failing to find Langmuir in, Whitney would likely move on to see Coolidge, who always showed up on time, even after his achievements had earned him the right to be late or stay home. He was still "Cool" to Whitney—the only nickname employed when the four leaders of the laboratory spoke to one another. The name still fit. His Yankee reserve gave no hint that the triumphs of the past fifteen years had been mixed with sadness and strain: the death of his young wife, the weariness of long days in court undergoing tough cross-examination in defense of his tungsten patent. "It is of great importance that Dr. Coolidge should be well and strong when he has to go on the stand in Toronto in the fall," patent attorney Albert G. Davis had written Whitney in 1922.

> In the weak and nervous condition in which he was when he gave his last testimony in that case he might have made a most unfavorable impression on the court and since the issue in the case is very largely a question of his veracity and recollection as distinguished from Dr. Fink's, it is of utmost importance that the impression which he makes should be good.[46]

Like Langmuir, Coolidge had earned a freedom to work on pure science of his choice, and he exercised it by developing high-energy electron accelerators and studying the effects of the fast moving particles. But he too responded willingly when Whitney came around with a more practical problem. For example, after Whitney's letter to Theodore Quinn had helped keep GE refrigerator problems close to home, Whitney had tapped Coolidge to lead a team of scientists through the refrigerator manufacturing plant to look for possible process improvements. This mixture of science and applications offered at GE continued to suit Coolidge. He turned down offers to direct other laboratories and remained Whitney's quiet, reticent, productive assistant director.[47]

Among the five leaders of the laboratory, then, there remained respect, mutual loyalty, and an unspoken understanding of research priorities. Whitney, for all his come-in-rain-or-shine cheerfulness, had no hesitation about asserting his executive prerogatives when the situation demanded it. A story illustrating this comes down through the laboratory's oral tradition via a chemist who joined the staff in the early 1930s. It describes a situation where Whitney found himself opposed on an issue by Langmuir, Hull, Coolidge, and Dushman. Whitney allegedly looked at the four of them and proclaimed: "this laboratory has two assistant directors, and two associate directors, but only one director, and what he says goes." Whether things really happened this way or not, the story certainly reflects the way the staff perceived the relationship among its five most eminent members.[48]

The relations among the five also reflected their personalities. Langmuir, Coolidge, and Hull all embodied the endothermic nature popularly associated with their Scotch and Yankee roots. Dushman, like Whitney, was more the exothermic type. But the energy he gave off came mixed with a bit of pomposity. Whitney loved to puncture it, and the quarrels between the two were not always in fun. The five leaders understood each other and worked together in harmony. But they went their own ways.

After his tour of the laboratory, Whitney's way typically took him to lunch at Schenectady's most exclusive men's club, the Mohawk Club. Most likely it was a business lunch, perhaps entertaining a visitor who had spent the morning on his own tour of the laboratory. From the time of its inception, the Research Laboratory had been a company showplace, where prominent visitors such as Walther Rathenau, scion of the founder of the German counterpart electrical manufacturing firm AEG, were taken to be shown that General Electric put a strong emphasis on scientific research. The guest list came to include the leaders of world science, too, including William H. Bragg, Ernest Rutherford, J. J. Thomson, Madame Curie, and Paul Ehrenfest.[49]

These visits helped spread around the world the laboratory's image as a model for the performance of science in industry. Writing to Whitney in the mid-1920s from Rutherford's laboratory at Cambridge, a physicist from Schenectady's Union College noted:

> You can understand how tickled a Schenectadian is when Rutherford refers, as he frequently does, to the Research Laboratory of the General Electric Company and names its leading men. Hardly a lecture passes, certainly no week passes, without one or more such references.[50]

A few years earlier, Rutherford's former colleague, chemist Frederick Soddy, had said in a public address that "some of

the finest research in pure physical science that is being produced today emenates from the General Electric Company's
Research Laboratories at Schenectady, New York." And evidence that the GE example exerted influence on the continent
shows up in a 1922 letter from the Dutch physicist Balthazar
Van Der Pol to British colleague Edward Appleton. Discussing
a job offer he recently received from the Philips Company,
Van Der Pol writes: "new laboratories are being built in the
American G.E.C. fashion . . . my job would be wholly independent of the works. Working in this general scientific way
already pays. They have the example of Langmuir."[51]

Whitney's direct contact with these European leaders did not
necessarily involve discussion of the major issues of world science. When theorist Paul Ehrenfest came to Schenectady in
1923, for example, he asked Whitney to locate for him the inventors of the snapless fastener and the Van Heusen collar, so
Ehrenfest could gaze on the face of men capable of making
such epochal inventions. (Whitney did, and the visits were a
great success.) Ehrenfest retained an appreciation of Whitney's accomplishments and approach to research. As Ehrenfest wrote a few years later, concerning a Whitney speech published in *Science*.

> I am so wholeheartedly grateful to you for saying simply and
> forcefully that we do not know the sense and value of research.
> In contrast to the self-assured rationalization which has such great
> power in the world and which threatens so much of the finest
> in our youth, it is splendid that a man who has accomplished
> what you have, and who, in such a respectable position always
> simply and warmly smilingly says: "oh, let us admit honestly to
> one another that precisely the most valuable, truest and most
> faithful is accomplished by us when our work is filled with the
> self forgetting seriousness that is found in its purest form in the
> solitary play of a child."[52]

These European contacts served an important purpose to
Whitney and General Electric. The Company still followed the
lead taken in Europe in both science and technology. Its agents
in Europe sent back a stream of reports on the latest Euro-

pean inventions and discoveries. And at almost any time in the 1920s at least one member of the laboratory's staff was touring Europe's outstanding laboratories. And Whitney thought even more was needed. "I want a man like myself, you, Coolidge, or Langmuir, here in Berlin half the time," he wrote to Hawkins in 1923.[53]

When Whitney wrote that letter, he was on his first European trip in seventeen years. It contrasted sharply with his previous visit in 1906, when he went to bargain over metal filament lamp patents. This time he took a leisurely tour of the great laboratories from London to Berlin and got a warm welcome at each stop. And at each stop, he collected hints for future work and suggestions for future collaboration. At the Cavendish Laboratory, Whitney looked on with fascination as C. T. R. Wilson demonstrated his apparatus for following the course of atomic collisons by the vapor trails they left in a cloud chamber. He ordered a model for his own laboratory. Then he negotiated with Rutherford an agreement whereby General Electric provided a small stipend to support research. Whitney had hoped to support the work of a single individual, but Rutherford insisted on having the money with no strings attached.[54]

Following a number of other British visits, it was off to the continent. In Paris, Whitney visited Madame Curie's laboratory to view experiments on the effects of X-rays on cells. Madame Curie had long been a recipient of gifts of GE electronic equipment, and she too would get more research support following this visit. And as Whitney mingled with scientific leaders, he also collected technological hints. "My view of the talking movie has also entirely changed since I saw Gaumont's work on them," Whitney wrote from Paris. "It is only a question of a short time when they will be common." In the succeeding years, work on talking movies at Schenectady picked up markedly, leading to the invention of a movie sound system by 1927. A dynamic loudspeaker under development in France also drew Whitney's interest. He sent back to Coolidge a description, a sketch, and the note "you might tell Chester

R. about this. Two years later, Chester Rice and his colleague Edward Kellog unveiled their own dynamic speaker. It went on to replace the earphones and horn that had previously been standard for RCA's radio sets. On across the continent, Whitney observed work that either suggested new paths or confirmed the views of the engineers back in Schenectady. The wireless picture transmission work being done by Belin in Paris paralleled Alexanderson's efforts in the direction of facsimile and television. The hermetically sealed refrigerator system with a cylindrical compressor on top that Whitney saw at the Escher-Wyss Company in Switzerland bears a close resemblance to the refrigeration system that GE introduced in the United States two years later. And advances in the design of mercury rectifiers at the Swiss Company Brown-Boveri suggested new directions for GE.[55]

But the highlight of Whitney's 1923 trip was his return to Germany. That nation presented two faces to the world. On one side, Germany continued to lead the world in advanced science and technology. "It's perfectly clear to me now," Whitney wrote Hawkins in April 1923, "that Germany is still, in spite of all its crimes and troubles, the most active in learning and in doing new things of any country." At the same time, a spiraling inflation had begun to threaten the income of Germany's scientists, many of whom were on fixed salaries at universities or state research institutes. The scientists, Whitney wrote Hawkins "are only half a stage above beggars, and three stages below artisans and it isn't right." He mingled with the leaders of Berlin's scientific community ("Einstein talked very interestingly about local politics. . . . Nernst was very friendly as were all the others"). A picture of the plight of German science and the possible contribution General Electric might make to helping relieve it began to emerge.[56]

Under Germany's Weimar Republic, support of scientific research came from two main sources: a union of institutions of research called the *Notgemeinschaft der Deutschen Wissenschaft* (NGW) and an association of large industrial firms, the Helmholz *Gesellschaft*. Although the NGW contributed about four times as much as the industrial fund, the support of the industrialists had become valued by the scientists, particularly as inflation and political instability mounted. "The rapprochement between industrialists and academics was part of a tacit social and political alliance," historial Paul Forman has written. "Both groups felt threatened by the new political order."[57]

Whitney remained impressed with the high morale of the investigators he observed, whether it was pure research, such as the studies being made by Freundlich at the new Astrophysical Laboratory at Potsdam to test Einstein's concepts of the red shift, or the more applied studies of young chemists Michael Polanyi and Hermann Mark on single crystals of zinc, tin, and aluminum. (GE made repeated efforts over the next few years to attract Polanyi's interest in part-time industrial research but never succeeded. Polanyi would later write: "You cannot serve two masters; you must choose between dedication to the advancement of knowledge, which requires freedom, or the pursuit of applied science, which requires subordination.")[58] By the end of March 1923, Whitney had decided that General Electric ought to help fund German science. Support of applied research of benefit to GE appeared to be a good investment, since the exchange rate of currencies had reached more than 20,000 marks to the dollar. "Buildings are here, apparatus is here, mechanics and offices are here," Whitney wrote Hawkins on April 1: "What would have to be paid for good scientific workers will be very small in proportion to the value of the results."[59]

But Whitney wanted to do more than merely gain immediate advantages from temporary German distress. He also wanted General Electric to contribute to the support of the foundations of German science—as he put it: "keeping alive, through hard times, those purely scientific undertakings and those young workers who have no company back of them." A precedent already existed. A Japanese industrialist, Hajime Hoshi, was donating $1,000 a month to help support scientific work in physical chemistry, and the money was doled out to applicants by a committee that included Haber and physicist Max Planck.[60]

Whitney and Rice, who had accompanied him to Berlin, considered two approaches to research support: the specific grant to fund applied work of commercial interest and the general grant to help keep German science healthy. They recommended that GE do both. They negotiated with Nernst to fund studies on the breakdown of wire insulation. And in cooperation with the major German incandescent lamp manufacturers, General Electric contributed $12,500 per year to the support of "pure electro-physical research" through a committee that included Planck, Haber, Nernst, and Max von Laue.[61]

Whitney returned to the United States in mid-1923 with the satisfaction of having made at least a small gesture toward aiding the scientific community that had provided him with a scientific education and that had given the world so many advances in knowledge and invention. Back at Schenectady, over the next few years, the thank you letters would come in. Max Planck would write in appreciation of "your generous contributions to German research in the field of electrophysics." Dr. Heinrich Luders of the Prussian Academy of Sciences would add his gratitude. And Fritz Haber would describe the gift as "the helping hand which came when we were most glad to grasp it."[62]

So by the mid-1920s, the scientific and personal contributions of the General Electric Research Laboratory and Whitney had made them known throughout the world of science. Whitney's luncheon that hypothetical day in the mid-1920s might turn into an informal reception for prominent visitors and reflect this stature. But after lunch, it was back to the office and back to the business of the General Electric Company.

Whitney's office door remained open to people throughout that company, not just to the staff of the Research Laboratory. Through that door came manufacturing engineers from the Works in need of troubleshooting help, inventors and designers with new ideas, and company executives up to and including the company's president, Gerard Swope.

The high mutual regard Whitney and Swope held for each other traced back to their days as instructor and student in an

MIT chemistry class in 1893. Swope had graduated as an electrical engineer and gone to work for the Western Electric Company in Chicago. There he quickly revealed a talent for administration and organization. He also lived and worked at the Hull House Settlement and married one of its residents, Mary Hill. His progressive tendencies—his concern about employee health, for example—stood in strong contrast to the conservative tendencies of the old-line General Electric management when he joined that company in 1918. Swope still stood out as an anomaly when he accepted the GE presidency in 1923. But in Whitney he had an ally.[63]

Whitney admired Swope's skill at organization and administration. It fit his elitist views that any large entity, whether a company or a country, ought to be run by expert specialists, not by committees or elected representatives. "Nowadays, the specialist dominates every part of the business," Whitney wrote in an admiring portrait of Swope he published in MIT's *Technology Review* in 1922.

Swope epitomized the emerging specialist in management. And he, in turn, both respected Whitney's skill at managing research and warmed to him as a person. The letters from Swope to Whitney became progressively friendlier in tone from 1923 through 1933, the salutation evolving from "Dear Dr. Whitney" to "Dear Old Doc," and the content coming to include a standing monthly lunch invitation in New York and an invitation for Whitney and Evelyn to spend a weekend at the Swope home at Storm King.

Swope rarely burdened letters with insincere gestures. When he wrote Whitney in 1928 that "as I have often said to you, the outstanding quality which endears you to everyone is that you are such a fine human being, irrespective of your qualities and attributes in other directions," he probably meant it. His public references were even more flattering. "Willis R. Whitney, head of our research department, a Tech boy of '90, is worth more to the General Electric Company than I am, even if I do get a larger salary," Swope told a group of MIT alumni in 1923.[64]

On Whitney's side, the respect and regard created a strong sense of loyalty. As he wrote to Hawkins from Berlin in 1923:

> I've also decided during my hours of worry over here, to work for the *Co.* and to back Mr. Swope as long as he is pres. (this is strictly for you). His job is a *white whale.*[65]

Swope made occasional visits to the laboratory but seldom personally intervened in lab policy. Describing a visit of Rice and Swope to the laboratory in September 1925, Whitney noted "latter in general o.k.'d what I had in mind."[66] Whitney, in turn, visited New York to sit on the advisory council, a group of top company leaders that advised Swope on major business matters. But he seldom added his voice to the council's deliberations. That advisory council was the most important of dozens of committees that permeated GE's centralized organizational structure, providing forums where strong-minded leaders of the company's main functional specialties, sales, engineering, finance, and manufacturing, could thrash out their differences. Whitney belonged to many of these committees. He served as a conciliating force on them, helping to cool off individuals such as mechanical engineer W. L. R. Emmet, who was likely to explode with impatience at committee procedures, walk angrily from the meeting, and then write Whitney the next day:

> What I said was all nonsense. I like every man on that committee and particularly you. . . . I have always been galled by the waste and stupidity I see about me.[67]

The waste and stupidity that became evident at committee meetings may have galled Whitney too. We have already heard his view that "committees cannot invent, and responsibility divided is as good as shifted." But he kept his temper and his sense of humor at such meetings and kept the admiration and respect of the GE executives who sat alongside him there. Though many testimonials attest to this respect, solider evidence does also. By 1925 Whitney received a salary of $20,000 a year, a very large one for the times. Less than 1 percent of all Americans made as much, and certainly few if any scientists did. In addition, he was one of about 500 of GE's valued employees to be included in an incentive compensation plan that paid a bonus varying with GE's profitability. By the mid-1920s, that bonus added about another $13,000 to his pay.[68]

The basis for Whitney's highly respected position in the company went beyond his sunny disposition and the growing scientific reputation of his laboratory. In the 1920s the work of the laboratory provided a foundation for the most profitable business of General Electric, the lamp business. And the patents on the laboratory's inventions served as a bulwark against those who would try to reduce the profitability of that business by application of the antitrust laws.

In 1922, for example, the formidable investigating lawyer Samuel Untermeyer directed the attention of New York State's Lockwood commission to the GE lamp business. He asserted that General Electric controlled, directly or indirectly, 95 percent of the U.S. lamp business and enjoyed a profit amounting to 34 percent of sales on that business. That meant lamps accounted for only one-fifth of GE's sales in 1920 but more than two-thirds of its profits. Appearing for GE, vice president Anson W. Burchard did not dispute Untermeyer's figures, remarking only that 1920 had been an unusually bad year in the nonlamp businesses. But GE's spokesman to the press had another answer. "The company does a large part of the incandescent lamp business" he explained

> only because the public demands the efficient tungsten lamps which are the result of the extensive work of the General Electric laboratories.[69]

Confident that GE's business strength in lamps rested on patented, legally protected technology, GE challenged the government to investigate the situation. The government did. The case made its way to the Supreme Court, where GE won a resounding victory. Speaking for the court, in 1926, Chief Justice William Howard Taft concluded:

The (General) Electric Company is the holder of three patents—one of 1912 to Just and Hanaman, the basic patent for the use of tungsten filaments in the manufacture of electric lamps; the Coolidge patent of 1913, covering a process of manufacturing tungsten filaments by which their tensile strength and endurance are greatly increased; and third, the Langmuir patent of 1916, which is for the use of gas in a bulb by which the intensity of the light is substantially heightened. These three patents cover completely the making of the modern electric lights with the tungsten filament, and secure to the (General) Electric Company the monopoly of their making, using, and vending.[70]

Resting on this contribution to the defense of GE's profitability, Whitney commanded respect from GE colleagues, whether or not they approved of the personalized brand of management he exercised.

Whitney welcomed visitors and valued opportunities to learn more about GE needs. But he was probably also glad when they left, for he valued the time he could spare, perhaps late in the afternoon of our hypothetical day at the office, for his own experimental work. Keeping to his determination not to compete with his researchers, that work typically involved subjects related only remotely, if at all, to General Electric's immediate business interests. For example, in 1925 he directed his personal assistant Albert Page to build apparatus for a study of electrolysis of water into hydrogen and oxygen by means of light-assisted reaction. He also was carrying out what he called "fool stunts on the age of flints"—heating arrowheads to a high temperature and testing whether their resulting color changes correlated with their age. This would have been a valuable tool for archaeologists if it had worked, but apparently it never did.[71]

Such "fool stunts" might occupy Whitney up to the close of the work at 5:00. But as he got into his Ford and drove out of the Schenectady Works, he did not necessarily head for his Niskayuna home. He might instead have a dinner and speaking engagement before a local civic or professional organization. Both local and national organizations sought Whitney's presence on the podium. The appearances enabled him to present his views on research and its uses to the public and to keep up and extend his acquaintance with leaders of science, business, and the professions.

Whitney's speeches do not read as well as they sounded. His enthusiasm brought ideas to life that, in print, often look forced or trite. The addresses rarely developed a theme in organized fashion. This was a consequence of Whitney's method of putting them together. He would not start from an outline or plan but would instead assemble in his memorandum book or commonplace book some anecdotes, analogies, or assertions. When the day of the speech came, he would link them together into a chain of thoughts of about the right length and present them. In print, fragments sometimes generate interest, but the whole speech rarely sustains it.

His primary message proclaimed the glory of research. "As architects or sculptors or hewers of stone we may be retrogressing, and in any selected development we may have passed zeniths," he told an audience of chemists in 1921:

> but all the time the knowledge of the universe and of each atom in it, from the tiny flower of the crannied wall to the sun which brings it forth and the stars which so immensely exceed this, has been rapidly increasing. The only perpetual motion is the growth of truth.[72]

"I should identify the search for scientific truth," he went on to say in the same talk, "with the highest religious aim, no matter what the cult." But research was more than religion. It was service to the public, carried out by corporations at a risk, and often at a loss. "The public always wins," he told a 1928 audience of businessmen, "but the company supporting research, much like the unfortunate inventor of the past, may still suffer in some cases.

> For example, the atomic or inherent energy of a drop of oil properly utilized, would be sufficient to drive the engines of a liner for a complete transatlantic trip. Suppose some research laboratory made the feat possible, it is still a question whether

the discovery would yield anything to the company which supported the research. Many reasons for such failure might be found, both in the actions of the owners and in those of their competitors. But there is one sure winner, and his name is public.[73]

Whitney believed thoroughly in the established United States system of large-scale business organization. Big business meant big research, and big research meant big benefits for the public. "I have always wanted about five minutes time before a good audience far removed from my own home town, and near the brain center of the United States," he began a 1922 speech fragment,

> in which to speak a little piece of my own composition. It is in favor of American trusts and large corporations. Without them this country would soon become third class in interest and industry. With their help, as I see it, the upper limit to our advance in knowledge and in appreciation of old and new laws of nature will be the elasticity of our collected or selected activities.[74]

Whitney's platform message, then, was simple. Research is religion and good business combined, and the organization that supports it, the giant corporation, is doing a public service. Seldom in the 1920s did Whitney present detailed descriptions of his management methods or of the payoffs from GE research, the subjects of his speeches in 1909–1915. He rarely mentioned national defense, his preoccupation in 1916–17. No longer did he campaign at the podium for government support of science, as he had done in 1917–1920. He had become an after-dinner philosopher, quoting Francis Bacon, Franklin, Emerson, and John Burroughs and embodying through his own enthusiasm the spirit of research.

And when he stepped down after the speech to mix with his audience, Whitney exercised another of his important roles, that of scientific statesman. He remained a leader of the maturing old guard of American chemistry, the group that included Little, Baekeland, Bancroft, Charles H. Herty, Floyd L. Parsons, and Noyes. He occupied a special position among them, partly for his integrity. "Whitney does not need a code of Ethics, no more than he needs a police code, or any code of laws, or a ready made religion," Baekeland had written to Little in 1915. And Whitney also commanded respect for his technical judgment. Floyd Parsons alleges that the adoption in the United States of the Casale process, one of the main variants of the Haber process of nitrogen fixation, resulted largely from the positive verdict Whitney gave when the backers asked for his opinion.[75]

Whitney's sociability got exercised mainly at these dinners and speaking engagements. On other evenings he probably did not visit or entertain. Instead, he preferred a quiet evening at home. In spring or summer, he took advantage of the evening light to pursue his experimental hobbies: growing a corn crop through holes in plastic sheets placed on the ground as a labor-saving method of killing weeds; stimulating the swelling of a plant gall by induction heating of bits of iron imbedded in a tree branch; or simply observing the activities of a colony of ants in a large anthill beside his driveway. Evening visitors were not always welcomed. One community social leader was sent packing when she drove uninvited down the Whitney driveway and her headlights played on and disturbed the ant colony.[76]

Whitney's home life never attained the happy serenity that he remembered from his own Jamestown childhood and had hoped to recapture. But it did stabilize. Evelyn became reconciled to life in the country. She had her visitors to talk to, her sister Harriet began to come again to spend the summers, and she enjoyed occasional evenings of talk with friends such as Research Lab physicist Gorton Fonda. Ennin had her farm, within easy drive of the Whitney home.

The day closed, then, on a man who had to a great extent achieved what he had set out to do a quarter century earlier. His life did represent a successful compound of many activities. The prizes he had won—the Chandler, Perkin, and Gibbs medals, and membership in the National Academy of Sci-

A Statistical Picture of the GE Research Lab in the Whitney Era.

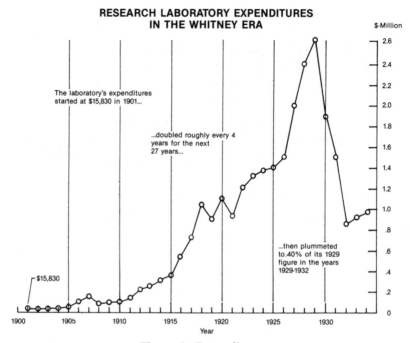

Figure 1. Expenditures.

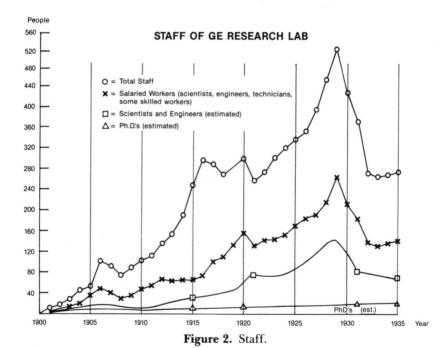

Figure 2. Staff.

EXPENDITURES OF GE RESEARCH LAB AS % OF GE SALES AND NET EARNINGS

Figure 3. Expenditures as Percentage of GE Sales and Net Earnings.

**% OF RESEARCH LAB EXPENDITURES
COVERED BY CREDITS, 1907-1927
(Credits are the sales of products made in the Research Lab—
for example, carbon resistance rods and tungsten contacts)**

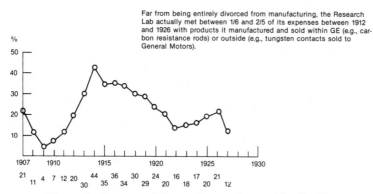

Far from being entirely divorced from manufacturing, the Research Lab actually met between 1/6 and 2/5 of its expenses between 1912 and 1926 with products it manufactured and sold within GE (e.g., carbon resistance rods) or outside (e.g., tungsten contacts sold to General Motors).

Figure 4. Percent of Expenditures Covered by Credits.

ences, for example—marked him as a leader of the American scientific community. The attention given to his words by after-dinner audiences, newspaper reporters, and magazine writers marked him as a public figure—the "molder of genius" and keeper of the "House of Magic." That reputation rested on a solid foundation of achievement. The laboratory he directed had defended GE's most profitable business; had launched new ones in the fields of radio, appliances, and X-rays; and had gained the respect of scientific leaders around the world for its contributions to knowledge.

Whitney had come up with a workable solution to that problem central to industrial research: achieving productivity without stifling innovation. He had done it through personal leadership. The Whitney method featured three main elements. First, he maintained a close connection between the laboratory and the company that supported it. The system for financing research that he created ensured accountability. He maintained an open door through which company leaders were encouraged to bring their problems. Second, he controlled the activities of the researchers in the laboratory through negotiation, not through dictation. He would peddle the problems of General Electric among the researchers and evaluate the results. But the choice of methods of attack on the problems and the decision whether or not to seek a scientific result that could be published were left to the researcher. And, third, he kept up a highly personal relationship with the major contributors through his regular visits to their laboratories, playing the gadfly, the catalyst, and the "homeopathic surgeon."

This method of directing research served as an inspiration for many who followed Whitney as industrial research directors. But it should not be viewed as a model that all American industrial research followed, or as *the* solution to the problem of combining productivity and innovation. It was one solution. It depended on a particular business climate that emerged in the 1920s, featuring prosperity, the diffusion of technological innovation, and wide public support for scientific research. It depended on the support of a corporation whose most profitable product was especially defensible by organized research. And it depended on a research director with an exothermic personality, an empirical approach to science, and an unshakable and simple faith in the value of research. In other business climates, in other companies, and in other hands, different solutions to the fundamental problem of industrial research would emerge. Those solutions would take account, not only of the virtues of the Whitney method, but of its limitations as well.

10/

Pikers in Audacity

Whitney's method of directing research had its limitations. In his occasional reflective moments he recognized them. On March 23, 1923, he wrote from Paris to Hawkins about work he saw that day in the transmission of pictures by radio. He reflected on the cautious approach GE had taken toward the subject and concluded: "we've got to take care not to be a lot of 'pikers in audacity.' "[1]

The phrase did not appear again in his writings. Unlike others he coined—"fortuitary gland" and "nut power," for example—it did not show up in a later speech. But it is one he might well have thought more about. Whitney and his laboratory stood at the summit in the mid-1920s. But a summit can be a place to rest, and a research organization that rests can be left behind. The General Electric Research Laboratory grew from 273 people in 1919 to more than 500 in 1929. The list of projects lengthened—from 47 in 1921 to more than 70 by the end of the decade. But the way the laboratory grew suggested that its leaders were becoming pikers in audacity. While many good scientists joined the staff, Whitney recruited no one with the inventive skill of Coolidge or Hull or with the scientific distinction of Langmuir or Dushman. Nor was there an explosion into new fields that matched the laboratory's entry during the previous decade into electronics, X-rays, and surface chemistry.

Whitney had opportunities to direct the laboratory toward such fields, but he drew back. He had reasons for doing so. He witnessed the fate of other laboratories that had proclaimed too exclusive a devotion to pure research or had attempted to assert too much independence in the introduction of new products. He saw American science continue down the path Hale, Millikan and Noyes had begun to mark out after the war. That path diverged as much from his views on science policy as the new X-ray diffraction apparatus in Noyes' Caltech laboratory differed from the microscope Whitney used to study worm galls and arrowheads. There is no way to assess, even with hindsight, whether he was right or wrong in choosing a cautious strategy. Perhaps a bolder course might have led sooner to important new discoveries—to radar or to fluorescent lamps, for example. But perhaps it might instead have turned the laboratory into the university-in-exile Whitney prevented it from ever becoming, and destroyed the lab's good reputation with GE's leaders.

Whitney's choice of a cautious strategy was defensible, but he did not defend it. Instead he spoke publicly as if the laboratory was in fact the "House of Magic" and center of pure research that the newspapers depicted. As a research director in the 1920s, Whitney said one thing and did another. The research director who stated "pure research to be good is usually random (beyond the edge of knowledge) and is usually activated inquisitiveness," did not devote a large portion of his own laboratory's research budget to pure research.[2] The research director who compared himself to a mining entrepreneur, grubstaking his scientific prospectors for their explorations into the unknown, began to look more like the owner of the company store, advancing tools and cash to scientific sharecroppers so they could produce staple crops in familiar fields. Whitney, a self-proclaimed empiricist and much-honored spokesman of science, failed either to submit his policies to empirical test or to explain them to the public. Instead, he came by 1929 to express an uncritical and complacent view of industrial research as the engine of uninterrupted progress. Whitney remained an inspiring and beloved figure through the 1920s. But by 1929 his paternalistic leadership and unquestioning faith in the soundness of the economic system began to look more like substitutes for, rather than spurs to, scientific creativity.

When Whitney used the expression "pikers in audacity" he

may have had in mind some occasions when he and his colleagues had begun prospecting on the frontiers of science but drew back. The quest for the chemical atom provides a good example.

In the 1920s, Langmuir's work on surfaces had led him to new ideas about the structure of atoms and the fundamental forces that held them together and bound them to one another. Hull and Dushman joined in the quest. Hull became a world leader in the determination of atomic structure by X-ray diffraction. In Dushman's laboratory notebooks, long stretches of attempts to account for the arrangement of electrons in atoms begun in 1918 crowded out accounts of more practical work on cable insulation and vacuum tubes.[3]

But the GE scientists worked on the assumption of a "chemical atom—a static arrangement of localized, identifiable electrons resembling tiny billiard balls arranged in cubes or spherical shells around a massive nucleus. This remains the mental picture most people summon up even today in response to the word *atom*. But by 1920 most physicists had passed beyond it into the more shadowy world of quantum theory.

Whitney remained one step behind. By 1920 he made the full transition from the lingering antiatomism of an Ostwald disciple to a firm belief in the reality of molecules and atoms. "Without blushing," he wrote in a 1920 address, "we nowadays refer to the number of molecules of gas per unit volume and know that whatever complications they may individually involve they are separate and discrete and numbered accurately."[4] He could not give up this orderly atomic world and plunge into the confusion that the physicists seemed mired in as they worked their way toward a new picture of matter.

Whitney did make one tentative step toward linking the work of his laboratory with the world of quanta. One place where the new theories might directly impact General Electric products was lighting. The laboratory had built impregnable patent protection for the tungsten lamp, but were there radically different alternatives, based on the new theories? Those theories explained for the first time the efficient process used by the mercury arc and other discharge lamps to turn electrical energy into light. Might this knowledge become the basis of a new light? To find out, Whitney chose Saul Dushman, the GE scientist with the deepest interest in the new physics, to run a new lighting laboratory established in August 1922 at the GE lamp plant in Harrison, New Jersey.

By October 1922 Dushman reported to Whitney on initial activities. Applied efforts remained in Schenectady, while the Harrison group concentrated on "purely scientific work." Its own researchers investigated areas such as electrodeless discharge and light emission resulting from thermal ionization. At Whitney's suggestion, Dushman offered Princeton physicist Karl Compton a consulting agreement under which GE would pay the cost of an assistant to work in Compton's laboratory.[5]

Compton became and remained a GE consultant. But Dushman's laboratory, begun with so much promise, rapidly disappeared. Perhaps the cause was a reorganization of the GE lamp department that phased out the Harrison plant. But whatever the reason, Dushman did not push on to attempt to explore quantum theory and bring back its results for use in electric lighting. The Research Laboratory's focus returned to incremental improvements on incandescent and discharge lamps. Instead of exploring quantum physics, the laboratory ran a lamp inspection program called a Mazda service. It involved no real research but remained there in the early 1920s solely because GE ran an advertising campaign that associated the trademark *Mazda* with the efforts of the Company's Research Lab. To provide a broader view of lighting problems, Whitney kept up the lamp vacuum committee that he had established back around 1910 to bring together the lab's lighting researchers for regular discussions. But if an anonymous satire written in the early 1920s is an indication, the committee meetings had become a drag on rather than a spur to creative work. Under the title "The Committee of Vacuums," the satire describes the participants taking up stereotyped positions in timeworn debates, such as Dushman's theoretical leanings against Whitney's empiricism. "Fonda opens very business like," it begins

> letting Dushman loose. No warming up necessary—starts at full speed making epsilon and omicron play tag in a lamp bulb. . . . Dr. Whitney insists on Dushman shaking around some broken milk bottles in a perfectly good lamp.[6]

In X-ray research the Lab fared somewhat better. GE's X-ray business took over routine tasks of tube design and inspection. Coolidge received considerable freedom to develop advanced tubes that accelerated electrons to hundreds of thousands of electron volts of energy. These could be used as sources of either extremely penetrating X-rays or energetic electron beams. The laboratory's strength in what might be termed early electron accelerators provided it with new links to the world science community. Scientists such as William H. Bragg and J. S. Townsend of Britain and Karl Siegbahn of Sweden wrote to obtain Coolidge tubes for use in their X-ray diffraction work. Rutherford corresponded with Hull, Langmuir, and Coolidge as he sought man-made methods of accelerating subatomic particles.[7]

In 1920 Whitney hoped to build on this expertise and establish the laboratory as a world center of advanced X-ray research. He aimed both to support GE's business and to pioneer in the physical and biological sciences. A handwritten draft he wrote asks "why should the GE Company start and even pay for a radiographic Institute in Schenectady?" and answers:

> Leaving out of account, as far as is possible, all reasons based on philanthropic motives, general welfare, and the natural wish for anyone to do some really useful human service. I claim that from a purely selfish and practical standpoint a Radiographic Institute is worth something between a hundred thousand dollars and a million to the Company.[8]

Much of this potential value would come from the institute's role as an "effective serviceable adjunct to the manufacture of X-ray tubes" and as a source of information for advertising "of the most direct and useful kind." But it could also establish for GE research a foothold in the life sciences. Shortly before 1920 Whitney had become interested in the mechanism of heredity. The work of Thomas Hunt Morgan at Columbia attracted him. Whitney thought X-rays might be a good way to induce genetic mutations in the fruit files Morgan was using in his experiments. He visited Morgan's lab and discussed the idea. "He was wonderfully helpful and interested," Whitney recalled a decade later, "but he warned me that he had tried X-rays on fruit flies and had made a mistake in reporting some effects which he later saw were spurious."[9] Whitney returned to Schenectady and took the same idea to biologist James Mavor at Union College. Mavor took up the project and carried out some pioneering work with the technique. It later became a standard part of the geneticist's repertoire.

Study of this and other biological effects of X-rays might be one area for the new institute's work. Other promising topics for research included the use of the Coolidge tube in cancer therapy; as the source of the intense X-rays needed to make images of organs, the interior of the head, or the circulatory system; and in industrial radiography. That final service, Whitney suggested in his 1920 memo, could be sold by the new laboratory to GE businesses and might bring in enough money to pay for the fundamental work.[10]

The X-ray laboratory would have extended GE research significantly in the direction of fundamental studies. But it never was established. No evidence suggests that Whitney even converted his handwritten draft into a formal proposal. Instead of building on GE's strong position in X-rays, Whitney allowed it to deteriorate during the 1920s. Laboratory researchers made only a few scattered studies of the physiological effects of X-rays. Coolidge put a thin nickel window on the end of one of his high-voltage tubes, letting out the electron beam, and proceeded to "ray" substances such as rubber plant leaves, rabbit ears, fruit flies, bacteria, castor oil, cane sugar, calcite crystals, diamond, fused quartz, snails, cockroaches, and geraniums. The random empirical efforts yielded little of value. Hull had wanted to make more sophisticated diffraction analyses with X-rays, but as already indicated, Whitney and Langmuir steered him back to vacuum tubes. As a result GE came to lack the skill to contribute to advanced biological work. When biologist Michael Heidelberger wanted to determine the structure of hemoglobin crystals in the 1920s, he took his best crystals to Schenectady to make use of the powerful X-ray tubes there. But he "came back disappointed because the technique was not up to it."[11]

So in fields such as atomic structure, quantum theory, and advanced X-ray studies, Whitney considered taking a true pioneering role but drew back. Why did he take a piker's approach to these fields? To begin with, the dean of industrial research was now one of America's oldest research directors, turning fifty-five in 1923. His heavy load of committee and board meetings, speaking engagements, and special company assignments left him little time to think about pure science. But age and growing responsibility do not explain it all. His academic contemporaries—Rutherford and Nernst in Europe, Millikan and Noyes in the United States—were all also in their fifties. They all had left their most productive research years behind and belonged to many boards and committees. But they continued to direct their laboratories by the stars of the future, rather than cling to the shores of past success.

Whitney was not, however, running an academic laboratory. Any attempt to increase the share of pure science in the lab's mixture of activities might look like an attempt to create the "philanthropic asylum for indigent chemists" that he had resolved not to establish back in 1901. And an attempt to push new technologies too vigorously might look like an abandonment of the teamwork with company businesses that he valued so highly. Whitney had advised the creators of other industrial laboratories. He had seen some try to be purists in science and others attempt to assert too much inventive entrepreneurship. He had observed the fate of both alternate strategies.

Charles Skinner, for example, planned in 1915 to turn the laboratory the Westinghouse Electric and Manufacturing Company founded in 1903 into a true research lab. By 1919 Skinner's efforts were well launched, with researchers such as Arthur H. Compton given broad leeway to explore new fields of science. They were placed under no pressure for immediate results. But after two years of this policy, the short, sharp depression of 1921 struck. The company's management needed to cut expenses and saw a laboratory making no contribution to company profits. They cut back sharply on the laboratory's freedom and its budget. Skinner had to restructure it on more practical lines, and as we have seen, Compton took his devotion to science into academic life.[12]

General Electric, too, had experienced an episode that warned Whitney about the dangers of scientific aloofness. Back in 1908, the National Electric Lamp Association, a group of lamp producers nominally independent, but in fact owned 60 percent by GE, had created a laboratory in Cleveland. Its first director, Edward P. Hyde, had come to GE from the National Bureau of Standards. "Pure research is something of a hobby with me," he wrote to Whitney, and for the next dozen years he used his industrial laboratory as a place to ride that hobby.[13] The laboratory's work ranged from the physics of light sources to the physiology of vision. In 1921 Yale physicist Ernest F. Nichols succeeded Hyde. Writing of his appointment in the journal *Science,* he said:

> The position offers complete freedom in the choice of research problems, and places at my unhampered disposal such human and material resources as no university I know of can at present afford.[14]

The organization he directed even got a new name, the "Pure Research Laboratory" to emphasize its distinctness. But Nichols died suddenly in 1924, and General Electric reexamined the Cleveland lab's policies. Whitney, for one, was not favorably disposed toward them. He wrote to Swope in 1925 that:

> apparently they have become accustomed to thinking of research patterned along the lines of Dr. Hyde's where scientific work is kept strictly apart from all practical applications. We in Schenectady have never worked that way.[15]

The Cleveland researchers would not work that way much longer. GE reconsidered its policy, removed the "Pure Research" label from the laboratory, and forced it to blend its efforts with the lamp development and engineering groups. It disappeared as a separate entity, becoming instead a section of the lamp engineering department.[16]

Excessive devotion to a laboratory's own technological innovations presented similar dangers. Kettering had been a visitor to the GE Research Laboratory after 1912, looking into the use of tungsten contacts for automobile electrical systems and advising on a power supply for Coolidge's portable X-ray tube.[17] By 1919 Kettering's laboratory had become part of General Motors and was hard at work on a radical automobile innovation, a new type of air-cooled engine. But Kettering did not adopt Whitney's policy of establishing strong ties of mutual consultation with company engineering departments. Instead, he assumed that the technical merits of his new engine were so pronounced and obvious that the GM engineers would automatically accept it. They did not. Instead, they viewed Kettering's initiative as an invasion of their territory. Tension arose between researchers and engineers in GM, and when technical difficulties with the engine arose, the engineers killed it as a product. The setback nearly killed Kettering's career as a research director too. When the project was discontinued in 1923, his spirits, according to a long-time aide, "reached the lowest point in his research career," and he asked GM president Alfred P. Sloan to relieve him as research director at "as early a date as possible." Sloan did not comply. He kept Kettering at his post but reduced his independence by setting up a general technical committee to coordinate the work of the Research Laboratory with that of the automobile manufacturing divisions.[18]

Awareness of the rocks on which such contemporaries as Skinner and Kettering had foundered helped Whitney steer a safe course through the 1920s. One danger was too exclusive a devotion to pure research; another was too aggressive an assertion of an inventor's independence. A third was too lavish spending on a research laboratory in a time of economic stringency. In the 1907 recession, the need to cut back sharply on laboratory expenses had come as a shock to Whitney. By the depression of 1921, he was taking that need in stride. Writing to Langmuir in October of that year, he noted casually:

> There doesn't seem to be much here to write about. We did reduce the staff by 10%, but letting some of the personnel go equivalent to 10% of the salary list, and we also have a 10% salary reduction beginning Nov. 1. This is all of interest, but not amusing or exciting.[19]

Even when prosperity returned, Whitney remained cautious. A little discovery, he believed, could serve as the foundation for a large amount of invention. "One Faraday a century would have us hurrying to keep up," he had written in 1911.[20] The priorities he set in the 1920s indicated that view persisted. Writing to Swope in November 1923, he raised four questions about the future of the laboratory. The first asked how fast it should continue to grow in size. The second, and the one receiving the most attention, concerned "the semicommercial development building" that Whitney had been proposing for several years "for the purpose of completing the commercial development, and often, for carrying on for a time the manufacture of products derived from research work." Whitney noted that radio and X-ray tubes had undergone this pilot-scale manufacturing in "old car barns" and other temporary buildings where "cleanliness is impossible." Without a new building, developments would not get to the GE businesses fast enough to beat competition to the marketplace. The third and fourth issues involved increased cooperation with MIT and conversion to the metric system.[21]

Swope accepted Whitney's recommendations on the first three issues. The laboratory staff grew at an average rate of 7 percent a year during the 1920s. A new building went up in 1925–26 across Works Avenue from the laboratory's headquarters. Whitney, Swope, and other prominent MIT alumni at GE worked closely with the Institute to build up its electrical engineering and physics departments. But the most interesting thing about the list of priorities is the absence of anything suggesting new directions in fundamental research.

Whitney emphasized development at a time when his most prominent academic contemporaries emphasized pure research. With the support of large philanthropic foundations, America was finally establishing a position as a contributor to basic science commensurate with the nation's place in world resources, industry, and politics. Whitney remained one of the most visible symbols of American science. A recent study places him alongside Millikan, Hale, Jewett of Bell Laboratories, and Charles D. Walcott of the Smithsonian Institution at the summit of "the public leadership of American science" in the 1920s. But he did not play an important role on the inner councils that guided national science policy toward an emphasis on pure research.[22]

Consider, for example, the most ambitious effort undertaken in the 1920s to secure permanent financial support for American basic science. In 1925 Hale and Millikan proposed a National Research Endowment—a permanent fund whose $20 million principal would be donated by industry and whose annual interest would finance scientific investigations. The idea quickly gained the backing not only of the nation's scientific leadership but also of businessman Julius Rosenwald and statesmen Elihu Root and Herbert Hoover. The fund's proponents appealed, not to industry's philanthropic urge, but to its self-interest. The prosperity of the 1920s, they argued, was built on the scientific discoveries of the past. More scientific discoveries would be needed in the present to ensure prosperity in the future.[23]

The fund's advocates recognized that corporations could not legally give their stockholders' money away for charitable or aesthetic purposes but could make contributions that promised "substantial, direct and proximate" benefits. And they also knew that some industries could use scientific contributions as a form of advertising to improve their public image. As Hoover put it in describing the trade association of the electric utility industry:

> Don't fool yourself that they care a damn for pure science. What they want is to get into their reports, which will soon be examined by the Federal Trade Commission, that they are giving money for pure science research.[24]

To present this case to industry, science needed good salesmen. No American in the 1920s was better at selling science than Whitney. So one learns with surprise that he seems to have played virtually no role at all in the National Endowment campaign. Jewett and John J. Carty of Bell Laboratories and AT&T seem to have taken on the job of industrial research representatives of the endowment. Why was Whitney absent?

In part, he may have stayed away because the effort had little chance to succeed. Even in the period of prosperity between 1925 and 1929, industry's pledges lagged far behing the fund's goals. Also, Whitney may have retained his 1919 view that "it would be better if the democracy could be brought to pay its own expenses," through a government program of support for science paid for out of tax revenues. And he may also have remained aloof from the efforts of Hale, Millikan, and their colleagues because he disagreed with their conception of the practical value of scientific research.

The research program the National Endowment Fund would have supported embodied the view of science already arrived at by the National Academy of Sciences leadership and the heads of major foundations. Wyckliffe Rose of the Rockefeller Foundation summed it up in these words: "make the peaks higher." From the scientific peaks—at Berkeley, Caltech, Harvard, Princeton, and a few other select institutions—enough knowledge would trickle down to meet the needs of industry.[25]

Whitney would not have entirely disagreed with this point of view. But he objected to carrying it to an extreme that denied any scientific role to industrial laboratories. And there is some evidence that Hale, Millikan, James Angell of Michigan, and other university-based scientific leaders did carry it to that extreme. A major foundation official, Robert S. Woodward of the Carnegie Institution, detected this in 1921. "Many of them," he wrote to Whitney:

> look upon the work of your great establishment, for example, as work in "impure" science, and as lacking in the divine afflatus. Have you not read the puerile claims of our friends Angell and Millikan for universities in respect to research?[26]

Millikan and Noyes shaped the policies of the rapidly growing California Institute of Technology in the 1920s by a trickle-down theory of science. They put into operation the elitist views that Noyes had fought for and been defeated on at MIT around the turn of the century and that Millikan had pushed before the wartime National Research Council (NRC). "If the institute (Caltech) is to make a new contribution to the educational development of the country" Millikan wrote to Hale in 1921, "it has to be done, I think, through making engineering grow out of physics and chemistry."[27]

This did not mean that Millikan denied the value of industrial research. He had helped AT&T put its research efforts on a more scientific basis in 1911 and remained on the payroll as a consultant. But it did mean that he thought ideas would flow in only one direction: from the best universities to the research laboratories.

Millikan's view oversimplified the science-technology relation, as his own experience illustrated. Even in the twentieth century, independent inventors often continued to beat trained scientists to major breakthroughs. The main role of the scientists continued to be improvement and explanation, not invention. For example, in the search for a telephone amplifier, the eventually triumphant idea of the three-element vacuum tube came, not from Millikan or the student he had sent to work for AT&T, Harold D. Arnold, but from De Forest, who had abandoned science (he was a Yale Ph.D.) for invention. Arnold's crucial role had been to explain the principles of De Forest's tube and to adapt it to telephone use.[28]

Millikan's relations with Whitney and General Electric also showed that important new ideas did not always flow smoothly from science to industry. In the mid-1920s, Millikan and his colleague Royal Sorenson applied their knowledge of the behavior of matter at low pressures to invent a new type of circuit breaker for use on electric power systems. They licensed the idea to General Electric in 1927. Scientists at the GE Research Laboratory spent three years and more than a million dollars proving that the idea was ahead of its time and that industrially practical vacuum techniques were not up to the demands of the invention. Only in 1959 had those techniques advanced sufficiently to turn the Millikan-Sorenson invention into a product.[29]

Millikan's picture of a one-way flow of ideas also neglected the reverse current of new techniques from industrial to scientific laboratories. In pushing toward a million-volt X-ray tube, Coolidge made breakthroughs in the design of high-energy equipment. America's pioneers in experimental high-energy physics, such as Gregory Breit and Merle Tuve of the Carnegie Institution, and Millikan's own colleague Charles C. Lauritsen, made use of Coolidge's inventions in their apparatus.[30]

The relation of science to industry had become more complicated in the 1920s than the rhetoric of Millikan and other supporters of the National Research Endowment portrayed it. Whitney agreed with them on the need for society to support science. He accepted the elitist view of scientific research that regarded the work of the few outstanding leaders in each field as more worthy of support than the work of the great majority of their less creative colleagues. But, as in the previous decade, he emphasized the education and training of researchers, rather than the centralized control of research funding. Rather than take an active part in the National Endowment effort, General Electric set up its own program, the Coffin Foundation, named for GE's first president. Representing Whitney on an early meeting of the fellowship and research committee of that foundation, Laurence Hawkins reported to him in February 1923 that:

> It was definitely agreed that the money would be used to make it possible for good men to continue or undertake research— men who, without help, would be unable to go on.[31]

The Coffin Fellowships took their place alongside those of the NRC and the Guggenheim Foundation in funding the rise of American science. But they also made Whitney's immediate task as a research director more difficult. By providing promising scientists with a new way to embark on a career in research, they provided a new reason not to go to work in an industrial laboratory.

In the previous generation, America's most promising young scientists typically went to Europe for their graduate education and came back to find a job as best they could. Back in 1909 so talented a scientist as Langmuir could find himself in a dead-end teaching position in his postdoctoral years and see industrial research as his only salvation. By the 1920s, this had become far less likely. A researcher would more likely apply to the Rockefeller and Guggenheim Foundations for a postdoctoral fellowship. In the 1920s, recent Ph.D. recipients such as Linus Pauling of Caltech and John Slater of Chicago could pursue their ideas on the application of quantum theory to chemical bonding under Guggenheim Fellowships, rather than be forced to enter industry or to plunge immediately into full-time teaching at an institution with little interest in research.[32]

Whitney appears to have recognized that he had little chance to attract the best students from institutions such as Caltech. "I am not in as close touch with Dr. Millikan's students as I might be," he admitted to Swope in 1924.[33] The Research Laboratory maintained the recruiting system that had brought it Langmuir and Hull. It invited a dozen or two promising young scientists to spend the summer, in the hope that a few of them would show enough talent and enough interest to merit and accept offers to join the full-time staff. But most of the best summer workers in the 1920s—individuals such as David Dennison of Michigan, who came in 1920 to study the crystal structure of ice, and Ernest O. Lawrence, who came in 1929 to work on electron physics—did not come to stay. "I like the laboratory, but don't like the idea of eight hours a day with two weeks vacation per year," Lawrence wrote to a colleague.[34] The new system of foundation-supported research gave him an alternative, and he seized it.

As the Research Laboratory became less able to compete with the universities for the services of the best young scientists, its identity as a scientific institution began to diverge further from the university model. Three aspects of its scientific strategy illustrate this continuing change. In the universities, physics became increasingly the model and the foundation for other sciences such as chemistry and metallurgy; the GE Research Lab put less emphasis on its "physics department" than university labs of comparable reputation did. Theory became more important in academic science; Whitney continued to stress experiment. Publication, already well established by the turn of the century as the mark of a scientist, increased in quantity and quality across U.S. science; Whitney continued to put little if any pressure on his staff to publish results. Let us look at each of these areas in a little more detail.

Whitney's relative neglect of physics can be seen in the comparison of his practices to those of his teacher Noyes in their mutual field of physical chemistry. At Caltech, Noyes, according to a recent study, encouraged his students "to be current with the latest physical concepts and techniques" and to "continually adapt to the changing state of physics." Whitney showed more interest in a candidate's resourcefulness and experimental skill. While GE was allowing its capability in X-ray structure determination to fall behind the times, Noyes supported the building up of that capability to support his department's work in the study of chemical bonding and the structure of matter.[35]

Whitney tended to recruit people with versatility, rather than specialized scientific training. The continually changing focus of industrial work put a premium on flexibility, not on depth. "Aside from metallurgists," notes Ernest E. Charlton, who joined the laboratory's staff in 1920, "they [Whitney and his associates] looked for generalists for the laboratory. They looked for people who could fit into as many fields as possible."[36] Increasingly, as the summer tryout method proved incapable of bringing in enough recruits to support the laboratory's 7 percent annual growth in the 1920s, Whitney brought in experienced industrial scientists from other companies or other parts of GE and engineers from GE's postgraduate training programs. He lured Charlton away from Du Pont; brought in metallurgists Truman Fuller and Samuel Hoyt from the GE lamp department; and hired engineers Anthony J. Nerad, David C. Prince, and William Westendorp from the GE "test" program. While their more famous contemporaries such as Langmuir continued to uphold the public image of the laboratory as a place where physicists and chemists were having fun and playing around with atoms and molecules, these new recruits were carrying more and more of the daily load of the laboratory. And that load consisted of getting immediate answers to practical problems. "The old (i.e., pre-World War II) lab had been mostly applied research," notes Nerad, a mechanical engineer who led a team of laboratory scientists and engineers helping the GE turbine department develop a new boiler for electricity generation using mercury in place of water as a working fluid. And Westendorp, an electrical engineer who specialized in new circuits for lighting and X-ray systems, adds:

> People sometimes talk about the old lab as if everyone was allowed to do what he wanted. Well it wasn't that way at all. Most people did what they were told to do. This talk about there being a lot more fundamental research then and more applied work

now [1975] just isn't the way things were. Of course Langmuir could do what he wanted. . . . And Albert Hull did what he wanted probably. But not most people.[37]

Whitney appears to have tried at first to correct the short-sightedness and fragmented nature of the laboratory's work and the lack of fundamental science expertise among those who administered it. In 1923 he attempted to limit Hawkins only to the job of keeping up relations between the laboratory and the company and to substitute in the role of internal adminis-trator the Cornell physicist F. K. Richtmyer. He would bring to laboratory administration a different tone than Hawkins, whose degrees in engineering and law dated from the turn of the century. Part of Richtmyer's job would be as an expert ad-viser in patent cases, lifting some of the burden of testimony from other scientists. But he would also have responsibility for "connecting the discoveries of one group to those of an-other."[38] As Whitney noted, the lab needed someone to pick out and emphasize the common themes:

What Kelley does on the 3rd floor will often help Dushman on the fourth, Coolidge on the first, or Rice on the fifth, but if you think this filters automatically through our concrete floors you don't know concrete. We need a daily colloquium.[39]

Richtmyer appeared in mid-1923 to have accepted the po-sition as scientific consultant in what Whitney told him "is going to be the best research institution in the world." But Richt-myer never took over the job, and Hawkins continued his double duty. Like the earlier initiatives in the direction of the lighting laboratory and the Radiographic Institute, Whitney never pursued this idea of bringing in an academic scientist to stimulate research and teamwork. A similar opportunity oc-curred in 1926 when the GE program of support for German science that Whitney helped initiate in 1923 came to an end. Fritz Haber suggested that it be converted into a temporary exchange of scientists. Gorton Fonda of GE, whom Whitney had sent to discuss the matter with Haber, agreed. He mentioned as a candidate Michael Polanyi, whose work in Berlin on crystal studies had so impressed Whitney three years earlier. "A clean cut fellow," Fonda wrote

> with clear expression, keen and acute in mental grasp and in statement—and at the same time brought up under such foreign influence that he would be a lion in the drawing room.[40]

Again, however, no exchange program was arranged. Whitney abandoned the idea of invigorating the scientific effort at Schenectady by importing a stimulating outside influence.

A second divergence of Whitney's research policy from that of his university colleagues concerned the role of theory. By the 1920s, Americans were finally beginning to make sustained and significant contributions to the development of new theories of matter. But as such work became an increasing concern at Caltech, Chicago, Harvard, and Berkeley, theory remained far less important to industry. This deemphasis partly stemmed from the nature of industrial effort. Except in a few specialized fields such as lighting, quantum theory, for example, could hardly contribute directly to the solution of industrial problems. The few theorists who entered industry—for example, physicist Lewi Tonks at GE—concentrated on carrying out the complex classical physics calculations required to describe the activities of electrons and ions inside vacuum tubes, rather than on more advanced studies.

But Whitney's personal view of research carried the distrust of theory even farther at GE than industrial needs might have dictated. For Whitney, the experiment was everything. Ceramist Louis Navias recalls:

> Dr. Whitney was mainly interested in experiments and in people who performed them. . . . He was concerned about the expert who knew too much about his subjects, and so at times found it unnecessary to try an experiment which he knew would not work. Dr. Whitney could recite many instances in which less knowledgeable people made them work.[41]

"He was primarily an experimentalist," Ernest Charlton adds:

> I'm always reminded, thinking about him, of a saying of Kettering of General Motors: "try the next bottle on the shelf." That was what Whitney was always interested in—trying things to see what would happen.[42]

Whitney recognized his empirical bias and at times tried to correct for it. In 1921 he even gave a speech in praise of theory, asserting:

> There are big theories and little theories, proved and discarded theories, but we must not admit that there are useless theories. It is so difficult to acquire the habit of theorizing and it is so seldom encouraged or produced or taught, that there is little danger from useless theories if they exist.[43]

He made occasional efforts to help his staff acquire that habit of theorizing. For example, in June 1925, he hired Professor Leigh Page, a Yale theoretical physicist, to visit the laboratory as a consultant, "talking math physics to Langmuir, Hull, Mott-Smith, Kingdon, Tonks, and Dushman."[44] But such infrequent initiatives did not balance the overwhelmingly experimental bias of the laboratory's efforts. And by his personal example, Whitney continued to emphasize the opportunistic, unguided random walk of experiment, rather than mapped-out research programs.

He illustrated this in the best known of his personal research efforts of the 1920s, the use of electromagnetic radiation for medical purposes. He began it in late 1925. Laboratory researchers had noticed that high-power radio tubes produced localized heating effects. One engineer, William Teare, had made a high-frequency outfit to kill cockroaches by steaming them to death. Whitney became interested in this for various reasons. First, as he noted, "if you could heat animals thus without heating the room you might conceivably electrically heat houses cheaply."[45]

"This I considered bizarre," he admitted, but some shorter range applications of the localized heating effect appeared more promising. He had observed that the swelling up of galls on tree branches was due to the presence of insect larva. Did the heat from the larva cause the swelling? He decided to try out the idea by putting a piece of metal inside a branch and heating it from the outside by electromagnetic induction. No swelling similar to a gall resulted, but Whitney now was hooked on the subject of heating by radio.

He soon was repeating Teare's earlier insect experiments, this time on flies. He observed that flies subjected to high power died. But those subjected to lower power merely slowed down their activity. This he interpreted as being a consequence of the radiation's having induced a fever in the fly. He found the hypothesis difficult to verify, having no means on hand to take a fly's temperature. But some inadvertent experiments on human beings supported the conjecture. GE researchers working on high-power radio tubes began to complain of localized pains. Doctors diagnosed the problem as localized fevers induced by electromagnetic energy.[46]

So Whitney now had a means of producing a fever, and he next looked for a way to use it. He learned of the work of the German physician Werner Jauregg in treating syphilis by means of inducing fevers in the patient. Jauregg had used a dangerous method of giving the patient a fever: giving him malaria. Whitney proposed to replace the malaria germ with radio waves.

The idea worked. Whitney encouraged physician Charles Carpenter and psychiatrist Leland Hinsie to take on the task of—in the overheated prose of journalist Paul de Kruif— "proving that fever—stoked by letting victims lie in the field of this shortwave broadcasting apparatus—would save some of them from the insane doom of syphilis!"[47] Whitney earned much favorable publicity for this excursion into medicine. Its anticlimatic sequel was less frequently cited. Radiofrequency heating proved an unreliable and difficult-to-control therapeutic tool. Researchers at the Miami Valley Hospital in Dayton, Ohio, working with Charles Kettering, became impatient with their temperamental radiofrequency apparatus. They suddenly discovered that a properly designed cabinet for circulating moist hot air over a patient maintained a fever without need for the radio waves. That became a frequently applied treatment for syphilis until finally replaced by antibiotics in the 1940s.[48]

Whitney returned to radiofrequency heating for other purposes, trying it as a treatment for bursitis and arthritis. These experiments produced some apparent cures. But he made no real tests of the technique that could have withstood critical analysis. The entire effort exemplifies Whitney's research style in the 1920s: humanitarian in intent, narrow in vision, empirical in procedure. He moved from one idea to the next by dead reckoning, rarely pausing to take a theoretical bearing. The project illustrated by example his belief in the superiority of Baconian empiricism to expert theorizing.[49]

The third divergence of Whitney's laboratory from the main trend of U.S. science showed up in its publication practices. The idea of carrying out research not directly connected with factory needs and publishing the results had been the GE Research Laboratory's claim to uniqueness back at the time of its founding at the turn of the century. "When we began electrical research we called ourselves the first research laboratory in our industry," Whitney wrote in 1931:

> Admittedly others have done research and new engineering work, but we knew of no laboratory in industry where random scientific research was going on, and where publication of research was incidentally an aim.[50]

But how central to the laboratory's evolving character by the 1920s did that incidental aim of publication become? Whitney made no explicit publication policy. But the evidence on the rate of publication of the laboratory staff supports Charlton's statement that "I don't think Whitney was really interested in publication." In the years 1925–27, surviving records indicate that the ninety or so trained scientists and engineers on the laboratory staff produced about fifty papers per year. Even allowing for multiple authorship and the failure of some papers to find their way into the laboratory's reprint file, the average productivity per staff member was still well below one paper per year. As a source of scientific papers, the GE Research Laboratory more closely resembled a small college rather than one of the outstanding research universities such as Caltech, Chicago, or Princeton.[51]

GE's publication practices mirrored those of all of U.S. industrial research. Industrial laboratories may have grown faster than academic science departments in the 1920s, but their role as sources of scientific publications did not. The share contributed by industrial laboratories to publication in physics and chemistry had peaked by 1920 or earlier and remained well below that peak afterward. Industrial laboratories contributed more than 20 percent of the papers in the 1920 *Physical Review*, for example, compared to 10 percent a decade earlier; but this share declined from 1920 on and fell to 5 percent in 1935. A less nearly comprehensive sampling of the *Journal of the American Chemical Society* suggests that the contribution of industrial laboratories rose from about 7 percent in 1895 to about 15 percent in 1910 but had fallen to about 5 percent by 1915 and stayed at or below that level subsequently. The scientific role of industrial research varied from leadership in areas such as electron physics, for example, to a virtual absence in areas such as quantum theory. And, as in universities, a few individuals wrote a disproportionate share of the papers. At GE, for example, even when the research staff had passed the ninety mark, Langmuir's name still appeared on about one in ten of the Research Laboratory's publications.[52]

The publication data support the view that Whitney's approach to scientific research and to laboratory organization had diverged noticeably from that of his academic contemporaries. He did not try to incorporate the methods of physics into fields such as chemistry and metallurgy. He encouraged experiment more than theory. And he left the decision to publish or not up to the individual researcher, rather than treat it as a primary goal of the laboratory.

Whitney did not force his scientists into a single mold. He offered the incoming scientist or engineer a wide range of roles. If he had the energy and ambition, the scientist could emulate Langmuir and squeeze out of each problem both the technological value to General Electric and the scientific value that could be expressed in a steady stream of publications. At the other extreme, he could treat the position as just another industrial job, carry out routine analyses or troubleshooting tasks, and maintain little contact with his professional peers outside the laboratory. Between these extremes, a number of specialized identities emerged. Some researchers earned outstanding reputations as valued consultants to company businesses in areas such as mechanics or heat transfer. Others became known as inventors, originating a steady stream of patentable products and processes.

Under Whitney's leadership, the GE Research Laboratory had become an important part of the mechanism that put science and technology to work in a productive American economy. But that mechanism did not resemble an orderly assembly line or automobile transmission, with academic science at one end supplying the raw materials or the power, factories at the other end putting out a final product based on the new science, and industrial laboratories somewhere in the middle acting as a sort of conveyor or gearbox. The connections were more diverse and multiple. Ideas and objects could be created at any point within the system and could flow in many directions. The incremental improvements originating in the factory itself, for example, probably played a larger role than new scientific discoveries in increasing American productivity. New apparatus coming out of industrial laboratories, such as Coolidge's high-voltage X-ray tubes and accelerators, became incorporated in the experiments academic scientists used to probe the structure of matter. Academic laboratories patented inventions, such as the Sorenson-Millikan vacuum switch. Important inventions continued to enter the system from foreign sources. Two of GE's major innovations in the late 1920s, for example, Carboloy cutting tools and Alnico magnets, grew out of ideas and patents obtained and licensed from Germany and Japan.

Research laboratories assumed an important place in American industry precisely because the system was complex. That complexity forced laboratories to take on many roles. They widened the array of career choices facing an individual with scientific interest and talent who did not care for a life of teaching or for the high-pressure career of an individual entrepreneur. They provided a meeting place for the experts in marketing, who knew what the consumer wanted; the production experts, who understood manufacturing costs; and the researcher, with knowledge of technical possibilities. On the many committees within GE or other large companies, such specialists could meet to consider new directions for industrial effort. And research laboratories also provided a point of contact for academic scientists with the system—whether it was Ernest Lawrence returning from his summer job at GE with a suitcase full of electronic tubes given to him by Albert Hull, or Karl Compton collecting an annual retainer from GE for consulting services while receiving enthusiastic endorsements from GE's Whitney and Swope when considered for the presidency of MIT.

Industrial research also played a more controversial role in the U.S. economy in the 1920s. Despite the efforts of the NRC to encourage smaller companies to support research, it remained an activity dominated by a few large firms. GE and AT&T, for example, employed between them some 40 percent of the physicists working in industry in 1925. The economic impact of this research concentration is harder to assess. Certainly, as historian Paul Uselding has suggested, corporations tried to use research to reduce the competitive uncertainty they faced.[53] They used patents coming from research to retain control over fields where they were already strong, as GE did in lighting and AT&T did in long-distance telephony. They used research as the basis of new ventures into unfamiliar fields, as GE did in cutting tool materials and GM did in tetraethyl lead. Did the competition-reducing effects of continuing patent-based strength in established fields, and the attempt to duplicate that strength in new fields such as radio, outweigh the competition-increasing effects of research-based diversification? Decades of debate have failed to answer that question. The most thorough case studies, such as historian Leonard Reich's work on the role of research and patents in radio, indicate how tangled the issue is. GE and AT&T certainly tried, through the creation of RCA, to establish business control of radio. Patent considerations certainly shaped the research efforts of both companies. But for all their research strength, both companies proved dismayingly unable to control the course of events. When AT&T tried to reenter the broadcasting business, an area it had agreed to stay out of in 1920, it was decisively repulsed. GE let its position as the manufacturing arm of RCA slip away in the 1920s, as that company's leader David Sarnoff exerted its independence. And the patent pool established by AT&T, GE, and Westinghouse did not prevent a number of independent companies, such as Philco, Zenith, and Atwater-Kent, from entering radio manufacture and making a strong showing.[54]

So industrial research had proved a complex institution, both in its performance and in its economic effect. It could not simply be characterized as a stop on the technological assembly line or a university-in-exile. It did not simply serve as an agent of monopoly or as an angel of competition. As the principal public spokesman for industrial research, Whitney might have been expected to convey to the public some useful guidance for understanding the institution. The titles of his publications on the subject suggest he wanted to. They include "The Relation of Physics and Chemistry to Industry," "Stimulation of Research in Pure Science Resulting from the Needs of Engineers and of Industry," and "Encouraging Competent Men To Continue in Research."

But looking for the meat those titles promise, one finds only the leftovers from the after-dinner speeches we have already

glanced at, with all their easy generalization, uncritical optimism, and incoherent organization. In the world depicted in
Whitney's publications between 1925 and 1930, research-based
progress is automatic:

> I will try to convince you that experiment and change for the
> better have been continuous since the creation, and that what
> we now call the application of chemistry and physics to industry
> has always been a part of scheme.[55]

The relation of science to industry presents no problems;
"science and industry are part of right living, and not separa-
ble from each other." Innovation came almost solely from the
minds of researchers, not as a response to the needs of the
factory or the consumer:

> Man usually does not know what he wants until he has it. . . .
> He has seldom realized the want first and then gone directly to
> produce the thing wanted.[56]

The best way to run a research laboratory is simply to gather
competent scientists and turn them loose:

> encouraged curiosity is the safest criterion of an improving civ-
> ilization. . . . The principle of random research, call it the blind
> principle if you will, is evident everywhere.[57]

Not progress, or profit, but paper is these laboratories' most
important product. Discussing "Langmuir's work," in 1928,
Whitney says:

> Above everything else I place his published scientific work, be-
> cause it is a kind on which he and others will continue to build
> serviceable structures, and we know that such mental and spir-
> itual advances as it marks are superior to technical ones.[58]

Scientific publication is the equivalent of "the artistic painting, the beautiful poem, the enduring sculpture," and "the most

altruistic and far-seeing leaders recognize the importance of its encouragement."[59]

But aesthetically pleasing as the immediate results of research are, in the Whitney view, they were not mere works of art. They were the heralds of utopia. "If we control our fears and taboos, as now seems possible through more educated inquisitiveness," he concluded:

> we may look forward to interesting occupations provided for everyone, mechanical work everywhere, but only for machines, and perhaps permanent world peace.[60]

What's wrong with this picture? Simply this: it clashed with Whitney's practice. He was a realist, not a utopian. His practices included heavy emphasis on development and meeting immediate company needs, a growing divergence from the research methods and interests of academic and individual laboratories, a predominance of experiment over theory, and an ambivalence toward publication. These were sensible adaptations by Whitney to reality. He had good reasons for being a piker in audacity. But rather than explain those reasons, he painted a rhetorical picture of the scientist as unfettered explorer.

Whitney's rhetoric, and the similarly oversimplified picture painted by Langmuir, have fooled a few historians into depicting the GE Research Laboratory as a university in exile. "The atmosphere at GE was strikingly similar to the atmosphere of G. N. Lewis' department at Berkeley," one writes in the midst of an otherwise insightful article on Langmuir's theory of the chemical atom. Another asserts that "at such (industrial) laboratories . . . "research work was placed under the direction of men who were purely scientific in their interests, and who managed to instill much of the university atmosphere into the industrial situation . . . in laboratories of this type advanced research was clearly distinguished from development."[61]

These distorted descriptions of industrial laboratories in the 1920s are harmless and easily corrected. But the divergence of

Whitney's rhetoric from reality appears to have created a more serious problem. Long before he fooled historians, Whitney seems to have at least partly fooled himself. By 1929 he seems to have convinced himself that he had created permanent and stable answers to the questions that had accompanied him to General Electric in 1900: what can the scientist do for the corporation, and what can the corporation do for the scientist? His public, and some of his private, pronouncements show him still depicting the laboratory as a combination of a happy small-town family and a turn-of-the century German scientific laboratory, long after it had in fact turned into something more original and interesting. He came more and more to pose as a homespun philosopher, combining idealism and practical advice, long after his management practices had conformed to the needs of a giant corporation and the society in which it operated.

The picture of his laboratory as a happy family remained more than a mere image. Whitney continued to take a personal interest in the people he worked with. He lent them money, referred them to medical specialists (and sometimes paid the bill), and listened to their problems. He kept the lab colloquium going, widening its scope by bringing in speakers such as historian Dixon Ryan Fox and a cotton futures broker named George Fabyn who thought he had proved that Bacon wrote the works of Shakespeare. Each summer he held a corn roast at his farm. While the staff members socialized, he would be down by the pond with their children, giving them bread crumbs to feed to the ducks and turtles or whittling them wooden toys. The day would end with singing around the campfire.[62]

The family feeling did persist through the 1920s, but it became progressively harder to sustain and less than complete. A staff of five hundred people made too big a family. Whitney could not get around to see each of them on his daily tour or get to know each of them by name. A growing share of them never got asked if they had any fun or felt comfortable about venturing through Whitney's always open door. Whitney had to establish a representative council to discuss the laboratory's work. The lab had grown too big for any single individual to know first hand about everything that was going on.[63]

His own family, like the laboratory family, continued to diverge from the image of it he continued to paint. Describing Ennin and her husband Van in a 1928 speech, Whitney said: "they are still, farmers, and I can truthfully say that they have lived happily 'ever after.' " But in fact, Ennin and Van's farm had added to the strain between Whitney and his daughter. Despite their Cornell education, she and her husband could not turn the farm into a paying proposition or even keep it running smoothly. Ennin continued to take in more horses and cats and to allow upkeep of the house and grounds to deteriorate. Whitney's weekly visit became more and more difficult to endure, as he picked his way carefully through the littered yard to join his daughter and her husband for strained conversations in a cluttered kitchen. Although they continued to accept his financial support, they repulsed his other gifts. The electric stove and refrigerator he had given them sat unused in the barn. The daughter of the director of research of the General Electric Company refused to have her house wired for electricity.[64]

But by the late 1920s, most of the United States outside of its farms was wired for electricity, fully equipped with radios, and increasingly supplied with automobiles and refrigerators. Whitney took on himself the job of assuring the nation that this sweep of progress had become perpetual and that the science it was based on did not conflict with religious values. Responding to a 1927 question from advertising man Bruce Barton, Whitney joined Will Durant, Rev. William T. Manning, and Vernon Kellogg in assuring the nation that science posed no challenge to religion. "Man has apparently only just begun to know and appreciate," he wrote

> he will continue indefinitely in a growing understanding, appreciation and utilization of the infinite creation. If anything is clear, it is that evolution . . . cannot conflict with religion. . . .
> It would seem a poor religion indeed, which depended upon

our feeble, continually changing, though growing science, or which made a scientist any more eligible than a child for any blessings it provides.[65]

Whitney's pronouncements on religion drew increasing national attention. When he looked at a demonstration of a metal ring levitating in a magnetic field and commented that it was held up by "the hand of God," the pronouncement drew favorable editorial comment and even an admiring poem.[66]

When Whitney looked upon the secular, as well as the spiritual, side of life in the United States, he found that also good. "In our expanding stock markets, our Stock Exchange and the 'curb,' we have a perfectly natural growth" he wrote in 1929

> because more and more people take stock in these things which they find by experiment to be helpful . . . everyone may take part nowadays in "big business" . . . the machinery which at first merely relieved man of the hardest kinds of mechanical work now has become complex enough to reward him literally for the loan of an equivalent of that mechanical work.[67]

His personal experience reinforced this optimistic view. As recently as 1925, his personal wealth had not been much over $100,000. But the money, largely invested in such apparently safe, conservative stocks as General Electric, and the electric utility holding company, Electric Bond and Share, was taking on a life of its own. Stock values doubled and redoubled, then doubled again. By the summer of 1929, Whitney had totaled up his holdings in a jotted note in his pocket diary and got a sum of more than a million dollars. The natural growth of the stock market had made him a millionaire.[68]

He had become a material success matching the most audacious dreams he might have held when he came to Schenectady three decades earlier determined to do some great thing for the General Electric. The great things he had accomplished made him a leader in a science-business partnership that had apparently found the secret of perpetual progress. The success of the American economy had won over observers far more skeptical than Whitney. Walter Lippman wrote that "the more or less unconscious and unplanned activities of business-men are for once more novel, more daring, and in general, more revolutionary than the theories of the progressives." Lincoln Steffens added that "Big business in America is pro-ducing what the Socialists held up as their goal: food shelter and clothing for all."[69]

If a businessmen could be described as more radical than progressives or socialists, then that most adventurous of busi-nessmen, a director of research, seemed the most radical of all, the one most directly responsible for prosperity. Whitney's practices of directing research may have been those of a piker in audacity. But his public image was that of a romantic, a free spirit, a man in touch with the future. He came to believe in that image. He incorporated it in his compound of values and motives. He put the new image alongside his picture of the Jamestown of his boyhood as a rural paradise; his conception of science as Baconian empiricism, carried on in a spirit of childlike curiosity; and his aim of creating an industrial labo-ratory that would combine the ideals of German science he thought he had glimpsed at Leipzig with the happy family of his boyhood. To them he added two additional elements: a faith in the capitalist system—in "our expanding stock markets, our Stock Exchange, and 'our curb' "—as the engine of national prosperity; and a confidence that American business viewed industrial research as essential insurance for the continuation of that prosperity.

Whitney cannot be faulted for accepting this faith. Better minds than his believed it. But he can be faulted for not ex-amining it more critically, or at least for not trying to express it in his own words. Instead, he took it ready made. Charac-teristically, when commenting on the state of the world in a late 1929 address, he lifted his words from the heading on a menu in a railroad dining car. "The year 1929," he quoted, "will be another milestone of achievement along the broad road of everlasting time. It should surpass all previous years in ma-terial progress."[70]

Between the day he wrote those words and the day they ap-peared in print, that broad road would turn sharply downhill.

11/

Come In, Rain

On Black Thursday, October 30, 1929, the "perfectly natural growth" in stock prices came to an abrupt end. General Electric's stock joined other industrials in a sharp decline. By the end of the day it fell $53 from its opening price of $252 a share. Whitney expressed his reaction to the stock market slide most graphically, not in a speech or a letter, but in one of the few sketches in his commonplace book. He changed a graph of declining stock prices, clipped from the *New York Times*, into the outline of an angry dragon.[1] The dragon of decline would do more than devour his paper profits. It would threaten his view of research and of himself. Between 1929 and 1932, Whitney sunk into a depression as deep as the nation's. He faced the task of presiding over a cut in the budget and staff of the Research Laboratory that wiped out the growth of the 1920s. He was challenged to defend the laboratory's character as a scientific institution, at a time when he found it difficult to eat, to sleep, and to face a day's work. The laboratory survived the Depression shaken but essentially intact. He did not. In 1932 he had to step down as director, ostensibly into honorable retirement, but actually in the grip of bitter personal defeat.

The theory that research and technology provided insurance against economic decline became one of the first casualties of the depression. New technology-based industries did not spring from the laboratories to take up the economic slack left by the drop in the production of automobiles, steel, houses, and the other established products of an industrial society. Business leaders began to view swollen research budgets, not as a cure to downturn, but as a luxury that ought to be cut back. U.S. spending on industrial research fell by an estimated 10 percent in the years 1929 to 1932. The GE Research Lab's budget would fall by 1932 to only 40 percent of its 1929 level.[2]

In December 1929, Whitney prepared a budget for the Research Laboratory in 1930 that totaled $1.9 million, an 18 percent drop from the 1929 budget.[3] As in 1907, carrying out this disagreeable task coincided with the onset of a serious illness that shook his faith in his vocation. At age 39 that faith could be restored. At age 61, it was too late.

Unlike 1907 this new illness was not preceded by clear signals. He would write in one subsequent letter that 1928 was the year his troubles began. But the evidence from his pocket diaries, commonplace book, and letters suggests that to be an error. Nothing more serious can be found before late 1929 than an occasional regretful note. ("I talked to Union (College) boys Mar. 20, '29," he wrote. "Left most unsaid. I was like a cheer leader.") and vague family recollections of a growing nervousness.[4]

The late 1929 illness took the form of a steep, continuing decline, not a sudden crisis as in 1907. By New Year's Day, 1930, he had collected his thoughts sufficiently to write about his condition. "I don't suppose I can correctly describe my feelings now," he wrote:

> but I want to try. I do it so that if I get back to normal I can believe that it is a possible thing to do. I have surely been sick. Perhaps it is nervous indigestion, ulcers of the intestine, even the duodenum. A depressing feeling in the stomach which is quite controlling. It has made a perfect coward of me, and removed me from about every vestige of interest in anything or in doing anything. Nothing seems worthwhile and almost everything seems impossible. This applies just exactly the same to the job at the lab as to the little things in the family or the planning about the house.[5]

He spent two weeks in Florida in January. The vacation did him little good. His weight fell from 165 to 150. He found it difficult to face the ordinary activities at the laboratory or to maintain his air of optimism. Writing apologetically in March 1930 to journalist George W. Gray, he explained: "When I see what I think is excessive weight given to modern science by the public I get into the unhealthy state of mind you had to witness."[6]

Despite Whitney's plea that his "individual philosophy" be reserved for "individual private use," Gray published an article picturing the optimistic pre-Depression Whitney and emphasizing his "come in, rain or shine" accessibility. It brought a shower of pleas for help. They deepened Whitney's sense of despair. "I have no regrets for the 'rain or shine,' he wrote in November,

> but I wish I had the wealth and wisdom to help all the people who have written me, honestly but despairingly, since the publication of Mr. Gray's story in the *Times*.[7]

He sought to turn off the flow of personal publicity. When Fred C. Kelly, another journalistic creator of the Whitney image, sought a new story in the fall of 1930, Whitney would reply:

> I have seen my name in print recently much more than I would like, and it would please me better if you could write an article on this or any other subject, without having to make it a personal interview with me.[8]

He now recognized the danger inherent in the image his laboratory had created. "There has been so much said about houses of magic and miracles lately that I personally would like to stop it," he told Kelly. "If I am anything, I am a worker, but not of miracles."[9]

Work seemed at first to be a cure. He took time off from the laboratory for manual labor around the farm. On July 5 he described a day of putting in cement around a flower bed. The rhythm of simple, repetitive movement under the hot sun helped drive away the cares for a while. For once, he tired himself out from work, rather than from worry. At just the right moment Evelyn appeared with a glass of ginger ale. The cool refreshment after wearying physical effort struck him as "the most enjoyable combination in the world." He felt "as though if I could work and get tired and let the brain rest I would be satisfied."[10]

But when he tried to return to the laboratory, the troubles came back. On July 23, 1930, he went to the Neurological Institute of New York for two weeks of physical and psychological examinations and physiotherapy treatments. The doctors could find no specific ailment and recommended rest and a change of scenery. He decided on a trip to Europe, accompanied by his friend Charles McMullen, a Schenectady surgeon. Swope wrote him an encouraging bon voyage note: "I hope you are going to find so many delightful new things to look at and new experiences that you will forget about the job. Stay away as long as there are new things to see."[11]

Seven years earlier, his European itinerary had taken him to see Rutherford in London, Madame Curie in Paris, Debye in Leyden, and Einstein, Haber, and Nernst in Berlin. The 1930 trip avoided the laboratories and the big cities. Instead, he and McMullen walked ten miles a day on the roads around Tavistock, until Whitney felt his strength returning and brought his weight back up to one hundred sixty. Then they toured resorts on the continent as summer gave way to early fall: ten days at Montreaux, four at Zermatt, three weeks in Italy, a leisurely tour from Milan to San Remo, and then to Genoa. On October 16, they boarded the liner *Augusta* to return to New York.[12]

Back in Schenectady, his personal troubles, those of his laboratory, and those of the country seemed to have stabilized. His stomach trouble had disappeared. His chronic sore throat was gone. His foot cramps had practically gone away. "Troubles reduced apparently to zero," he noted on November 3. "Bank balance good but that could not have been the cause of the worry."[13] The reduction of the laboratory's staff could have been a cause of the worry, but a large part of that reduction had now been accomplished. Some layoffs had been necessary, but he had succeeded in arranging a large transfer of personnel to GE's radio business when it was split off to join RCA. Radio manufacture dipped less seriously than other industries in the depression, so this move helped secure the jobs of the twenty or so engineers who made the move. A few employable young scientists lined up jobs at universities. So the reduction in total staff by nearly sixty people, half of them salaried, that Whitney carried out in 1930 was not as severe as the bare figures indicate.[14]

In the nation, too, the unrelieved gloom of the winter of 1929–1930 gave way to a mixture of good and bad news. In the spring of 1930, production indices rose slightly, and the stock market temporarily leveled off. GE president Swope put a company-funded unemployment compensation plan into effect. President Hoover took unprecedented, though in the outcome wholly inadequate, steps to meet the emergency: a temporary tax cut and a $400,000 public works appropriation. He also sought to reinflate the nation's confidence by bringing leaders of business and opinion to meetings and dinners at the White House. Whitney attended one such dinner there in December 1930, in honor of Vice-President Curtis.[15]

As that Washington trip indicated, Whitney had got back to work and back into his round of public activities. In that winter of 1930–31, he came back to the office. He traveled to Boston to discuss MIT affairs with Karl Compton and National Academy of Sciences matters with Harlow Shapley and to New York to meet Einstein. "I am perfectly well. So far as I can see, in both body and mind I am sound as a bell," he wrote on January 25, 1931. "I enjoy my work very much and am anxious to do more. . . ." He had new projects: a method of recording much longer stretches of spoken words than would fit on a standard disk record, and the "hot bed," an early electric blanket.[16]

He now awoke at 6:30 A.M. and immediately dressed and took a twenty-minute walk "largely to get the cobwebs of night dreams out of my head." He took a two- or three-hour nap on midweek afternoons. Braced by these measures, he noted by February that he was "feeling fine" and had "improved for months." By the spring he felt well enough to give a speech to the Chamber of Commerce of Boston—his first public address since 1929. It drew a good-natured complaint from Swope, who was trying to get him to pass up public appearance in favor of recuperation.[17]

Swope himself became more aware than Whitney that the mixed signals of 1930 represented only a pause in a serious and deteriorating situation. As late as mid-1930, he still hoped that GE's strong financial position could carry the Company through the Depression without major salary reductions or layoffs. "If we ever come to a reduction of salaries," he told a group of the Company's leaders in July "it will be a reflection that we have not done our job, including myself." But in October GE's works managers had requested permission to lay off the least efficient of the Company's veteran workers. "It would be cruel to let go these men," Swope protested—but he agreed to the step.[18] As Whitney emerged toward recovery in January 1931, Swope went on a vacation cruise and scribbled out on telegraph forms and the backs of envelopes an ambitious plan of national economic revival. Trade organizations chartered by the government would regulate working conditions and gather production data within individual industries, in much the same way that GE's patent licensing policy regulated production and prices in the light bulb business. The Federal Government would oversee these cartel-like arrangements. Always an advocate of cooperation and planning, Swope stood ready to jettison competition to lighten the economic ship and help it survive the storm.

Swope consented to ship-lightening measures at GE, too. But throwing overboard a worn-out Whitney was not one of them. Swope showed a genuine concern for Whitney's health. As good as that health appeared on the surface, it still mirrored the nation's economy and the state of his laboratory. In both, surface indicators masked underlying unsoundness. The best measure of the nation's economic health was not the slight upturn of production but the more than six hundred fifty banks that closed their doors in the fall of 1930 alone. The best measure of the health of Whitney's laboratory was not enthusiastic public pronouncements but a look at its list of projects. The lab issued a monthly confidential report to the GE lamp department of its efforts of possible interest to the lamp and vacuum tube businesses. In October 1929, the list had run to twenty-three items, including areas of research studies such as the Raman effect, the Barkhausen effect, and high-frequency plasma oscillations. By mid-1931, the list was down to ten items, all of them directly concerned with improving lamps or finding new applications for them (such as sterilizing water with ultraviolet radiation). By mid-1932, the list would fall to four projects.[19]

Whitney also lowered his personal expectations as he returned to health. He became reluctant to allow his face and cheery quotations to appear in magazine discussions of science and religion. Whe F. S. Mead of the *Christian-Herald* requested such an interview in February 1931, Whitney wired back:

> Sorry to disappoint you but scientists seem to me no better than children for your object and they may do harm by thoughtless talk.[20]

Even in prosperous times he had felt uncomfortable about the "house of magic" label. Now he tried to detach it from the laboratory he directed. "I don't believe in magic," he wrote in preparation for his March 1931 speech in Boston. He recognized that his recovery remained incomplete. "I am not such an active, radical, and fertile leader as I wish I were," he wrote in February 1931.[21]

In 1931 Whitney seemed to have made a successful adjustment to economic downturn and his own ill health. It looked like the 1908 experience all over again. On September 4 he announced a major reorganization of the laboratory. He had transferred "certain classes of engineering work"—the remainder of the vacuum tube effort, for example—to the company's engineering departments. The number of laboratory development sections had been reduced to four, each now to be managed by a veteran researcher. G. M. J. MacKay would direct work on electrical cables and insulation. Fonda would manage the applied lamp work. William Ruder would manage the magnetic materials effort. Fuller would direct the projects in applied metallurgy. The research side remained under the guidance of the assistant and associate directors, Coolidge, Langmuir, Hull, and Dushman. The laboratory's total employment had come down to 374 by the end of 1931, about three-quarters the size of its peak in 1929. This reduction paralleled that undergone by the entire company's work force. GE had eliminated Saturday morning work, with a proportionate reduction in pay.[22]

But the worst appeared to be over. In July 1931 GE had held its annual "Camp Engineering." It brought together the company's leadership and its "promising young men" for meetings and sports on Association Island in Lake Ontario. Coats and ties were left at home, and for a few days a relaxed, informal Swope and his top associates mixed informally with their subordinates on the playing field and in the "Black Cat" bar. Whitney felt well enough to resume his usual role at this gathering. He delivered an inspirational talk (indeed, it is titled "Inspirational Talk") describing how economic troubles were temporary, but the progress inspired by science went on forever. Right now, he suggested, it was leading toward a technological revolution in the application of electricity to farming and a scientific revolution in biology.[23]

"Been perfectly well all month," he wrote in his commonplace book in August 1931, "and working every day but one or two when I had a cold caught on the island in July.

> The throat trouble only occurs once or twice a month for just a moment's reminder. I weigh about 163 most of the time. . . . Worry don't "sink in" very deep now and I can't see but that I am as well as I was 20 or 10 years ago . . . my own efforts seem to be great medicine.[24]

By the winter of 1931–32 he had regained an interest in the laboratory's new projects. The character of such projects had changed since the onset of the depression. Rather than look toward the long-range development of new business areas—for example, aircraft navigation or advanced X-ray applications—they typically aimed at quick, easy applications of electrical and materials technology to immediate product opportunities. Technician William Kearsley had now built an electric blanket, and Whitney used his daily nap to test it out in his office. The laboratory's metallurgists used the new cutting tool material Carboloy to design a razor blade sharpener and a new type of phonograph needle. Other engineers and scientists built polarized light headlights and electric hot plates and corn poppers.

These efforts never got beyond the laboratory in the 1930s. Research could not generate new products, revive consumer spending, and put people back to work. It proved as insufficient to meet the emergency as Swope's unemployment relief and Hoover's combination of a tax cut, public works, and exhortation. The economy had not yet struck bottom. Instead, the failure of large Austrian and German banks in the spring of 1931 had turned the Depression into a worldwide emergency. Foreign trade slumped, adding to domestic problems. The second half of 1931 brought steep declines in commodity and stock prices and a new fall in the level of industrial production.[25]

People were now losing hope that business as usual could bring the nation's economy back to health. Research, sound management, and other established methods were not enough. New solutions put forward to meet the crisis in 1931 called for fundamental changes in the nation's economic structure and operations. Swope unveiled his plan of industrial reorganization to the public in September 1931. By then he was only one of a flock of advocates of national planning as a substitute for competition. Others taking the same position ranged from conservative financier Bernard Baruch to liberal historian and social critic Charles A. Beard. And a second type of solution, urged by economists William T. Foster and Waddell Catchings, looked to vastly increased government spending as the cure.[26]

But as the debate about long-range solutions went on into early 1932, businessmen had to take short-range action. Swope and his associates at GE looked upon factories producing only

25 percent as many turbines, motors, lamps, and other electrical products as they had turned out in 1929. Sales no longer met expenses. Only two methods presented themselves for making up the difference: cutting expenses—mainly by cutting wages and releasing workers—or passing up the dividend to the company's stockholders. Each step would affect a constituency of roughly 70,000 people, though with greatly different impact in each case.

Swope and his colleagues did not hesitate. They chose to preserve the dividend and with it the Company's financial integrity. In 1930 a teacher at Mount Holyoke had written to Swope:

> Is it true that the question was put to the General Electric stockholders whether they should pass the dividends and keep the factory going, or pay the dividends and shut down the factory and they voted to shut down the factory and pay the dividends?[27]

Swope could answer honestly: "no such question was ever put up to the stockholders of the General Electric, nor to the directors." It would simply not have occurred to the Company's leadership that the workers of the company had a prior claim on profits to the shareholders. When the renewed downturn of late 1931 and early 1932 came, the company embarked on a new round of wage cuts, reductions of the work week, and layoffs.

At first, the Company could convince itself that it was only getting rid of its inefficient workers. Not everyone who lost his place agreed with that assessment. Paul Adeler, a twenty-two-year veteran, came back to work from an illness in March 1932 to find that he no longer had a job. "They were laying them off in the hundreds," he said:

> Of course, I laid it to the foreman. Him and I had a little trouble quite a few years back, and he told me he would get me. I went back to see Mr. Spicer (Schenectady Works Manager) and they shoved a $500 settlement under my nose. I said, Mr. Spicer, what would you do. He said, I would not take it.[28]

But in fact the laid-off workers had little choice but to take their lump sum severance pay. Protests proved futile. In May a group calling itself the "Provisional Committee of Laid Off Workers of the GE" held a mass meeting at the Turnverein Hall in Albany. But beyond getting newspaper coverage for its charges that the company had laid off seven thousand workers recently, while paying $41 million in dividends in 1931, the committee could accomplish nothing.[29]

By now, the Company's management had to admit that the layoffs were more than a housecleaning. "At this time," wrote Corporate executive E. O. Shreve to district and department managers in May 1932, "thru elimination from payroll, our organization should be free of ineffective employees." He instructed that further layoffs should be on the basis of a furlough rather than a separation. Instead of receiving a lump sum severance payment, the discharged employee would now get a promise that he would be considered for reemployement if conditions improved within twelve months.[30]

These were the conditions Whitney faced in early 1932. He had followed the company in cutting the work week back to four days. He no longer had the opportunity to cushion the effect of further cuts, as he had done in 1930, by transferring groups of researchers to the slightly more prosperous portions of the company such as the radio department. He would have to make budget cuts and staff reproductions bigger than before, with no bottom in sight.

He expressed no objection to Swope's policies for meeting the Depression. In fact, the difficulties seemed to bring the two closer together. Since the Depression's start, Swope had gone out of his way to express confidence in the Research Laboratory. "Research is the search for new methods," he had told a group of lamp department managers in July 1930:

> and the question is how much can you advantageously spend. The best guide of that is our experience in the past. And our past experience has been fraught with great satisfaction.[31]

Whitney in his turn retained his confidence in and support for Swope. "We have a bold and ambitious president. His aims are exactly our own," he wrote in 1931. "His boldness is just enough, his willingness to try experiments in insurance is just enough . . . he is an incessant worker." In February 1931, the corporate office sent out its annual request to the members of the advisory committee to rate each other for the purpose of salary determination. As always, the rating was done in the form of a number expressing the respondent's view of each committee member's relative value. Whitney not only rated Swope the highest but gave him twice the score give to the next one on his list, Board Chairman Owen D. Young. Through the depression, Whitney loyally carried out all Swope's policies without complaint. Not all the company's senior statesmen did the same. In April 1932 Swope wrote to fifteen of GE's recently retired leaders, asking them to accept a temporary reduction in their pensions to share the burden of the depression with GE's workers. Thirteen of the fifteen refused, including Swope's predecessor as GE's president, Edwin W. Rice, Jr.[32]

Whitney's response to the renewed onslaught of budget cutting and layoffs in early 1932 came not in the form of opposition to company policies or attempts to invent novel responses. Instead, as in 1907 and 1930, he turned on himself. His pocket diary indicates that he carried on his usual busy schedule of meetings, trips, and laboratory work through January. Then in February his activity comes to a halt. "Vacation get well" reads the entry for February 4, prefacing three weeks in Nassau.[33] He returned to work in March but found he could not face his daily tasks. He was preoccupied by returning stomach pains, insomnia, dropping blood pressure, and weight loss. He lost interest in any form of work. The long period of identification of Whitney with the General Electric Research Laboratory—the period when, in Hawkins' words, "Whitney was the laboratory and the laboratory was Whitney" was coming to an end. Unlike the situation in 1907, the questions of whether Whitney could recover from his illness and the accompanying depression and whether the laboratory could recover from its malaise became two separate questions, rather than parts of the same one.[34]

The laboratory's illness did not appear terminal; even in the spring of 1932, General Electric showed no signs of ceasing to support research. But would the character of research change? Would short-range "fire-fighting" crowd out science? And would the habit of looking over one's shoulder at the economic situation and the state of the company become so ingrained as to make creativity impossible? On April 19 Swope convinced Whitney to take an official leave of absence and put Coolidge temporarily in charge of the laboratory. Coolidge immediately asked Swope for guidance on the laboratory's program. "He wants us to draw in some on both lines, pot boiling and fundamental," Coolidge was told. Swope also instructed him to make reductions in staff, working hours, and salaries in concert with the rest of the Schenectady Works.[35]

The laboratory did not have a great deal of fundamental work to draw back on. And with their own engineering staffs increasingly idle, the Company's product departments had less reason than in times of prosperity to bring potboilers to the laboratory. The lab's major efforts concerned neither potboiling nor research but new product and process development work. The Depression threatened the continuation of such projects. Some appeared unlikely to be commercially successful in a time of business downturn, no matter how good they were technically. For example, the laboratory's work on a mercury vapor power system for electricity generation had helped create a new type of power plant with a substantially improved efficiency. But with fuel cheap, and the beleaguered utility companies lacking both money and the will to make large capital investments, who would buy it? Other developments might find a market if technically successful. But on these, the laboratory was running into technical problems. In 1932 the lighting researchers were trying to build a sodium vapor lamp for highway lighting in imitation of one that the Philips Company had already introduced in Europe. "It is clear that we don't know how to build the lamp," Coolidge admitted in August. By the time they learned, the sodium lamp was on the way to being bypassed by the mercury vapor fluorescent. Similarly, GE had correctly focused on the need for a better cooling fluid for refrigerators than the currently used sulfur dioxide. But the laboratory's candidate, methyl formate, proved inferior to the fluorocarbon refrigerants invented at General Motors and introduced by Frigidaire.[36]

This period of low productivity of the lab's technical efforts corresponded to challenges to its traditional role as an autonomous research unit. One proposal that surfaced in 1932 called for the lab to begin selling its services outside General Electric. A trial in this direction had already begun, with the laboratory's chemists taking on a consulting assignment with the Curtis Publishing Company to study the use of ozone for drying printing ink. A second proposal came from Theodore Quinn, the aggressive and highly successful manager of the refrigerator department. He suggested that the laboratory accept the job of inspecting refrigerators and putting a research laboratory stamp of approval on them. This paralleled the old Mazda service for light bulbs. It essentially meant using the scientific prestige of the laboratory as an advertising gimmick.[37]

Swope rejected both of these proposals for diluting the Research Laboratory's role. He did not want to see the lab working for other companies, even if that would bring in money. He wanted the advantages of strength in advanced science and engineering to be applied to General Electric. And as for the stamp-of-approval proposal, "Mr. Swope felt that it would make engineers of us," Coolidge noted. Albert G. Davis also presented a more practical objection to the scheme. "It was now poor advertising," Coolidge reported him as saying. In the 1920s, the approval of science may have sufficed to sell anything; in the 1930s, the public had turned skeptical.[38]

Defense against such onslaughts only partly solved the laboratory's problems. It needed not only to preserve its existing role but also to find the spark of new ideas and renewed interest that would lead to achievement. In personal terms Whitney faced a parallel problem. Ceasing to come to the office in April 1932 could relieve him of the immediate pressures that accompanied his deteriorating health. But mere withdrawal could not reignite his enthusiasm.

Perhaps medicine could provide the answer. On April 26,

Charles McMullen, the surgeon and friend of Whitney's who had accompanied him through Europe in 1930, referred him to Dr. Llwellys Barker at the Psychiatric Institute at Johns Hopkins. The physical symptoms accompanying Whitney's mood disturbances—for example, the fall in his blood pressure from its usual 150 to 98—suggested to McMullen that the problem might be endocrine disturbances. Whitney entered the hospital at Baltimore. Barker and his associates gave him a full physical examination. They found, Coolidge reported to Swope, "nothing organically wrong but an exhausted nervous system." They kept him at Johns Hopkins through May, prescribing total isolation from mail and visitors, a regimen of massage, and the occupational therapy of bookbinding.[39]

As busy as Swope was between his stewardship of GE and his growing role as a national adviser, he took a personal interest in Whitney's condition. Coolidge had sensed from talking to Whitney before his departure for Baltimore that worry about the expenses of hospitalization added to the strain. "For Dr. Whitney's future peace of mind," he wrote Barker on May 9:

> I hope that the expense of his treatment is not going to be more than he can afford. . . . Dr. Whitney, like most scientists, is far from being a rich man, and has, I know, worried considerably about expenses lately. As I told him last night, he is so conscientious that when I discussed money matters with him recently he was unwilling to entertain the idea of accepting money from the Company during his leave of absence.

Coolidge conveyed these concerns to Swope. The next day Swope wrote to Barker expressing his concern. "Dr. Whitney is very dear to me, personally, as I have known him for many years," he began. He explained to Barker that he had seen Whitney just before the trip to Baltimore, to "relieve his mind of worry" about the technical side of his job. He assured Barker that Whitney's salary would continue indefinitely during his leave of absence, in spite of Whitney's request to the contrary.[40]

The hospital stay lasted six weeks. Both of Whitney's doctors, McMullen and Barker, recommended that it be followed by an "entire separation from the laboratory for several months." Whitney complied. But his condition at first continued to worsen. Looking back on it later, it seemed to him that he "struck bottom" mentally toward the end of June. He had no appetite and no interest in anything. His brave hopes of eventually returning to the research director's job now began to vanish. The height of his ambition now was to stand and hoe corn in his garden for an hour a day. "I suggested you grant me several months absence without pay," he begged Swope again in late June.

> By that time I may know better what to expect of myself . . . I cannot bear the thought of having no GE work but it may be best to appoint Dr. Coolidge director for he deserves it.[41]

Carefully phrased advice from Baltimore contributed to Whitney's decision. "You have psychomotor acceleration and less inhibition than usual," Dr. Barker wrote him in early August. That represented not so much an explanation as a rephrasing of Whitney's complaint. His mind now worked too hard, generating a flood of mental associations, and making it impossible to concentrate on any subject. But gradually, he was able to bring the condition under control. On September 6, he returned to the laboratory for the first time since April. He planned to spend mornings in his office and to sit in on some of the most important technical conferences. But at the same time, he gradually began to prepare Coolidge to turn his temporary post as research director into a permanent one.[42]

This gradual passing on of authority coincided with a continuing decline in the laboratory's fortunes. On the same day that Whitney told Coolidge to expect, not six months, but two to three years as acting director, the laboratory's colloquium was discontinued—ending temporarily an institution dating back to 1901. And on the day that the matter of turning the laboratory into a quality control bureau of appliances came up for discussion, on October 21, Whitney told Coolidge "that he had asked Mr. Swope to make me Director. This is to take effect November 1."[43]

In his formal letter to Swope confirming the request, Whitney put it this way:

It is my plan to continue to do what I can in the laboratory, but at present it will probably have to be done forenoons only. When I can work full time I want to do so, but I cannot see any difficulty in doing that with Dr. Coolidge directing. The combination of Coolidge as director with Whitney helping as much as he can, is certainly better than the present set up with Whitney out half the time.[44]

Swope accepted Whitney's request, with one important modification. Whitney would retain the position of vice president of research. On October 28, Swope cleared the official announcement with Whitney and released it to the press:

Owing to ill health and the doctor's orders that he give up some of the strenuous burdens that he has been carrying so enthusiastically, Dr. W. R. Whitney has asked to be relieved of the directorship of the Research Laboratory, but, I am glad to say, will continue as Vice-President in general charge of the research work of the Company.
Effective November 1, 1932, Dr. W. D. Coolidge is appointed Director of the Research Laboratory.[45]

The suggestion that Whitney was going out with his enthusiasm undiminished was a final considerate gesture by Swope. He did his best to make sure that the world did not know about the bitter feeling of exhaustion and failure that had overtaken Whitney in the past year. And indeed, the public versions of Whitney's retirement carried this intended message. The *New York Sun* ran an editorial about the announcement that read:

Dr. Whitney retire? Pooh! . . . . Dr. Whitney in seclusion, Dr. Whitney in retreat, Dr. Whitney withdrawn from circulation—these are unthinkable. The Whitney intellect had served knowledge too long to be suspended in its operations by a mere rearrangement of opportunities. The Whitney curiosity has so persistently projected into the abyss of man's ignorance that no shifting of titles can restrain it from future excursions into that fascinating unplumbed gulf. The Whitney utilitarianism is too robust to be manacled by assignment to nonroutine duties. The Whitney spirituality is too pervading to be definitely engrossed on a scroll and filed away in a cabinet.[46]

On the staff of the Research Laboratory, a different version prevailed. "When the depression forced personnel cuts throughout the Company," engineer John H. Payne, a member of the laboratory staff since 1913, wrote later, "Whitney was asked to prepare a list of Research Laboratory people who could be released. His comment was 'put my name first.' "[47]

But the facts fit neither the *Sun*'s picture of Whitney steaming off into retirement with his fires still burning nor Payne's implication that Whitney left in a combined gesture of protest and self-sacrifice. The manner of his departure had, in fact, been designed both to speed his recovery from depression and to retain his connection with the laboratory. By the end of the year, the cure had begun to work. "I feel better all the time," he wrote in his commonplace book on December 27, 1932. He continued to spend mornings at the laboratory and afternoons at home. As he put it:

I can do as much good at the Lab'y (Coolidge made director Sept. 32) and have spent most of the afternoons out of doors. By noon even yet I find I am nervously exhausted, but moderately happy while I know I would not feel so well if I worked inside all (day?). Today Wednesday after the good rest Friday to Tuesday I had a happy day all day with much of the feeling of physical comfort and mental happiness through many of the nervous (high?) speed phenomena I know.[48]

The "psychomotor acceleration" apparently persisted. The official message Christie had been putting out depicted Whitney as perfectly happy, mentally well, and rapidly recovering from his physical problems. Not all of his many correspondents were convinced by it. "I know exactly what is at the root of your indisposition," wrote Jewett, the first president of the Bell Laboratories, in July 1932.

> I am presently in the throes of much of what you have already gone through. How it will come out so far as the gang or some of us individually are concerned time alone can tell.[49]

Jewett probably exaggerated the perfection of his understanding of Whitney's troubles. He had refrained from enthusiastic speechmaking and personal identification with the new prosperity in the 1920s, so he had less reason than Whitney to look at the economic downturn as judgment on himself. But like Whitney, he had faced the need to cut staff and budgets and had not tried to avoid or protest the task. By mid-1933, the Bell Labs work force was on a four-day week, salaries were down more than 25 percent, and Jewett had put in place a separation allowance system for discharging employees too young to receive a pension.

Across the industrial research community, the timing and depth of the depression's impact varied greatly. U.S. Steel had only recently established a true scientific laboratory on the GE model and decided to preserve it in spite of the depression. Its lab remained on a five-day week and at full strength, although salaries were cut by 35 percent. American Cyanamid, William D. Coolidge noted, was spending a million dollars per year on research, had not decreased development and research at all, and had hired away one of General Electric's best chemists, George M. J. MacKay, to serve as research director. Some companies drew the erroneous conclusion they were Depression-proof and boosted research spending. The A. O. Smith Company, with a strong backlog of orders for pipe in 1932, hired away GE metallurgist Samuel Hoyt and increased its research force to one hundred people. But when the Depression struck it in full fury in 1934, it cut that staff back to sixty (again according to Coolidge's information).

In some companies, the percentage of annual sales dedicated to research remained steady or even increased. Kodak's research spending went up from 1.25 percent of sales to 1.5

percent. Du Pont's research spending remained at the relatively high level of 4.7 percent of sales (GE spent only .5 percent of sales on its research laboratory). According to Coolidge, "Du Pont generous on salaries and large bonuses—discharge in droves with brutality." GE's most important competitor, Westinghouse, experienced perhaps the most severe impact on research of any U.S. corporate giant in the 1930s. It underwent cuts similar to those Whitney carried out between 1929 and 1932. But then, in 1934, when other laboratories were stabilizing their situations, Westinghouse apparently carried out another deep cut. William C. White reported to Coolidge that the head of physics research at Westinghouse was "forced to make much more drastic reduction in force now than during worst of depression," a cut that reduced the staff by 25 percent to 33 percent.[50]

It is difficult to convert this impressionistic information about the major laboratories into a comprehensive picture of industrial research in the Depression. Historian Spencer Weart has made the most careful attempt to do so. He estimates that employment of "research workers" in industry, based on a sample he examined, fell by about 20 percent in the years 1930–33. That is less than the 30 percent drop in total U.S. nonagricultural employment. Weart could not tell whether fundamental research suffered more than applied work. At Bell Labs, some scientists used their extra day off a week to study the quantum mechanics of solids, the subject that would a dozen years later provide that laboratory with the scientific basis for the transistor. Similar initiatives may have occurred elsewhere.[51]

At GE, the Depression had never threatened to eliminate research altogether. The real question was its impact on the balance between the more fundamental work and "potboiling." This now became an issue for Coolidge and Swope, with Whitney cheering from the sidelines. The evidence suggests that the GE leaders seized the earliest opportunities they could to reaffirm the role of pure science and innovation in industrial research.

The first opportunity to do so came fortuitously and symbolically. In December 1932, a month after Whitney's retirement and as the economy headed for new depths, word came from Stockholm that Langmuir had become the first American industrial scientist to win a Nobel Prize. In spite of the Depression, and in the face of possible adverse criticism from heads of other departments, Coolidge—with Swope's concurrence—sent Langmuir on a fully paid three-month tour of Europe to receive the prize and visit the major European scientific centers. Of course, such a move was more than a reaffirmation of basic science. For publicity reasons alone, it now became more important then ever to keep Langmuir happy so that he would not consider leaving GE for the university post he could obtain so easily. But it did at least remind the company of the strength of its scientific assets.[52]

Coolidge began immediately to make more concrete initiatives too. He encouraged advanced work in electronics, such as the studies by electrical engineer Chester W. Rice on two-centimeter radio waves—far shorter wavelengths than any of potential commercial importance. He supported physicist Kenneth Kingdon's efforts to explore new types of electron accelerators, although at a very modest level. These initiatives were balanced by a need to continue cutting the staff through the winter of 1932–33. Among Coolidge's early official actions, as research director beginning November 30, were letters to five scientists and engineers informing them of their coming termination of employment. And he prepared a budget for 1933 that was just half what the laboratory's budget had been only two years earlier.[53]

But these early and severe cuts were the last drastic ones Coolidge had to make. Employment stabilized in 1933 at about two hundred and seventy people (about seventy-five of them scientists and engineers, and about twenty-five of them Ph.D.'s). By the end of 1933, Swope was ready for new initiatives. Just before Christmas he rode the train from Schenectady to New York City with Coolidge and Whitney to attend a Nobel Centenary Dinner. The talk naturally turned to research. As Coolidge reported it afterward:

> Mr. Swope would like to see us add 4 or 5 chemists to our staff to develop new products—he refers for illustrative purposes to cellophane of Du Pont. . . . Doesn't want us to exceed budget.[54]

By February 1934 Collidge had converted this encouraging hint into a proposal for increased fundamental research in chemistry. He took the case to Swope in his New York office. GE's president first had to be reminded what Coolidge meant by that term *fundamental research*. But when he understood, he went along, "Mr. Swope OK'd my trying out the four Harvard chemists located by Marshall," Coolidge noted, "even if we keep two or three of them and even tho we exceed budget in so doing." This initiative in a new field of fundamental research taken in a time of Depression would pay big dividends for GE. The research effort Coolidge put underway under Dr. Abraham L. Marshall led GE into a new field, the chemistry of man-made materials. That research, over the next twenty years, launched businesses in areas such as silicones, plastics, and even man-made diamond. By 1980 the area contributed more than a billion dollars to GE's annual sales.[55]

So Whitney could note with satisfaction that the type of laboratory he had established would survive the Depression. He sought to make sure that the spirit of teamwork, the open door, and optimism survived as well. He resumed his tours of the laboratory, neither hiding nor emphasizing his own personal problems, but focusing on encouraging the researchers he visited. His approach in the mid-1930s might be summed up in the ancient Greek epitaph:

> A shipwrecked sailor on this coast
> Bids you set sail
> Full many a gallant bark, when I was lost
> Weathered the gale.[56]

The bark of industrial research weathered the gale. Whitney had lost his place at the helm. But he would soon have been forced to step down by advancing age in any case. He took it as his remaining task to contribute what moral support he could, while adjusting his personal compound of activities to a life on the sidelines. For a man who had written in 1929 "I must serve to live," this was a major adjustment.[57]

His health began to stabilize. He underwent a hernia operation in early 1933. By the middle of the year he felt able to enter into his commonplace book one of those announcements of recovery that had by now become periodic. "By working forenoons only since the operation for hernia," he noted,

> I certainly have been coming back. I get so much more interest in doing things that I do not feel like starting "health notes" like this. I believe I can do a lot better, tho recently some of the old throat trouble has turned up and signs of a cold, but generally I feel so much encouraged that I take on new ideas and seem to have more ideas than usual recently.[58]

Touring the laboratory in the afternoons, he seemed himself again. Looking back much later on the 1930s, GE researcher Vincent Schaefer could not recall any sharp break in Whitney's cheerful and regular visits to the lab bench where Schaefer assisted Langmuir. As far as he could tell, though Coolidge headed the laboratory, Whitney seemed to go on playing the same role as ever.[59]

But the visits began to be restricted to a narrower circle of the laboratory veterans. And although Whitney freely offered his advice, Coolidge was clearly and completely in charge. The replacement of the exothermic Whitney by the endothermic Coolidge might have been expected to shift the laboratory toward more conservative policies. But this did not occur. At times it was Coolidge who felt able to begin initiatives into new research areas that Whitney—still, in many ways, a piker in audacity—thought risky or irrelevant. For example, when physicist Kenneth Kingdon expressed an interest in experimental nuclear physics in 1933, Coolidge noted:

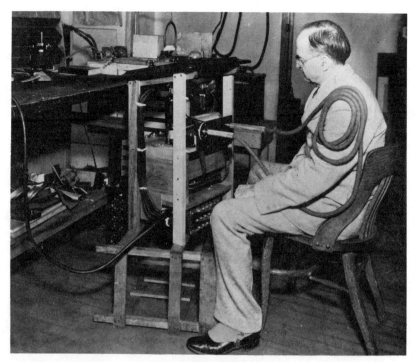

Whitney ready for experiment with high-frequency heating coil on his shoulder.

Dr. Whitney feels that it might be better to have Kingdon working on metal receiving tubes for radio than on atomic disintegration. He felt a little differently about it, however, on seeing that I had some definite ideas as to how Kingdon could start at disintegration work and how we *might* use his early tubes as an X-ray generator for medical work.[60]

In the event, Kingdon's work led indirectly, not to new X-ray tubes, but to his participation in early U.S. efforts on nuclear power, and ultimately to a job for him after World War II as director of GE's first nuclear power research laboratory. As in the case of the new chemistry research efforts, Coolidge's championship of fundamental research helped lead to new opportunities for General Electric's diversification.

Whitney now concentrated his personal research efforts on his hobbies and hunches. As his interest and enthusiasm revived in 1933, he resumed work on the inductotherm, his radiofrequency heating device. It had proved useful in heat treatments for shoulder injuries suffered by a couple of members of the laboratory staff, and Whitney became interested in the possible reasons for these successes. This led him into the study of bursitis, a painful condition of the shoulder due to inflammation of a small sac of tissue called the bursa.[61]

By 1935 he had developed a hypothesis to explain both the cause of the condition and the efficacy of the inductotherm. As earlier in his research career, he had turned to an electrochemical mechanism. He pictured continuing muscular exercise raising levels of lactic acid in the bloodstream in the vicinity of the shoulder. That acid dissolved away portions of bone. Somehow—and here the Whitney theory became vague—at the bursa, the acid and bone concentrations, and the local temperatures became just right for the bone to deposit again. The grating of this bone deposit caused bursitis pain. The heat delivered by the inductotherm helped dissolve away that deposited bone, taking away with it the pain and stiffness.

The composition of the deposits in the bursa provided one test of the theory. They were undoubtedly calcium salts, but were they identical to bone? His hopes of finding out brought Whitney to a long-delayed recognition of the value in biological studies of X-ray diffraction. Briefly, he put aside his microscope and took up this technique. It provided evidence that supported his hypothesis. The bursitis deposits showed an X-ray diffraction pattern identical to that of bone and clearly distinguishable from the patterns of other calcium and phosphate compounds. He wrote up these results for the *GE Review* in an uncharacteristically technical paper, drawing so heavily on technical terms that the editor saw fit to publish with it a glossary that ran from "acute fulminating" to "vitro." The paper carried a full array of footnotes, and the proper theory-procedure-results-conclusion organization. But in spite of this bow to scientific etiquette, it seems to have had little permanent impact on bursitis treatment.[62]

It was the closest Whitney came to a final return to professional science. His interest in life and science had returned by the mid-1930s, but from then on his productivity and his mental stability remained tenuous. Although his commonplace book entries report good physical and mental health, his family saw a different picture. "He had breakdown after breakdown," his niece Agnes Wendel recalled later. "He was always trying to make Evelyn think he'd gotten over it." Additional physical ills emerged, such as a callus-like growth on his forehead in 1937. Only in between these bouts could he become his old self. Only then could his interest in the scientific and personal lives of his old laboratory colleagues remain high. Only then could he keep up the hobbies—hunting for arrowheads; building a heated birdhouse in a vain effort to keep the songbirds in the North for the winter; and, above all, the turtles.[63]

In 1937, the *American Magazine* prevailed on Whitney to make some of his thoughts on life and science again available for publication. The thoughts were characteristics of the man. He described his electrically heated birdhouse; his ant colony; his experiments on goldenrod galls; how to find cricket eggs in moss, hatch them in the basement, and have singing crickets by Christmas; and an idea for making mother-of-pearl inlays in conch shells. He took a quick swipe at the sit-down strikers at General Motors ("the happy faces of sit-down strikers which I see in newspaper photographs led me to believe that the workers are not striking for just a few dollars more a week. They are simply having a good time—creating a drama and playing in it"). He reviewed his recent studies in neurology; his observations on the oak-trimmer; his latest suggestions on things that should be invented—a pain meter and disposable tableware; and, finally, some findings from his long study of turtles: "every piece of knowledge is like the branch of a tree," he concluded: at the end of which another branch grows—on and on.

"We begin one research in the laboratory, only to find that another waits at the end of it. Electron tubes such as those used in the radio were developments of the incandescent lamp, which, in turn, was a product of man's struggle with the darkness.

> Have you ever investigated anything just for the pleasure of it? If your inquiries have been merely a part of your job, you have missed most of the kick of life. There is no method that you need here observe, no laws. You simply let your mind travel inquisitively as it will. You need only be yourself—the child that is within you. If you insist that nothing comes of it, then I must write at the bottom of your report a line I wrote many years ago on hundreds of reports from my chemistry students. After the routine experiment of putting a piece of ignited charcoal in a jar of oxygen, they would note such incomplete observations as "it burned." Always on such papers I wrote this instruction: "Repeat the experiment and note the glow.' "[64]

To illustrate the article, the magazine sent a photographer out to the Niskayuna farm. He found Whitney with a neighbor boy, nine-year-old Paul Gundrum, and a turtle. He sat Whitney on an upturned log and stood Paul beside him, offering Whitney the turtle. The picture achieved its purpose. It established at a glance the theme of the story: a world-famous scientist in retirement has turned into a homey rural sage who befriends local children and introduces them to the scientific wonders of nature. It was used with the article and subsequently widely reprinted.

But the picture achieves an unintended purpose, too. It completes a series of three photographs that span and portray his life's journey. Sixty years earlier, Whitney as a boy had positioned himself on a packing box in a photographer's studio and had left an image of youth posed within an artificial studio version of an idyllic rural boyhood. Thirty-two years earlier, he had posed leaning against a rail fence beside his daughter Ennin. He stood proudly, a handsome, confident, thirty-six-year-old man, his legs crossed and chest out, father and daughter looking at each other with smiles that suggested a close relationship and shared secrets. The final picture, at a cursory glance, appeared to complete the series. The scientist

Whitney and his young neighbor Paul Gundrum pose with a turtle for a photographer from the *American* magazine, 1937.

and father had come safely home to leisurely and honored retirement.

But a closer look at the picture conveys suggestions that a closer look at Whitney's retirement confirms. There is nothing exothermic about the old man in that 1937 picture. He looks stiff and tired in his old suit and stiff collar, peering self-consciously half at the turtle, half at the boy, obviously posing. For Whitney, retirement meant a pleasing surface image but beneath it barely hidden disappointments and discomfort. The mental and physical difficulties that began in 1929 never really went away. The neighborhood children such as Paul Gundrum were no substitute for the grandchildren he never had. Indeed, he scarcely had a family at all now. Ennin, grown increasingly eccentric, withdrawn, and mired in the squalor and confusion of her out-of-control farm, rarely came to visit her father. Evelyn too spent most of her time away from the home she had never really adjusted to. She preferred trips to her sister's in Boston or long drives in the family's chauffered Buick. General Electric honored its senior scientific statesman and kept an office and a laboratory room for him at its research laboratory. But it had little real use for him.

All that was really left were the hobbies—the farm and the turtles. The message in that photograph was in one way correct. Whitney was happy touring his beloved farm, with a young companion to listen to a nonstop monologue something like the one that used to echo through the halls of the research lab. "He never seemed to slow down," Paul Gundrum recalls. "He only said he wished he had more time." He would lead Paul through the gardens and along the stream and then stop to feed the goldfish in the pond. Then it was off to the woods to follow the trail of the turtles. Whitney would stride briskly ahead. Paul would struggle to catch up, his galoshes sticking in the spring mud. Some of the old exothermic enthusiasm might return, and Whitney might begin humming his favorite tune, "There's an Old Spinning Wheel in the Parlor." Then the man and the boy would plunge into the woods at the edge of the ploughed field and disappear from view.[65]

Epilogue

It is a thirty-minute drive from the old Research Laboratory buildings at General Electric's Schenectady Works to the old Whitney place on the Lisha Kill. One route between the two passes through the "GE plot" a mile west of the Works. No longer are its spacious homes filled by some of GE's top executives and their families. They have long since moved on, to the Company's new headquarters in Fairfield, Connecticut, or to hundreds of manufacturing sites dispersed around the world. The roughly 17,000 GE employees now in Schenectady still make it GE's largest single site. But where it once accounted for fully one-third of GE's employment, now it is less than 5 percent and falling.

The route continues on past Ellis Hospital, where Whitney died on January 9, 1958, at 89. Until a few years earlier, he had kept active. During World War II, he had gone back to the laboratory bench to study metallurgical problems in support of the war effort. He learned welding from Research Laboratory craftsman Sam Loposino and studied welding corrosion problems.

He kept up his other interests: the turtles, arrowheads, and speculations about the workings of the mind. He read James Breasted's books about ancient civilizations, and he reread Herodotus and Aristotle. He kept up his correspondence with his shrinking circle of old friends and made new friends with his still-breezy letterwriting style.

And he kept coming in to the laboratory. In 1949, the *Wall Street Journal* sent a reporter to Schenectady to prepare a feature story on GE research and its current hot topics—atomic energy, electronics, and man-made precipitation. But that reporter's lead sentence dealt with an 81-year-old man playing around with an electronic "sniffer" designed for detecting refrigerator leaks. Forty-nine years after he had joined the company, Whitney still provided the best copy in General Electric.[1]

Whitney at age 80 in the study of his home at Niskayuna, New York, 1948.

And seventeen years after giving up formal management duties he still roamed the laboratory, a homeopathic surgeon of science dispensing encouragement and advice. "Whitney used to think it wise for each man in Res Lab to have a minor field to work on when tired out from his exertions," a young physicist wrote in his notebook in 1946. Another recalls Whitney discussing with him the thesis that a cluttered desk means a cluttered mind. Whitney decided to subject the idea to an empirical test, searched the lab for its most cluttered desk, found that it belonged to a young chemist with high promise and a highly disciplined mind, and judged the old saw refuted. Another physicist recalls showing Whitney a photomicrograph of a metallic structure with an unusual and regular pattern. A few days later, Whitney came back with a strikingly similar pattern—an enlargement of a portion of a magazine photo showing a tweed jacket worn by the Duke of Windsor.[2]

He tried not to become a bore. "At my age, I can talk any

listener to death and it will get worse as I go along," he wrote in 1943.[3] The occasion was his refusal to accept the suggestion by former GE board chairman Owen D. Young and submit to a ghostwritten autobiography. He resisted a few more times but finally gave in on his own terms. He allowed a long-time GE colleague, John D. Broderick, to serve as his Boswell rather than his ghost. The resulting book captures his still nimble spirit, as he leaps mentally from crag to crag of an eventful life: from worm galls, to turtles, to his Jamestown boyhood, to stainless steel rake handles, to research policy, to boyhood walks to Jamestown swimming holes, to speaking engagements in the 1920s and 1930s, and back to midnights in the Boston of 1886 and the eating of Sennet's all surpassing wheat cakes.

After that book appeared, in 1945, Whitney had five more years of nearly full activity left. Then the 1950s brought him one health problem after another. The most annoying was a chronic case of the hiccups. His doctors could neither find its cause nor cure it. He ceased visiting the laboratory and fell prey to more serious and debilitating ailments. His death in 1958 came as a release from an increasingly burdened and long since completed life.

A monument to the achievements of that life lies five miles northeast of Schenectady, in the suburb of Niskayuna and on the route to Lisha Kill. The General Electric Research and Development Center now occupies a tree-shaded campus on a knoll overlooking the Mohawk River. Its sprawling main building and cluster of specialized facilities hold working space for more than 500 scientists and engineers and more than 1,000 supporting workers. Some 500 more employees occupy the two old laboratory buildings at the main Schenectady plant and outposts around the world, from Sao Paulo to Singapore.

A walk down the front drive of the main Niskayuna laboratory site, beneath an arch of elms, and toward a glass facade etched with portraits of Whitney, and by his two successors Coolidge and C. Guy Suits, provides a good setting for reflection on those questions with which we began. Could the corporation's chemist truly remain a chemist? Would the ideals of

The "old guard" of the GE Research Lab in 1950. Left to right, Saul Dushman, Willis R. Whitney, Irving Langmuir, Albert W. Hull.

science prove compatible with those of industry? And how would the attempt to answer those questions shape the life of an individual?

The experiment Whitney began has proved conclusively that the professional scientist can find a place in industry and remain a scientist. Hundreds of thousands of trained scientists are employed in U.S. industry today. The great majority of them carry out jobs involving mainly routine analysis, administration, or the application of scientific results. But a significant minority, tens of thousands of them, do real research. Most of that research makes only small and unsurprising additions to the store of knowledge (as does most of the research of their academic counterparts). But discoveries of fundamental importance have emerged from industrial laboratories. In fields such as solid state physics and polymer chemistry, the work of industrial scientists has kept up with or even outpaced that of the universities. Two scientists from the laboratory that Whitney founded, Langmuir and Ivar Giaever, have won the Nobel Prize. They have been joined as Nobel laureates by eight employees of the much larger Bell Laboratories.

Industry has supported science, not to establish philanthropic asylums for indigent chemists, but because science pays. Quantitative studies performed by scholars such as economist Edwin Mansfield show that industrial innovation, based largely on the work of research and development laboratories, pays both an attractive rate of profit to industry and an even more attractive "social rate of return" to society as a whole.[4] Specific examples of that payoff include ductile tungsten, the modern type of X-ray tube, man-made diamond, and the engineering plastics Lexan and Noryl from General Electric; the transistor, the charge-coupled device, magnetic bubbles, and dozens of other contributions to electronics, communications, and information processing from Bell Laboratories; Nylon, Orlon, Teflon, and other materials innovations from Du Pont; Kodacolor film from Kodak; tetraethyl lead and freon refrigerants from General Motors; and scores of other important innovations from other companies.

American industrial science has been able to record these achievements because the ideals of science have proved sufficiently compatible with those of industry for industrial laboratories to attract and retain talented professional scientists. An individual wanting to retain professional status, to serve practical ends, and to gain the high salary of an industrial employee can do all three things at once. He or she finds in industry neither a university-in-exile, nor an impersonal research assembly line staffed by scientific proletarians. Instead, industrial research remains the institution Whitney pioneered: a middle way, blending the goals and methods of the corporation and the academic laboratory.

Whitney's successors, both in General Electric and throughout American industry, steer the same couse he did. Like him, they do not insist on total independence from the factory but welcome the requests and advice of company engineers and managers. Like him, their potboilers outnumber their explorations, and their lemons outnumber their peaches. Like him, they seek to create an atmosphere of teamwork, rather than secretiveness and competition. Like him, they encourage the publication of research results, though only after company proprietary interests have been protected.

But if the Whitney strategy remained a guiding one for industrial research, the Whitney style did not. Even in his own lifetime, the world of science had begun to pass him by. That world began to have less and less room for the exothermic generalist, the romanticist, the researcher who preferred the microscope to the complex apparatus and quantitative data of the modern laboratory. Even in the role that Whitney pioneered, the director of industrial research, his style became obsolete. The endothermic manner of leaders such as his successor Coolidge at GE and Jewett at AT&T, became the model for future managers of industrial laboratories.

In part the growing scale of industrial research made this change in style necessary. Under Coolidge's successor, C. Guy Suits, the GE laboratory moved to that sprawling campus outside Schenectady, far from the bustle of GE's biggest works. The halls there were too long for a research director to roam. The staff of more than 1,000 became far too big to remain a happy family. Arthur M. Bueche, Suit's successor, took on the daunting task of combining the Research Lab with an equally large engineering laboratory and making the combination even more effective than ever before at meeting the technical needs of General Electric. But in the process he had to jettison even more of the Whitney style.

Roland W. Schmitt, who succeeded Bueche in 1978, views Whitney's personal style of directing research as something impossible to recapture. "Whitney could walk through and become acquainted with a fairly sizeable fraction of the plant, and a fairly substantial number of the people who worked in his laboratory," he notes.

He could exert quite a direct personal influence on what they did, and make personal decisions about programs and directions at the level of the individual scientist. Today, the number of people involved and the number of different businesses GE is in preclude this. And that is a fundamental reason for the strong emphasis in GE, and here at the R&D Center, on the planning process. It's an attempt to try to put some discipline into what has become too big or too broad in scope for any single individual to make detailed decisions about.[5]

The findings of scholars who have studied the management of U.S. industrial research echo Schmitt's view. Planning, strategy making, structuring, and selling research have become more important tasks for the research manager than daily tours of the lab and a personal familiarity with the work of subordinates. The full calendar has replaced the open door. Manipulating the researcher's environment has become more important than becoming the researcher's substitute father, homeopathic surgeon, or friend. To sociologist William Kornhauser, the key to research management is creating a productive tension between the individual researcher's need for autonomy and the professional group's need for integration. Psychologists Donald Pelz and Frank Andrews have conducted studies showing that a researcher becomes more productive if presented with a variety of responsibilities—research, development, consulting, even a bit of management—rather than channeled into a single specialty.[6]

And to management expert Edward B. Roberts, the personal style of the research director has no effect on the productivity of the laboratory. "The evidence for difference in productivity among groups," he concludes, "rests not on motivational skills but, rather, on the technical competence of the first-line performer's boss."[7]

A tour of that R&D Center near Schenectady that is the successor to Whitney's laboratory provides evidence that the principle Roberts enunciated remains very much in force. But is it truly the final answer? Should the unique spirit Whitney brought to the corporation be wholly replaced by formal planning procedures? Should the question "Are you being productive?" wholly replace the question Whitney used to ask: "Are you having any fun?"

Whitney ran a laboratory with a record of productivity that has never been surpassed. But he did not settle for a cool compromise between the ideals of the laboratory and those of the board room. His life was an exothermic reaction, creating a human compound. True, the reaction did not go to completion, and the compound proved neither as inclusive nor as stable as he had hoped. But his errors, omissions, and failures were those of a warm person reaching out to make contact with others, not those of a cold manager seeking to manipulate others into serving his goals or those of the company.

In the laboratory that stands as Whitney's monument, and in the thousands of others that profited by his example, one hopes that spirit has not been wholly lost. Somewhere in that national research establishment, one hopes, the spirit of a playful boy peering into his first microscope persists—just as, in a dusty cabinet in a small room off the GE R&D Center's main lobby, among the mementos of the career of the corporation's chemist, there remains a beautifully crafted metal image of one of Doc Whitney's turtles.

Appendix A
Major Dates in the Life of
Willis R. Whitney

1868	born August 22, Jamestown, N.Y.
1886	matriculated at MIT
1890	graduated from MIT, B.S., chemistry; married Evelyn B. Jones; joined MIT faculty as assistant instructor of chemistry
1891	his daughter Evelyn born
1894–96	did graduate work at University of Leipzig, Germany, earning Ph.D. in chemistry
1900	joined the General Electric Co. as director of its Research Laboratory
1904	moved permanently to Schenectady, N.Y.
1928	named vice president-research, General Electric Co.
1932	retired as director of GE Research Laboratory; named honorary vice president of GE.
1958	died, January 9, Schenectady, N.Y.

Appendix B
Major Honors Received by
Willis R. Whitney

Member, National Academy of Sciences (elected, 1917)
President, American Chemical Society, 1909
President, American Electrochemical Society, 1912
Willard Gibbs Medal, American Chemical Society
Chandler Medal, American Chemical Society
Perkin Medal, American Chemical Society
Edison Medal, American Institute of Electrical Engineers
John Fritz Medal, American Society of Mechanical Engineers
Chevalier of the Legion of Honor, France
Gold Medal, National Institute of Social Sciences

Notes

1/ THE CORPORATION'S CHEMIST

1. Whitney describes his turtle studies in John Broderick, *Willis R. Whitney*, pp. 221–32.

2. His neighbors' views of Whitney were told to me by his former neighbors John Lake (interview March 11, 1976) and Paul Gundrum (interview April 6, 1976).

3. *Industrial Research Laboratories*.

4. Whitney, "Research and the Newlands Bill," p. 6.

5. The figure of 40 patents is given in Broderick, *Willis R. Whitney*, p. 271. Whitney's bibliography in C. Guy Suits, "Willis Rodney Whitney, 1868–1958," *National Academy of Sciences Biographical Memoirs* (1960), vol. 34, lists more than 100 items, but more than 75 of them are published versions of Whitney's popular addresses on research management and science policy. Only about 25 are scientific research papers.

6. Arthur D. Little, "Presentation Address," p. 26.

7. Wilder D. Bancroft, "Wilhelm Ostwald," p. 611.

2/ THE MANUFACTURING REPUBLIC

1. The photograph is in John Broderick, *Whitney*, opposite p. 65.

2. Alfred D. Chandler, *The Visible Hand*, pp. 240–58.

3. Herbert G. Gutman, "Class, Status and Community Power," p. 11.

4. Paul A. Spengler, "The Development of a Furniture Industry"; interview with B. Dolores Thompson, Feb. 8, 1980.

5. Details of the family history, unless otherwise indicated, are from an interview with Mrs. Agnes Wendel, July 19, 1980; from the Whitney genealogy and accompanying letter sent by Mrs. Wendel to the author, Nov. 24, 1980; and from the genealogy file, Fenton Historical Society, Jamestown, N.Y.

6. These details are from the interview with Mrs. Wendel cited above.

7. Vernille A. Hatch, *Illustrated History of Jamestown*, pp. 25–31; Spengler, "Yankee, Swedish, and Italian Acculturation."

8. *History of Chautauqua County* pp. 4; 11–13.

9. Jamestown *Evening Star*, Feb. 7, 1873.

10. Andrew M. Young, *History of Chautauqua County*, pp. 346–49.

11. George Cook, *Industrial Jamestown*, p. 8.

12. Interview with Agnes Wendel, July 19, 1980.

13. Broderick, *Whitney*, p. 21.

14. Jamestown *Evening Star*, Dec. 29, 1873.

15. Whitney to I. B. Cohen, undated, ca. 1950, Whitney B papers.

16. Whitney, "The Biggest Things in Chemistry," p. 7.

17. Whitney to Ida Schulze, April 3, 1895, Schulze letters.

18. Broderick, *Whitney,* p. 19.

19. Whitney to M. J. H. Gibbons, Oct. 2, 1913, Whitney papers, box 4, c-101, 1913.

20. Jamestown *Evening Star,* Feb. 25–26, 1885.

21. Jamestown *Evening Star,* April 4–5, 1873.

22. Jamestown *Evening Star,* Mar. 7, 1885.

23. Broderick, *Whitney,* p. 19.

24. Whitney, "Daily Reminder," p. 60, Whitney B papers.

25. Broderick, *Whitney,* p. 288.

26. Whitney, "The Biggest Things in Chemistry," p. 7.

27. Whitney, "Strikes," 1885 school composition in Whitney B papers.

28. The 1885 diaries are in the Whitney B papers.

29. Whitney to Parke-Davis, Nov. 22, 1886, Whitney B papers.

30. Jamestown *Evening Star,* June 25, 1886.

31. Whitney to James P. Munro, Mar. 17, 1917, MIT Archives; Whitney's status as a special student is indicated in the 1887 MIT Catalogue.

32. Interview with Agnes Wendel, July 19, 1980.

33. Whitney to I. B. Cohen, undated, ca. 1950, Whitney B papers.

34. Interview with Agnes Wendel, July 19, 1980.

3/ TECHNOLOGY

1. John W. Servos, "Physical Chemistry in America," p. 159.

2. Samuel C. Prescott, *When MIT was Boston Tech,* p. 129.

3. Whitney's MIT "report cards" for the first term of 1886–87 (dated Feb. 26, 1887) and the second term of 1886–87 (dated June 2, 1887) are in the Whitney B papers.

4. John Broderick, *Willis R. Whitney,* p. 205. The $9-a-week rented room is mentioned in Virginia Veeder Westervelt, *The World Was His Laboratory,* p. 90.

5. Servos, "Chemical Engineering at MIT," pp. 531–44.

6. Helen Wright, *Explorer of the Universe,* p. 55.

7. C. R. Cross to Henry S. Pritchett, June 10, 1903, C. R. Cross papers, MIT Archives.

8. On Cross' consulting, see Robert V. Bruce, *Bell: Alexander Graham Bell,* pp. 93, 112, 131; and Robert Conot, *A Streak of Luck,* p. 282.

9. Albert G. Davis to Owen D. Young, Feb. 8, 1919, O. D. Young File Prior to January 1920), #9–6, O. D. Young papers, GE R&D Center.

10. Albert L. Rohrer, "Address to Camp Engineering, 1937," A. L. Rohrer Papers. Rohrer was an early associate of Thomson's and this speech describes Thomson's early efforts to recruit college-trained engineers.

11. Quoted in Daniel Kevles, *The Physicists,* p. 43. See also Stanley Guralnick, "The American Scientist," pp. 99–135.

12. Linus Pauling, "Arthur Amos Noyes," p. 322; Julius Steiglitz, "Gibbs Medal Award to A. A. Noyes," p. 5.

13. Pauling, "Arthur Amos Noyes," p. 322.

14. Arthur A. Noyes, "A Talk on Teaching," p. 659.

15. *Ibid.*

16. Noyes to H. M. Goodwin, Feb. 20, 1890, H. M. Goodwin papers, MC121-folder 1, Correspondence, 1888–1897, MIT Archives.

17. Williams Haynes, *The American Chemical Industry,* p. 396.

18. John D. Miller, "Rowland's Physics," p. 45.

19. Prescott, *When MIT was Boston Tech,* p. 115.

20. Broderick, *Whitney,* p. 33.

21. *MIT 22nd Annual Catalogue,* 1886–87 (Boston, 1886).

22. Whitney's MIT chemistry classrooms are described in the MIT *Technique* for 1889, p. 154. His senior thesis is on file at the MIT Archives.

23. Noyes, "A Talk on Teaching," p. 663.

24. Noyes to Whitney, Jan. 24, 1888, Whitney B papers.

25. The posts reached by Whitney's classmates are listed in *Bulletin of MIT,* (March 1911) vol. 46; and *Register of Former Students* (MIT, 1925). Of the 102 graduates of the class of 1890, 16 were company presidents, 4 were chief engineers, and 2 were treasurers.

26. Whitney's wedding is described in the Jamestown *Post Journal,* Thursday, June 26, 1890. Information on the Whitney marriage comes from the interview with Agnes Wendel, July 19, 1980, as supplemented by sketchier and more secondhand comments by Whitney's former neighbors George Barker, Paul Gundrum, and John Lake.

27. Noyes to Goodwin, Nov. 1, 1888; Feb. 20, 1890; Jan. 5, 1890; Goodwin Papers, MC121-folder 1, Correspondence, 1889–1897, MIT Archives.

28. Servos, "Physical Chemistry in America," pp. 10–60; Edwin Hiebert and Hans-Gunther Korber, "Wilhelm Ostwald," pp. 456–465; F. G. Donnan, "Ostwald Memorial Lecture," pp. 316–32.

29. Wilder D. Bancroft, "Wilhelm Ostwald," p. 611.

30. R. G. A. Dolby, "Debates Over the Theory of Solutions," p. 306.

31. Servos, "Physical Chemistry in America," pp. 10–60; Dolby, "Debates Over the Theory of Solutions," pp. 296–404.

32. Whitney, "The Biggest Things in Chemistry," p. 8.

33. *Ibid.*

34. Noyes and Whitney, "Kryoskopische Unterschungen," pp. 694–98.

35. Servos, "Physical Chemistry in America," pp. 22; 69–70; 80.

4/ AND NOTE THE GLOW

1. The "repeat and note the glow" story is detailed in a typescript by Whitney, undated but written around 1950. It is in the Whitney B papers.

2. Whitney to G. V. Wendell, December 20, 1910, Whitney papers, box 1 (1910).

3. Whitney to Henry S. Pritchett, August 6, 1901. Office of the President, 1887–1930, box 7, MIT Archives.

4. *Ibid.*

5. *Annual Report of the President and Treasurer of MIT,* December 11, 1889, p. 39, MIT Archives.

6. John W. Servos, "Physical Chemistry in America," p. 148, cites "the need for competent and versatile faculty members to handle the bloated enrollments in introductory science courses" as the main source of academic demand for physical chemists.

7. After the death of Ida Schulze Rebel, her husband sent a packet of letters to her from Whitney to the GE R&D Center, where they remain on file today in the Communications Operation. The "almost improper" remark is in Whitney to Ida Schulze, September 26, 1898, in that collection.

8. Whitney to Schulze, September 30, 1894; March 27, 1897, Schulze letters.

9. Whitney to Schulze, February 22, 1895, Schulze letters.

10. Whitney's translation of Max Le Blanc's *A Text Book of ElectroChemistry* was published by MacMillan in 1900 and again in an enlarged edition in 1907 with additional translation by John W. Brown.

11. Wilder D. Bancroft, "The Relation of Physical Chemistry to Technical Chemistry," p. 1107.

12. Servos, in "Physical Chemistry in America," p. 63, quotes Paul Walden, *Wilhelm Ostwald,* as describing Ostwald in his prime "walking quickly from table to table. . . . Each student's work held interest for him . . . his personal laboratory was no sanctuary."

13. Erwin N. Hiebert, "The Energetics Controversy," pp. 72–76; Bancroft, "Wilhelm Ostwald," pp. 609–12.

14. Whitney to Schulze, January 20, 1895, Schulze letters.

15. Whitney to Schulze, April 3, 1895; September 9, 1895; September 29, 1895; November 2, 1895; Schulze letters.

16. Whitney to Schulze, August 4, 1896; Whitney describes his visit to Moisson in an undated typescript, probably written between 1945 and 1950, in the Whitney B papers.

17. Whitney, "Research," p. 116.

18. Hugh Hawkins, "Transatlantic Discipleship," p. 197.

19. Whitney, "Research," p. 116.

20. L. F. Haber, *The Chemical Industry,* pp. 38–50.

21. *Ibid.,* p. 45; Joseph W. Ben David, "The Profession of Science," pp. 362–83 and "The Universities and the Growth of Science," pp. 1–35.

22. Whitney, "Research," p. 115.

23. Haber, *The Chemical Industry,* pp. 26–37; Robert F. Bud, P. Thomas Carroll, Jefferey L. Sturchio, and Arnold W. Thackray, "A Quantitative Analysis of American Chemistry, 1876–1976," unpublished ms., December 1979; and *Chemistry in America.*

24. Bud, Carroll, Sturchio, and Thackray, "A Quantitative Analysis," figure 3–7.

25. Charles Albert Brown and Mary Elvira Weeks, *A History of the American Chemical Society,* pp. 37–47. Jefferey L. Sturchio, "Charles Chandler, the

ACS and Club Life in Gilded Age New York," presented to the History of Science Society, New York City, 1977.

26. Brown and Weeks, *A History of the American Chemical Society;* Bud, Carroll, Sturchio, and Thackray, *Chemistry in America.*

27. Brown and Weeks, p. 32; *Review of American Chemical Research,* vol. 3 and 4, 1897, contributed by members of the Massachusetts Institute of Technology, A. A. Noyes, ed. (Chemical Publications, Easton, Pa., 1897).

28. Servos, "Physical Chemistry in America," pp. 246, 346; A. Findlay, "Wilder Dwight Bancroft," p. 2506.

29. Whitney to Schulze, March 27, 1897, Schulze letters.

30. Whitney to Schulze, March 27, 1897; September 22, 1897; Schulze letters.

31. Whitney, "Willard Gibbs Medal Award Acceptance," p. 559.

32. Noyes and Whitney, "The Rate of Solution of Solid Substances," pp. 930–34.

33. Whitney, "The Corrosion of Iron," pp. 394–406.

34. The genesis of Whitney's corrosion studies was told to me by Dr. Herbert Uhlig, interview August 13, 1980, who had discussed this with Dr. Whitney while on the staff of the GE Research Lab in the 1940s. Dr. Uhlig also provided me with background information on the place of Whitney's work in the field of corrosion studies.

35. Wilhelm Palmaer, "Uber die Auflosung von Metalen," (1901) 39:1; (1903), 45:182; (1906), 46:689.

36. Noyes to Harry Goodwin, January 15, 1891, H. M. Goodwin Papers, Massachusetts Institute of Tehcnology Archives.

37. Reese Jenkins, *Images and Enterprise,* pp. 180–200.

38. Servos, "Physical Chemistry in America", p. 103, indicates that the work was begun in 1896. Whitney's letters to Ida Schulze do not mention it until 1898. The first surviving contract for the work dates from 1899, but since that covers the manufacturing plant, the research must have begun earlier.

39. Sketchy deatils of the process are given in a letter from "Harold" to Whitney, June 13, 1901, Whitney B papers (Harold must have been the superintendent of the Whitney-Noyes plant). Various colloido-chloride and solvent recovery processes are described in Edward C. Worden, *Nitrocellulose in Industry, II.*

40. John J. Beer and W. David Lewis, "Professionalization of Science," pp. 110–30.

41. "Agreement Between Willis R. Whitney and Arthur A. Noyes and the American Aristotype Company," July 3, 1899, in possession of Mrs. Agnes Wendel.

42. Whitney to Schulze, September 26, 1898; Noyes to C. D. Walcott, January 22, 1903, Carnegie Institution of Washington Files; Henry G. Pearson to V. Bush, March 22, 1939, Carnegie Institution of Wahington Files. I thank John W. Servos for supplying me with the two Carnegie Institution references.

43. Jenkins, *Images and Enterprise,* p. 200; "Agreement between Willis R.

Whitney and Arthur A. Noyes and American Aristotype Company to April 2, 1904," in possession of Mrs. Agnes Wendel.

44. Arthur D. Little, "Presentation Address—Perkin Medal."

45. Whitney complains about that turndown as late as 1921 in "The Biggest Things in Chemistry."

46. Whitney to Schulze, May 2, 1897, Schulze letters.

47. Whitney to Schulze, May 2, 1897; October 23, 1898, Schulze letters.

48. Whitney to Schulze, August 6, 1897, Schulze letters.

49. Interview with Agnes Wendel, July 18, 1980; Interview with George Barker, May 10, 1980.

50. Elihu Thomson to Whitney, October 10, 1900, reel 5.1, microfilm, GERLA.

5/ INDUSTRIAL RESEARCH EXPERIMENT

1. *Who Was Who in America* (Chicago, 1942), 1:299.

2. "Edwin W. Rice, Jr.," *Biographical Sketches of Some Outstanding General Electric Men* (GE, Schenectady, 1947); David O. Woodbury, *Beloved Scientist*, pp. 117–18; *Who Was Who in America* (Chicago, 1942), 1:1026.

3. Albert G. Davis, Interview with John Winthrop Hammond, 1926, Hammond file, Item L2991, GE Main Library.

4. The 1900 figure is from a chart in the *General Electric Review* (1921), 25:43; the 1979 figure is from "GE Says Light Bulb It Designed Cuts Use of Energy by One-Third," *Wall Street Journal*, June 15, 1979, which estimates 1979 incandescent lamp sales in the United States at 1.5 billion lamps.

5. Quoted by Charles L. Clarke in Francis Jehl, *Menlo Park Reminiscences*, 2:862.

6. John Eddy, "Edison the Scientist," pp. 3737–49.

7. Matthew Josephson, *Edison*, p. 278.

8. On Upton's role with Edison, see Upton Collection, Cabinet 12, shelf 6, and Thomas A. Edison to Upton, January 2, 1886, Upton E 6285, Edison Papers, Edison National Historic Site. On other trained scientists employed by Edison, see Jehl, *Menlo Park Reminiscences*, 1:269–70.

9. David A. Hounshell, "Edison and the Pure Science Ideal," pp. 612–17; Simon Newcomb to Thomas Edison, February 24, 1880, "Electric Light Filaments, 1880," Edison papers.

10. The surviving papers of William Stanley are at the Stanley Library, General Electric Co., Pittsfield, Mass. See especially Stanley to C. F. Scott, October 7, 1915. For a summary of Stanley's career, Henry Douglas, *William Stanley* (New York, 1903); and T. C. Martin, *Life of William Stanley*, typescript, 1922. There remains no good biography of Nikola Tesla, though Harold C. Passer, *The Electrical Manufacturers*, puts his contributions into context.

11. "Memorandum of Bradley Contracts" (1895), on file at the GE R&D Center; and "Development of the Rotary Converter: Mr. Charles S. Bradley's Recollections," October 14, 1927, L 2939, Hammond file. On Ernst

Danielsen, see John A. McManus, "50 Years of Induction Motor Manufacture"; and "Ernst F. W. Alexanderson Interview with Clyde Wagoner and Ernest Hill," January 14, 1951, on file at the GE R&D Center.

12. Stanley to George Westinghouse, December 18, 1886, William Stanley Papers, Stanley Library, General Electric Co., Pittsfield, Mass.

13. Eaton and Lewis to John Kruesi, February 27, 1890, on file at GE R&D Center.

14. Alfred D. Chandler, *The Visible Hand*, pp. 287–337.

15. For statistics and background on the wave of mergers at the turn of the century, see Chandler, *The Visible Hand*, ch. 10, "Integration by Way of Merger."

16. The story of Howell and the Maligniani patent is given in J. W. Hammond, *Men and Volts* (typescript edition, 1935), p. 227. The best history of the incandescent lamp is Aaron A. Bright, *The Electric Lamp Industry*.

17. The NELA story is in 272 US 476, *U.S. v. General Electric Co. et al.*, #113, argued October 13, 1926, pp. 808–63; "Circuit Court of the U.S. for the Northern District of Ohio, *The U.S. of A., petitioner, v. General Electric Co. and Others, Defendants,* filed March 3, 1911.

18. GE lamp research spending by year was: 1894, $9,166; 1895, $4,878; 1896, $15,296; 1903, $28,820. M. S. Willson to J. Klenke, October 5, 1927, L 3357, Hammond file. On the purchase of patents, see John W. Howell, "The Past, Present, and Future of the Incandescent Lamp" (1900), L2821, Hammond file.

19. On the Nernst lamp and other early rivals to the carbon-filament lamp, see Bright, *The Electric Lamp Industry*, pp. 220–30.

20. K. Mendelsohn, *The World of Walther Nernst*, p. 45.

21. Henry G. Prout, *A Life of George Westinghouse*, pp. 234–36.

22. Charles P. Steinmetz, "Review of Engineering Progress During November and December, 1898," L 5458–5467, Hammond file. I thank Rondal Klein for this reference and for many useful suggestions about the role of Steinmetz. Steinmetz also visited the Cooper Hewitt laboratory, but since the reference to that visit, L 5533, Hammond file, is undated, it is impossible to determine if that visit occurred before or after the 1898 proposal.

23. Martha Moore Trescott, *The Rise of the American Electrochemicals Industry*, p. 186.

24. "Verbatim Extracts from a letter from C. P. Steinmetz to E. W. Rice," September 21, 1900, L2986, Hammond file.

25. "Verbatim Extract from a letter from A. G. Davis to Edwin W. Rice, Jr.," September 21, 1900, L2987, Hammond file.

26. "Verbatim Extract from a letter of September 24, 1900, written by Professor Elihu Thomson to Edwin W. Rice, Jr." L2988, Hammond file.

27. John J. Beer, "Coal Tar Dye Manufacture," pp. 137–38.

28. Summaries of the history of American industrial research are given in Kendall Birr, *Pioneering in Industrial Research*; Birr, "Industrial Research Laboratories"; Birr, "The General Electric Research Laboratory," pp. 6–42; Harold Vagtborg, *Research and American Industrial Development;* and John Rae, "The Application of Science to Industry," pp. 249–68. The count of re-

search laboratories established before 1900 is based on 1941 survey data and published in Robert F. Bud, P. Thomas Carroll, Jeffrey L. Sturchio and Arnold W. Thackray, *Chemistry in America*, p. 364.

29. Beer, "Coal Tar Manufacture," pp. 137–138.

30. Charles Dudley, "The Dignity of Analytical Work," p. 89.

31. William Burton, "Chemistry in the Petroleum Industry," p. 483, and the article by C. H. Herty on Burton in "William Burton: Perkin Medal Award," pp. 159–162.

32. Quoted in Leonard Reich, "Radio Electronics," p. 19.

33. William Haynes, *American Chemical Industry*, p. 395.

34. Edwin W. Rice, Jr., "A Tribute to Willis R. Whitney," p. 3.

35. "Verbatim Extracts of letter from C. P. Steinmetz to E. W. Rice, Jr.," September 21, 1900, L2486, Hammond file.

36. Cross's recommendation of Whitney is described in Albert G. Davis to Owen D. Young, February 18, 1919, O. D. Young file, "Prior to January, 1920," file #9–6, Swope/Young Collection.

37. Whitney, "Cooperation and Corporations," p. 133.

38. Robert M. Powers, "Schenectady, N.Y., A Streetcar City." I thank Professor David Nye for pointing out this reference to me.

39. The Steinmetz biographies are John W. Hammond, *Charles Proteus Steinmetz;* Jonathan N. Leonard, *Loki;* and John Anderson Miller, *Modern Jupiter.* I thank Ronald Klein, who is currently working on a new Steinmetz biography, for useful suggestions.

40. Steinmetz, "The Law of Hysteresis," pp. 3–51; Donald B. Martin, "Steinmetz and His Discovery," p. 544. On anticipations of Steinmetz's findings, see J. A. Ewing, "On the Production of Transient Electric Currents in Iron and Steel Conductors," *Proceedings of the Royal Society* (1881), 33:21, and "On the Effects of Retentiveness on the Magnetization of Iron and Steel," *Proceedings of the Royal Society* (1882), 34:39.

41. The comment about Steinmetz' paper's being suitable for the Physical Society or Royal Society was made by Thomas D. Lockwood, chairman of the meeting where he first read the paper. See *Transactions of the AIEE* (1892), 9:49, "Discussions," Arthur Kennelly added that the paper was "likely to become classical."

42. G. Windred, "Complex Quantities," pp. 337–39, puts Steinmetz' contribution into perspective. The 1893 paper was eventually published as Steinmetz, "Symbolic Representation of General Alternating Waves," pp. 289–316.

43. Harold S. Black, "Inventing the Negative Feedback Amplifier," p. *58*, describes a 1923 lecture by Steinmetz as follows:

> Dr. Steinmetz was 20 minutes late, but he was given a standing ovation as he walked down the center aisle dressed in blue overalls and a blue shirt with short sleeves and smoking the largest cigar that I had ever seen. . . . I was so impressed by how Steinmetz got down to the fundamentals that when I returned home I restated my own problem.

44. Whitney to Ida Schulze, March 9, 1901, Schulze letters.

45. The salary figure is given in John Broderick, *Forty Years With General*

Electric (Albany: Ft. Orange Press 1929), 1893. *Historical Statistics of the U.S.,* Part 1, p. 1921, gives the average income of a U.S. family in 1901 as $651.

46. Whitney to Schulze, March 9, 1901, Schulze letters.

47. Interview with Frank Lang, January 5, 1977, on file at GE R&D Center.

48. Whitney's initial efforts on the mercury lamp are detailed in his lab notebook #1, on file at the GE R&D Center. His reaction to Steinmetz's poker game is given in Broderick, p. 41.

49. Early recruits are listed in Whitney, notebook #1, June 9, 1901. The failure to hire Coolidge is described in Whitney to Steinmetz, April 2, 1901, GERLA, microfilm 13.2.

50. Whitney to Agnes Whitney, June 21, 1901, in possession of Agnes Wendel.

51. Whitney to Schulze, March 9, 1901, Schulze letters.

52. Samuel C Prescott, *When MIT Was Boston Tech,* p. 178, gives the date of Whitney's promotion to assistant professor.

53. Whitney, "Cooperation and Corporations," p. 133.

54. Whitney and J. E. Ober, "The Precipitation of Colloids," pp. 842–63.

55. Whitney to H. S. Pritchett, August 6, 1901, Office of the President, AC55, MIT Archives.

56. Arthur A. Noyes to H. M. Goodwin, July 13, 1901, MC7, Goodwin Collection, MIT Archives.

57. Servos, "Physical Chemistry in America," p. 179.

58. *Ibid.,* pp. 185, 298. Dr. Servos kindly provided me with a copy of Whitney's grant application to the Carnegie Institution.

59. Prescott, *When MIT Was Boston Tech,* pp. 184–86. Servos, "Physical Chemistry in America," pp. 224, 225, 246.

60. On the German Electrochemical Society, see *50 Jahre AEG* (Berlin: AEG 1950), p. 99.

61. On the founding of the American Electrochemical Society, see *Journal of the Electrochemical Society,* (1901), 1:1–13. On that society's role as a meeting place for chemists with varied interests, see Trescott, *The Rise of the American Electrochemicals Industry* pp. 280–305.

6/ BURNT-OUT BULB

1. Interview with Ginger Adams, 1940, microfilm 5.1, "Lab Affairs—General—40th Anniversary," GERLA.

2. Interview with John T. H. Dempster, 1940, "Lab Affairs—General—40th Anniversary," GERLA.

3. "Verbatim Extract of a Letter from C. P. Steinmetz to E. W. Rice," September 21, 1900, item 2986, Hammond file.

4. Whitney notebook #1, July 9, 1901; July 10, 1901; pp. 59–65.

5. General Electric Co., *Annual Report for 1902* (New York: 1903), p. 13.

6. Whitney notebook #1, p. 15; October 24, 1901, p. 160, Ezekiel Weintraub, "Metallic Vapors," pp. 85–124.

7. Whitney notebook #2, May 23, 1903.

8. For a discussion of the advantages of alternating and direct current, and the importance of a method of converting between them, see Harold C. Passer, *The Electrical Manufacturers*, pp. 297–320.

9. Chester Biesterfield, *Patent Law*, pp. 132–48.

10. William Stanley, "The Inventor and the Trust," p. 597.

11. Kendall Birr, "The General Electric Research Laboratory," p. 159; *New York Times*, April 20, 1911, p. 6; "Resolution of the Executive Committee, October 18, 1918" (in which A. G. Davis recommends acquisition of Cooper Hewitt Co. for $250,000), box 7 folder 5, Swope papers.

12. Whitney notebook #2, February 18, 1904.

13. Birr, "The General Electric Research Laboratory," p. 220 (based on interview with Whitney, February 25, 1950). The "bear pit" remark is quoted in John Anderson Miller, *William P. Coolidge: Yankee Scientist*, p. 50.

14. Entries in Whitney's notebooks for March 7, 1903; January 31, 1903; October 16, 1903; September 26, 1902; May 19, 1903, give the monthly salaries of foreign-born scientists with Ph.D.s as follows: Ossian Kruh, $65/month; John Harden, $75/month; Erland Zell, $85/month, and "Dr. Selzer from Germany," an offer of $75/month (he did not accept). By contrast, Roy T. Wells, a new PhD. of American birth, got $125/month; Charles F. Lindsay, also a new Ph.D. of American birth, got $125/month; and Emery Gilson, an MIT B.S., got $125/month. The major exception to the tendency to give foreign-born scientists lower salaries was Ezekiel Weintraub, who got $250/month.

15. William Weedon, "A Contribution to the Study of the Electric Arc," pp. 171–87; Whitney, "Arcs," pp. 291–99; Whitney notebook #1, July 1902; December 12, 1901.

16. Whitney notebook #1, December 7, 1901; Whitney, "The Theory of the Mercury Arc Rectifier," pp. 619–21. On p. 620, Whitney writes:

A promising theory postulates negative ions passing within the wire. It would not seem more impossible than the phenomena evidently occurring in aqueous solutions or in gases when these conduct the current. In the case of solutions, an early demonstable motion of ponderable material, the electrochemist's ions, always accompanies the flow of direct curent, and there is a motion of material in both directions.

17. Whitney quotes J. J. Thomson's theory in Whitney, "Arcs," pp. 291–99.

18. Whitney notebook #1, November 15, 1901. At the first colloquium, Whitney notes: "Dr. Weinbtaub, Wood, and Arsem presented abstracts of work on electron theory. . . . Weintraub discussed J. J. Thomson's experiments on the conductivity of gases."

19. Whitney notebook #1, December 7, 1901.

20. Whitney, "Arcs," pp. 291–99; Weedon, "A Contribution to the Study of the Electric Arc," pp. 177–87.

21. Weedon, *ibid.*, p. 182, refers to Thomson's work.

22. Whitney to John Trowbridge, April 19, 1911, Whitney Collection.

23. Weedon, "A Contribution to the Theory of the Electric Arc," *supra*, note 20.

24. "Discussion," *Transactions of the American Electrochemical Society*, (1909), 16:224.

25. Whitney to "Dear Folks," July 18, 1903, letter in possession of Agnes Wendel.

26. Whitney notebook #1, September 20, 1902, lists twenty-nine "subjects" and fourteen "men."

27. Interview with Ginger Adams, "Lab Affairs, General—40 Anniversary, 1940," microfilm 5.1 GERLA.

28. Edna May Best Sexton to Whitney, April 10, 1905; April 21, 1926, Whitney B papers.

29. The list of twenty-nine projects is in Whitney notebook #1, September 20, 1902.

30. Whitney notebook #1, July 10, 1901; September 11, 1901; September 14, 1901; September 26, 1901; September 20, 1901; February 21, 1902; July 18, 1902; notebook #2, January 16, 1903.

31. The resistance rod story is given in Whitney notebook #1, September 1, 11, 14, 19, 20, 20, 23, 26, 1901.

32. *Ibid.*

33. Whitney, "Address on the Occasion of the Presentation of the Edison Medal" (nd., ca., 1925).

34. Whitney notebook #2, December 19, 1903; January 1, 1904. The popular accounts Whitney later gave of this discovery inadvertently reverse the sequence of events, making it sound more "serendipitous" than the notebooks indicate that it was.

35. The "two masters" quote is in Whitney's notebook #1, September 27, 1902. The "good and evil" quote is in notebook #2, May 19, 1904.

36. Whitney to parents, January 27, 1906; letter in possession of Agnes Wendel.

37. Whitney to Mr. William Ward and Mr. Benedict Grafton, Alplaus, undated, ca. 1950, Whitney B papers.

38. The photo is currently in the possession of Mrs. Agnes Wendel.

39. Interview with Agnes Wendel, July 16, 1980; William D. Coolidge to mother, March 6, 1907, Coolidge papers.

40. Whitney to "Dearest Folks," July 14, 1904, letter in possession of Agnes Wendel.

41. *Ibid.*

42. David O. Woodbury, *Beloved Scientist*, p. 251.

43. Albert D. Chandler, *The Visible Hand*, p. 429.

44. Harold Passer, *The Electrical Manufacturers*, pp. 335–45; Whitney notebook #1, October 5, 1903.

45. Maxwell W. Day to E. W. Rice, Jr., May 18, 1904, data folder 438, Technical Information Exchange, GE R&D Center, Schenectady, N.Y.; G. F. Steele to D. W. Niven, March 6, 1926, L3030, Hammond file.

46. Whitney to "Dearest Folks," January 29, 1905, in possession of Mrs. Agnes Wendel.

47. Whitney notebook #2, August 29, 1904; September 1, 1904; September 9, 1904.

48. Aaron A. Bright, *The Electric Lamp Industry*, p. 170, gives the following lamp efficacies: carbon (1881) 1.68 lumens/watt; improved carbon (1906) 3.4 lumens/watt; GEM (1908) 4.25 lumens/watt; osmium (1898) 5.9 lumens/watt; tantalum (1902), 4.8 lumens/watt; squirted tungsten (1906), 7.75 lumens/watt; Coolidge ductile tungsten (1911) 10 lumens/watt. See also John W. Howell and Henry Schroeder, *History of the Incandescent Lamp*.

49. Whitney notebook #2, October 2, 1904.

50. Bullock and Cranshaw to Thomas A. Edison, April 2, 1879, "Electric Light-Filaments, 1879," Edison Archives, Edison National Historic Site.

51. Transcript of Record in U.S. Court of Appeals for the 3rd. Circuit, No. 2615, October term, 1920, *Independent Lamp and Wire Co.* v. *General Electric Co.*, Appeal from the District Court of U.S. for the District of New Jersey, Vol II, Defendant's Record, September 18, 1920, pp. 621–25.

52. Whitney, "General Notice," July 11, 1903, 5.1 Lab Affairs General, GERLA.

53. H. C. Pollock was told this by Whitney, and he told this to me.

54. These reports of work and patent letters are now on microfilm at the Whitney Library, GE R&D Center.

55. Whitney notebook #1, July 30, 1903; Notebook #2, February 25, 1904.

56. Whitney notebook #2, January 10, 1905; June 7, 1905; Whitney to A. G. Davis, February 7, 1905, reel 12.1 GERLA.

57. Whitney notebook #2, March 7, 1905.

58. Whitney notebook #1, December 28, 1902; Frank Cameron, *Cottrell, Samaritan of Science*, p. 102.

59. Coolidge to Whitney, September 5, 1904, Whitney B papers. The biographies of Coolidge are in John A. Miller, *Yankee Scientist;* Herman A. Liebhafsky, *William D. Coolidge;* and William D. Coolidge, "Autobiographical Notes," on file in the Communications Operation, GE R&D Center.

60. Coolidge makes the statement that his GE salary initially was twice his MIT salary in "Biography of William D. Coolidge," GE News Bureau, July 25, 1942, on file at Communications Operation, GE R&D Center.

61. Transcript of Record in the U.S. Court of Appeals for the 3rd Circuit, No. 2615, October Term, 1920, *Independent Lamp and Wire Co.* v. *General Electric Co.*, Appeal from the District Court of the U.S. for the District of New Jersey, Defendant's Record, September 18, 1920, II, 467.

62. *Ibid*, p. 623.

63. Coolidge, "Historical Report on the Development of Ductile Tungsten," March 26, 1912, reel 17, microfilm of Laboratory Reports of Work, Whitney Library, General Electric R&D Center.

64. Whitney to Alexander G. Neave, October 29, 1942, reel 5.1 GERLA.

65. Recollections of Samuel Ferguson, undated, ca. 1920, L6443, Hammond file.

66. Details of the negotiations are given in A. G. Davis to Neave, May 20, 1925, box 6, file 3, Swope/Young papers, GE R&D Center. See also District Court of U.S. District of New Jersey, *U.S.* v. *General Electric*, Civil Action No. 1364, March 20, 1946, pp. 1047–1236.

67. Davis to Neave, May 20, 1925, Swope-Young papers, box 6, folder 3.

68. *Ibid.* states that GE paid $100,000 for the Auer Process in 1906. Circuit Court of the U.S. for the Northern District of Ohio, the *U.S. of A. Petitioners* v. *General Electric Co., and others, defendants,* filed March 3, 1911, in 272 U.S. 476, *US.* v. *General Electric Co., et al.,* No. 113, argued October 13, 1926, p. 819, says that in 1906 GE paid $100,000 for the Auer process and $250,000 for the rights to tantalum. Only three years later, in 1909, did GE buy the three principal squirted tungsten patents, paying $250,000 for the Just and Hanaman patent, $240,000 for the Kuzel Patent, and $175,000 for the Bergmann patent.

69. Copy of Bulletin No. 3643, October 10, 1906, from Mr. Franklin Terry, Whitney B papers; "Number of Incandescent Lamps Sold in U.S.," *GE Review* (1921), 25:43.

70. Kuzel's 1906 offer is discussed in Coolidge to mother, May 6, 1906, Coolidge papers.

71. Whitney notebook #2, September 6, 1906.

72. Coolidge to mother, May 26, 1906, Coolidge papers.

73. Coolidge to mother, March 5, 1906, Coolidge papers.

74. New York *Commercial,* August 18, 1907; John Broderick, *Willis R. Whitney,* p. 204.

75. Coolidge to mother, December 23, 1906, Coolidge papers.

76. Coolidge to mother, February 10, 1907; August 6, 1906, Coolidge papers.

77. Coolidge to mother, March 6, 1907, copy from Vincent D. Manti.

78. Whitney notebook #2, March 5, 1907.

79. Coolidge to mother, August 14, 1907, Coolidge papers. Whitney's bibliography lists ten speeches or reviews of earlier work, but no papers describing new work, between 1907 and 1912.

80. Whitney to Ennin, July 24, 1906, in possession of Agnes Wendel.

81. Coolidge to mother, August 3, 1907, Coolidge papers.

82. The original papers describing this incident have disappeared, but it is described fully by Birr, "The General Electric Research Laboratory," pp. 151–52, who saw those papers.

83. Whitney notebook #2, September 13, 1907.

84. Interview with Agnes Wendel, July 19, 1980.

85. May Best Sexton to Whitney, April 10, 1905, Whitney B papers.

86. Whitney, "Diary, 1908–1912," Whitney B papers.

87. Coolidge to mother, November 20, 1907; December 21, 1907, Coolidge papers.

88. Arthur A. Noyes to Whitney, February 1, 1908, Whitney papers. Only the Noyes half of the exchange survives, but in it he summarizes Whitney's letter.

7/ REDESIGNING THE EXPERIMENT

1. Arthur A. Noyes to Whitney, February 1, 1908, Whitney B papers.

2. Coolidge to Whitney, March 2, 1907, Patent Letters, reel 12.1, GERLA

3. Coolidge to mother, March 11, 1907, Coolidge papers.

4. Coolidge to mother, December 15, 1907, Coolidge papers.

5. Transcript of Record in the U.S. Court of Appeals for the Third District, No. 2615, October Term, 1920, *Independent Lamp & Wire Co.* v. *General Electric,* Appeal for the District Court of the U.S. for the District of New Jersey, Vol II, Defendant's Record, September 18, 1920, pp. 173–85.

6. *Ibid.,* pp. 185–90; 528–37.

7. Coolidge to Whitney, Patent Letters, reel 12.1, GERLA

8. Whitney to A. G. Davis, June 9, 1909; Coolidge to Whitney, June 21, 1909, Patent Letters, reel 12.1, GERLA

9. Herman A. Liebhafsky, *William D. Coolidge,* ch. 3, summarizes the tungsten patent cases.

10. Coolidge to Whitney, May 24, 1909, Patent Letters, reel 12.1, GERLA.

11. *Ibid.* Actually, the additives used commercially to prevent excessive crystal growth in ice cream include carrageen, guar gum, and sodium carboxymethyl cellulose. See Terry Dunkle, "The Cold Facts About Ice Cream," *Science 81* (July/August 1981), p. 45.

12. For a description of the Coolidge process, see John W. Howell and Henry Schroeder, *History of the Incandescent Lamp,* pp. 102–17.

13. Circuit Court of the U.S. for the Northern District of Ohio, *The United States of America, Petitioner,* v. *General Electric Company and Others, Defenders* filed March 3, 1911, quoted in full in 272 U.S. 476, *U.S.* v. *General Electric Co., et al.,* argued October 13, 1926, decided November 23, 1926, pp. 854–63.

14. An estimate of "20 trained Research Chemists" working on the tungsten problem, along with an acknowledgement of Fink's contribution, appears in Coolidge, "Ductile Tungsten," pp. 961–65. Whitney alludes to Fink's claims and expresses the firm view "the development of ductile tungsten, as I knew it, was the work of Dr. Coolidge," in WRW to Arthur D. Little, November 21, 1913, Whitney papers, box 4-C, 101–1913.

15. Whitney notebook 2, February 29, 1908.

16. Whitney to "Dear Folks" (John and Agnes Whitney), May 9, 1908, in possession of Agnes Wendel.

17. Whitney, "Diary, 1908–1912," Whitney B papers.

18. Photos of Whitney's 1909 office are on file at the GE R&D Center.

19. Ferguson's appointment is noted in Whitney's notebook #2, April 25, 1908.

20. W. F. Hillebrand, "Present and Future Status of the Chemical Society," pp. 1–18.

21. *Transactions of the American Institute of Chemical Engineers* (1908), 1:1–9.

22. Charles Albert Brown and Mary Elvira Weeks, *History of the American Chemical Society,* pp. 81–96.

23. Whitney, "Organization of Industrial Research," pp. 71–78, delivered as an address on September 17, 1909; "Research as a Financial Asset," pp. 325–30.

24. "Organization of Industrial Research," p. 72.

25. *Ibid.*, p. 73; Whitney notebook #1, February 25, 1904.

26. Whitney, "Organization of Industrial Research," p. 75.

27. Whitney, "Research as a Financial Asset," p. 326.

28. A detailed accounting of the statistics that form the basis for this speech is given in "Value of Apparatus and Materials Originated in the Research Lab," January 29, 1912, Lab Affairs General 5.1, GERLA.

29. GE figures are based on my count of the reprint file at the Whitney Library of the GE R&D Center. Those typical of a physics laboratory in the United States (or elsewhere) ca. 1900 are given in Paul Forman, John L Heilbron, and Spencer Weart, "Physics Circa 1900," *Historical Studies in the Physical Sciences* (1976), 5:127.

30. Langmuir's biography is Albert Rosenfeld, *The Quintessence of Irving Langmuir,* vol. 12 of *The Collected Works of Irving Langmuir,* C. Guy Suits and Harold Way, eds. It will be supplemented by Leonard Reich, "Irving Langmuir," pp. 199–221. The quote about being "free to do research as I wish" is from Rosenfeld, p. 42.

31. A description of Langmuir's work at Stevens is given in Langmuir to Mrs. Sadie C. Langmuir, August 3, 1905; August 7, 1906; March 27, 1907; October 3, 1906; February 1, 1907, Irving Langmuir Collection, Library of Congress.

32. The sequence of events leading to Langmuir's employment at GE is given in Langmuir to Whitney, June 20, 1909; Whitney to Langmuir, February 2, 1909; Langmuir to Whitney February 22, 1909; March 15, 1909; June 15, 1909; Langmuir to Mrs. S. C. Langmuir, July 16, 1909, all in the Langmuir Collection, Library of Congress.

33. Langmuir to "Robb," October 26, 1908, Langmuir Collection.

34. Langmuir, notebook 180, pp. 1–148, July 19–October 26, 1908.

35. Langmuir to S. C. Langmuir, January 17, 1910, Langmuir Collection.

36. Langmuir to S. C. Langmuir, December 5, 1909, Langmuir Collection.

37. Whitney, "Electrical Conduction," p. 18.

38. Whitney, "Vacua," pp. 1207–16.

39. Albert Rosenfeld, "Irving Langmuir," p. 363.

40. Langmuir, "A Chemically Active Modification of Hydrogen," *Journal of the American Chemical Society* (1912), 34:1310; "The Dissociation of Hydrogen into Atoms," *ibid.,* p. 860.

41. Langmuir, "Chemical Reactions at Very Low Pressures, I," *ibid.* (1913), 35–103.

42. U.S. Circuit Court of Appeals for the 2nd Circuit (April 1920), *General Electric* v. *Nitro-Tungsten Lamp Co.,* Brief for the Patent Appellee, pp. 26–28.

43. John W. Howell, chief engineer of GE's Harrison, N.J., Lamp Works, claimed previous knowledge of the effects of water vapor in a letter to Whitney, August 6, 1913.

44. U.S. Circuit Court of Appeals for the 2nd Circuit (April 1920), *General Electric* v. *Nitro Tungsten Lamp Company,* Brief for the Patent Appellee, indicates (pp. 70–75) that the use of nitrogen to retard filament evaporation

was known to Edison in 1883 (U.S. Patent 274,295) and was the subject of a British patent in 1889. Neither patent resulted in a practical product.

45. *Ibid.*, p. 29, indicates the importance to the gas-filled lamp of Langmuir's work with Stanley. The results of that work were published in Langmuir and G. S. Meikle, "Flow of Heat Through Furnace Walls; the Shape Factor," *Transactions of the American Electrochemical Society* (1913), 24:53; and Langmuir, "Convection and Radiation of Heat," *ibid.* (1913), 23:293.

46. Langmuir and J. A. Orange, "Tungsten Lamps of High Efficiency," *Collected Works*, 2:176–202, an article initially published in two parts in the *Transactions of the American Institute of Electrical Engineers* in 1913.

47. The gas-filled lamp was initially introduced only in large sizes, for such uses as street lamps. It took decades to reduce the cost of argon and improve manufacturing methods sufficiently to introduce it in the smaller sizes.

48. The figures of one bulb per four people in 1910 and four bulbs per person in 1925 are taken from "GE Lamp Engineering Report for 1925," p. 15.

49. GE does not release data on sales or profits in individual lines of business. However, the 1920 figures came out in a series of articles in the *New York Times*, January 7, 1922, p. 7; January 13, 1922, p. 1; January 16, 1922, p. 1; January 18, 1922, p. 24; January 20, 1922, p. 1; January 21, 1922, p. 3, and GE confirmed their correctness.

50. Discussing Langmuir's work, Daniel Kevles, *The Physicists* p. 99, repeats an allegation by Kendall Birr, *Pioneering in Industrial Research*, p. 66, that "suspicious stockholders scrutinized the accounts of Willis R. Whitney," but neither presents any evidence that any such scrutiny actually occurred.

51. Langmuir describes how his light bulb work led to the surface chemistry work that led to his Nobel Prize in Langmuir, "Nobel Lecture" (Stockholm, December 14, 1932), *Collected Works*, 8:158–60.

52. Langmuir, *Collected Works*, 12:255.

53. Dushman describes this first visit to the GE Research Lab in his memoir "An Album of Memories," (undated, ca. 1950), on file at the GE R&D Center.

54. Whitney to Hull, December 17, 1913, reel 13.2, GERLA

55. Birr, *Pioneering in Industrial Research*, p. 82.

56. Broderick, *Willis R. Whitney*, p. 226. Whitney later wrote in his commonplace book, February 3, 1929: "I think I played with my turtles because I could do a line of research myself and alone."

57. Whitney to Ennin, December 7, 1911, in possession of Mrs. Agnes Wendel.

58. Whitney to Ennin, December 8, 1911, December 15, 1911, in possession of Mrs. Agnes Wendel.

59. Whitney to Ennin, December 11, 1911; February 6, 1912; March 30, 1913, in possession of Mrs. Agnes Wendel.

60. Whitney to Ennin, November 21, 1912, in possession of Mrs. Agnes Wendel.

61. Charles Dudley, "The Dignity of Analytical Work," *Journal of the American Chemical Society* 20 (1899), 89. For further support of the view that

German industrial chemistry laboratories did little if any fundamental research, see Georg Meyer,-Thurow, "The Industrialization of Invention," pp. 363–81. Meyer-Thurow states:

> Truly basic research not directed towards industrially and commercially valuable products was left to private or state research institutions. . . . Bayer's management rarely allowed research chemists to publish scientifically interesting results, even when company secrets were not involved (pp. 379–80).

8/ ON A WIDER STAGE

1. The Compton-Whitney Correspondence is in the Whitney papers and was reprinted in full in *Physics Today* (July 1976), pp. 13–15. The "very bright fellow" remark is in a letter from Whitney to Gerard Swope, undated, reel 13.2 GERLA.

2. Arthur Compton's role as a GE consultant is described in George Inman, "Fluorescent Lamps," p. 36. Karl T. Compton's work as a GE consultant is described in Saul Dushman to Whitney, October 2, 1922, Whitney B papers. Robert A. Millikan's career is described in his *Autobiography* and in Robert Kargon, *The Rise of Robert Millikan* (Ithica, 1982). On George E. Hale, see Helen Wright, *Explorer of the Universe*, and Daniel Kevles, "George Ellery Hale," pp. 278–88. On James B. Conant, see his autobiography, *My Several Lives* pp. 25–26.

3. Frank B. Jewett, *Temporary National Economic Committee Hearings*, part 3, Patents (Washington, DC, 1939), p. 949, quoted in Spencer Weart, "The Rise of Prostituted Physics," p. 14.

4. On the advisory board, see A. G. Davis to A. C. Neave, May 20, 1925, Swope/Young papers, box 6, file 3.

5. Flat irons and toasters first appear in the GE *Catalog of Supplies* in 1907. On the Chicago Electrical Exhibit, see the Schenectady *Evening Star*, January 13, 1906.

6. The development of Calrod is described in Louis Navias, "Partial History of Ceramics Research and Development," pp. 56–60. The suggestion to make the primitive hot plate is in Whitney notebook #13, February 27, 1911, p. 87.

7. The development of vacuum tubes at GE is described by a participant in William C. White, "History of Radio and Electronics." Whitney's "disproved by Soddy" remark is on a sheet in his "Reports of Work" file at the Whitney Library, GE R&D Center, undated but ca. 1909.

8. Gorton Fonda et al., "Come in Rain or Shine," *GE Research Lab Memo* (spring, 1958), p. 10.

9. A. H. Barnes, "Study of Tungsten Lamps as to Influence of Voltage and Temperature on Edison Effect," report of work, October 7, 1910–October 22, 1910, Whitney Library.

10. G. M. J. MacKay, notebook, October 1, 1912, quoted in U.S. Patent Office, *Langmuir Priority Record, Arnold v. Langmuir*, Interference #40380, p. 127.

11. Quoted in Albert Rosenfeld, "The Quintessence of Irving Langmuir," 12:121. Members of the Langmuir family state that some years after showing excerpts of the Langmuir diaries to Rosenfeld, the diaries were destroyed.

12. U.S. Patent Office, Brief on Behalf of Irving Langmuir, Appellee, *Arnold* v. *Langmuir*, Interference #40380, pp. 105–110; 134.

13. The paper appeared as "The Effect of Space Charge and Residual Gases on Thermionic Currents in High Vacuum," *Physical Review* (1913), 2:450. Rather than rush into print with his initial space charge findings in late 1912, Langmuir held on to those results and expanded them while giving GE patent attorneys a chance to file for key patents on electron tubes using pure electron discharges. As a result, this paper appeared at the end of, rather than the middle of, 1913.

14. Langmuir priority record, p. 112, notes that on November 21, 1912, Langmuir gave a short talk on "Leakage Current in Lamps" to the lamp vacuum committee. Langmuir testified in "GE, Appellant, and Fama Radio Ltd., Respondent, an Appeal from the Supreme Court of Canada, Privy Council 74 of 1928," that "Mr. Hawkins arranged that I should meet Mr. Alexanderson and talk these problems over with him, and we did on several occasions in 1913."

15. On Arnold's work on the Audion, see F. B. Jewett to T. D. Lockwood, December 7, 1912, and "Arnold Testimony, October 25, 1926, before U.S. Supreme Court," both in Lloyd G. Espenscheid Collection, box 5, Smithsonian Institution, and Lillian Hoddeson, "The Emergence of Basic Research," pp. 512–44.

16. Coolidge, in his laboratory notebook entry of December 19, 1912 (quoted in W. C. White, "The Coolidge X-Ray Tube," unpublished, September 30, 1957) explicitly credits Langmuir for the key hint. He acknowledges this again in "A Half Century of X-Ray Generators," *American Journal of Roentgenology, Radium Therapy and Nuclear Medicine* (1956), 75:166, as he did consistently in several publications about the "Coolidge Tube" from 1914 on.

17. White, "Memorandum for Zenith Suit," August 30, 1957, p. 21, on file at GE R&D Center.

18. A. G. Davis to Ernest Thurnauer (GE executive) December 26, 1913, Coolidge X-Ray Tube papers, on file at GE R&D Center.

19. Whitney to E. W. Rice, Jr., March 17, 1916, Coolidge X-Ray Tube papers.

20. Coolidge to G. D. Bliss, July 1, 1926, Coolidge X-Ray Tube papers.

21. Whitney to J. R. Lovejoy, October 24, 1912, "Lab General," reel 5.1, GERLA.

22. Reese Jenkins, *Images and Enterprise*, p. 310.

23. T. A. Boyd, ed., *Prophet of Progress*, quotes Kettering on managing research in a June 1916 speech "Science and the Future of the Automobile," pp. 61–75, in which Kettering gives a detailed account of the ductile tungsten project as a model of industrial research. Kettering visited GE at about this time to investigate the possible use of tungsten in spark plugs. Whitney's notebook 13, December 27, 1910, p. 40, notes: "Mr. Darling of DuPont Pow-

der to spend day with us at laboratory." On the assistance to Eli Lilly, Curtiss, and Hyatt, see Birr, "The General Electric Research Laboratory," p. 478.

24. Whitney expresses his admiration for Roosevelt in Whitney to H. Garland, February 18, 1919, Whitney papers.

25. The comments on food quality are in Whitney to William McMurtie, January 24, 1912, box C101, 1912, Whitney papers. The comments on an endowment fund are in Whitney to F. J. Metzger, June 14, 1911, Whitney papers.

26. Whitney to R. M. Thomson, January 21, 1913, box C101, 1913, Whitney papers.

27. Whitney to J. M. Cattell, December 9, 1911, box 2, C101, 1911, Whitney papers.

28. Accounts of the origins and efforts of the Naval Consulting Board include Lloyd N. Scott, *The Naval Consulting Board;* Richard G. Hewlett, "Technology for War"; Thomas Hughes, *Elmer Sperry*, p. 273 et seq.; and Daniel Kevles, *The Physicists* p. 102 et seq.

29. Whitney to S. S. McClure, September 18, 1915, box 6, C101, 1915, Whitney papers.

30. Hewlett, "Technology for War" and Kevles, *The Physicists;* see n. 28.

31. For a parallel discussion of the need for a coordinated approach to the development of new weapons, see I. B. Holley, *Ideas and Weapons* (New York, 1950), an account of the development of military aviation by the United States in the World War I period.

32. I have relied on a bibliography prepared by Miles Martin and C. Guy Suits for their biographical memoir on Whitney published by the National Academy of Sciences.

33. Whitney to Dennis English, April 19, 1915, box 6, C101, Whitney papers.

34. Quoted in Helen Wright, *Explorer of the Universe*, pp. 287–88.

35. Scott, *The Naval Consulting Board*, p. 67.

36. *Ibid.,* pp. 68–69; L. A. Hawkins to John Frazier, April 19, 1948, 13.2 GERLA; "Report on General Electric Work on the Submarine Problem," 1919, General Electric Co., unpublished, in possession of Edmund E. Eveleth.

37. "Tests at Nahant, May 7–8, 1917," Whitney B papers.

38. "Lectures on Antisubmarine Devices," U.S. Naval Experimental Station, Bulletin 100 (1918), Whitney B papers.

39. Millikan, *Autobiography*, p. 138.

40. *Proceedings of the National Academy of Sciences* (1917), 3:531.

41. Millikan, *Autobiography*, p. 138.

42. "Lectures on Antisubmarine Devices"; Scott, *The Naval Consulting Board*, p. 69.

43. Whitney to Josephus Daniels, June 16, 1917, NRCM ExCom, Sub Comm. on Sub Detection, general file, quoted in Kevles, *The Physicists*, p. 121.

44. "Shipping Situation," October 14, 1917, unpublished memo, Whitney B papers.

45. C. E. Eveleth to Langmuir, December 24, 1917, Whitney B papers.

46. C. E. Eveleth to Whitney, December 25, 1917, Whitney B papers.

47. R. S. Leigh, USN, to Commander of U.S. Naval Forces Operating in European Waters, January 9, 1918, Whitney B papers.

48. The problem of submarine chasers is discussed at length in Thomas Robins to Josephus Daniels, March 18, 1918, Whitney B papers.

49. Ashley Adams, September 6, 1918, quoted in Admiral William Sims, circular letter #18, December 24, 1918, Whitney B papers.

50. Ibid.

51. Action Report #26, October 14, 1918, Whitney B papers.

52. I have relied mainly on the account of the wartime nitrogen project in L. F. Haber, The Chemical Industry.

53. Whitney to Charles H. Herty, November 1, 1918, Charles H. Herty papers, special collections department, P. W. Woodruff Library, Emory University, Atlanta, Ga.

54. Haber, The Chemical Industry, p. 205.

55. David K. Allison, New Eye for the Navy; the Naval Research Laboratory and the Development of Radar (Washington, Naval Research Lab, 1980).

56. Kevles, "George Ellery Hale," pp. 427–37.

57. Millikan quotes this earlier statement of his in his Autobiography, p. 196.

58. John W. Servos, "The Industrial Relations of Science," pp. 531–49; and "The Knowledge Corporation; A. A. Noyes and Chemistry at Cal-Tech, 1915–1930; AMBIX (1976), 23:175–86.

59. George Ellery Hale to Whitney, October 3, 1915, Hale papers, I-32, California Institute of Technology Archives, Millikan Library, California Institute of Technology.

60. On National Academy of Sciences attitudes toward applied scientists, and especially toward Edison, see Rexmond G. Cochrane, The National Academy of Sciences; pp. 283–84.

61. Kevles, "Federal Legislation for Engineering Experiment Stations," pp. 182–89.

62. Whitney, circular letter to George Ellery Hale et al., April 26, 1916, Hale papers, I-32.

63. Kevles, "Federal Legislation for Engineering Experiment Stations," p. 184.

64. Whitney to Noyes, June 19, 1916, Hale Papers, I-32.

65. Whitney repeats this message over and over in his 1916 speeches, which include "Research and the Newlands Bill," "Water Power and Defense," "The Call for Research," and "Preparedness."

66. Kevles, "Federal Legislation for Engineering Experiment Stations," p. 184.

67. Whitney to Hale, January 9, 1917, Hale papers, I-32.

68. Hale to Whitney, June 19, 1918, Hale papers, I-32.

69. Whitney to Hale, June 11, 1918, Hale papers, I-32.

70. Lance E. Davis and Daniel J. Kevles, "The National Research Fund," describe Whitney's 1918 view as "stating the importance of internalizing externalities of benefits and the advantage of externalizing costs in the financial support of research" (p. 220). That is, they say Whitney was interested in getting the public to pay for research that benefited GE. But a reading of

the full letter and other Whitney remarks at the time make it clear that he was supporting the Newlands Bill and other government initiatives as a way of increasing America's number of trained scientists, not as a way of subsidizing research. Whitney seems to have been motivated more by the impact of a greater scientific effort on the nation as a whole than by its impact on GE.

71. Whitney to Hale, June 11, 1918, Hale papers, I-32. See also "Meeting of the Advisory Committee on Industrial Research," May 29, 1918, National Research Council, typescript, Whitney B papers.

72. Whitney, "American Engineering Research," pp. 115–27.

73. Whitney to Colin G. Fink, February 6, 1923, C101-1922, Whitney papers.

9/ PEAK OF AUTHORITY

1. Maurice Holland, *Industrial Explorers,* p. 13.

2. Stuart Leslie, "Thomas Midgley and the Politics of Industrial Research," pp. 480–503.

3. Lillian Hoddeson, "The Roots of Solid State Research," pp. 22–30, and "The Emergence of Basic Research," pp. 512–44; Leonard Reich, "Radio Electronics."

4. Holland, *Industrial Explorers,* pp. 13–22.

5. A. W. Greene to Gerard Swope, January 28, 1925, Swope papers, 4/5 GE R&D Center.

6. See, e.g., Sumner A. Schlicter, "The Current Labor Policies of American Industries," *Quarterly Journal of Economics* (May 1929), reprinted in John T. Dunlap, ed., *Potentials of the American Economy* (Cambridge, Mass., 1961), pp. 184–212.

7. "General Electric Co.: Its Contributions to a Better Life for Its Employees," (Schenectady, und. ca. 1925).

8. David Loth, *Swope of GE.*

9. Herbert C. Pollock heard this from Dr. Whitney and told it to me.

10. Spencer Weart, "The Rise of Prostituted Physics," p. 14.

11. Clyde Wagoner, "The General Electric News Bureau," undated, ca. 1955.

12. F. W. Davis to Whitney, August 5, 1922, Whitney B papers.

13. Holland, "Highlights of 50 years of R&D Management," p. 421.

14. John Rae, "The Application of Science to Industry," pp. 244-68; Kendall A. Birr, "Industrial Research Laboratories," pp. 156-80.

15. Herbert Bruher, "Scientific Research at Schenectady," p. 46.

16. Herman Liebhafsky told this story to me.

17. Whitney, "Education," p. 1. The role of Mary Christie was described to me in interviews with C. G. Suits, April 28, 1981; Vincent J. Schaefer, May 24, 1977; and Bertha Lloyd, February 6, 1981.

18. The laboratory financial system is described in H. L. Warner to E. L. Spalding, August 28, 1925, GERLA 13.2.

19. "Laboratory Budget, 1901–1949," on file at the GE R&D Center.

20. See table 1.

21. For the early history of radio I have relied on Gleason L. Archer, *History of Radio;* and William C. White, "A History of Radio and Electronics," and "Memorandum for Zenith Suit," August 30, 1957, both at GE R&D Center.

22. White, "History of Radio and Electronics," p. 6.

23. *Ibid.*, p. 7.

24. Whitney to L. A. Hawkins, December 12, 1922, box 12-C101-1922, Whitney papers.

25. Reich, "Radio Electronics," pp. 166–67.

26. Hawkins to Whitney, September 8, 1922, Whitney B papers.

27. Whitney to George E. Emmons, June 25, 1918, Whitney B papers.

28. Theodore K. Quinn, *Giant Business, Threat to Democracy*, p. 93.

29. Whitney to T. W. Smith, November 5, 1920, box 9, C101–1919, Whitney papers.

30. Whitney makes a plea for support to Union College in "A Plea To Extend Postgraduate Work at Union College" (1925). On his support for students, see Whitney to A. S. Ferguson, July 12, August 25, January 1, 1917, box 7, C101–1916–18, Whitney papers; Whitney to A. E. Freeman November 15, 1915; Whitney to Dean Barton, MIT, March 14, 1912, box 3, C–101–1912; Whitney to A. Vogel, June 19, 1913, box 4, C101–1913, Whitney papers; and H. P. Talbot to Whitney, February 26, 1926, Whitney B papers.

31. GE Personnel Accounting, "Staff of the Research Laboratory, 1900–1946."

32. Louis Navias, "Memories of the Research Lab," July 24, 1970, on file at GE R&D Center; interview with Willem Westendorp, June 25, 1975.

33. John Broderick, *Willis R. Whitney,* pp. 90–91.

34. Interview with Samuel Hoyt, October 13, 1977.

35. Interview with Truman S. Fuller, March 22, 1922.

36. These handwritten charts, undated but clearly from the mid-1920s, survive in the Whitney B papers.

37. Whitney, "Research Director," August 23, 1947, Whitney B papers.

38. Taken from "Research Lab Budgets, 1900–1949," on file at the GE R&D Center.

39. Whitney to Charles H. Herty, January 18, 1928, Herty Papers, special collections department, P. W. Woodruff Library, Emory University, Atlanta, Ga.

40. On the importance of the metal tube, see James Brittain, "Power Electronics at General Electric," p. 438.

41. Whitney to F. K. Richtyer, July 24, 1923, Whitney B papers

42. Saul Dushman, "An Album of Memories," (undated, ca. 1950), on file at GE R&D Center.

43. Albert Hull, "Autobiography" (undated, ca. 1950), on file at GE R&D Center and Center for History of Physics.

44. Interview with Harold Mott-Smith, March 1, 1977.

45. Albert Rosenfeld, "The Quintessence of Irving Langmuir," pp. 117–61, describes Langmuir's work in the 1920s.

46. Albert G. Davis to Whitney, August 2, 1922, Whitney B papers.

47. John Miller, *William D. Coolidge: Yankee Scientist* pp. 125–42.

48. This story was told to me by Herman A. Liebhafsky.

49. A guest book from the 1920s is on file at the GE R&D Center.

50. Edward Ellery (professor of physics, Union College) to Whitney, March 5, 1926, Whitney B papers.

5,1. Frederick Soddy, "Ideals of a Scientific School," Farewell Address to the Scientific Association, Aberdeen University, June 20, 1919, reprinted in Soddy, *Science and Life;* F. L. H. M. Sliphers, "Some Notes on the Correspondence," I thank George Szasz for supplying this reference.

52. Paul Ehrenfest to Whitney, April 14, 1927, Whitney B papers. I thank Herman A. Liebhafsky for translating this and other German lettes in the Whitney B collection.

53. Whitney to Hawkins, April 2, 1923, box 12, C101, Whitney papers.

54. Whitney to Coolidge, undated, ca. December 1923; Whitney to Hawkins, December 13, 1923, box 12, C101, Whitney papers.

55. Whitney to Hawkins, March 9, 1923; March 14, 1923, box 12, C101, Whitney papers.

56. Whitney to Hawkins, March 28, 1923; April 20, 1923, box 12, C101, Whitney papers.

57. Paul Forman, "Financial Support and Political Alignment," pp. 39–66, quote on p. 48.

58. Whitney's interest in the work of Polanyi and Mark is given in Whitney to Hawkins, April 1, 1923, box 12–C101, Whitney papers. Polanyi's quote is from John R. Baker, "In the Cause of Freedom of Science," *New Scientist* (July 12, 1979).

59. Whitney to Hawkins, April 1, 1923, box 12, C101, Whitney papers.

60. Whitney to Hawkins, April 1, 1923, box 12, C101, Whitney papers.

60. Whitney to Hawkins, April 1, 1923, box 12, C101, Whitney papers.

61. Copy of letter from Fritz Haber to Einstein, Von Laue, Planck, October 23, 1926, in G. R. Fonda to Whitney October 25, 1926, Whitney B papers.

62. M. Planck to Whitney, January 31, 1924; Whitney to Heinrich Luders March 4, 1924; Haber to Einstein, Von Laue, Planck, October 23, 1926 in Fonda to Whitney, October 25, 1926, all in Whitney B papers.

63. Loth, *Swope of GE.*

64. Swope to Whitney, December 18, 1928; George L. Gilmore to Whitney, April 30, 1932, Whitney B papers.

65. Whitney notebook 122, p. 153, September 21, 1921; Whitney to Hawkins, January 21, 1923, C101–1922–23, Whitney papers.

66. Whitney notebook 1422, September 17, 1925.

67. W. L. R. Emmett to Whitney, undated, ca. 1922–23, Whitney B papers.

68. Income tax returns in Whitney B papers state that Whitney's salary

was $20,000 a year in 1925. The bonus of $13,232.24 for the year 1923 is mentioned in F. C. Pratt to Whitney, March 31, 1924. (Pratt was General Electric's vice president for engineering.)

69. *New York Times,* January 13, 1922, p. 8; January 7, 1922, p. 7; January 20, 1922, p. 2.

70. *U.S.* v. *General Electric et al.,* 272 US 476 (1926).

71. Whitney notebook 1422, December 31, 1925.

72. Whitney, "The Biggest Things in Chemistry," p. 43; Whitney, "Electrical Research and Progress," p. 12.

73. Whitney, "Electrical Research and Progress."

74. Whitney, undated., ca. 1922, Whitney B papers.

75. Charles L. Parsons to Whitney, October 23, 1923, Whitney papers.

76. Interview with Truman Fuller, March 22, 1978.

CHAPTER 10/ PIKERS IN AUDACITY

1. Whitney to L. A. Hawkins, March 3, 1923, box 11, Whitney papers.

2. Whitney, "Stimulation of Research in Pure Science," p. 21.

3. Irving Langmuir, "The Structure of Atoms and the Octet Theory of Valence," *Proceedings of the National Academy of Sciences* (1919), 5: 252; Albert W. Hull, "Autobiography," (undated, ca. 1950), on file at GE R&D Center and the Center for History of Physics; Saul Dushman, notebook #1, pp. 109–25, on file at GE R&D Center.

4. Whitney, "The Littlest Things in Chemistry."

5. Dushman to Whitney, October 2, 1922, Whitney B papers.

6. "The Committee of Vacuums," undated memo in Whitney B papers, a satire on a meeting of the lamp vacuum committee written by an insider—perhaps Whitney himself.

7. Whitney to W. H. Bragg, March 22, 1921; Coolidge to K. Siegbahn, September 2, 1916; J. S. Townsend to Coolidge, October 28, 1924, Coolidge X-Ray Tube Papers, GE R&D Center. Hull to Ernest Rutherford, December 3, 1921, quoted in Norman Feather, *Lord Rutherford* (Glasgow, 1940), p. 167.

8. "Why Should the GE Company Start and Even Pay for a Radiographic Institute in Schenectady?" April 1, 1920, Whitney B papers.

9. Whitney, commonplace book, June 1929, p. 259.

10. Whitney, "Why Should the GE Company Start,"

11. On Coolidge's "raying," see "The Laboratory's History in Electron Chemistry," *GE Research Lab Digest,* #1 (summer, 1957), pp. 31–33. On Hull's X-ray diffraction work, see Hull, "Autobiography." On Heidelberger's work and disappointment with Schenectady, see *Proceedings of the Conference on Historical, Biochemical, and Molecular Biology* (Brookline, Mass., 1971), p. 94, quoted in Robert Olby, *The Path to the Double Helix* (New York, 1974), p. 269.

12. Skinner's Westinghouse Laboratory is described in Marjorie Johnston, ed., *The Cosmos of Arthur Holly Compton,* (New York, 1967), pp. 24, 239–42.

13. Edward P. Hyde, "The Aims, Organization and Work of the Nela Re-

search Laboratories," (undated clipping, ca. 1910); Hyde to Whitney, November 16, 1918, Whitney B papers.

14. Quoted in Spencer R. Weart, "The Physics Business in America," p. 303.

15. Whitney to Swope, October 23, 1925, GERLA 13.2

16. The disappearance of the Pure Research Lab was mentioned to me by C. Guy Suits, in an interview June 9, 1977, and confirmed by lamp department engineering reports.

17 Coolidge's work with Kettering is described in John A. Miller, *William D. Coolidge; Yankee Scientist,* pp. 74–75; 96–97.

18 Stuart W. Leslie, "Charles F. Kettering"; T. A. Boyd, *Professional Amateur,* p. 123; Stuart W. Leslie, *Boss Kettering.*

19 Whitney to Langmuir, October 18, 1921, reel 5.1, GERLA.

20 Whitney to John T. Trowbridge, April 9, 1911, box 2–C101–1911, Whitney papers.

21 Whitney to Swope, November 23, 1923, reel 13.2 GERLA.

22. The quote on "leadership" is from Daniel J. Kevles, *The Physicists,* p. 170.

23. Lance E. Davis and Daniel J. Kevles, "The National Research Fund," pp. 207–20.

24. Hoover is quoted by George E. Hale in Hale to Millikan, March 15, 1928, Millikan mss., box 24, which is in turn quoted by Kevles, *The Physicists,* p. 214.

25. Wyckliffe Rose, quoted in Raymond B. Fosdick, *Adventure in Giving,* quoted in Kevles, *The Physicists,* p. 192.

26. R. S. Woodward to Whitney, June 16, 1921, Whitney B papers.

27. Robert W. Seidel, "The Origin of Academic Physics Research in California," pp. 1–47.

28. U.S. Patent Office, *Arnold v. Langmuir,* Interference #40,380, "Thermionic Devices and Methods of Constructing and Operating the Same," Arnold Record, testimony taken in New York, October 1917. See also Lillian Hoddeson, "The Emergence of Basic Research," pp. 534–537.

29. James M. Lafferty, ed., *Vacuum Arcs.* Lafferty's preface, pp. v–xiv, gives a history of the development of the vacuum switch.

30. Gregory Breit and Merle Tuve, "The Production and Application of High Voltages," pp. 535–36; Coolidge, laboratory notebook, March 28, 1928.

31. Hawkins to Whitney, February 26, 1923, box 12–C101–GE#2, Whitney papers.

32. Stanley Coben, "Foundation Officials and Fellowships, pp. 225–40.

33. Whitney to Swope, December 15, 1924, reel 13.2, GERLA.

34. See, e.g., Ernest O. Lawrence to Leonard B. Loeb, June 1, 3, 1929, Loeb Papers, 76/3, The Bancroft Library, University of California at Berkeley (I thank Dr. Arthur Norberg for locating these letters and sending me copies).

35. John W. Servos, "Physical Chemistry in America," pp. 371–76.

36. Interview with Ernest E. Charlton, July 22, 1976.

37. Interview with Anthony J. Nerad, July 2, 1975; interview with Willem Westendorp, June 25, 1975.

38. Whitney to F. K. Richtmyer, July 24, 1923, Whitney B papers.

39. *Ibid.*

40. Gorton R. Fonda to Whitney, October 25, 1926, Whitney B papers.

41. "Historical Recollections of the Research Laboratory," Louis Navias, July 24, 1970, on file at GE R&D Center.

42. Interview with Ernest O. Charlton, July 22, 1976.

43. Whitney, "Theories,"p. 884.

44. Whitney notebook #1422 (1925), p. 109.

45. Whitney notebook #1422 (November 25, 1925), p. 163.

46. Neil B. Reynolds, "Some Significant Steps," pp. 171–73.

47. Paul de Kruif, *The Fight for Life,* p. 261.

48. The conversion of Whitney's radiotherm to Kettering and Edwin C. Sitter's fever box is described in T. A. Boyd's *Professional Amateur,* pp. 178–80, and Leslie, *Boss Kettering,* pp. 282–84.

49. Whitney, Bursitis, X-rays, High Frequency," pp. 70–76.

50. Whitney, "Research, Theory and Practice," pp. 147–54.

51. The statement is from an interview with Ernest Charlton, July 22, 1976; the estimate is from my count of the reprint file at the Whitney Library, GE R&D Center.

52. I made a compilation of the affiliations of authors of the first 500 pages of the *Journal of the American Chemical Society* in 1895 (vol. 17);1900 (vol. 23);1905 (vol. 28); 1910 (vol.32); 1915 (vol. 37); 1920 (vol. 42); and 1925 (vol. 47), tabulating the affiliation of the authors (in most cases it was listed). The industry share was: 1895: 7%; 1900: 12%; 1905: 10%; 1910: 15%; 1915: 6%; 1920: 5% 1925: 3%. Two qualifications should be offered. The sample of papers is small (500 pages is typically 40 to 60 papers). And the American Chemical Society, as mentioned earlier, deliberately set up a journal in 1909 under the title *Industrial and Engineering Chemistry* to publish papers by industrial chemists on industrial topics. So paper counting in the Journal of the ACS tell us only how many industrial scientists attempted to publish their best work in the profession's most prestigious "pure" research journal—not how many published at all. In spite of these drawbacks, the tabulation stands as a first rough indicator of the relative role of industry in the production of American "pure" research in chemistry.

53. Paul Uselding, "Business History," p. 450.

54. Leonard Reich, "Industrial Research" pp. 503–29.

55. Whitney, "The Relation of Physics and Chemistry to Industry," p. 1.

56. *Ibid.,* p. 3.

57. Whitney, "Stimulation of Research in Pure Science," p. 4.

58. Whitney, "Langmuir's Work," p. 329.

59. Whitney, "Encouraging Competent Men To Continue in Research," pp. 310–12.

60. *Ibid.*

61. Robert E. Kohler, Jr., in "Irving Langmuir and the 'Octet' Theory of

Valence," pp. 34–67, writes of GE (p. 44) that Whitney allowed his "most able chemists to work on anything that interested them without regard to immediate payoff to GE," and "the atmosphere at GE was strikingly similar to the atmosphere of G. H. Lewis' department at Berkeley." John J. Beer and W. David Lewis in "Aspects of the Professionalization of Science," in Kenneth S. Lynn, ed., *The Professors in America* (Boston, 1965), pp. 110–30, write "at such laboratories (i.e., GE and Bell) research work was placed under the direction of men who were purely scientific in their interests . . . research was clearly distinguished from development." And for an even more nearly complete acceptance of the Whitney speeches as an accurate record of Whitney's history in industrial research, see Elting Morison, *From Knowhow to Nowhere* (New York, 1975); and Daniel Boorstin, *The Americans,* vol. 3. (New York, 1974).

62. John Broderick, *Willis R. Whitney,* p. 104; Birr, *Pioneering in Industrial Research,* p. 79.

63. The Laboratory's representative council is described in Truman S. Fuller to Whitney August 27, 1927, reel 4.2, GERLA. In various interviews I have learned that Whitney's practice of visiting the researchers was far from universal and that by the late 1920s, fewer and fewer researchers were being visited. Former laboratory executive engineer Dudley Chambers told me of the complaint of one veteran of the later Whitney years: "he never asked *me* if I was having any fun!"

64. The "happily ever after" quote is in Whitney, "Appreciation of Creation." Corrections on that assessment were told to me by George Barker (interview 12/31/79) and Agnes Wendel (interview 7/6/80).

65. Whitney is quoted in Bruce Barton, "The Conflict Between Science and Religion," p. 12.

66. *Literary Digest,* January 17, 1931. A copy of the poem, unfortunately undated, is in Whitney's commonplace book. Its author is Roselle Mercier Montgomery, and it concludes: "let earthbound ones, their eyes upon the sod. Broadcast today the cry 'there is no God.' The scientist discovers God again."

67. Whitney, "Cooperation and Corporations," p. 133.

68. The tantalizing hint that Whitney became temporarily a millionaire is contained in an entry he wrote in his pocket calendar for June 14, 1929:

250,000	B.S.
600	GE
50	(illegible)
50	misc.
1,030,000	

Though the addition comes out wrong, a plausible interpretation of this note is that it is Whitney figuring up the current value of his stock holdings, B.S. being Electric Bond and Share, and GE being General Electric.

69. Steffens' and Lippman's 1929 statements are quoted in William F.

Leuchtenberg, *The Perils of Prosperity* (Chicago, U. of Chicago Press, 1958), p. 202.

70. Whitney, "Industrial Progress Made Through Research," p. 586.

CHAPTER 11/ COME IN, RAIN

1. The sketches of the dragon are inserted in Whitney's commonplace book, p. 43.

2. Spencer Weart indicates that U.S. industrial research expenditures rose until 1931, and dropped only about 10 percent from 1931–34, while the number of research workers in industry dropped by about 20 percent. This takes into account the continuing creation of new laboratories in industries less severely hurt by the Depression. As footnote 3 indicates, the drop was sharper in established laboratories. See Weart, "The Physics Business in America," p. 306.

3. Kendall Birr estimates in "The General Electric Research Laboratory" that the GE Research Lab's budget fell 40 percent from 1929 to 1933. John Broderick, in *Willis R. Whitney*, p. 172, estimates a 60 percent drop. The lab's records bear out Broderick. The 1933 budget was only 40 percent that of 1929.

4. The "cheer leader" remark is in Whitney's commonplace book for March 20, 1929, p. 352. The nervousness is remembered by Agnes Wendel, July 6, 1980.

5. Commonplace book, January 1, 1930.

6. Whitney to George Gray, March 8, 1930, Whitney B papers.

7. Whitney to Otto Gutentag, November 18, 1930, Whitney B papers.

8. Whitney to Fred C. Kelley, November 19, 1930, Whitney B papers.

9. *Ibid.*

10. Commonplace book, July 5, 1930, p. 362.

11. Swope to Whitney, August 14, 1930, Whitney B papers; commonplace book, January 25, 1931, p. 363. The Whitney B papers contain an invoice for Whitney's stay at the Neurological Institute of New York.

12. Commonplace book, pp. 362–63, describes the European trip.

13. Whitney pocket memo for 1930, November 3, 1930.

14. William C. White, "A History of Radio and Electronics," p. V-9, describes the transfer of "some 20 people active in tube work" from the Research Lab to RCA's Harrison, N.J., tube plant.

15. The national situation for 1929–30 is described in Ellis W. Hawley, *The Great War and the Search for Modern Order*, pp. 180–86. Commonplace book, December 21, 1930, p. 198, mention's Whitney's dinner at the White House.

16. Commonplace book, January 20–25, 1931, pp. 362–63.

17. Commonplace book, p. 361. Swope wrote to Whitney, May 8, 1931, reel 13.1, GERLA: "I thought that one of the inhibitions that as you mention . . . I had imposed is that you would not give any more speeches that I did not approve."

18. Gerard Swope to W. H. Burrows, October 28, 1930. Swope papers 10/19; S. Whitestone to Swope, November 3, 1930, Swope 10/19.

19. Confidential progress reports, Research Laboratory NR 278#2, 1929–1935, on file at GE R&D Center.

20. Whitney to F. S. Mead, February 9, 1931, Whitney B papers.

21. Commonplace book, p. 257; February 14, 1931, p. 242.

22. Whitney to staff of Research Laboratory, September 4, 1931, reel 4.2, GERLA.

23. "Inspirational Talk," Camp Engineering, 1931, typescript in Whitney B papers.

24. Commonplace book, August 23, 1931, p. 265.

25. Ellis W. Hawley, *The Great War and the Search for a Modern Order* pp. 192–201.

26. *Ibid.*, p. 201.

27. Jeanette Marks to Gerard Swope, October 30, 1930; Swope to Marks, November 5, 1930, Swope Papers 9/22. See also David Loth, *Swope of GE*, p. 196.

28. Paul Adeler, Statement at Stockholder's Meeting, Rice Hall, Schenectady, April 21, 1936, Swope 9/10.

29. A clipping dated May 26, 1932, describing the meeting is in the Swope papers, 10/26.

30. E. O. Shreve to district managers and department managers, May 25, 1932, Swope 10/26.

31. Swope to Whitney, May 8, 1931, reel 13.1 GERLA. See also Swope to Camp INCAS, July 25, 1930, Swope papers, 11/2.

32. Whitney, "Speech to Elfuns" (1931), Whitney B papers Whitney's rating of the top executives is noted in pencil on the letter Swope to Whitney, February 21, 1931, Whitney B papers. The request to the retired executives is in Swope to C. Patterson et al, April 15, 1932, Swope papers 10/113.

33. The comment "Vacation get well," is on February 4, 1932, in Whitney's pocket diary for 1932, followed by the notation for February 7–28: "Nassau."

34. Commonplace book, December 27, 1932, p. 363. In *Adventure Into the Unknown*, p. 5, Laurence A. Hawkins writes: "At its beginning, the Research Laboratory was Whitney, and Whitney was the Research Laboratory. In one very real sense that has been true throughout the Laboratory's history."

35. Coolidge notebook #2304, April 19, 1932, p. 49.

36. The mercury vapor turbine is described in an as yet unpublished manuscript to Dr. H. A. Liebhafsky, "Quicksilver and Steam" (1980). On the sodium lamp, see Coolidge notebook #2304, August 30, 1932, p. 85. On other projects, see *ibid.*, pp. 49, 59, 83

37. Coolidge notebook #2304, October 21, 1932, p. 121.

38. *Ibid.*

39. Whitney to Swope, April 26, 1932; May 9, 1932, reel 13.1 GERLA.

40. Coolidge to Lwellys Barker, May 9, 1932; Swope to Barker, May 10, 1932, reel 13.1, GERLA.

41. Whitney's pocket diary for 1932 indicates "left the hospital after 7 weeks" on June 18, 1932, and on June 22, 1932, indicates "worst day." An undated note in Whitney B papers, placed near letters written in 1932, notes: "physically I am apparently perfectly all right, but mentally I struck bottom last week" and notes that Dr. Barker recommended an entire separation from work.

42. Lwellys Barker to Whitney, August 3, 1932, Whitney B papers.

43. Coolidge notebook #2304, October 21, 1932.

44. Whitney to Swope, October 25, 1932, reel 13.1 GERLA.

45. Swope, "Organization Announcement," October 28, 1932, reel 13.1, GERLA.

46. *New York Sun,* November 1, 1932.

47. Payne tells this version in "Come in . . . Rain or Shine," *GE Research Lab Memo,* 1957, p. 6.

48. Whitney commonplace book, December 27, 1932, p. 363.

49. Frank B. Jewett to Whitney, July 19, 1932, Whitney B papers.

50. Coolidge, notebook #2304, May 8, 1933, pp. 176–77; January 11, 1934, p. 222; February 12, 1934, pp. 233–35; January 25, 1934, p. 329.

51. Weart, "The Physics Business in America," pp. 316–17. Weart notes that expenditures at Bell Laboratories fell nearly 30 percent between 1930 and 1933.

52. Coolidge notebook #2304, November 23, 1932; April 18, 1933.

53. Coolidge notebook #2304, March 7, 1933; November 30, 1933.

54. Coolidge notebook #2304, December 19, 1933, p. 225. An undated listing from the personnel accounting department of the GE Research Laboratory says that the salaried staff leveled off at about one hundred thirty five people in 1936, down from two hundred sixty-five in 1929. The total staff, including hourly paid laborers, secretaries, etc., also nearly fell in half. The impact on the top echelon is harder to assess. Surviving organization charts for the 1930s indicate that between 1931 and 1935, while the salaried staff fell by about 15 percent (from one hundred seventy-two to one hundred forty) the number of Ph. D.s actually increased from twenty-three to twenty-seven.

55. Coolidge notebook #2304, February 21, 1934, p. 235; August 21, 1934, p. 298. These entries show that eight of Marshall's "new men" had been hired on a trial basis. Three of them (Winton Patnode, Herman Liebhafsky, and Murray Sprung) would be key men in GE's next generation of chemistry research.

56. Quoted in William James, *Pragmatism* (Cleveland, 1965), p. 191.

57. Whitney, commonplace book, January 23, 1929, p. 346.

58. Whitney, commonplace book, June 18, 1933, p. 257.

59. Interview with Vincent Schaefer.

60. Coolidge notebook #2304, August 25, 1933, p. 214.

61. Whitney, "Bursitis, X-Rays, High Frequency," pp. 70–76; Neil B. Reynolds, "Some Significant steps," pp. 171–73.

62. Whitney, "Bone, Bursitis, and X-Ray Diffraction," pp. 517–22.

63. Interview with Agnes Wendel, July 19, 1980.

64. Whitney, "Things I've Been Thinking About," pp. 102–11.
65. Interview with Paul Gundrum, April 6, 1976.

EPILOGUE

1. *Wall Street Journal*, September 6, 1949, p. 1.
2. The quote is from W. C. Dunlap, lab notebook #4144, February 20, 1946, p. 61, on file at GE R&D Center. The other two stories were told to me by GE physicists Charles P. Bean and Benjamin W. Roberts.
3. Whitney to Owen D. Young, March 3, 1943, Whitney B papers.
4. Edwin Mansfield, "Contributions of R&D to Economic Growth in the United States," *Science* (February 4, 1972), 175: 477–86, summarizes Manfield's own findings and those of Terelycki, Grilliches, Hollander, and others. Mansfield concludes:

> Although econometric studies of the relationship between R&D and productivity increase have been subject to many limitations, they provide reasonably persuasive evidence that R&D has an important effect on productivity increase in the industries and time periods that have been studied.

For other aspects of the economics of industrial research, see Richard R. Nelson, "The Simple Economics of Basic Research," *Journal of Political Economy* (June 1957), 67: 297, and Kenneth Arrow, "Economic Welfare and the Allocation of Resources for Invention," in *The Rate and Direction of Inventive Activity* (Princeton, 1962), which explain in economic terms why a research director is likely to become a "piker in audacity." C. Freeman, "Economics of R&D," in I. Spiegel Rosing and D. de Solla Price, eds., *Science, Technology and Society* (Beverly Hills, 1977), pp. 236–58, summarizes more recent findings.
5. Roland W. Schmitt, interviewed by Michael Wolf, "A View from 1980," *Research Management* (March 1980), p. 3.
6. William Kornhauser, *Scientists in Industry* (Berkeley, U. of California Press, 1966), especially pp. 97–201; Donald Pelz and Frank Andrews, *Scientists in Organizations* (New York, Basic Books 1966). Other valuable discussions of the organizational principles, management, and sociology of industrial research include Simon Marcson, *The Scientist in American Industry* (Princeton, Princeton U. 1960); Frank Andrews et al., *Scientific Productivity* (New York, Basic Books 1979); Norman R. Baker, Jack Stegnon, and Alfred Rubenstein, "The Effects of Perceived Needs and Means on the Generation of Ideas for Industrial Research and Development Projects," *IEEE Transactions on Engineering Management*, EM-14-4 (December 1967), pp. 156–62; Clagget G. Smith, "Consultation and Decision Processes in an R&D Laboratory," *Administration Science Quarterly* (1970),15: 203–15; Todd R. LaPorte, "Conditions of Strain and Accommodation in Industrial Research Organization," *Administration Science Quarterly* (1965–66), 10: 21–38.
7. Edward B. Roberts, "What Do We Really Know About Managing R&D?" *Research Management* November 1978), 10: 6–11.

Bibliography

Primary Sources

Coolidge, William D. Papers. In possession of Elizabeth Coolidge Smith, Portland, Ore.

Edison, Thomas A. Papers. Edison National Historic Site, West Orange, N.J.

Eveleth, Charles. Papers. In possession of Edmund E. Eveleth, Dothan, Ala.

Fenton Historical Society. Geneological and Jamestown history files. Jamestown, N.Y.

General Electric Collections. Main Plant and Research and Development Center of General Electric Co. Schenectady, N.Y.:

    Coolidge X-ray tube papers. GE R&D Center.

    General Electric Research Laboratory Archives (GERLA). Microfilm. GE R&D Center.

    Hammond, John Winthrop. File (indicated in footnotes as "Hammond file"). Main Library, General Electric Co. Schenectady, N.Y.

    Historical file. GE R&D Center (items from here are indicated in footnotes as "on file at GE R&D Center.

    Laboratory notebook collection. GE R&D Center (items from here are indicated in footnotes by person who kept the notebook and by notebook number).

    Reports of GE lamp engineering department. GE R&D Center.

    Reports of work file. Whitney Library. GE R&D Center.

    Schulze, Ida. Letters (correspondence between Ida Schulze and Whitney). GE R&D Center

    Swope-Young papers (business correspondence of Gerard Swope and Owen D. Young), GE R&D Center.

    Whitney B papers (a collection of photocopies of Whitney's business correspondence; originals in possession of George Barker, Charlton, N.Y.). GE R&D Center

Hale, George Ellery. Papers. California Institute of Technology Archives. Millikan Library. California Institute of Technology. Pasadena, Calif.

Herty, Charles H. Papers. Special Collections Department. P. W. Woodruff Library. Emory University. Atlanta, Ga.

Langmuir, Irving. Collection. Library of Congress. Washington, D.C.

Loeb, Leonard B. Papers. Bancroft Library. University of California at Berkeley. Berkeley, Calif.

MIT Archives. Massachusetts Institute of Technology. Cambridge, Mass.:

Annual reports of the president and the treasurer.

Cross, Charles R. Papers.

Goodwin, H. M. Papers.

Papers of the Office of the President, 1897–1930.

Rohrer, Albert L. Papers. Chatham Booksellers. Chatham, N.J.

Stanley, William. Papers. Stanley Library. General Electric Co. Pittsfield, Mass.

Wendel, Agnes. Collection (indicated in footnotes as "in possession of Agnes Wendel, Swampscott, Mass.).

Whitney, Willis R. Papers. On loan to the Schenectady Archives of Science and Technology. Union College. Schenectady, N.Y. (since my use of them, they have gone into possession of Agnes Wendel, Swampscott, Mass.)

Legal Documents

U.S. Circuit Court of Appeals for the Second Circuit. Brief for the Patent Appellee. *General Electric* v. *Nitro Tungsten Lamp Co.* April 1920.

U.S. Court of Appeals for the Third Circuit. No. 2615. October Term, 1920. Transcript of Record. *Independent Lamp and Wire Company* v. *General Electric Co.*

U.S. of A., Petitioner, v. *General Electric Co. and Others, Defendants.* Filed March 30, 1911. Circuit Court of the U.S. for the Northern District of Ohio. In 272 US 476. *U.S.* v. *General Electric Company et al.* No. 113, pp. 854–63.

U.S. Patent Office, *Arnold* v. *Langmuir*. Interference #40380. 1917.

Interviews (Notes or tapes on file at GE R&D Center, Schenectady, N.Y.)

Barker, George. Charlton, N.Y. May 10, 1980.
Charlton, Ernest E. Schenectady, N.Y. July 22, 1976.
Fuller, Truman. Fairfield, Conn. March 22, 1978.
Gundrum, Paul. Schenectady, N.Y. April 6, 1976.
Hoyt, Samuel. La Jolla, Calif. October 13, 1977.
Lake, John. Schenectady, N.Y. May 11, 1976.
Lloyd, Bertha. Schenectady, N.Y. Feb. 6, 1977.
Mott-Smith, Harold. Schenectady, N.Y. March 1–2, 1977.
Nerad, Anthony J. Alplaus, N.Y. July 2, 1975.
Schaefer, Vincent J. Schenectady, N.Y. May 24, 1977.
Suits, C. Guy. Pilot Knob, N.Y. June 9, 1977 and April 28, 1981.
Thompson, B. Dolores. Jamestown, N.Y. February 8, 1980.
Uhlig, Herbert. Boston, Mass. August 13, 1980.
Wendel, Agnes. Swampscott, Mass. July 19, 1980.
Westendorp, Willem. Schenectady, N.Y. June 25, 1975.

Secondary Sources

Abrahams, Harold J. and Marion B. Savin, eds. *Selections from the Scientific Correspondence of Elihu Thomson* (Cambridge, MIT Press. Mass., 1971).

Archer, Gleason L. *History of Radio* (New York, 1938).

Bancroft, Wilder D. "The Relation of Physical Chemistry to Technical Chemistry." *Journal of the American Chemical Society* (1900), 22: 1107.

——"Wilhelm Ostwald, the Great Protagonist." *Journal of Chemical Education*" (1933), 10: 611.

Barton, Bruce. "The Conflict Between Science and Religion." *Popular Science Monthly* (October, 1927), p. 12.

Baruch, Bernard. *The Public Years* (New York, 1960).

Baker, John R. "In the Cause of Freedom in Science." *New Scientist* 86, 203–205. (July 12, 1979).

Beer, John J. "Coal Tar Dye Manufacture and the Origins of the Modern Industrial Research Laboratory." In Thomas P. Hughes, ed. *The Development of Modern Technology Since 1500* (New York, 1964).

Beer, John J. and W. David Lewis, "Aspects of Professionalization of

Science." In Kenneth S. Lynn, ed. *The Professions in America,* (Boston, 1965).

Ben David, Joseph W. "The Profession of Science. *"Minerva* (1968), 7:1–35.

Ben David, Joseph W. "The Universities and the Growth of Science, *Minerva* (1968), pp. 1–35.

Biesterfield, Chester H. *Patent Law* (New York, 1949).

"Biographical Sketches of Some Outstanding General Electric Men," (Schenectady, N.Y., GE: 1947).

Birr, Kendall. "The General Electric Research Laboratory, A Case Study In the History of Industrial Research." Ph.D. dissertation. University of Wisconsin, 1951.

——"Industrial Research Laboratories." In Nathan Reingold, ed. *The Sciences in the American Context* (Washington, D.C., 1979).

——*Pioneering in Industrial Research* (Washington, D.C., 1956).

Black, Harold S. "Inventing the Negative Feedback Amplifier." *IEEE Spectrum* (December 1977), 14:58.

Boyd, Thomas A. *Professional Amateur* (New York, 1957).

Boyd, Thomas A., ed. *Prophet of Progress* (New York, 1961).

Breit, Gregory and Tuve, Merle. "The Production and Application of High Voltages in the laboratory." *Nature* (April 7, 1928), 121:535–36.

Bright, Aaron A. *The Electric Lamp Industry* (New York, MacMillan, 1949).

Brittain, James E. "C. P. Steinmetz and E. F. Alexanderson:Creative Engineering in a Corporate Setting." *Proceedings of the IEEE* (1976), 64:1414–20.

——"Power Electronics at General Electric, 1900–1945." *Advances in Electronics and Electron Physics* (1980), 50:408–48.

Broderick, John. *Willis R. Whitney* (Albany, N.Y., Ft. Orange Press 1945).

Brown, Charles Albert and Mary Elvira Weeks. *A History of the American Chemical Society* (Washington, D.C., 1952).

Bruce, Robert V. *Bell: Alexander Graham Bell and the Conquest of Solitude* (Boston, Little, Brown 1973).

Bruher, Herbert. "Scientific Research at Schenectady." *Review of Reviews* (February 1931), p. 46.

Buckley, Oliver E. "Biographical Memoir of Frank Baldwin Jewett (1879–1949)." *National Academy of Sciences Biographical Memoirs* (1952), vol. 27.

Bud, Robert F., P. Thomas Carroll, Jeffrey L. Sturchio, and Arnold W. Thackray. *Chemistry in America, 1876–1976.* Report to the National Science Foundation. Prepared under grant #SOC 75-14952.

Burton, William. "Chemistry in the Petroleum Industry." *Journal of Industrial and Engineering Chemistry* (June 1918), 10:483.

Cameron, Frank. *Cottrell, Samaritan of Science* (Garden City, N.Y., Doubleday 1952).

Canada. Privy Council 74 of 1928. "An Appeal from the Supreme Court of Canada, General Electric Co. Appellant and Fadu Radio Ltd., Respondent" (1928).

Chandler, Alfred D. *The Visible Hand* (Cambridge, Mass., Harvard 1975).

Coben, Stanley. "Foundation Officials and Fellowships: Innovation in the Patronage of Science." *Minerva* (1976–77), 14: 225–40.

Cochrane, Rexmond. *The National Academy of Sciences; the First 100 Years* (Washington, D.C., 1978).

"Come in Rain or Shine." *General Electric Research Laboratory Memo* (1958).

Compton, Arthur H. *The Cosmos of Arthur Holly Compton* (New York, 1967).

Compton, Karl T. "Elihu Thomson, 1853–1937." *NAS Biographical Memoirs* (1939), vol. 21.

Conant, James B. *My Several Lives* (New York, Random House 1970).

Conot, Robert. *A Streak of Luck* (New York, Seaview, 1979).

Cook, George. *Industrial Jamestown* (Jamestown, N.Y., 1890).

Coolidge, William D. "Ductile Tungsten," *Transactions of the American Institute of Electrical Engineers* (1910), vol. 29, part 1, 961–65.

Davis, Lance E. and Daniel J. Kevles. "The National Research Fund: a Case Study in the Industrial Support of Academic Science." *Minerva* (April 1974),12:206–20.

de Kruif, Paul. *The Fight for Life* (New York, 1938).

Dolby, R. G. A. "Debates Over the Theory of Solutions. *Historical Studies in the Physical Sciences* (1976),7:296–404.

Donnan, H. G. "Ostwald Memorial Lecture." *Journal of the Chemical Society* (1933), 13: 316–32.

Dudley, Charles. "The Dignity of Analytical Work." *Journal of the American Chemical Society* (1901), 20:89–95.

Eddy, John A. "Edison the Scientist." *Applied Optics* November 15, 1979), 18:3737–49.

Fifty Years of AEG (50 Jahre AEG) (Berlin, AEG 1950).

Findlay, A. "Wilder Dwight Bancroft, 1867–1953." *Journal of the Chemical Society 31* (1953), p. 2506.

Finn, Bernard, R. Friedel, C. Ellis, and M. J. DeWalt. *Lighting a Revolution* (Washington, D.C., Smithsonian, 1979).

Forman, Paul. "Financial Support and Political Alignment of Physicists in Weimar Germany." *Minerva* (1974), 12:39–66.

Forman, Paul, John L. Heilbron, and Spencer Weart. "Physics Circa 1900." *Historical Studies in the Physical Sciences* (1976), 5:127.

General Electric Co., *Annual Report for 1902*.

Guralnick, Stanley. "The American Scientist in Higher Education." In Nathan Reingold, ed. *The Sciences in the American Context* (Washington, D.C., Smithsonian 1979), pp. 99–135.

Gutman, Herbert G. "Class, Status and Community Power in Nineteenth Century Industrial Cities—Paterson, New Jersey as a Test Case." In Blanche Wiesen Cook et al., eds. *Past Imperfect* (New York, 1973), pp. 10–25.

Haber, L. F. *The Chemical Industry, 1900–1930* (Oxford, England, Oxford U. Press 1971).

Hammond, John W. *Charles Proteus Steinmetz* (New York, 1932).

——*Men And Volts* (New York, 1939).

Hatch, Vernille A. *Illustrated History of Jamestown* (Jamestown, N.Y., 1900).

Hawkins, Hugh. "Transatlantic Discipleship: Two American Biologists and Their German Mentor." *ISIS* (1980), 31:197–210.

Hawkins, Laurence A. *Adventure into the Unknown* (New York, 1950).

Hawley, Ellis. *The Great War and the Search for Modern Order* (New York, 1979).

Haynes, Williams. *American Chemical Industry* (New York, Van Nostrand 1954).

Herty, Charles H. "William Burton: Perkin Medal Award." *Journal of Industrial and Engineering Chemistry* (1922), 14:159–62.

Hewlett, Richard G. "Technology for War." To appear in the *Proceedings of the Centennial of the Electric Light Symposium* (held October 20, 1979, Newark N.J.).

Hiebert, Erwin N. "The Energetics Controversy and the New Thermodynamics." In H. D. Roller, ed. *Perspectives in the History of Science and Technology.* (Norman, Okla., 1971), pp. 72–86.

Hiebert, Erwin N. and Hans-Gunther Korber. "Wilhelm Ostwald." In *Dictionary of Scientific Biography* (New York, 1971), supp. pp. 456–65.

Hillebrand, W. F. "Present and Future Status of the Chemical Society." *Journal of the American Chemical Society* (1907), 29:1–18.

History of Chautauqua County, New York, and Its People (Jamestown, N.Y., 1921).

Hoddeson, Lillian H. "The Roots of Solid State Research at Bell Labs." *Physics Today* (March 1977), pp. 22–30.

——"The Emergence of Basic Research in the Bell Telephone System, 1875–1915." *Technology and Culture* (July 1981), 22:512–44.

Holland, Maurice. *Industrial Explorers* (New York, 1928). ——"Highlights of 50 Years in R and D Management." In Harold Vagtborg, ed. *Research and American Industrial Development* (New York, Pergamon 1976), pp. 421–26.

Hounshell, David A. "Edison and the Pure Science Ideal in 19th Century America." *Science* (1980), 207:612–17.

Howell, John W. and Henry Schroeder. *History of the Incandescent Lamp* (Schenectady, N.Y., Maqua 1927).

Hughes, Thomas P. *Elmer Sperry, Inventor and Engineer* (Baltimore, Johns Hopkins, 1971).

—— *Networks of Power* (Baltimore, Johns Hopkins 1983).

Industrial Research Laboratories of the United States, ed. 16. (New York, 1979).

Inman, George. "Fluorescent Lamps." *GE Review* (1954), 57:36–40.

Jehl, Frances. *Menlo Park Reminiscences* (Dearborn, Mich. 1939).

Jenkins, Reese. *Images and Enterprise* (Baltimore, Johns Hopkins 1975).

Jewett, Frank B. "Industrial Research." Paper read at the Royal Canadian Institute, Toronto, Canada, February 8, 1919.

Josephson, Matthew. *Edison* (New York, McGraw Hill, 1959).

Kevles, Daniel J. "Federal Legislation for Engineering Experiment Stations." *Technology and Culture* (1971), 12:182–89.

——"George Ellery Hale, the First World War, and the Progress of Science in America." In Nathan Reingold, ed. *Science in America Since 1820.* (New York, 1976), pp. 278–88.

——*The Physicists* (New York, Knopf 1978).

Kingdon, Kenneth. "Irving Langmuir, 1881–1957." GE Research Lab Report GP-151 (Schenectady, N.Y. 1960).

Kohler, Robert E., Jr. "Irving Langmuir and the 'Octet Theory of Valence." *Historical Studies in the Physical Sciences* (1974), 4:34–67.

"The Laboratory's History in Electron Chemistry." *GE Research Lab Digest* (summer, 1957), pp. 31–33.

Lafferty, James M., ed. *Vacuum Arcs* (New York, 1980).

Langmuir, Irving. *The Collected Works of Irving Langmuir.* C. Guy Suits and Harold Way, eds. (New York, 1960), 12 vols.

Layton, Edwin. "Mirror Image Twins: the Communities of Science and Engineering in 19th Century America." *Technology and Culture* (1971), 12:562–80.

LeBlanc, Max. *A Test Book of Electrochemistry* (New York, 1900).

Leonard, Jonathan N. *Loki* (New York, 1929).

Leslie, Stuart. *Boss Kettering* (New York, 1983).

——"Charles F. Kettering and the Copper Cooled Engine." *Technology and Culture* (October 1974), 20:752–78.

——"Thomas Midgley and the Politics of Industrial Research." *Business History Review* (1980), 54:480–503.

Liebhafsky, Herman A. *William D. Coolidge, a Centenarian and His Work* (New York), 1974).

——*Quicksilver and Steam.* Unpublished ms., 1981.

Litchfield, P. W. *Industrial Voyage* (New York, 1954).Little, Arthur D. "Presentation Address—Perkin Medal." *Chemical and Metallurgical Engineering* (January 19, 1921).

Loth, David, *Swope of GE* New York, 1958).

McManus, John A. "50 Years of Induction Motor Manufacture at the Lynn Works of the General Electric Co." (Lynn, Mass., 1943).

Martin, Donald B. "Steinmetz and His Discovery of the Hysteresis Law." *General Electric Review* (1912), 15:544–48.

Mendelsohn, Kurt. *The World of Walter Nernst* (Pittsburgh, U. of Pittsburgh 1973).

Meyer-Thurow, Georg. "The Industrialization of Invention: a Case Study from the German Chemical Industry." *ISIS* (1982), 73:363–81.

Miller, John A. *Modern Jupiter* (Schenectady, N.Y., 1958).

——*William D. Coolidge: Yankee Scientist* (Schenectady, N.Y., 1963).

Miller, John D. "Rowland's Physics." *Physics Today* (July 1976), 29:45–50.

Millikan, Robert A. *The Autobiography of Robert A. Millikan* (New York, 1950).

Navias, Louis. "Partial History of Ceramic Research and Development in the Research Laboratory of the General Electric Company." 65-GP-0315M, GE R&D Center (Schenectady, N.Y., 1965).

Noble, David. *America by Design* (New York, Knopf 1977).

Noyes, Arthur A. "A Talk on Teaching." *Science* (1908), 27:659.

Noyes, Arthur A. and Willis R. Whitney. "Kryoskopische Untersuchungen mit Aluminaten und Boraten von Alkalimetallen." *Zeitschrift for Physikalische Chemie* (1892), 15: 694–98.

——"The Rate of Solution of Solid Substances in Their Own Solutions." *Journal of the American Chemical Society* (1897), 19:930–34.

Olby, Robert. *The Path to the Double Helix* (New York, 1974).

Palmaer, Wilhelm. "Uber die Auflosung von Metallen. "I,II,III, *Zeitschrift fur Physikalische Chemie* (1901) vol. 39; (1903) vol. 45; (1904) vol. 46.

Passer, Harold C. *The Electrical Manufacturers, 1875–1900* (Cambridge, Mass. Harvard, 1953).

Pauling, Linus. "Arthur Amos Noyes." *National Academy of Sciences Biographical Memoirs* (1958) vol. 31.

Powers, Robert M. "Schenectady, New York, a Streetcar City." (Unpublished undergraduate honors paper, Union College, 1977.

Prescott, Samuel C. *When MIT Was Boston Tech* (Cambridge, Mass., 1954).

Prout, Henry G. *A Life of George Westinghouse* (New York, 1921).

Quinn, Theodore K. *Giant Business, a Threat to Democracy* (New York, 1953).

Rae, John. "The Application of Science to Industry." In Alexandra

Oleson and John Voss, eds. *The Organization of Knowledge in Modern America, 1860–1920* (Baltimore, 1975), pp. 189–206.

Reich, Leonard. "Industrial Research and the Pursuit of Corporate Security: the Early Years of Bell Laboratories." *Business History Review* (1968), 54:503–29.

——"Irving Langmuir and the Pursuit of Science and Technology in the Corporate Environment." *Technology and Culture* (1983), 24:199–221.

——"Radio, Electronics and the Development of Industrial Research in the Bell System." Ph.D. dissertation, The Johns Hopkins University, 1977.

Remsen, Ira. "Development of Chemical Research in America." *Journal of the American Chemical Society* (1910), 37:5–10.

Reynolds, Neil B. "Some Significant Steps in the Development of the Inductotherm." *General Electric Review* (1937), 40:171–73.

Rice, Edwin W., Jr. "A Tribute to Willis R. Whitney." *General Electric Review* (January 1933), 36:3–5.

Rosenfeld, Albert. "Irving Langmuir." *Dictionary of American Biography,* supp. 6, 1956–1960 (New York, 1980), p. 363.

——*The Quintessence of Irving Langmuir,* vol. 12 of *The Collected Works of Irving Langmuir,* C. Guy Suits and Harold Way, eds. (New York, 1962).

Scott, Lloyd N. *The Naval Consulting Board of the United States* (Washington, D.C., 1920).

Seidel, Robert W. "The Origin of Academic Physics Research in California." *Journal of College Science Teaching* (1976), 6:

Servos, John W. "The Industrial Relations of Science: Chemical Engineering at MIT, 1900–1939." *ISIS* (1980), 71:531–49.

——"The Knowledge Corporation: A. A. Noyes and Chemistry at Cal Tech, 1915–1930." *AMBIX* (1976), 23:175–86.

——"Physical Chemistry in America." Ph.D. thesis, Princeton University, 1979.

Sliphers, F. L. H. M., "Some Notes on the Correspondence Between Sir Edward Appleton and Balth. Van der Pol." *Philips Research Reports* (1975), 30:344–56.

Soddy, Frederick. *Science and Life* (London, 1920).

Spengler, Paul A. "The Development of the Furniture Industry in Jamestown, N.Y." Unpublished ms., 1978.

——"Yankee, Swedish and Italian Acculturation and Economic Mobility in Jamestown, New York, from 1860 to 1920." Ph.D. dissertation, University of Delaware, 1971.

Stanley, William. "The Inventor and the Trust." *Electrical World and Engineer* (March 28, 1903), p. 597.

Steiglitz, Julius. "Gibbs Medal Award to A. A. Noyes." *Journal of Industrial and Engineering Chemistry* (May 1915), 7:5.

Steinmetz, Charles P. "The Law of Hysteresis." *Transactions of the American Institute of Electrical Engineers* (1892), 9:1–48.

——"Symbolic Representation of General Alternating Waves and Double Frequency Vector Products." *Transactions of the American Institute of Electrical Engineers* (1899), 16:289–316.

Trescott, Martha M. *The Rise of the American Electrochemicals Industry, 1880–1910* (Westport, Conn., Greenwood 1981).

Uselding, Paul. "Business History and the History of Technology." *Business History Review* (1980), 54:450–55.

Vagtborg, Harold. *Research and American Industrial Development* (New York, 1976).

Weart, Spencer. "The Rise of Prostituted Physics." *Nature* July 1, 1976), 262:14.

——"The Physics Business in America, 1919–1940: a Statistical Reconaissance." In Nathan Reingold, ed. *The Sciences in the American Context: New Perspectives* (Washington, D.C.: Smithsonian Institution Press, 1979), pp. 298–325.

Weedon, William. "A Contribution to the Study of the Electric Arc." *Transactions of the American Electrochemical Society* (1904), 5:171–87.

Weintraub, Ezekiel. "Metallic Vapors in an Exhausted Space." *Philosophical Magazine* (1904), 7:85–124.

Westervelt, Virginia W. *The World Was His Laboratory*, (New York, Julian Messien, 1964).

White, William C. "A History of Radio and Electronics at the General Electric Company." Unpublished ms., Schenectady, N.Y., 1950.

Whitney, Willis R. "American Engineering Research." *Proceedings of the American Institute of Electrical Engineers* (1918), 38:115–27.

——"Appreciation of Creation." Annual Dinner of the National Institute of Social Sciences, May 3, 1928.

——"Arcs." *Transactions of the American Electrochemical Society* (1905), 7:291–99.

——"The Biggest Things in Chemistry." *Chemical and Metallurgical Engineering* (1921), 24:43.

——"Bursitis, X-Rays, High Frequency." *General Electric Review* (1935), 38:70–76.

——"Cooperation and Corporations," *General Electric Review* (1929), 32:133–36.

——"The Corrosion of Iron." *Journal of the American Chemical Society* (1903), 25:394–406.

——"Education." *Industrial and Engineering Chemistry* (1909), 1:6.

——"Electrical Conduction." *Transactions of the American Electrochemical Society* (1912), 21:18–19.

——"Encouragement of Competent Men To Continue in Research." *Science* (1929), 69:310–12.

——"Industrial Progress Made Through Research and Its Economic Importance." *General Electric Review* (1929), 32:586–89.

——"Langmuir's Work." *Industrial and Engineering Chemistry* (1928), 20:329.

——"The Littlest Things in Chemistry." Reprint, Chandler Award Address, Columbia University, New York, 1920.

——"Organization of Industrial Research." *Journal of the American Chemical Society* (1910), 32:71–78.

——"The Relation of Physics and Chemistry to Industry." In Michael Pupin et al., eds. *Physics and its Relations* (New York, 1924).

——"Research." *General Electric Review* (1917), vol. 20.

——"Research and the Newlands Bill." *Metallurgical and Chemical Engineering* (1916), 14:61–64.

——"Research as a Financial Asset." *General Electric Review* (1911), 14:325–30.

——"Stimulation of Research in Pure Science Resulting from the Needs of Engineers and of Industry." *Mechanical Engineering* (February 1927), vol. 28, 101–113. 4.

——"The Theory of the Mercury Arc Rectifier." *General Electric Review* (1911), 14:619–21.

——"Things I've Been Thinking About." General Electric Publication #211, January 1948, reprinted from the *American Magazine,* 1937.

——"Vacua." *Transactions of the American Institute of Electrical Engineers* (1912), 31:1207–16.

——"Water Power and Defense." *Transactions of the American Institute of Electrical Engineers* (1916), 35:431–39.

——"Willard Gibbs Medal Award Acceptance." *Journal of Industrial and Engineering Chemistry* (1916), 8:559.

Whitney, Willis R. and J. E. Ober, "The Precipitation of Colloids by Electrolytes." *Journal of the American Chemical Society* (1901), 23:842–63.

Wise, George. "Physics Yesterday: A Career in Research." *Physics Today* (May 1976), 29:13–15.

——"A New Role for Professional Scientists in Industry: Industrial Research at General Electric, 1900–1916," *Technology and Culture* (1980), 21:408–29.

——"Ionists in. Industry: Physical Chemistry at General Electric, 1900–1915." *ISIS* (1983), 74:7–21.

Windred, G. "Complex Quantities." *Electrician* (1936), 115:337–40.

Woodbury, David O. *Beloved Scientist* (New York, 1944).

Worden, Edward Chauncey. Nitrocellulose in Industry (New York, 1911).

Wright, Helen. *Explorer of the Universe: A Biography of George Ellery Hale* (New York, 1966).

Young, Andrew W. *History of Chautauqua County, New York,* (Buffalo, N.Y., 1875).

Index